A History of the
National Intelligencer

A History of the
National Intelligencer

by William E. Ames

The University of North Carolina Press
Chapel Hill

Manufactured in the United States of America.
Printed by Kingsport Press, Kingsport, Tennessee.
ISBN 0–8078–1178–5.
Library of Congress Catalog Card Number 75–109462.

To Jan, my coauthor

Preface

During much of the first half of the nineteenth century, Washington, D.C., was the journalistic capital of the United States. This was the period when the political newspaper dominated the publishing field and when governmental funds provided the financial base that allowed the publications to stay in business.

The aristocrat of Washington, D.C., journalism was the *National Intelligencer*, founded by Samuel Harrison Smith in 1800, but edited and published during most of its life by Joseph Gales, Jr. and his brother-in-law, William Winston Seaton. The printing press of the *Intelligencer* began to the accompaniment of the hammers, planes, and saws that built the nation's capital out of the swampland along the Potomac. The newspaper died in the period following a civil war that threatened the political union that had been so ingeniously tied together following the separation between the colonies and England.

For most of its life the *Intelligencer* depended on the federal government for its financial support. Printing patronage allowed it to continue for sixty-five years as a political newspaper, yet the longest lasting of its rivals endured no more than a decade and a half. Partly the long life of the *Intelligencer* was due to the high journalistic standards, the quiet dignity, and the strong intellectual character of the paper throughout the Gales and Seaton period. Partly it was due to the editors' knowledge of the workings of federal patronage, which allowed them to piece together publishing projects that enabled the *Intelligencer* to remain in the capital even though political enemies occupied the White House and controlled both houses of Congress. For sixty-two years three men who headed the publication were associated intimately with the workings of the United States government. At times they were almost part of it.

Anyone attempting to equate the *Intelligencer*'s role with that of a newspaper of the mid-twentieth century would fail to understand the aristocrat of Washington journalism. Throughout its existence the *Intelligencer* endeavored to inform the nation on the workings of the federal government. In addition the editors sought to persuade readers to adopt the particular political decisions they reached. Entertainment had no place in such a newspaper, which was filled with columns of proceedings of Congress, official proclamations and advertisements, leaders ranging from one or two paragraphs to full pages, and the always-present letters to the editor.

The years of the *Intelligencer* spanned a period that saw much of American journalism change its financial base from political party and government patronage to the industrial system of the nation. Circulation grew from four-digit to six-digit figures, and the entire content of the newspaper underwent revolution, the likes of which the print media had not seen before and have not witnessed since.

It was a quiet, staid, and even stoggy type of journalism the *Intelligencer* represented. It was a personal journalism which directly reflected the views and ideas of the men who published it. These were men who carried political journalism to its zenith and who clung to the political format long after the rest of the nation had moved to a new type of journalism built on sensational reporting, hard-hitting editorials, and a frantic drive for mass circulation. Its editors came to prominence as liberals in the political revolution of 1800 and parted with the *Intelligencer* long after it had ceased to be attuned to the dynamic changes reflected in the nation in the period surrounding the Civil War.

For the most part this account of the *Intelligencer* is the story of Gales and Seaton, whose influence dominated the paper from 1807 until 1865. These were the men who for over half a century influenced not only the journalistic world but also the political spheres of the nation and the District of Columbia. In addition, they made a major contribution to the historical scholarship of the nation in providing three major documentary sources: the *Annals of Congress*, *The Register of Debates*, and *The American State Papers*. All bore the publishing stamp of Gales and Seaton.

This is also the story of Samuel Harrison Smith, the young

Philadelphia publisher who succeeded in winning the friendship of Thomas Jefferson and in establishing Washington's most influential paper during the first half of the nineteenth century. It was Smith who started the *Intelligencer* in its devotion to the principles of Jeffersonian Democracy and the Constitution of the United States. It remained for Gales and Seaton to reinterpret the Jeffersonian principles to enable the newspaper to espouse the cause of Clay's American System and the dominance of industrial capitalism.

Many persons contributed greatly to the research that has gone into this manuscript. Philip Jordan, Department of History, University of Minnesota, not only suggested the research topic, but gave most generously of his time and advice. My debt to him is great. I am especially grateful to Dr. Elizabeth Gregory McPherson, whose interest in her fellow North Carolinian, Joseph Gales, Jr., helped locate much material used in this writing.

This biography of a newspaper is written to help fill the wide gap in historical information for the period when Washington, D.C., was the journalistic capital of the United States and government patronage was the financial base. It is an attempt to show that political journalism, rather than being the dark ages of the American newspaper, offered a higher quality information and interpretation of American society than at any other time in American history.

Contents

[xi]

A History of the
National Intelligencer

CHAPTER 1

Washington Beckons

Clouds of dust rose from the wheels of a stagecoach that wound its way between the groves of trees, past the stagnant swamps. It finally rounded a curve and came into view of the crude and unfinished settlement known as Washington City, the nation's new capital. The time was late September, 1800, and in the carriage rode a newly married couple, Mr. and Mrs. Samuel Harrison Smith of Philadelphia, bound for Washington City to start the settlement's first newspaper—already named the *National Intelligencer and Washington Advertiser.*

Although Smith had warned his wife that the city that was to be their first home was unfinished, she was scarcely prepared for what surrounded her. As she peered from the carriage she saw the beginnings of the capitol, with carpenters and masons hurrying to give the building some semblance of readiness for the meeting of Congress in December. To the west lay the president's home, occupied by President and Mrs. John Adams, but even this was not complete. No wonder Mrs. Adams complained bitterly about the lack of comfort in the new surroundings. Between the capitol and the president's house a narrow road skirted the swamps so numerous in the District of Columbia. To the south lay the Potomac River, which contributed to the humid, hot atmosphere that settled over the area.[1]

Just to the south of the capitol a cluster of fifteen or sixteen wooden houses served as dwellings and business places for the new city. Albert Gallatin described them as rough little structures hardly better than shanties. One housed a tailor, another a shoemaker, a third a washerwoman. A grocery store, a dry goods shop, and an oyster shop stood nearby.[2]

Government officials arriving in town found few and inadequate homes for themselves, let alone their families. They lived, for the most part, in boarding houses until better accommodations became available. As the Smiths soon learned, some two miles to the west stood Georgetown, a growing town located on the north bank of the Potomac River. First settled about 1700, Georgetown offered better chances for lodging and more complete shopping facilities. Yet the entire population of the District of Columbia numbered only about 14,303.[3] In May, 1800, Washington City boasted only 372 buildings—109 of brick and 263 of wood.[4]

In one of these crude frame buildings, between D and E streets on New Jersey Avenue, the newly married couple set up their first home, and in the adjoining building Smith established his printing plant.[5]

To most Americans the accommodations offered by the city seemed crude, but to Mr. and Mrs. Smith, used to the finest social circles of Philadelphia, the setting was a trifle less than shocking. Probably only their newly wedded bliss enabled the young couple to adjust to their new surroundings.

1. Albert J. Beveridge, *The Life of John Marshall, Conflict and Construction, 1800-1815* (Boston, 1919), 3:6.

2. Raymond Walters, Jr., *Albert Gallatin: Jeffersonian Financier and Diplomat* (New York, 1957), p. 127.

3. Wilhelmus Bogart Bryan, *A History of the National Capital* (New York, 1914), 1:355.

4. *American State Papers*, Miscellaneous Papers (Washington, D.C., 1834), 1:256-57.

5. Samuel Harrison Smith to Margaret Bayard, August 22, 1800, Margaret Bayard Smith Papers, vol. 6, Library of Congress, Washington, D.C.

Until leaving for Washington City, Smith's entire life had been bound to Philadelphia, where he was born in 1772.[6] He was descended from prominent and respectable stock. Samuel's father was Jonathan Smith, son of Samuel Smith, originally from Portsmouth, New Hampshire. The Smiths moved to Philadelphia before Jonathan's birth on February 12, 1742, and there the family engaged in the mercantile business. Jonathan was graduated in 1760 from the College of New Jersey, entered business in Philadelphia, and married Susannah Bayard, daughter of Samuel Bayard of the famous Maryland family. Following his marriage Jonathan added Bayard to his legal name.[7]

Samuel was well acquainted with the early history of the Republic, for his ardently anti-British father had served as a delegate and secretary to the Provincial Congress, which helped conduct the war in Pennsylvania,[8] had chaired a meeting of the real Whigs on December 2, 1776, which ordered all persons between sixteen and fifty to be put under arms to defend the city,[9] and later was elected to the Continental Congress,[10] where he served on the publications committee.[11] In addition Smith also served as a member of the Council of Safety,[12] as auditor of Public Accounts,[13] and as a colonel in the Second Troop of the Philadelphia City Cavalry.[14] He strongly supported the Articles of Confederation but was not active in national political events following the end of the

6. A search of the Smith manuscripts, the University of Pennsylvania files, and the American Philosophical Society files failed to produce the date and month of Smith's birth.

7. John Hill Martin, *Martin's Bench and Bar of Philadelphia* (Philadelphia, 1883), p. 58.

8. Francis Von A. Cabeen, "The Society of the Sons of Saint Tammany of Philadelphia," *The Pennsylvania Magazine of History and Biography* 26 (1902):345; and *Pennsylvania Archives*, series 2, 3 (1875): 676-77.

9. *Pennsylvania Archives*, series 1, 3 (1853): 83-84.

10. Cabeen, "Society of the Sons of Saint Tammany," p. 345; and "Diary of James Allen, Esq., of Philadelphia, Counsellor-at-law, 1770-1778," *The Pennsylvania Magazine of History and Biography* 9 (1885): 278-79.

11. Herbert Friedenwald, "The Journals and Papers of the Continental Congress," *American Historical Association Annual Report* (Washington, D.C.,1897), 1:97; and Friedenwald, "The Journals and Papers of the Continental Congress," *The Pennsylvania Magazine of History and Biography* 21 (1897): 176.

12. *Pennsylvania Archives*, series 2, 3 (1875): 685-86.

13. Ibid., p. 692.

14. W. A. Newman Dorland, "The Second Troop Philadelphia City Cavalry," *The Pennsylvania Magazine of History and Biography* 49 (1925): 183n.

Revolution.[15] In addition, the elder Smith was prothonotary of the court of common pleas,[16] and between 1778 and 1788 served successively as justice of the court of common pleas and as a Philadelphia alderman.[17] He was also active in the Sons of Tammany,[18] and was grand master of the Masons of Pennsylvania, a member of the American Philosophical Society, and a trustee of the college of New Jersey and the University of Pennsylvania.[19]

Coming from such a family, it is little wonder that Samuel should have inherited capabilities and that he should have been given the best education the day afforded. Although, unfortunately, little is known of the nature of his early training, he was graduated from the University of Pennsylvania in 1787 with the degree of Bachelor of Arts. Three years later, without additional class work and as the result of passing an examination, the University conferred upon him the degree of Master of Arts.[20] In 1797 he received an M.A. degree, *gratiae causa*, from the College of New Jersey. His father then served on the Board of Trustees.[21]

The young man who appraised the world in 1790 in search of a life's occupation was not dynamic. Indeed, he was quiet and introspective, a rather tall, slender person with a sparse crop of hair, small eyes, and a prominent nose. Diligence, together with a serious countenance, marked everything Smith undertook.[22]

Smith possessed the necessary journalistic background for

15. For a Biography of Jonathan Bayard Smith, see *Dictionary of American Biography* 17:308-9, 1956.

16. Martin, *Martin's Bench*, p. 58; *Pennsylvania Archives*, series 1, 11 (1855): 423.

17. "Jonathan Bayard Smith," *Dictionary of American Biography* 17:308-9.

18. Cabeen, "Society of the Sons of Saint Tammany," pp. 339, 450; "Extracts from the Diary of Jacob Hiltzheimer of Philadelphia, 1768-1798," *The Pennsylvania Magazine of History and Biography* 16 (1892): 170; "Jonathan Bayard Smith," *Dictionary of American Biography* 17:308-9.

19. John MacClean, *History of the College of New Jersey* (Philadelphia, 1877), 2:26, 34; Samuel W. Pennypacker, "The University of Pennsylvania in Its Relations to the State of Pennsylvania," *The Pennsylvania Magazine of History and Biography* 15 (1891): 98.

20. Samuel Harrison Smith File, Alumni Records Office, University of Pennsylvania, Philadelphia. The University Archives, University of Pennsylvania, show Smith's fee payment records but give no indications of his course of study.

21. University of Pennsylvania, *General Alumni Catalogue* (Philadelphia, 1922), p. 10.

22. For a picture of Smith, see Mrs. Samuel Harrison Smith, *The First Forty Years of Washington Society* (New York, 1906), insert between pp. 40 and 41.

his Washington City experience, for he entered the Philadelphia printing business in 1791[23] and in 1794 proposed publishing an American edition of the *English Monthly Review*. Evidently the plans failed; no record can be found of any such publication. He also was connected with the *American Universal Magazine*, a literary publication established in Philadelphia in January, 1797. The first issues showed S. H. Smith as the printer for Richard Lee, with offices located at 131 Chestnut Street. In later numbers of the first two volumes his name disappeared, but in the last number of volume two, dated June 13, 1797, Smith again was listed as the printer and continued through volumes three and four. The fourth and last volume was published on March 7, 1798.[24]

Smith's journalistic endeavors faced tough competition both from the Philadelphia papers within the Republican party and those supporting the opposing Federalist views. The leading Republican newspaper at this time was the *Aurora General Advertiser*, popularly known as the *Aurora*. It was founded on October 1, 1790, by Benjamin Franklin Bache, a grandson of Benjamin Franklin. Bache and Smith undoubtedly were acquainted, since the two received their B.A. and M.A. degrees from the University of Pennsylvania in the same years.[25] However, it is difficult to ascertain the professional relationship that actually existed between the two men.

Bache and Smith had entirely different views on editing a political newspaper. Bache was bold, brash, and outspoken in his mannerisms and in the paper he produced. When first established, the *Aurora* played a subordinate role to the *National Gazette*, edited by the poet Philip Freneau, in advocating the Republican cause, but after the failure of the Freneau paper in 1793,[26] Bache and his *Aurora* championed the Republican philosophy.

Bache frequently attacked the Federalists; not even George Washington was free from the bitter criticism of the paper. The *Aurora* backed France in its war with Great Britain and

23. Joseph Sabin and Wilberforce Eames, *Bibliotheca Americana* (New York, 1928), 20:547.

24. Ibid., pp. 547-48.

25. University of Pennsylvania, *General Alumni Catalogue*, p. 10.

26. For an account of the life of Philip Freneau, see Lewis Leary, *That Rascal Freneau: A Study in Literary Failure* (New Brunswick, N.J., 1941).

criticized the Washington administration's refusal to aid the French.[27] On Washington's retirement, Bache's *Aurora* shocked many with an uncharitable editorial. Bache wrote: " 'Lord now lettest thou thy servant depart in peace for mine eyes have seen thy salvation' was the pious ejaculation of a man who beheld a flood of happiness rushing in upon mankind." Bache was certain that if ever there was a time to repeat this exclamation, that time had arrived, "for the man who is the source of all the misfortunes of our country is this day reduced to a level with his fellow citizens and is no longer possessed of power to multiply evils upon the United States." He contended this was a period for rejoicing.[28] Needless to say, Washington held no affection for Bache and thought his paper was an outrage to "common decency."[29]

The Federalists had good reason for disliking Bache intensely, for his paper constantly irritated them. In 1795 he committed one of his gravest offenses when he published the text of Jay's treaty with Great Britain while the controversial document still was being debated by the Senate.[30] His pro-French sympathies largely accounted for his troubles with the Washington and Adams administrations and earned for him the reputation of being among the leading Jacobins in the United States. Bache so bitterly criticized John Adams that Mrs. Adams, only slightly anticipating the Alien and Sedition laws of 1798, thought Bache should be presented by "the grand jurors."[31]

Feelings against the *Aurora* ran so strong during 1798 that twice Bache's house was attacked by mobs, and on two other occasions Bache was physically beaten. Both attacks on his home were led by groups demonstrating anti-French feelings.[32] Abel Humphreys, son of the builder of the frigate *United States*, and John Ward Fenno, son of the editor of the

27. For a discussion of the United States' relationship to the war between Great Britain and France, see Samuel Eliot Morison and Henry Steele Commager, *The Growth of the American Republic* (New York, 1962), 1:345-69.

28. *Aurora*, March 5, 1795.

29. Jared Sparks, ed., *Writings of George Washington* (Boston, 1836), 10:359.

30. *Aurora*, June 30, 1795.

31. James Morton Smith, *Freedom's Fetters: The Alien and Sedition Laws and American Civil Liberties* (Ithaca, N.Y., 1956), p. 191; and Mrs. Abigail Adams to her sister, April 7, 1798, as quoted in Stewart Mitchell, ed., *New Letters of Abigail Adams, 1788-1801* (Boston, 1947), pp. 153-55.

32. *Aurora*, May 9, 1798; *Gazette of the United States*, May 10, 1798.

Federalist *Gazette of the United States*, both outraged by Bache's editorial attacks, physically assaulted Bache.[33]

Charges that the French Directory employed Bache were climaxed in June, 1798, when the *Aurora*'s editor published a conciliatory note from Talleyrand before it had been submitted to Congress. The letter, which offered to negotiate with the XYZ representatives in France at that time, was received in the United States only two days before Bache published it, and Federalist editors claimed the letter was received directly from the French Directory, proof that the French employed Bache.[34]

Shortly after this the famous Sedition Laws of 1798 were passed, and the Federalists used Bache's publication as one of the chief arguments for urging passage of the bill. Bache was arrested before the bill actually was signed into law and charged with libeling the president and the executive government. Before he could be brought to trial, however, he died of yellow fever on September 10, 1798, during the horrible epidemic that ravaged Philadelphia.[35]

Bache's death altered only slightly the character of the brash *Aurora*, for his associate editor, William Duane, took charge. Duane, born in New York State, obtained his newspaper experience both in England and in India before arriving in Philadelphia in 1796. He went to work for Bache shortly after arriving and contributed much to the fiery outpourings that appeared in the *Aurora*. Between 1798 and 1800 Duane edited the paper and led the bitter campaign against the Alien Act. Federalists' attempts to convict Duane under the Sedition Law, his efforts at evading prosecution, and later his indictment all kept the *Aurora* and its editor before the public eye.[36] Duane's wife also died in the epidemic of 1798, and on June 28, 1800, Duane and the widow Bache were married. Duane then became sole owner of the paper.[37]

The Federalist press that opposed Smith was as colorful as

33. Smith, *Freedom's Fetters*, p. 193.
34. Ibid.; *Aurora*, June 16, 21, and 22, 1798.
35. J. Thomas Scharf and Thompson Westcott, *History of Philadelphia, 1609-1884* (Philadelphia, 1884), 3:1977; and James C. Miller, *Crisis in Freedom: The Alien and Sedition Acts* (Boston, 1951), p. 96.
36. Smith, *Freedom's Fetters*, pp. 277-306.
37. Margaret Woodbury, "Public Opinion in Philadelphia, 1789-1801," *Smith College Studies in History* (Northampton, Mass., 1919-20), 5:26-27.

that which supported the Republican cause. Until 1798 John Fenno edited the leading Federalist paper, the *Gazette of the United States*, which he moved to Philadelphia from New York in 1790.[38] The *Gazette* supported Washington and was considered rather aristocratic in tone.

On March 4, 1797, a much more dynamic editor than Fenno appeared on the Philadelphia scene: William Cobbett, an Englishman who had gained a reputation as a political pamphleteer in the United States before starting his paper, *Porcupine's Gazette*.[39] Cobbett, writing under the pseudonym of "Peter Porcupine," was as scurrilous in his attacks on individuals as was either Bache or Duane, and he probably was far less careful with the truth.[40] Many Federalists, including President Adams's wife, applauded *Porcupine's Gazette*,[41] but Cobbett's abusive attacks on Dr. Benjamin Rush for his treatment of yellow fever eventually led to a sensational libel trial and to Cobbett's conviction. He fled the country, and this ended the most colorful of the Federalists' papers in the national capital.[42]

With such lively competition, Smith's first two attempts at newspaper publishing met little success. On August 15, 1796, Smith began the *New World*, a twice-daily news sheet innovative to Philadelphia journalism of that day.[43] Pledged to support Jefferson and the Republican party, the paper was changed to a daily on October 24, 1796, and its size altered from a quarto to a folio.[44]

The *New World*, in its first issue, promised that the editor would encourage political discussion as long as it was connected with "principles and the general good." Party malevolence and personal resentment would be rejected, making

38. Ibid., p. 11.
39. For a life of Cobbett, see L. T. Melville, *The Life and Letters of William Cobbett in England and America* (London, 1913); also the articles by William Reitzel, "William Cobbett and Philadelphia Journalism," *The Pennsylvania Magazine of History and Biography* 59 (1935): 223, and "William Cobbett," *Littell's Living Age* 41 (1854): 61.
40. Scharf and Westcott, *History of Philadelphia*, p. 1979.
41. Mitchell, *New Letters of Abigail Adams*, p. 142.
42. For a detailed account of the libel trial, see Winthrop and Frances Neilson, *Verdict for the Doctor: The Case of Benjamin Rush* (New York, 1958); see also Woodbury, "Public Opinion in Philadelphia," pp. 15-20, for a briefer account of the suit.
43. Clarence S. Brigham, *History and Bibliography of American Newspapers, 1690-1820* (Worcester, Mass., 1947), 2:927.
44. *New World*, October 26, 1796.

Smith's paper radically different from those of his competitors.[45]

What prompted Smith to start the *New World* or who his supporters were is not clear, but undoubtedly his attachment to the Republican party and his interest in the election of 1796 played some role in establishing the paper. Editorials, most signed with Greek noms de plume, heaped extravagant praise on Jefferson, preferred Pinckney to Adams if a Federalist had to be elected, and criticized the retiring President Washington. Smith seems to have contributed little, if any, comments himself. The views expressed in the *New World* were those of subscribers and readers.[46]

The *New World* ceased publication on August 16, 1797,[47] and not until two years later did Smith turn his attention to another journalistic venture: the *Independent Gazetteer*. The *Gazetteer* had been founded in April, 1782, by Eleazer Oswald, was published weekly on Saturdays, and had the reputation of being a lively newspaper. Following Oswald's death, the paper was sold to Joseph Gales, Sr., a refugee political editor from England.[48] Gales continued to publish the *Gazetteer* until the summer of 1797, when he sold it to Smith, and in 1799 he moved to North Carolina to begin publishing the influential *Raleigh Register*.[49]

Smith changed the name of the *Gazetteer* to the *Universal Gazette* on November 16, 1797,[50] but did not alter its general format. He continued to print news of the nation's capital in Philadelphia and to publish the usual letters bearing classical signatures from unidentified contributors. He wrote few editorials. Obviously intended for readers outside Philadelphia, the paper contained a minimum of local news. Politically it supported the Republican party, yet partisan expressions were couched in moderate and inoffensive language.

45. Ibid., August 15, 1796.
46. See *New World*, October 26, 1796, for a particularly lively political issue of the paper.
47. Ibid., August 16, 1797.
48. For a more complete discussion of Gales and his coming to America, see Chapter 5.
49. Winifred and Joseph Gales' Recollections, Gales Family Papers, University of North Carolina Library, Chapel Hill, N.C., p. 139; Woodbury, "Public Opinion in Philadelphia," p. 31; Scharf and Westcott, *History of Philadelphia*, pp. 1975-76.
50. Files of the *Universal Gazette* are available at the Pennsylvania State Historical Society, Philadelphia, and at Duke University, Durham, N.C.

Smith's mild political stand, however, did not reflect any lack of commitment to the Republican party. Smith believed a newspaper should present both sides of controversial issues rather than just one, and he was critical of party papers so tied to one political view that they would permit no writings from opposing politicians.

Smith's policy of not making personal comments on contemporary issues at times frustrated him, for he strongly opposed the Alien and Sedition Acts of 1798.[51] Yet he hesitated to say so. Also, he was convinced that Jefferson was the man the United States needed to head its government, but Smith's policy stopped him from supporting and defending Jefferson.

Gazette readers, few as they were, were annoyed with the policy of editorial neutrality. To make matters worse, subscribers were distributed over a number of states, which made collections difficult, as Joseph Gales, Sr., had found to his regret when he published the *Independent Gazetteer*.[52]

Smith therefore began in the summer of 1799 to investigate other publishing opportunities, and his eyes followed the nation's capital from Philadelphia to Washington City. If he went there, he reasoned, he could cover news from the seat of government, he would come into contact with the nation's leading political and social personalities, and he might even capture the lucrative plum of public printing.

He needed to think seriously about his future, for he was engaged to his second cousin, Margaret Bayard, and the pair hoped to be married soon.[53] A vivacious young lady of twenty-two, Margaret had sharp eyes and rather attractive features.[54] She was a dynamic person who, although contending she preferred solitude, mingled graciously with people and could be counted upon as a valuable asset to almost any career.

Margaret, born February 29, 1778, when the American Revolution engulfed the energies of the country, was the

51. For a complete text of these acts, see *United States Statutes at Large*, statute 2 (Boston, 1845), 1:570-72, 577-78, 596-97.
52. Gales' Recollections, pp. 155-57.
53. Samuel Harrison Smith to Margaret Bayard, January 3, 1800, Margaret Bayard Smith Papers, vol. 5.
54. Smith, *First Forty Years*, frontispiece.

seventh child[55] of John Bubenheim Bayard, a Philadelphia mercantilist and Maryland plantation owner. John Bayard was the son of James Bayard, who had moved the family to Maryland from New York, where the original Bayards settled after leaving France.[56]

John Bayard, father of Margaret, left Maryland when he was eighteen years old and entered the counting house of John Rhea in Philadelphia. Here he met and married Margaret Hodge, daughter of a prominent Philadelphian, and here also he achieved considerable financial success before he became deeply involved in the colonial activities that eventually led to the revolt against England.[57] In 1765 Bayard took his first protest action when he signed a nonimportation agreement against England.[58] Later he served in the Provincial Congress, in the Convention for the Province, which encouraged domestic industry, and finally in the Pennsylvania assembly, of which he was speaker in 1777.[59] He early joined the Sons of Liberty and urged the choice of Washington as commander in chief of the colonial forces. His activities, however, were not limited to administrative and legislative action, for he also saw considerable military service and served as a colonel at the battles of Brandywine, Germantown, and Princeton.[60]

Margaret undoubtedly heard much about the activities of her father and was familiar with the difficulties suffered by the rest of her family during the long conflict. When hostilities began, John Bayard moved his family from Philadelphia

55. Margaret's brothers, none of whom is mentioned prominently in any of her writings or diaries, included James Asheton Bayard, who died in 1788; Andrew, a merchant, who was president of the Commercial Bank of Philadelphia; John, who owned an estate in Monmouth County, New Jersey; Samuel, who served as clerk of the United States Supreme Court and in numerous other federal and local governmental offices; and Nicholas, an eminent physician. Margaret's two sisters were Jane Kirkpatrick, wife of the chief justice of New Jersey, and Anna Maria, who married a New York lawyer. Her three foster brothers and sister, James Asheton, John, and Jane Bayard, were considerably older than Margaret, and only James is mentioned in her correspondence. The family genealogy is given by General Jas. Grant Wilson, "Colonel John Bayard (1738-1807) and the Bayard Family of America," *The New York Genealogical and Biographical Record* 16 (April, 1885): 70-72.

56. Ibid., pp. 52-53.

57. Morton Borden, *The Federalism of James A. Bayard* (New York, 1955), p. 16.

58. Wilson, "Colonel John Bayard," p. 54.

59. Ibid., pp. 55-58.

60. Ibid.

to a farm on the Schuylkill, about eighteen miles from the city. During the family's stay there Margaret's oldest brother, James, was captured by the British while enroute home from college at Princeton, New Jersey. Mrs. Bayard went to Philadelphia and personally interceded with Washington to get her son released.[61] Later the Bayard farm was captured by the British, and for a time the family lived at Bohemia Manor, their Maryland plantation, until it was safe to return to Philadelphia and to the farm.[62]

Because of her age Margaret undoubtedly remembered little of this turmoil, and she probably had only vague recollections of her mother, who died when Margaret was four. Jonathan Bayard married twice after this, the last time to Johannah White, sister of General Anthony W. White, of New Brunswick, New Jersey. In 1788 Bayard retired from business in Philadelphia, and he was forced to sell Bohemia Manor because of the financial strain of the war and the extravagance of his oldest son.[63] He moved to New Brunswick and became active in the political and social affairs of that community. He served as mayor of New Brunswick, as justice of the court of common pleas of Somerset County, and as trustee of the College of New Jersey from 1778 to 1806. He also served in the state assembly and was active in the Presbyterian church.[64]

While in New Jersey Margaret received part of her education at home. She also attended the Moravian seminary at Bethlehem, Pennsylvania.[65]

Despite the fact that John Bayard was absent from home a good deal and exerted little influence over his family, he did succeed in indoctrinating them with his political views.[66] John Bayard was a Federalist of the Alexander Hamilton school, believing in a class of gentry to act as guardians of the people rather than to serve as representatives. He thought society must have class distinctions to function properly.[67]

61. Borden, *Federalism of James A. Bayard*, p. 16.
62. Wilson, "Colonel John Bayard," pp. 60-61.
63. Borden, *Federalism of James A. Bayard*, p. 20; Mrs. Jane Kirkpatrick, *The Light of Other Days: Sketches of the Past* (New Brunswick, N.J., 1856), p. 33.
64. Wilson, "Colonel John Bayard," p. 66.
65. *Appleton's Cyclopaedia of American Biography* 5:574, 1888.
66. Kirkpatrick, *Light of Other Days*, p. 33.
67. Wilson, "Colonel John Bayard," p. 64.

Margaret Bayard's Federalist beliefs sharply contrasted with Smith's Republican views, a point that caused some consternation on the part of her family. Other objections were raised to the engagement.[68] Margaret was reared a devout Presbyterian, while Smith, following Jefferson to the fullest, was a deist, a "non-believer."[69]

In addition, the Bayard family considered Smith a rather unsatisfactory mate for Margaret because of the general lack of financial success of his printing and newspaper ventures in Philadelphia. Therefore, in the summer of 1799, considerable attention was given to a plan to urge Smith to start a newspaper in New York. Margaret's brother Samuel especially urged Smith to leave Philadelphia, for he thought that the *Universal Gazette* had an unpromising future, and though the number of subscribers to the *Gazette* increased yearly, that the paper still was unproductive. Margaret supported her brother and campaigned to get Smith to move to New York.[70]

Smith was uncertain of the wisdom of moving to New York and of attempting to establish a paper there. He was concerned particularly about the financial risks. He estimated at least $12,000 to $15,000 would be needed to run the paper for a year, and he would be forced to borrow much of this amount. No wonder he dreaded such a gamble. He was willing to consider the venture, however, and was pleased that Samuel Bayard might give the needed financial support.[71]

But the proposed New York venture was eclipsed in June, 1800, when Smith first reported to Margaret that both Thomas Jefferson and Albert Gallatin had encouraged him to start a Republican newspaper in Washington City.[72] Smith,

68. Margaret Bayard to Samuel Harrison Smith, February 20, 1800, Margaret Bayard Smith Papers, vol. 5.

69. Margaret Bayard to Mary Ann Smith, August 16, 1800, Margaret Bayard Smith Papers, vol. 6.

70. Margaret Bayard to Samuel Harrison Smith, Friday (no date), March, 1800, and Margaret Bayard to Smith, April 9, 1800, and April 23, 1800, Margaret Bayard Smith Papers, vol. 6.

71. Samuel Harrison Smith to Margaret Bayard, March 31, 1800, Margaret Bayard Smith Papers, vol. 6.

72. Samuel Harrison Smith to Margaret Bayard, June 26, 1800, and Smith to Margaret Bayard, January 2, 1800, Margaret Bayard Smith Papers, vols. 6 and 5; see also Albert Gallatin to Thomas Jefferson, December 15, 1801, "Letters of William Duane," *Proceedings of the Massachusetts Historical Society* (Boston, 1906, 1907), 20:258-59.

Margaret learned, had caught Jefferson's eye in 1797 when both were active in the American Philosophical Society and when Smith had shared an award for the best essay on a system of national education with the Reverend Samuel Knox, a Presbyterian minister of Bladensburg, Maryland.[73] In 1798 Smith became secretary of the society, and Jefferson was president.[74] A friendship developed that eventually led to the proposed Washington newspaper.[75]

The Washington plan pleased Smith, but he made no decision until he had consulted his fiancée and received her permission. Margaret, perhaps to Smith's surprise, was perfectly willing to leave Philadelphia for Washington City. Chance for success and prosperity in the former city seemed unlikely, while Washington held promise. She explained to Smith's sister: "You ask me . . . what I think of the plan your brother has adopted; I answer you with pleasure that it meets with my fullest approbation." She was relieved of the possibility of living in Philadelphia. There, she reasoned, it would have been years before she and her husband could afford to live in the style of the "persons we must have been obliged to see. . . ." She could not have entertained and would have been considered "parsimonious and unhospitable." But in Washington all these "inconveniences" would be gone. "We will be unknown, and may live as we please."[76]

On July 30 Smith told Margaret that the move to Washington City was becoming more attractive and that he only awaited the removal of a few obstacles before making final plans.[77] For one thing, Smith's brother John objected to the wedding, saying a young bride should not be taken to the undeveloped District of Columbia. The lack of adequate accommodations, said John Smith, would seriously handicap

---

73. Margaret Bayard Smith, "Washington in Jefferson's Time, from the diaries and family letters of Mrs. Samuel Harrison Smith (Margaret Bayard)," ed. Gaillard Hunt, *Scribner's Magazine* 40 (July-December, 1906): 295; also quoted from Mrs. Smith's notebook in Smith, *First Forty Years*, p. 9; Bryan, *History of the National Capital*, 1:90.

74. *Proceedings of the American Philosophical Society*, part 3, no. 119 (Philadelphia, 1885), 22:246.

75. Smith, *First Forty Years*, p. 9.

76. Margaret Bayard to Mary Ann Smith, August 16, 1800, Margaret Bayard Smith Papers, vol. 6.

77. Samuel Harrison Smith to Margaret Bayard, July 30, 1800, Margaret Bayard Smith Papers, vol. 6.

the Smiths in Washington City. John's approval was important, for he had banking connections with a New York firm that had promised to finance the proposed paper. As Smith explained, "If he (John) choose to exert this influence . . . I may be seriously embarrassed."[78] Within ten days, however, John's objections were overcome, and wedding plans began in earnest.[79] Fortunately Margaret's family gave her a dowery of "sufficient sum to furnish the house genteely [sic]."[80] But the wedding date was not yet set.

Before the wedding Smith had much to do. He traveled to Washington City in mid-August to find a house for himself and his bride and also a suitable location for his print shop. Fortunately he rented two nearly completed buildings, one in which to live and the other for his business. He, like many another visitor, was surprised by the crudeness of the city. He wondered if Margaret would really be happy with her new home.[81]

Smith returned to Philadelphia to seek support for his new publication from top Republican leaders. He wrote James Madison soliciting aid, saying he hoped that Gallatin had told Madison of Smith's project. Madison was assured by Smith that he had promises of support, but Smith hoped that he might add Madison's name to the list of persons offering assistance.[82] Smith also ordered the necessary paper, type, and other materials, with delivery promised in Washington City by September 23.[83]

But all Smith's thoughts and attention were not devoted to soliciting aid for his new paper, and, despite his inclination to be rather matter-of-fact, his letters to his prospective bride were filled with many romantic thoughts and glances ahead at married life. He confided to Margaret this anticipation: "Much, very much, of, perhaps, the most precious felicity of our lives depend upon our cherishing our retirement, in our

78. Ibid., August 12, 1800.
79. Ibid., August 22, 1800.
80. Margaret Bayard to Mary Ann Smith, August 16, 1800, Margaret Bayard Smith Papers, vol. 6.
81. Samuel Harrison Smith to Margaret Bayard, August 22, 1800, Margaret Bayard Smith Papers, vol. 6.
82. Samuel Harrison Smith to James Madison, August 27, 1800, James Madison Papers, vol. 21, Library of Congress, Washington, D.C.
83. Samuel Harrison Smith to Margaret Bayard, August 28, 1800, Margaret Bayard Smith Papers, vol. 6.

own humble abode, unnoticed by the unobtrusive eye of curiosity. The first pledges of love—ah! my tenderest Margaret—how delicious are the feelings."[84]

Because of the suddenness of the decision to move to Washington City, the wedding date was not finally set until September 13, and even then the prospective bridegroom was not certain he would be able to make it to New Brunswick for the wedding. The bride too admitted she was trembling with anticipation of the event. On Friday, September 26, Smith arrived at Margaret's New Jersey home. On the following Monday, September 29, the nuptial vows were spoken, and the couple left by carriage for Philadelphia, where they took the stagecoach for Washington City.[85]

The young publisher and his wife, with much to be optimistic about, also faced great problems. The Smiths were gambling that Jefferson would become president and that his election would bring them a share of the federal printing. They were leaving the familiar surroundings in which they were reared and were moving into the uncertain but challenging society growing up around the new capital. The possibilities of success were promising but uncertain. However, if the *National Intelligencer* should fail, Smith still had the *Universal Gazette*, for he moved the subscription list to Washington City with him. He continued to publish the *Gazette* until he sold his newspaper interests in 1810.[86]

84. Ibid., September 4, 1800.
85. Margaret Bayard Smith to her family, October 3, 1800, and Samuel Harrison Smith to Mary Ann and Susan Smith, October 5, 1800, Margaret Bayard Smith Papers, vol. 6.
86. Brigham, *American Newspapers*, 1:106-7.

CHAPTER 2

Early Success

Smith probably little realized as his publishing venture got underway that fall in 1800 just how fortunate he was. He was about to begin publishing one of the nation's most influential newspapers, to be an important part of the Jefferson administration, and to play a major role in nineteenth-century journalism. All this was possible for the young editor if fortune should go his way. So much depended on Jefferson, his election, and his policies.

Smith's devotion to Jefferson, as his editorship proved, was unqualified and the young editor willingly risked all to serve the man he hoped would be the next president. As the campaign of 1800 developed, he was greatly encouraged by the triumph of the Jeffersonian Republicans in New York that spring and by reports from Maryland and Virginia that these states too would lead in throwing off the Federalist rule.[1]

1. The most recent treatment of the election challenges many long-held interpretations and adds many insights into the organization and functioning of the Republican party. See Noble E. Cunningham, Jr., *The Jeffersonian Republicans: The Formation of Party Organization, 1789-1801* (Chapel Hill, N.C., 1957). For a detailed account of the campaign, see pp. 145-210.

During the early weeks of October, 1800, the young editor worked frantically while waiting for his equipment and supplies to be shipped from Philadelphia. These were delayed by a storm on Chesapeake Bay, and not until October 31 did politicians and Washington townspeople see the first issue of the *National Intelligencer and Washington Advertiser.*

In general, readers and subscribers knew what to expect, for Smith, as was customary in his day, published a prospectus in Georgetown's *Centinel of Liberty* and in Philadelphia's *Universal Gazette* and the *Aurora.* The *Intelligencer* was to be a triweekly costing five dollars a year. Smith promised his readers the new paper would contain more opinion than his earlier publications. He intended to treat fairly all persons and political views but felt it his duty to carefully scrutinize "public measures and conduct of public men." Candor and truth, he promised, would be his guide.[2]

The *Intelligencer* was largely a one-man operation, with Smith handling all duties of the paper except mechanical reproduction. He wrote the news, took the debates, selected the exchange stories, handled the advertising and accounting, and in general, published the three issues a week nearly single-handed.

Beginning with the first issue, the paper's content was fairly well standardized.[3] In a small column on the front page Smith sometimes aired his opinions on happenings in the nation's capital. The remainder of the page reported congressional proceedings and contained advertisements. Small business notices were purchased mostly by Washington City storekeepers and slave owners whose property had run away.

Congressional proceedings as well as miscellaneous material, such as excerpts from current books, letters from subscribers, and lengthy political articles written by unidentified correspondents, along with clippings from other newspapers, filled page two of the *Intelligencer.* A second editorial column appeared on page three, and page four carried a variety of

2. For copies of the prospectus, see *National Intelligencer and Washington Advertiser* (Washington, D.C.), October 31, 1800; the *Universal Gazette* (Philadelphia) for August, 1800; and the *Aurora* (Philadelphia) and *Centinel of Liberty* (Georgetown) September and October, 1800. The *National Intelligencer and Washington Advertiser* is hereafter referred to as the *National Intelligencer.*

3. Nearly complete files are available at the Library of Congress. Microfilm of the paper is available at the University of Minnesota Library, Minneapolis.

material. Most of the paper was devoted to congressional proceedings, but stories clipped from exchange papers were found throughout the paper.

Small type for both headlines and text of stories characterized the paper's conservative makeup. Short, label headlines gave the same dull, grey appearance to each page. Much of the paper's text was printed in small six-point type, and lengthy debates ran for columns with nothing to break the solid blocks of printed matter.

Smith had many problems to overcome before the *Intelligencer* venture could succeed. First, and most important, was the question of whether Jefferson could win the presidential election in November. The paper itself was started too late to influence voters, and the complexities of the contest of 1800 proved trying indeed to the young publisher. Even after the November election showed the next president would be a Republican, the tie in electoral votes between Jefferson and Aaron Burr left the name in doubt. The campaign had been bitter and had been waged over a span of several years, not months, and many Federalists viewed the threat of Jefferson as president as a great risk. After all, he was to them an atheist, a Jacobin, a fanatic liberal—and a Virginian, which in the eyes of many in New England and in the Middle Atlantic states was as great an offense as any other accusation.[4]

Smith's paper gave no hint of the behind-the-scenes maneuvering carried on by many Federalist congressional members in an attempt to swing support behind Burr and thus to deprive Jefferson of the presidency. Smith perhaps knew little of the complicated web of secrecy woven around the election, but by the time the election reached the House of Representatives, he was keenly aware of the Federalist plot. He also must have realized that James A. Bayard, his wife's foster brother and his cousin, played a key role in the Federalist plans.[5] Strained family relations may have precluded any possibility of Smith or his wife influencing Bayard, holder of the single Delaware vote, away from supporting Burr. Apparently no

4. For the most complete account of the election, see Cunningham, *Jeffersonian Republicans.*

5. For a detailed account of the House of Representative's election, see Frank van der Linden, *The Turning Point: Jefferson's Battle for the Presidency* (Washington, D.C., 1962).

close ties existed between Mrs. Smith and her foster brother, and only occasionally did she mention his presence in her Washington home, and then in a most impersonal manner.[6] Bayard's correspondence had only one reference to his foster sister, despite the fact that many of his letters were addressed to her brother, Andrew.[7]

Mrs. Smith, writing years later of the tense election in the House of Representatives, claimed she and her husband thought little of the personal issues involved. Instead they feared for the future of the nation should the Federalists succeed in electing Burr. To her, Jefferson's election meant not only a question of war or peace but of the whole future of the nation.[8]

The Smiths waited together in their parlor as the balloting began on February 12 and continued throughout the night. A messenger brought hourly reports,[9] and as the time for each message approached, Mrs. Smith wrote, " '... my heart would almost audibly beat and I was seized with a tremour that almost disabled me from opening the door. . . .' "[10] Mrs. Smith's memory proved faulty in the time sequence involved, for the election was not determined on Friday, as she recalled,[11] but rather continued until the following Tuesday, when Bayard cast a blank ballot, other congressmen followed suit, and the Jeffersonian majority was achieved.[12]

Mrs. Smith was elated: " 'The dark and threatening cloud which had hung over the political horrison [*sic*], rolled harmlessly away, and the sunshine of prosperity and gladness broke forth. . . .' "[13]

Smith hoped that Jefferson's election might remove some

6. Mrs. Samuel Harrison Smith, *The First Forty Years of Washington Society* (New York, 1906), pp. 10, 24, and 26.
7. See "Papers of James A. Bayard, 1796-1815," ed. Elizabeth Donnan, *American Historical Association Annual Report*, 1913 (Washington, D.C., 1915), 2:145.
8. Mrs. Samuel Harrison Smith, quoted from her notebook in *First Forty Years*, p. 23.
9. For a description of the event, ibid., p. 24; see also Margaret Bayard Smith, "Washington in Jefferson's Time, from the diaries and family letters of Mrs. Samuel Harrison Smith (Margaret Bayard)," ed. Gaillard Hunt, *Scribner's Magazine* 40 (July-December, 1906): 298.
10. Mrs. Samuel Harrison Smith, quoted from her notebook in *First Forty Years*, p. 24.
11. Ibid., p. 25.
12. Donnan, "Papers of James A. Bayard," p. 132.
13. Mrs. Samuel Harrison Smith, quoted from her notebook in *First Forty Years*, p. 25.

annoyances caused by the Federalist-dominated Congress. He experienced none from President Adams's office, however, where the president had been cordial; information for the *Intelligencer* was courteously given despite Smith's support of Jefferson.[14]

But Smith's dealings with the House of Representatives proved less pleasant. In early December, 1800, when the congressional session opened, Smith prepared to report the debates and proceedings of the House of Representatives, the body considered more important by many Republicans because of the popular election of its members[15] and the body that remained under Federalist domination throughout this session.

Since no facilities existed in the new House chamber for reporters, or stenographers as they were then known, Smith spoke to the Speaker of the House, Theodore Sedgwick, of Massachusetts, requesting permission to place a desk inside the rail in order to better hear the debates. Smith ordered a desk built, and he and a Thomas Carpenter[16] sent a memorial to the House for admission within the bar.

Sedgwick, a closed-minded Federalist, stood poised to save the nation from the ruin threatened by the Jeffersonian Republicans and fought his rear guard actions with vigor.

In considering the request Speaker Sedgwick concluded that the dignity of the House and the convenience of the members could not be preserved if such permission were granted. He contended the area of the House chamber was too small for such action.[17] The matter was referred to a House committee, which reported on December 9 that " 'it is not expedient for this House to make any order upon the subject of the memorial of Samuel Harrison Smith and Thomas Carpenter. . . .' " A move to refer the matter to a committee of the whole was defeated.[18]

The debate that followed split the House, largely on party

14. Samuel Harrison Smith to Susan B. Smith, November 27, 1800, Margaret Bayard Smith Papers, vol. 6, Library of Congress, Washington, D.C.

15. Henry Adams, *History of the United States of America* (New York, 1930), 1:266.

16. I was unable to establish the identity of Carpenter. At this time a Thomas Carpenter did run a tailor shop in Washington, D.C., but whether this is the same person is not known.

17. *Annals of Congress*, Sixth Congress, Second Session (Washington, D.C., 1851), 10:797-99.

18. Ibid., p. 806.

lines, in opposition or defense of Smith's right to be admitted within the bar. The question, as those opposing the admission saw it, concerned the prerogatives of the Speaker; those favoring admission of the reporters viewed the problem as a matter of freedom of information.

Harrison G. Otis supported his fellow representative from Massachusetts and opposed taking away the Speaker's power of granting admission, a right previously given in 1797.[19] Otis admitted that in Philadelphia the one or two reporters at the sessions were admitted within the bar, but there was room. In Washington City there was not. Perhaps, he pointed out, the stenographers could occupy the space allowed for executive officers and foreign ministers when it was not taken. Otis was supported in his views by John Nicholas of Virginia, Roger Griswold of Connecticut, and George Thatcher of Massachusetts.[20]

Opposing the Speaker's stand were Joseph Nicholson, from Maryland, one of Jefferson's chief supporters in the House, and William H. Hill of South Carolina. Nicholson disagreed with the idea that the House had to abide by the Speaker's decision; the House had a right to decide on its own. Further, he wondered if secretaries of the executive department and foreign dignitaries should have greater rights than citizens of the United States. Let these officials sit in the galleries, Nicholson suggested.[21]

The vote on the committee's recommendation, however, resulted in a 45-45 tie, and by his vote Sedgwick retained the right to decide where the stenographers would sit in the House of Representatives.

Smith continued to report the debates from outside the bar and on December 23 witnessed and reported that Sedgwick ordered a James Lane arrested for disorderly conduct after he allegedly applauded a remark made during a House debate.[22] The incident occasioned some comment when the matter was brought before the House on January 6. Lane contended he was ordered from the chamber by the sergeant at arms, Joseph Wheaton, and accordingly left the building.

19. Ibid., pp. 808-9.
20. Ibid., pp. 806-13.
21. Ibid., pp. 809-11.
22. Ibid., pp. 880-82.

Outside he again was apprehended and then imprisoned in a room in the capitol until the session ended. Smith reported this version.

Wheaton and his supporters denied the second apprehension, and Speaker Sedgwick supported this account. Further, Sedgwick contended, the whole affair was grossly misrepresented in the Washington newspapers.

Smith questioned Sedgwick's version and defended the *Intelligencer*'s account of the incident, making a point against the unsatisfactory reporting conditions in the House as well as the confusion of the Speaker. "He (Smith) will not deny his inability to understand the meaning of the Speaker, even when he hears all his words. His consolation, however, is, that the misfortune is not peculiar to himself."[23]

This incident probably brought on the chain of events that saw Smith expelled completely from the House, for on January 12, when Smith took his usual place outside the bar, the "Serjeant at Arms," on instructions from the Speaker, ordered the editor to leave. No reason was given, and Smith withdrew to the upper gallery.[24]

Smith's expulsion from the House floor made him more determined than ever to obtain a convenient place for reporting the debates. He vowed: "Uninfluenced by personal feeling, and guided by a *due* respect for the *Speaker*, and a *sincere* respect for the *People* of the United States, he will not, while he retains the power, cease, by publishing a record of truth, whatever or whomsoever it may affect, to manifest to the people, on *whose* support he relies, a spirit of dignity and moderation that frowns of power can never dismay."[25]

On the day this was published the sergeant at arms brought from the Speaker a message demanding Smith to withdraw from the gallery. No reasons were given, and Smith left without creating a disturbance. Later he protested that he had assumed the galleries were for anyone.[26]

A few days later Smith approached Sedgwick and asked the reasons for his expulsion from the House. Had he been removed because he was a reporter? Or had he been removed

23. Ibid., p. 886.
24. *National Intelligencer*, January 14, 1801.
25. Ibid., January 14, 1801.
26. Ibid., January 16, 1801.

for other reasons? Sedgwick answered that Smith had been expelled because he had either intentionally or incompetently misrepresented the Speaker's conduct to *Intelligencer* readers. Sedgwick cited no specific incident but said he thought Smith and others were intentionally abusing the Speaker. However, while not allowing Smith within the House, Sedgwick gave the editor access to any papers the House clerk "pleases to let you have. . . ."[27]

To Smith this was censorship, an attempt on the part of the Speaker to conduct the legislative affairs of the country in secret. The editor wrote: "I have always believed . . . that the only respect which the government of a republican country ought to receive, is that, which flows from a knowledge of its acts, and of the manner in which those acts are passed; except in peculiar cases that may require secrecy."[28]

The Republican members of Congress rallied to Smith's cause, and on February 18 Thomas T. Davis, from Kentucky, introduced a resolution censuring Sedgwick's action. Two days later the censure was voted out of order 54-49.[29] A resolution introduced by Gallatin aimed at limiting the Speaker's right of expulsion also was defeated by a party vote.[30]

Smith was unable to regain admission during the session, but the *Intelligencer* continued to carry debates from the House. Where Smith received his reports is not clear, but some may have come from the representatives themselves and other material probably was taken from the House clerk.

Editors throughout the country watched Smith's battle for admission with interest, for already they were copying reports of congressional proceedings from the *Intelligencer*. Joseph Gales, Sr., editor of the *Raleigh* (North Carolina) *Register*, acknowledged indebtedness to the *Intelligencer* for congressional bulletins and thought his readers could not help "considering this conduct of Mr. Sedgwick as very arbitrary, since it may deprive the people of any account at all of congressional proceedings."[31]

Smith gained readmission to the House the following ses-

27. Ibid., January 19, 1801.
28. Ibid.
29. Ibid., February 23, 1801.
30. Ibid.
31. *Raleigh Register* and *North-Carolina State Gazette*, January 27, 1801.

sion when the Republican majority took control. Nathaniel Macon of North Carolina was elected Speaker and used his prerogative to permit Smith's return. But Smith never considered the facilities for reporting the debates satisfactory during his term as editor of the *Intelligencer*.

Newspaper reporters' admittance to the Senate floor was less dramatic. Smith made no attempt to cover the Senate proceedings during his first year as editor, but on January 5, 1802, he presented a petition for the right to report the debates. Permission was granted by a 17-9 vote. The resolution gave the Senate president the right to determine the space to allot reporters; a move to require them to post bonds was defeated.[32]

Smith was pleased by the Senate action and informed his readers that reporting that chamber's proceedings previously had been impossible, because he had been required to sit in the gallery. Now, for the first time, reporters would be allowed on the lower floor. Indeed, this was the opening of a new door to public information, Smith wrote.[33] The editor of the *Raleigh Register* agreed.[34]

In neither instance had formal permission been given for reporting the debates. In both cases the presiding officers were left to decide if there would be a place for reporters. Even Macon, who opened the House door to Smith, as late as 1807 did not feel the matter of news coverage was settled definitely. He wrote: "S. H. Smith will claim the right to detail the proceedings of the Court and of the Senate. . . . I will not therefore interfere with his claim nor dispute at this time the Claim itself. . . ."[35]

Although Jefferson's election solved Smith's problems in dealing with the executive and congressional branches of government, the Federalist-dominated judiciary gave the young editor trouble. His problems with the courts in Washington City began in June, 1801, when he published a letter criticizing the judiciary and the late appointments of President John Adams.

32. *Annals of Congress*, Seventh Congress, First Session (Washington, D.C., 1851), 11:22.
33. *National Intelligencer*, January 8, 1802.
34. *Raleigh Register* and *North-Carolina State Gazette*, January 10, 1802.
35. Nathaniel Macon to Joseph Nicholson, January 30, 1807, Joseph Nicholson Papers, vol. 3, Library of Congress, Washington, D.C.

The article, written by an unidentified contributor who signed himself "A Friend to Impartial Justice," contended that Federalist judges no longer administered law impartially as the Constitution intended. As a result of Adams's late judicial appointments under the judiciary bill of 1801, the article continued, the courts had become a threat to the power of the executive and legislative branches. The writer lamented the court situation that faced Jefferson when he took over the presidency: "He found the community divided; he found the asylum of justice impure—There, where reason and truth, unagitated, and unimpaired even by suspicion, ought to preserve perpetual reign, he contemplated the dominance of political and personal prejudice, habitually employed in preparing or executing partial vengeance."[36]

On June 22, 1801, at the first meeting of the Circuit Court for the District of Columbia,[37] Justices John Marshall and William Cranch, contrary to the opinion of Justice William Kilty, ordered the district attorney to institute a libel prosecution against "the Editor of the National Intelligencer for a publication of his paper of the 12th, entitled, 'Appointments by the President.' "[38]

Smith viewed the charge as a test of the guarantee of freedom of the press as promised by the Constitution. Justice Marshall took an opposite view, stating he was a friend to freedom of the press but an enemy to licentiousness of the press. Marshall observed that the printers in the country on both sides of the political questions "which agitated the public mind" had taken "most unwarranted liberties, and descended to the most shameful scurrility and abuse." It was difficult for him to say on which side of the fence they had been most abusive. Marshall avowed that as long as he was on the bench he would restrain those abuses on both sides and contended this was what the court was doing in its action against Smith.[39]

A bond of $1,000 "recognizance" was posted by Smith, but the court required no sureties, even though a number of

36. *National Intelligencer*, June 12, 1801.
37. The court records for the case against Samuel Harrison Smith have not been located by searchers.
38. *National Intelligencer*, October 25, 1801.
39. Ibid.

Washington and Georgetown citizens offered to raise the full amount if necessary.[40]

Smith based his editorial defense on the United States Constitution, which permitted no law abridging freedom of speech and of the press. Also, he cited in his defense the Maryland Constitution, which stated " 'That the liberty of the press ought to be . . . preserved.' "[41] He further argued that the article containing the alleged libel applied to a public rather than to a private person. A public officer was criticized only for his discharge of an official duty and was not censured as an individual. As Smith saw it, the charge against him really involved differences of opinion, and what arbiter was to decide who was right or wrong in such differences? *"Inasmuch as governments may err, every citizen has a right to expose an error in HIS OPINION com[m]itted by them."* Smith wondered if courts could punish persons for holding and expressing opinions.[42]

Because Smith had not written the article, he argued that he was being tried as a printer rather than as a writer. The editor admitted that the person who wrote the article might have erred in his opinions, but said he had the right to express his opinions. Smith further explained that the views regarding the courts as instruments of executive power expressed the thoughts of the letter writer and not necessarily those of the editor.

The bill of indictment sent by the attorney for the district to the September term of the grand jury was returned marked "Ignoramus." This did not necessarily mean the case had to be dropped, but evidently the charges against Smith were not renewed.[43]

Another problem that occupied Smith's attention during his first year of publishing concerned finances. The printing patronage Smith hoped to realize from Jefferson's election involved a considerable sum from both congressional and executive printing orders.

Although it is difficult to ascertain just how much money was involved for any single year, in 1801 the House printing

40. Ibid., July 1, 1801.
41. Ibid., October 26, 1801.
42. Ibid.
43. Ibid.

alone totaled about $4,000[44] and the Senate about half this amount.[45] Executive printing for this period also amounted to a considerable sum, with the printing for the State, Treasury, and War Departments for the 1794 session totaling $7,061.67.[46]

Three days after Jefferson's inauguration Smith wrote confidently that he now would receive the printing orders of the federal government. He confided to his sister, Mary Ann: "The executive arrangements are made, and we have every appearance of at least a short political calm. This to me is a source of indefinable pleasure. No longer obliged to stand in the painful attitude of opposition, I find myself the government printer! . . . Can you believe it? I scarcely can. It seems a mystery! A republican, printing the President's speech, etc. —Can it be possible? Truly these are strange times—. . . ."[47]

Mrs. Smith was not as convinced as her husband that the matter was completely settled, however. The day after her husband wrote Mary Ann, Mrs. Smith gave her sister quite a different picture:

Mr. S & I, are equaly [sic] averse to solicitation of patronage, so much so, that altho he has seen Mr. Jefferson, at least once a week the whole winter, & although, Mr. J. has given him several testimonies of his good will; he has not even mentioned to him his wishes of recieving [sic] his support, or employ. Mr. S. is on an intimate footing, with Galatine [sic] & several other leading men, but even to them he has not expressed his wishes.—And yet, we rely so entirely on the good opinion of these men, that I have not doubt, he will have a large portion of the printing of the government & I am certain Mr. J. will like him all the better for not having solicited it.[48]

The Smiths had a right to worry, for a powerful competitor, William Duane, editor of the Philadelphia *Aurora*, was

44. *Annals of Congress*, Seventh Congress, First Session, 11:336.

45. During this period the printing costs were listed in the contingency expenses for the House and Senate, making exact printing costs difficult to ascertain.

46. Robert W. Kerr, *History of the Government Printing Office* (Lancaster, Pa., 1881), p. 16.

47. Samuel Harrison Smith to Mary Ann Smith, March 7, 1801, Margaret Bayard Smith Papers, vol. 6.

48. Margaret Bayard Smith to Jane Kirkpatrick, March 8, 1801, Margaret Bayard Smith Papers, vol. 7.

working for support to move his paper to Washington City, where he hoped to become a printer for the government.[49] Duane gave yeoman service to the Republican party in Pennsylvania after he took over the *Aurora* from Benjamin Franklin Bache in 1798. As a result of his efforts he spent much of his time in 1801 in court defending himself and incurring heavy expense. He reasoned that the Republican party ought to share these expenses and that patronage represented one way to reimburse him.

Duane's threat was lessened by the end of 1801, and by the December meeting of Congress Smith held the printing for the House of Representatives as well as for some executive departments. The House printing, in question until this time, was awarded by the House clerk to the lowest bidder. The Senate contract was awarded to the printing firm of Way and Groff, who had held the contract before the government moved from Philadelphia.[50]

Despite the prosperous outlook, Smith still was uneasy about his relations to the federal government and complained because he still had not received "the official communications" he hoped to receive.[51]

Duane, of course, was displeased when he learned that the House printing had been awarded to Smith,[52] and the *Aurora* editor took his complaints to Gallatin. The new secretary of the treasury, too, thought Smith had received a bit more of the printing than he rightfully deserved and protested to Jefferson: "Why Mr. John Beckley [House clerk] did not divide the printing between Mr. Duane and Mr. Smith I do not know; but I am sure that most of our friends are so chagrined at it, that they speak of altering the rules of the house, so as to have the printer appointed by the House & not by the clerk. Mr. Smith came here before the fate of the election was ascertained, and at a risk. He was promised by myself and others every reasonable encouragement.

49. Worthington C. Ford, "Letters of William Duane," *Proceedings of the Massachusetts Historical Society*, series 2 (Boston, 1907), 20:258-80.

50. Gallatin to Jefferson, December 15, 1801, quoted, ibid., pp. 258-59.

51. Samuel Harrison Smith to Mary Ann Smith, December 15, 1801, Margaret Bayard Smith Papers, vol. 7.

52. Raymond Walters, Jr., *Albert Gallatin: Jeffersonian Financier and Diplomat* (New York, 1957), p. 158.

But this cannot be construed into an exclusive monopoly."[53]

Gallatin suggested that various department heads be encouraged to make their stationery purchases from Duane's Washington City office supply store. Duane continued to make pleas for help from the administration[54] and eventually did receive part of the printing for his plant in 1803.[55]

The House reaction, which Gallatin foresaw in his letter to Jefferson, took place on December 17, when John Randolph, Jr., of Virginia, asked for appointment of a committee to investigate the letting of the printing contracts. The group included Randolph, Joseph Nicholson of Maryland, and L. R. Morris, from Vermont. The following day the committee recommended appointment of a printer by House members rather than by the House clerk. Roger Griswold of Connecticut opposed the move on the grounds this would make the printer an officer of the House, which had enough such officers already. Thomas Lowndes of South Carolina feared that an official printer would make the sentiments of the elected editor appear official and on this point opposed the bill. The proposal was soundly defeated, with only about twenty supporting votes.[56]

Had the bill passed the House, the printing probably would have been divided between Smith and Duane. As it was, Duane printed the executive documents for the 1801 session and in 1803 took over the Senate printing from Way and Groff, a contract he held until 1806, when it was relinquished to R. C. Weightman, a printer who used the contract to amass a sizable fortune before he retired from the congressional printing field in 1814. Duane continued his stationery store after the loss of the printing.[57]

Smith held the House contract only until 1804, after which the contract was relinquished to A. and G. Way, Washington City printers not connected with newspaper publishing. The

53. Gallatin to Jefferson, December 15, 1801, quoted in Ford, "Letters of William Duane," pp. 258-59.

54. William Duane to James Madison, May 10, 1801, quoted, ibid., pp. 263-64; Duane to Jefferson, June 10, 1801, quoted, ibid., pp. 259 and 264-68.

55. See Noble E. Cunningham, Jr., *The Jeffersonian Republicans in Power: Party Operations, 1801-1809* (Chapel Hill, N.C., 1963), pp. 267-74.

56. *Annals of Congress*, Seventh Congress, First Session, 11:335-37.

57. Ford, "Letters of William Duane," p. 259.

move that undoubtedly accounted for Smith's loss of the printing was the passage of concurring resolutions that empowered the secretary of the Senate and the clerk of the House to advertise for proposals for printing, stationery, and fuel for the next Congress and to award the contracts to the lowest bidder.[58]

This move on the part of Congress effectively removed the newspaper publishers from contention for the printing contracts, and from 1804 until 1819 the large printing offices of the city, which had no connection with the newspapers, held the contracts and built sizable fortunes for such firms as Weightman, Way, William A. Davis, and E. De Krafft.[59]

Although Smith did hold the contracts for printing congressional documents during the first Jefferson term, his position was clearly that of the spokesman for the executive branch of government rather than of the legislative. Washington early became organized along these lines, in many ways socially as well as politically, so that to the Smiths, the White House rather than the capitol was the center of their very existence.[60]

Many of the problems about which Smith worried during the early period of founding the *Intelligencer* were overcome during the first months of the new publishing venture. But of even greater worry to him than his newspaper was the type of life his bride would have to endure in Washington City. She, used to wealth and social position and from a strong Federalist family, might find the crude Washington City life too difficult.

Mrs. Smith also worried somewhat about her ability to adjust to the new city and also to her new political surroundings. She did not share her husband's unqualified devotion to Thomas Jefferson, as her Federalist background had taught her that Jefferson was "an ambitious and violent demagogue, coarse and vulgar in his manner, awkward and rude in his appearance." Her reading and conversations with other Federalists had only confirmed this description.[61]

58. Senate Report 18, Fifty-second Congress, First Session.
59. Ibid., see also House Report 298, Twenty-sixth Congress, First Session.
60. For a study of the Washington establishment up to the Jacksonian period, see James Sterling Young, *The Washington Community, 1800-1828* (New York, 1966).
61. Mrs. Samuel Harrison Smith, quoted from her notebook, in *First Forty Years*, p. 6.

Although her husband gave Mrs. Smith quite a different view of Jefferson, she confessed she thought Smith's more favorable opinions were due largely to his devotion to the Jeffersonian party and especially to Jefferson himself. Smith tried to convince his wife that Jefferson was the great political leader the United States needed and upon whom the "security and welfare" of the country depended. Mrs. Smith, fully aware that her husband's fate was tied to Jefferson's election, clung to the unflattering view of the future president.[62]

Founding a home in this city required more of her attention than politics, however, and one morning as she sat in her parlor a gentleman dropped by to see her husband. She was not acquainted with the stranger but was impressed with his "dignified and reserved air," qualities Mrs. Smith generally found lacking in Washington society. She seated the visitor, relaxed, and engaged in a casual conversation. A few minutes later her husband entered the room, greeted the visitor, and then introduced his wife to Thomas Jefferson. Her conversion was complete as her "heart warmed to him with the most affectionate interest," and she became convinced that all her husband had told her about the man was true. "Yes, not only was he great, but a truly good man!"[63]

In many ways the challenges Mrs. Smith faced in their new life were no less than those confronting her husband. He was pioneering with a new government in a new city in a publishing role quite different from that which the Philadelphia editors had held. Mrs. Smith, because of her presence in the capital city, became a pioneer in the setting of the social structure, not only for the Jeffersonian period but for many years beyond.

It was not an unchallenging task that faced the new publisher's wife. In many ways the city was crude beyond belief, with only a few roadways carved out of the morass of swamps and timber that covered much of the city site. Far from being the intellectual or political center of the nation, Washington was regarded by politicians and government officials as a place of banishment from civilization during the period when government business required their attendance.[64]

62. Ibid., p. 7.
63. Ibid., pp. 6-8.
64. See Young, *Washington Community*, pp. 24-26 and 43-48.

Despite her early enthusiasm for moving to Washington City, Mrs. Smith was disappointed with the new home on New Jersey Avenue and the lack of social life she first experienced. Her reaction, however, was not as strong as that of Abigail Adams, wife of President John Adams, who was thoroughly depressed by the rustic nature of Washington City life.[65]

While her husband was with her Mrs. Smith did not mind the inconveniences and unfamiliarity of Washington, but publishing the paper took him from home much of his time. Mrs. Smith lacked company during the early days, as she confided to her sister Jane, wife of Chief Justice Andrew Kirkpatrick of New Jersey: "I have not met with a single woman, of any information, or who could be an agreeable companion for more than a day much less than a friend."[66] She hoped the social situation would improve. One couple, a Mr. and Mrs. Bell, seemed interesting, wealthy, and respectable. And, most important to Mrs. Smith, who was raised a Presbyterian, the Bells were "professors of religion," something unusual in Washington City.

But Mrs. Smith spent little time brooding about the lack of proper society in the newly founded city, and less than a month later she described a busy social schedule that included not only the Bells but also Mrs. William Thornton,[67] whose husband designed the capitol building and was superintendent of the Patent Office; Mrs. Thomas Tingey, who was married to a retired naval officer; and Mrs. Thomas Law, herself a granddaughter of Martha Washington and her husband a real estate speculator.[68]

Not only did Mrs. Smith find suitable company, but she found a real need for a woman's hand in the new city's activities. Families of congressmen, senators, and cabinet members had to be welcomed to the city, and newly arrived wives could

---

65. Abigail Adams to her sister, November 21, 1800, quoted in Stuart Mitchell, ed., *New Letters of Abigail Adams* (Boston, 1947), pp. 256-60.

66. Margaret Bayard Smith to Jane Kirkpatrick, October 19, 1800, Margaret Bayard Smith Papers, vol. 7.

67. For a detailed account of early social activities, see Mrs. William Anna Maria Brodeau Thornton Diary, entries during the years 1800 and 1801, William Thornton Papers, Library of Congress, Washington, D.C.

68. Margaret Bayard Smith to Jane Kirkpatrick, November 16, 1800, quoted in Smith, *First Forty Years*, pp. 1-5.

use help with housing, shopping, and servant problems. Mrs. Smith did her best to be of service.[69]

In addition, she succeeded in setting up her home as a social center in the city, and during the first official winter in the new capital many leading political figures of Washington frequented her hearth and table.[70] Mrs. Thomas Randolph and Mrs. John Eppes, daughters of Jefferson; Dolly Madison, wife of James Madison; and Mrs. William Cranch, wife of Justice Cranch, also became intimates of the young Mrs. Smith. Even a pregnancy failed to curtail Mrs. Smith's social activities to any great extent. She confided to Susan Bayard Smith her busy round of entertaining:

We have dined twice at the President's, three times at Mr. Pichons [the French Charge d'Affaires], and they have dined twice here, four times at Mrs. Tingeys and once at Genl. Mason's (the Island Mason). I have drank tea out three or four times and declined several invitations to balls. I have often gone out with the ague, sometimes with fever on me, so much has habit done in reconcilling [*sic*] me to this enemy. I know that nothing will keep off the fit, and may as well have it in one place as another. I very seldom now go to bed, but sit up, or lie down on the sopha [*sic*], have a bowl of tea and a basin by me, and then give no one further trouble, but take my fit with the greatest *sang froid.*[71]

The Smiths dined frequently at the White House, and the occasions greatly delighted Mrs. Smith especially. And so agreeable had affairs become in Washington City since Jefferson took office that Smith confided to his sister Mary Ann that in the capital city, at least, political differences were forgotten, and all politicians were "all Republicans and all Federalists," a remarkably myopic view for a publisher.[72]

69. Walters, *Albert Gallatin*, p. 212.
70. Helen Nicolay, *Our Capital on the Potomac* (New York, 1924), p. 60.
71. Margaret Bayard Smith to Susan Bayard Smith, December 26, 1802, quoted in Smith, *First Forty Years*, p. 33.
72. Samuel Harrison Smith to Mary Ann Smith, July 5, 1801, quoted, ibid., pp. 30-31.

CHAPTER 3

A Defense
of Domestic Policy

During the first years of Jefferson's administration domestic affairs occupied the center of the political stage as the young nation attempted to progress at home and to achieve dignity in the eyes of the world. In this period, for example, the federal judiciary became suspect, the cunning Aaron Burr alienated himself from the Republican party and later sought to split the union, and Jefferson acquired the wide expanse of the Louisiana country. Smith reported these major controversies in his news columns and commented upon them editorially; first, last, and always, he loyally supported Jefferson.

Despite Smith's obvious devotion to Jefferson and the Republican party, the editor continually contended the *Intelligencer* was nonpartisan.[1] In a day when both Republican and Federalist newspapers were filled with personal vituperation,

---

1. *National Intelligencer*, December 17, 1802.

Smith's *Intelligencer* carried few words of personal abuse, with the editor holding a high regard for individual rights and privileges. Smith seldom attacked political opponents as individuals; only their political views were questioned.

Coupled with Smith's belief in moderation was his lack of original political thinking. If he had ideas of his own, he submerged them in his complete support of Jefferson. Even Joseph Gales, once Smith's partner, contended that Smith was so bound to follow the directions of others that he would march directly into a brick wall if ordered to do so by a superior.[2] This blind adherence to authority also may have accounted for his general lack of imagination.

Smith's deficiency of creative power, his blind subservience to a cause, and his mild manner and moderation produced a paper with these same characteristics. The *Intelligencer* was read not because it was interesting but because as the quasi-official organ of the Jefferson administration it carried the official notices, proclamations, and advertisements for the government, along with detailed accounts of the proceedings and debates in Congress. It was especially valuable to newspapers outside Washington.

Its reputation as the journal for the Jefferson administration caused many people to regard the *Intelligencer* as merely a mouthpiece for the president and his party and void of any real character contributed by the editor. James Bayard viewed it as the official administrative organ "which is unquestionably under the direction of Mr. Jefferson and his party."[3]

Opposition papers, attempting to discredit the *Intelligencer*'s views, portrayed Smith as merely the tool of Jefferson's administration. The *New York Evening Post* frequently pointed to Smith's connection with Jefferson, and on one occasion said: "The absurdity and utter disregard to truth in the NATIONAL INTELLIGENCER . . . might be still further pursued and detected, but it is hoped enough has been done to impress every reader with the proper degree of estimation in which he ought to hold this paper; emphatically styled Mr. Jefferson's paper."[4]

2. Joseph Gales to Nicholas Biddle, March 7, 1831, Nicholas Biddle Papers, vol. 26, Library of Congress, Washington, D.C.

3. James A. Bayard to Richard Bassett, January 31, 1806, in "Papers of James A. Bayard, 1796-1815," ed. Elizabeth Donnan, *American Historical Association Annual Report*, 1913 (Washington, D.C., 1915), 2:165.

4. *New York Evening Post*, February 8, 1802.

Another time William Coleman, editor of the *Post*, referred to the *Intelligencer* as the "court journal of Jefferson," and Smith was given the unflattering description of "the little monkey."[5] Coleman obviously pictured Smith as a mere instrument of Jefferson—and not particularly effective at that.

Jefferson's estimate of the *National Intelligencer* is somewhat difficult to ascertain despite ample evidence that he made wide use of the newspaper. Even before taking office the president-elect indicated his favor for the *Intelligencer* by giving Smith the advance copy of his inaugural speech so that it might be distributed to the crowd at the capitol ceremony.[6] Within the first month of his administration he advised: "I recommend to you to pay not the least credit to pretended appointments in any paper, till you see it in Smith's. . . . He is at hand to enquire at the offices, and is careful not to publish them on any other authority."[7]

Vice President Aaron Burr also confirmed the close position of the *Intelligencer* to the Jefferson administration when he wrote: "The Washington paper edited by Smith has the countenance and support of administration. His explanations of the Measures of Government and of the Motives which produce them are, I believe, the result of information and advice from high Authority."[8]

As Jefferson admitted, contact between him and Smith was frequent and undoubtedly much information was given to the *Intelligencer* through conversation. Existing records also indicate that Jefferson used the *Intelligencer* not only to give the official point of view on issues but also to place before the newspaper's readers points of view he thought were important to be considered.[9]

Although politicians of the period made wide use of the

5. Allan Nevins, *The Evening Post* (New York, 1922), pp. 50-51.

6. Margaret Bayard Smith to Susan B. Smith, March 4, 1801, as quoted in Mrs. Samuel Harrison Smith, *The First Forty Years of Washington Society* (New York, 1906), p. 26.

7. Jefferson to John W. Eppes, March 27, 1801, as quoted in Noble E. Cunningham, *The Jeffersonian Republicans in Power: Party Operations, 1801-1809* (Chapel Hill, N.C., 1963), p. 261.

8. Burr to Barnabas Bidwell, October 15, 1801, quoted, ibid., p. 259.

9. For example, see Jefferson to Smith, October 23, 1802, and May 23 and October 8, 1803, Samuel Harrison Smith Papers, Library of Congress, Washington, D.C.; see also an exchange of letters between Madison and Jefferson on September 21 and 23, 1807, Jefferson Papers, Library of Congress, Washington, D.C.

press, it was considered unethical, or at least undignified, for an officer of government to be associated with political statements and actions, such as diverting pressure from administrative policies in Congress or announcing the removal of a Federalist office holder.[10]

It was not unknown for the president to intercede in getting articles published that were submitted by members of the cabinet. Secretary of the Treasury Albert Gallatin suggested that an article might be reprinted in the *Intelligencer*: "My idea was that Smith should obey the request of 'a plain citizen,' by reprinting his piece, and should add as his own remarks the substance of what I have written dressed in his own way and corrected as he may think fit. Will you be good enough to look at it and to see whether it wants any additions, corrections or curtailing? I mean as to facts and arguments, not as to style—this Smith must modify."[11]

But despite his use of the *Intelligencer*, Jefferson evidently felt impatient at the performance Smith gave as editor at certain times. On one occasion he reportedly told Senator William Plumer of New Hampshire that he considered newspapers vehicles of slander and falsehood and that no reliance could be placed on them. Plumer also reported that Jefferson believed "Smith's paper of this city was the most correct, but even that is sometimes very erroneous—And he requested the editor to be vigilant in correction, & frank in avowing his errors, when he discovered them."[12]

On another occasion he wrote even more bitterly of his distrust of the press: "I will add, that the man who never looks into a newspaper is better informed than he who reads them, inasmuch as he who knows nothing is nearer to truth than he whose mind is filled with falsehoods and errors."[13]

With regard to the *National Intelligencer*, Jefferson's use of the newspaper perhaps yields greater understanding of his regard for the publication than his views expressed. Smith, from all indications, continued throughout the Jefferson ad-

10. See Jefferson to Smith, March 2, 1808, and August, 1808, Samuel Harrison Smith Papers.

11. Gallatin to Jefferson, undated, Jefferson Papers.

12. Everett Sommerville Brown, ed., *William Plumer's Memorandum of Proceedings in the United States Senate, 1803-1807* (New York, 1923), p. 601.

13. Jefferson to John Norvell, June 14, 1807, as quoted in Cunningham, *Jeffersonian Republicans in Power*, p. 75.

ministration to receive the confidence of the president and his officers.

In no sphere were the ties between Jefferson and Smith more apparent than in the social relationship between the two men. Visits between the families within Washington City were frequent and on at least one occasion, the Smiths visited at Monticello. Following the Smiths' return to Washington, Jefferson wrote that he hoped they had "found the same pleasure in the excursion, which we have received from your agreeable visit believing such changes of scene equally advantageous to mind as to body, we cannot give up the hope of a repetition of it. . . ."[14] In later years similar invitations were declined.[15]

No place was Smith's devotion to Jefferson more obvious than in a statement made following Jefferson's inauguration. Smith assured his readers that he favored economy in pecuniary concerns, exemption from foreign entanglements, obedience to laws, and freedom of inquiry. Without these principles, Smith wrote, excessive taxation, intellectual debasement, uncontrolled power, and perpetual hostility with foreign nations would result. "Freedom of enquiry is the soul of republican institutions; and gloomy will be that period in which shall be suppressed its salutary influence."[16]

Two problems the *Intelligencer* reported during the first years of the Jefferson administration concerned the judiciary and Vice-President Burr. The courts' enforcement of the Alien and Sedition laws was unpopular with Smith because of the treatment some Republican editors received, but the additional offense of the Federal Judiciary Act of 1801,[17] passed during the closing days of Adams's administration, made the Federalist-controlled courts even more odious. Smith joined Jefferson in rating the courts high on the list of subjects needing republican treatment.[18]

Smith protested Adams's last-minute appointments, and a long article from a correspondent on the subject resulted in

14. Smith to Jefferson, September 11, 1810, Jefferson Papers, vol. 191.
15. Jefferson to Smith, August 15, 1813, and Smith to Jefferson, June 11, 1815, Jefferson Papers, vols. 199 and 203.
16. *National Intelligencer*, March 9, 1801.
17. *United States Statutes at Large*, statute 2 (Boston, 1845), 2:89-100.
18. Albert J. Beveridge, *The Life of John Marshall: Conflict and Construction, 1800-1815* (Boston, 1919), 3:20.

a charge of libel against Smith.[19] He strongly favored repealing Adams's judiciary act,[20] for he felt the will of the people of the United States was being subverted by entrenchment of the Federalists in the judiciary system.

Debates over the repeal of the judiciary measure occupied much of the congressional session that opened late in 1801.[21] Front pages and large portions of the inside pages of the *Intelligencer* contained comments of the partisans as they argued about the constitutionality of taking away offices from judges appointed under the 1801 judiciary bill. The laboriousness of the reporting caused Smith's wife to complain of the amount of time her husband spent on these lengthy debates.[22]

Smith editorialized on the brilliance of speeches he heard relative to the repeal of the judiciary bill and was especially impressed with talks of John Breckenridge, the new Jeffersonian from Kentucky, who had introduced the repeal bill, and of Gouverneur William Morris, of Pennsylvania, a staunch old Federalist who grew to fear Jeffersonian Republicanism as much as he feared Great Britain in 1776. Although Smith admitted he disagreed with Morris, he thought Morris's performance was "one of the most splendid specimens of eloquence."[23] The Senate passage of the repeal bill on February 3 was hailed by Smith as a great triumph of Republican principles.[24]

The *Intelligencer* expressed no opinion on the heated debate that developed in the House of Representatives as party members lined up behind William Branch Giles of Virginia, Republican, and James Asheton Bayard of Delaware, Federalist. Smith, however, was jubilant over the passage of the repeal measure on March 3: "Hereafter we may indulge the pleasing hope that the streams of justice, unpolluted by party

19. For a more complete discussion, see Chapter 2.

20. Max Farrand, "The Judiciary Act of 1801," *American Historical Review* 5 (July, 1900): 682-86.

21. For a discussion of the debates, see appropriate sections of *Annals of Congress*, Seventh Congress, First Session, vol. 11 (Washington, D.C., 1851); W. S. Carpenter, "Repeal of the Judiciary Act of 1801," *American Political Science Review* 9 (August, 1915): 519-28.

22. Margaret Bayard Smith Diary, 1803, Library of Congress, Washington, D.C.

23. *National Intelligencer*, January 20, 1802.

24. Ibid., February 5, 1802.

prejudice or passion, will flow pure." The editor was pleased by his conclusion that the Republicans had answered and had refuted all arguments the Federalists had advanced: "Can there be a stronger evidence that the violence of passion on the one hand was only equalled by the strength of reason on the other?" The national will would be obeyed, and judges created for political purposes and opposed to this will hereafter would cease to exist, Smith concluded.[25] If Smith saw any constitutional questions involved in the repeal of the Federalist act of 1801, he did not note them.[26] But the question of the court's right to decide the constitutionality of the acts was raised, and Marshall himself gave the answer in Marbury vs Madison.

Smith's goal was attained: the abolition of judgeships held by Federalists. He supported the drive to rid the judiciary branch of Federalist control but gave no indication he wished to go a step further in making the courts more responsive to the will of the people by electing judges. Neither he nor the Virginia leaders he followed proposed that such measures should replace the judiciary the Federalists had set up in 1801.[27]

The *Washington Federalist* looked with despair upon passage of the repeal bill and wondered what the Republican majority in Congress would do next to tear down the legal system. A Federalist editorial bid "Farewell, A Long Farewell, to All Our Greatness."[28]

The financial program presented by Gallatin, secretary of the treasury, was the other major issue that occupied the first Republican Congress. Smith, an "intimate" of Gallatin, followed and supported his financial policies, which were greatly affected by the threat of the involvement of the United States in the European war.

Gallatin's main objective on assuming the treasury post was to reduce the public debt without using the sinking fund

25. Ibid., March 5, 1802.

26. For a discussion of the constitutional issues involved in the judiciary debates and act of 1801, see Andrew C. McLaughlin, *A Constitutional History of the United States* (New York, 1935), 1:290-93; Homer C. Hockett, *The Constitutional History of the United States*, 1776-1826 (New York, 1939), pp. 302-6.

27. For a detailed discussion, see Henry Adams, *History of the United States of America* (New York, 1921), 1:255-98.

28. *Washington Federalist*, March 3, 1802.

favored by the Federalists. He dared not abolish the fund, although he favored such a plan. Secondly, Gallatin wished to reduce taxes. To do this he instigated a program of administration economy, particularly with relation to the War and Navy departments, since the threat of involvement in a European war had lessened.[29]

Smith, who unqualifiedly supported Gallatin's program, wrote: "We are persuaded that that government is the strongest which is free from debt, and free too from taxes beyond its necessary wants."[30]

With the adjournment of Congress, Smith finished his first session as editor of the Republican journal at the nation's capital. Nothing marked his performance as remarkable. He had supported the Jeffersonian cause, but the backing was not brilliant. He, like a junior senator, followed the straight party line and made few original comments. He seconded what the Republican leaders said and offered no variations on the goals these leaders were pursuing. At the same time, he made no bitter attacks on the opposition, nor did he personally attempt to answer any criticisms made by Federalist leaders.

Probably Smith's greatest contribution was his reporting of the proceedings of the two houses during the debates. Since foreign intelligence was scarce, *Intelligencer* readers were supplied column after column of the debates on the judiciary bill. Papers throughout the country found in the *Intelligencer* their most complete source of information on what was happening in Washington City.

The following session the judiciary was once again a topic of concern, for the bill passed by the Republicans in 1802 was not a victory—only a step in the campaign to rid the courts of their Federalist domination. Smith joined in applauding Republican attacks on Federalist judges, and even before the famous Marbury *vs* Madison decision, he attacked the Supreme Court's interference in such matters. He wrote: "The Supreme Court ought to have refused any instrumentality into this meditated, and we may add, party invasion of Executive functions."[31]

Smith noted with disbelief the decision itself, given on

29. Raymond Walters, Jr., *Albert Gallatin: Jeffersonian Financier and Diplomat* (New York, 1957), pp. 148-51.
30. *National Intelligencer*, December 30, 1801.
31. Ibid., February 2, 1803.

February 24, 1803.[32] He did not dwell on the issue, however, for as he had pointed out a few days earlier, the political nature the courts had assumed would cause such "gross" actions.[33]

In Smith's eyes Federal courts were less responsive to public will than when founded, a fact he abhorred. He joined enthusiastically the move to impeach judges whom he considered were using the courts for political gains rather than for administering justice. And in many cases the actions of the judges themselves were responsible for the strong feelings building up against the judiciary.[34]

Chief Justice John Marshall's impeachment may have been the aim of the Republicans, although constitutional historians cannot agree on the point. Whether or not Smith hoped for this goal, he supported the two impeachment cases involving judges who were tried and found guilty. In Pennsylvania Alexander Addison, described as an able but arrogant Federalist judge, was convicted of high crimes and misdemeanors.[35] This was followed by the trial of the insane judge John Pickering of the United States Court for the District of New Hampshire, who was found guilty by the Senate on the same charge.[36]

The next target of the Republican drive to rid the courts of Federalist domination was Associate Justice Samuel Chase, a judge who had engendered the hatred of many Republicans by his enforcement of the Alien and Sedition laws,[37] and who made himself even less popular with his famous charge to the grand jury at Baltimore on May 2, 1803.[38] Judge Chase had lectured the Republicans on the errors of democratic tendencies of the local and national governments when he addressed the grand jury.[39]

---

32. For a discussion of the Marbury vs Madison case, see Beveridge, *Life of John Marshall*, pp. 101-56; Hockett, *Constitutional History*, pp. 306-9: McLaughlin, *Constitutional History*, pp. 305-10.

33. *National Intelligencer*, February 21, 1803.

34. Beveridge, *Life of John Marshall*, p. 30.

35. Ibid., p. 163.

36. *Annals of Congress*, Eighth Congress, First Session (Washington, D.C., 1852), 13:315-68; Beveridge, *Life of John Marshall*, p. 167.

37. James Morton Smith, *Freedom's Fetters: The Alien and Sedition Laws and American Civil Liberties* (Ithaca, N.Y., 1956), pp. 317-56.

38. Adams, *History of the United States*, p. 148.

39. See John C. Miller, *Crisis in Freedom: The Alien and Sedition Acts* (Boston, 1952), p. 208.

Chase's remarks disturbed Smith's usual mild manner: "This Charge may be pronounced the most extraordinary that the violence of federalism has yet produced, and exhibits humiliating evidence of the unfortunate effects of disappointed ambition."[40]

Evidently Smith was in Baltimore, heard Judge Chase address the grand jury, and was called to testify during the Chase trial.[41] Just what Smith was expected to state during his testimony is not clear, but at least one senator, William Plumer, the famous diarist from New Hampshire, was disappointed. Plumer described Smith's appearance: "His nerves failed him—he stated that the sum of all he could say was contained in an affidavit he gave last winter to the Committee—& he requested & obtained liberty to read a printed copy of it which he had compared with the original."[42]

Smith attended the entire trial, where he and Thomas Lloyd, a Philadelphia printer, took stenographic notes and later published a two-volume account of the proceedings.[43] The final decisions, clearing Chase of all eight counts against him, failed to stir Smith. He felt that perhaps never before "in this country, or in any other, has a tribunal of justice exhibited more honorable traits of impartiality, or dignified deportment. During the whole progress of the trial a degree of order and decorum has persevered, which reflects high honor on the Senate of the United States, and the individual who presides over their deliberation."[44]

The editor was referring, of course, to Burr, vice-president of the United States, the central figure in the next major conflict between the Jefferson administration and the United States's federal courts. From the time he arrived in Washington, and perhaps before, Smith, like any Jeffersonian editor, opposed Burr. The editor suspected and feared Burr during the election of 1800. Mrs. Smith was so opposed to Burr that had he been elected in 1801 she was certain "civil commotions would have ensued."[45]

40. *National Intelligencer*, May 20, 1803.

41. *Annals of Congress*, Eighth Congress, Second Session (Washington, D.C., 1852), 14:235-36.

42. Brown, *William Plumer's Memorandum*, p. 288.

43. See Samuel H. Smith and Thomas Lloyd, *Trial of Samuel Chase*, vols. 1 and 2 (Washington, D.C., 1805).

44. *National Intelligencer*, March 5, 1805.

45. Mrs. Smith's notebook, quoted in Smith, *First Forty Years*, p. 10.

Except for praising Burr's conduct during the Chase trial, the *Intelligencer* generally treated Burr with stony silence as Republican leaders endeavored to rid their party of the man suspected of attempting to betray Jefferson in 1800. Even the duel fatal to Alexander Hamilton did not receive prominent display.[46]

By 1804 the Jeffersonians largely had succeeded, with considerable help from Burr, in their efforts to make the vice-president impotent politically. Yet the Republicans also sensed that as shrewd and as cunning a man as Burr was not without resources. Even when rumors circulated of Burr's plan to carve out an empire in the western United States, Smith's *Intelligencer* ignored the stories. Smith followed the Jeffersonian line of waiting until sufficient evidence of Burr's activities warranted his trial and destruction as a political opponent.[47]

The *Intelligencer* made no mention of stories about Burr moving down the Ohio and Mississippi rivers to New Orleans. But by December, when Jefferson officially noticed Burr's activities, Smith began to spread the party line. He wrote:

The obscurity, that has for some time enveloped the project of Aaron Burr, begins to give place to facts. From a great variety of information received from various quarters, we believe, it may be confidently said—

1. That a military plan has been formed; and

2. That Aaron Burr is the head of it.

. . . .

Our decided opinion is that there ought to be no reserve on this subject. Treason and traitors are entitled to no reserve; and the people of the United States, without being unnecessarily alarmed, ought to be enabled to appreciate the danger that menaces them.[48]

The climax to the Burr case came in Richmond, Virginia, in the summer of 1807, when Jefferson again faced his old

46. For details of Burr and his activities, see Nathan Schachner, *Aaron Burr* (New York, 1937); Walter Flavius McCaleb, *The Aaron Burr Conspiracy* (New York, 1903); Thomas Perkins Abernethy, *The Burr Conspiracy* (New York, 1954); Samuel H. Wandell and Meade Minnigerode, *Aaron Burr* (New York, 1925).

47. See Abernethy, *Burr Conspiracy*, for a discussion of Burr's activities and the reaction of the Jefferson administration. See also Morrison Shaforth, "The Aaron Burr Conspiracy," *American Bar Association Journal* 18 (1895): 669-72.

48. *National Intelligencer*, March 13, 1807.

adversary, Chief Justice Marshall. As the court proceedings moved through preliminary hearing, grand jury investigation, and the actual trial for treason, Jefferson and Marshall, rather than the accused Burr, appeared to be the main figures. In the hearing Marshall delivered his definition of what constituted treason under the United States Constitution, and President Jefferson was subpoenaed to appear. Eventually the trial ended with a "not guilty" verdict and a lengthy opinion by Justice Marshall. His famous statement regarding treason read: "The present indictment charges the prisoner with levying war against the United States, and alleges an overt act of levying war. That overt act must be proved, according to the mandates of the constitution and of the act of congress, by two witnesses. It is not proved by a single witness."[49]

All attempts to convict Burr were fruitless, and Smith and other Republicans felt further bitterness toward Marshall's decisions. Smith assured his readers that the trial was stopped by the Federalist court to prevent truths that would have embarrassed the Federalist party from being brought to light. Although Smith regretted this, he did not dwell long on the subject and praised the country's press for its calm treatment of the trial. He was pleased by the journals' reluctance to criticize the way the court conducted the case.[50]

In this same issue Smith bade an editorial farewell to Burr, noting erroneously that Burr was thought to have passed through Washington City on his way to Baltimore. Attention was called to Burr's activities only because Smith felt such a "dangerous person deserved close watching."[51] Actually Burr was still in Richmond, where various other charges against him were considered and tried.[52]

The other major event that attracted attention from the nation during Jefferson's first term touched both foreign and domestic affairs. Until the Louisiana Purchase was completed, Smith shared Jefferson's qualms about its constitutionality. But any doubt vanished from Smith's mind once

49. David Robertson, *Reports of the Trials of Colonel Aaron Burr* (Philadelphia, 1808), p. 443; see also E. S. Corwin, *John Marshall and the Constitution* (New Haven, Conn., 1921).
50. *National Intelligencer*, September 7, 1807.
51. Ibid.
52. Schachner, *Aaron Burr*, pp. 441-42.

Jefferson reached a decision that the purchase was constitutional.[53]

Smith's strong support for Jefferson's domestic program was bound to make the *Intelligencer* the target for vigorous political criticism. Not only were Smith's editorial stands attacked, but Smith was accused of political bias in reporting congressional proceedings. The editor of the Baltimore *Anti-Democrat* thought Smith "shamefully mutilated the speeches of the federal members." The *Anti-Democrat* editor ceased copying from the *Intelligencer* for this reason and instead took his debates from the Washington *Federalist*.[54]

Smith thought the criticism unjust and assured his readers: "It has been the invariable effort of the Editor of the National Intelligencer . . . to sustain the character of an impartial reporter. . . ." He went on to say that he wished "no impression to be made upon the public mind, other than that which is founded on the truth."[55]

Not all Federalist papers criticized the *Intelligencer* for being partisan. The *New York Evening Post*, a strongly Federalist paper, reluctantly preferred extracting from the *Intelligencer* rather than from the *Federalist*. This policy was changed, however, when the Washington *Federalist* hired a stenographer to report more detailed accounts of the debates. This hiring occasioned the *Post* editor to comment: "We are glad to hear this, because we have been not a little mortified that from the more ample and satisfactory manner in which the debates have hitherto appeared in the National Intelligencer, we have thought ourselves obliged to extract them from that paper, instead of the Washington Federalist."[56]

Since for many years Smith was the only *Intelligencer* stenographer, he was unable to report all the proceedings. Certain speeches from members in both houses of Congress were omitted. Also some of the speeches reported were furnished by the congressional speakers rather than taken down during the time the speech was given in Congress. John Bacon, a

53. *National Intelligencer*, July 8 and August 17, 1803.
54. Baltimore *Anti-Democrat*, quoted in the *National Intelligencer*, March 10, 1802.
55. *National Intelligencer*, March 10, 1802.
56. *New York Evening Post*, March 1, 1802.

representative from Massachusetts, defended the *Intelligencer* against criticism from the *Federalist*, saying that a portion of his speech had been given "extempore" and was not "furnished to Smith."[57]

No doubt mistakes were made in the reporting, but in general Smith seems to have done a conscientious job in a situation presenting many difficulties.[58]

More than political editing duties demanded Smith's time, and as the *Intelligencer* became more successful outside activities increased. Smith early involved himself in the social and political affairs of the rising young city, even to the point of joining a "dancing Assembly," because, as his wife confided to her sister, becoming well known was important and "the best way of getting business, is by being generally known, and by being connected with the most respectable people."[59]

Smith succeeded in his conscious efforts to make himself known in Washington; especially during Jefferson's first term he was involved in city governmental affairs. One of his first official jobs was that of city councilman. The *Intelligencer* carried a story in May, 1803, naming Smith as a possible candidate.[60] Mrs. Smith was absent from Washington at election time, and Smith wrote her of his success.[61] Mrs. Smith confided to her diary: "Mr. Smith was elected by his fellow citizens as a member of the city Council, & altho pleased & gratified by this testimony of their regard & respect for him, I regretted this new employment which by occupying every moment of his time completely seperated [*sic*] him from his family."[62]

Smith was reelected to the city council in 1804[63] and was named president of the First Chamber the same year.[64] He

57. *National Intelligencer*, March 19, 1802.

58. For a detailed appraisal of the reporting of the debates during this period, see Elizabeth Gregory McPherson, "The History of Reporting the Debates and Proceedings of Congress" (Ph.D. thesis, University of North Carolina, 1940).

59. Margaret Bayard Smith to Jane Kirkpatrick, November 16, 1800, quoted in Smith, *First Forty Years*, p. 4.

60. *National Intelligencer*, May 25, 1803.

61. Samuel Harrison Smith to Margaret Bayard Smith, June 10, 1803, Margaret Bayard Smith Papers, vol. 7, Library of Congress, Washington, D.C.

62. Margaret Bayard Smith Diary, undated entry.

63. *National Intelligencer*, June 6, 1804.

64. Ibid., June 13, 1804.

was defeated for a third term and never again held a city office.[65]

But duties other than those of city government took much of his time. In 1803 Smith served on a planning committee for celebrating Independence Day. Celebration of July 4 during the early days of Washington meant a great undertaking with national figures as well as local citizens taking part in the speeches, parades, and numerous other activities.[66]

The young editor's interest in education undoubtedly was responsible for his appointment in 1805 to a group for the "Permanent Institution for the Education of Youth in the City of Washington."[67] Jefferson served on this same committee and was notified of his appointment by Smith.[68] In July, 1806, Smith became a trustee of Washington Academy.[69]

By the end of Jefferson's first term Smith had experienced considerable success. He was encouraged by his flourishing newspaper and by the achievements of the political administration he so strongly supported. But all this was to tarnish within the next four years as the nation turned to meet pressing foreign relations problems.

---

65. Ibid., June 5, 1803.
66. Ibid., June 27, 1803.
67. Ibid., April 29, 1805.
68. Samuel Harrison Smith to Jefferson, July 23, 1805, Jefferson Papers, vol. 151.
69. *National Intelligencer,* July 23, 1806.

CHAPTER 4

The *Intelligencer* Changes Owners

Political editing had lost much of its appeal for Smith by the end of Jefferson's second term, and by 1807 the editor offered the *Intelligencer* for sale. But devotion to Jefferson kept Smith on the paper until 1810 while the nation sought, through a complicated system of economic sanctions, to avoid active involvement in the war between Great Britain and France. On the same terms on which Smith shared Jefferson's triumphs of the first administration, he staunchly defended Jefferson's second-term foreign policy, which was exceedingly unpopular in certain sections of the United States.

The major foreign-policy issue during Jefferson's first administration was the Louisiana Purchase,[1] which increased the president's popularity within the United States. Yet the

---

1. For a record of official treatises and other papers relating to Louisiana, see James A. Robertson, ed., *Louisiana Under the Rule of Spain, France and the United States, 1785-1807*, vols. 1 and 2 (Cleveland, Ohio, 1911).

transaction gave this country some uneasy moments as it sought to tread the delicate balance of power between France and England.

Louisiana, of course, was a Spanish possession during the early part of Jefferson's administration, but the Treaty of San Ildefonso returned the territory to France. Jefferson and his advisors greatly dreaded this turn of events,[2] for they feared that French possession of Louisiana would, as they said, forever wed the United States to the British fleet for protection.[3]

Yet during this period Republican spokesmen did not view Great Britain too unfavorably. Smith followed his leader's sentiments and went so far as to cite England as a great moral leader in the world. He thought the English should be credited for shedding their blood to establish "the invincibility of reason, the triumph of principle, which . . . proclaim more loudly than ever the right of every nation to form for itself such a government as it pleases. . . ." He was sure the example never would be forgotten.[4] He believed the United States had little to fear from either France or England.[5]

Smith's optimism was unfounded, for about the time he expressed these sentiments hostilities began again between England and France after the brief period of peace following the Treaty of Amiens.[6] Resumption of the struggle between the European powers brought up the old problems of neutral rights and British impressment, which after 1806 dominated thinking and political activity in the United States. This country, as an important neutral carrier, particularly of foodstuffs, scarcely could avoid conflict with the two warring European nations.[7]

The hostilities sent the United States searching for methods of maintaining peace, and Smith followed Jefferson completely as he led the nation on the much-criticized policy of

2. Thomas A. Bailey, *A Diplomatic History of the American People* (New York, 1958), pp. 102-3.

3. Jefferson to Robert E. Livingston, April 18, 1802, quoted in A.A. Lipscomb, ed., *Writings of Thomas Jefferson* (Washington, D.C., 1904), pp. 311-16.

4. *National Intelligencer*, November 30, 1801.

5. Ibid., April 6, 1803.

6. Henry Adams, *History of the United States of America* (New York, 1921), 1:355.

7. Bailey, *Diplomatic History*, p. 116.

"millions for Defence, but not a cent for tribute." Smith hailed a bill appropriating money for two vessels as a wise and patriotic move which demonstrated the administration's energy "not by vain vaunting of prowess: but by actions. . . ."[8]

Between 1805 and 1807 Smith witnessed the steady worsening of United States–British relations until war was narrowly averted in 1807. Smith's paper recounted the increased raiding on United States' shipping, stepped-up impressment activity, the Non-Importation Act of the United States,[9] Napoleon's Berlin and Milan Decrees, and the British Orders in Council.[10] The United States' refusal to accept the Monroe-Pinckney treaty negotiated with Great Britain in 1807 stalled diplomatic attempts at settling difficulties and increased tensions between the two countries.[11]

Tempers in the United States peaked in July, 1807, when the British man-of-war, the *Leopard*, attacked an American frigate, the *Chesapeake*, off the American Coast.[12] Smith felt the incident called for war unless immediate settlement were made. Hurriedly called cabinet meetings issued strong protests.[13] All this faded into ineffective negotiations, and the United States and Great Britain flirted with war for months and then delayed action five years.[14]

The *Chesapeake-Leopard* affair aroused Smith as had no other event. He was annoyed by the Federalist papers, which feared Jefferson might use the incident as an excuse for war with Great Britain, and he especially criticized editors of Philadelphia's *United States Gazette* and of Boston's *Repertory*.

For weeks Smith printed accounts of the nation's reaction to the *Chesapeake* affair. One issue of his paper contained reports of forty-eight meetings, mostly in the Middle Atlantic

8. *National Intelligencer*, March 23, 1804.

9. *United States Statutes at Large*, statute 1 (Boston, 1845), 2:379-81, 469.

10. A. T. Mahan, *Sea Power in Its Relations to the War of 1812* (Boston, 1905), 1:141-202; Samuel Flagg Bemis, *A Diplomatic History of the United States* (New York, 1965), pp. 138-58.

11. Anthony Steel, "Impressment in the Monroe-Pinckney Negotiation, 1806-1807," *American Historical Review* 57 (January, 1952), pp. 352-69.

12. Claude G. Bowers, *Jefferson in Power: The Death Struggle of the Federalists* (Boston, 1936), pp. 426-31.

13. Raymond Walters, Jr., *Albert Gallatin: Jeffersonian Financier and Diplomat* (New York, 1957), p. 195; Jefferson to Gallatin, quoted in Paul Leicester Ford, ed., *The Writings of Thomas Jefferson* (New York, 1898), 9:86-87.

14. Mahan, *Sea Power*, pp. 157-71.

and southern states, at which resolutions were passed calling for a strong stand against the British.[15] Time passed and Smith eased away from the drastic action he called for immediately following the incident when he felt the country was sufficiently united to strike a telling blow at Britain's most vulnerable possession in North America—Canada.[16]

The *New York Evening Post* was worried for fear the *Intelligencer* articles reflected the administration's intentions to go to war, and the Boston *Repertory* thought Smith's views were ridiculous. "It is mortifying," said the *Repertory*, "that at a moment, when the whole country is in a state of consternation and looks to the National Intelligencer, as the Index of the Executive mind, that we are fobbed off with dreams which really throw an air of burlesque and ridicule on the most momentous concerns of the Republic." The writer thought Smith's contention that the United States would have no difficulty conquering Canada and the West Indies was unreasonable.[17] The *Post* editor criticized: "The National Intelligencer continues its speculations on the consequences to this country of a war with Great Britain. Whether they come from the pen of Mr. Jefferson, or little Smith, the editor, we know not." The article continued that there was little hope of avoiding war.[18]

By the end of July Smith was fully in support of his mentor when he recommended economic sanctions against Great Britain. He was sure that "nothing could . . . more decisively manifest" the strength of the United States than a resolution not to hold "any commercial intercourse with her until she acceded to those principles of justice and reciprocity to which we are in every respect entitled."[19]

These economic reprisals became law in December, 1807, when Congress passed the famous Embargo Act,[20] which for the most part froze American shipping activities with other nations.[21] The *Intelligencer* warmly supported the embargo as

15. *National Intelligencer*, August 7, 1807.
16. Ibid., July 17, 1807; see also July 24 for Smith's views on the united front the country presented.
17. *New York Evening Post*, July 28, 1807.
18. Ibid.
19. *National Intelligencer*, July 29, 1807.
20. *United States Statutes at Large*, statute 1, 2:451-54.
21. For a thorough analysis of the embargo and its effect and reception in the various sections of the country, see Louis Martin Sears, *Jefferson and the Em-*

a measure "peculiarly adapted to the crisis" at hand. Smith felt sure trade restrictions would be popular throughout the country and would keep the nation out of war.[22]

But while Smith and other Republican editors acclaimed the embargo, a hue and cry against the measure sounded from the Federalist press throughout the country. The *Intelligencer* editor attempted to counter, as bitter rantings from the New England shipping interests began. The opposition, the editor wrote, was not from the agricultural and manufacturing interest. Virginia, which Smith called the greatest exporting state, was not violently opposed. The opposition came, he noted, from Federalist New England and mainly from the Federalist leaders. Smith wrote that the complaints from New England towns needed evaluation. Much foreign capital was invested in these shipping concerns, and these interests frequently received foreign protection. The "*bona fide* American traders," however, risked their all because of British and French policies, Smith contended.[23]

Loyalty to Jeffersonian policies blinded Smith to any objective appraisal of the results the embargo actually accomplished, although had the embargo continued long enough, Jefferson's goal might have been achieved.[24] Smith tried desperately to serve as a catalyst in building the morale of the country and as a balm in quieting the dissident sections—particularly New England. In April the editor defended the embargo measure as preferable to war—the choice the United States faced.[25] By May he felt the benefits had become even more startling. He wrote: "The outrages perpetrated on us by the belligerent powers of Europe, and their restrictions on our trade, are already producing the most striking effects in the growth of manufactures."[26] Smith hailed the appointment of a committee in Baltimore to look into the development of manufacturing as wise and judicious. He commented:

bargo (Durham, N.C., 1927). Sears also covers the subject in the following articles: "Philadelphia and the Embargo of 1808," *Quarterly Journal of Economics* 35 (February, 1921): 354-59; "The South and the Embargo of 1808," *South Atlantic Quarterly* 20 (July, 1921): 254-75; "The Middle States and the Embargo of 1808," *South Atlantic Quarterly* 21 (April, 1922): 152-69.

22. *National Intelligencer*, December 23, 1807.
23. Ibid., January 18, 1808.
24. Bailey, *Diplomatic History*, p. 129.
25. *National Intelligencer*, April 4, 1808.
26. Ibid., May 20, 1808.

"We rejoice to perceive this spirit rising in the United States. The time has certainly come when every effort in our power should be made to render ourselves independent of the nations of Europe. . . ."[27]

Smith's optimism was not shared in the New England and Middle Atlantic states. Idle ships, idle sailors, and idle ports all contributed to a restlessness created by an economic depression that needed more than reassuring words to overcome.[28] New England legislatures, town meetings, and private citizens joined in the cry against the embargo, and memorials continued to pour into Washington protesting the detested shipping control. At first Smith was hurt and bewildered by the attacks on his beloved president. Finally, with the passage of a resolution by the Massachusetts legislature calling for the repeal of the embargo and the substitution of naval protection to American shipping, Smith exploded:

Submission! Good God! Can the idea enter into the minds of any Americans? Can it more than all enter into the minds of the sons of Massachusetts? Can they who have been rocked by their illustrious and patriotic forefathers in the cradle of revolutionary independence, . . . who risqued their property, their lives, in seventy-six, when we were weak, poor, and disunited, can these men in eighteen hundred and eight, when we are a powerful, a rich, an united people, submit to the same nation, to the same chains forged for us, and others still more galling? The idea is too monstrous. It were treason against liberty to harbor it for an instant. It would prove that commerce had made us another Carthage: and that wealth and liberty were incompatible.[29]

Smith, well aware of the pressure Jefferson experienced, viewed the memorials submitted to the president demanding repeal of the embargo as traitorous. The president, who was at Monticello during the late summer of 1808 when demands were greatest, was "overwhelmed with petitions" from Massachusetts. In desperation Jefferson turned to Smith with a plea for 150 printed replies to the petitions. He cautioned Smith to make sure these were printed in "large good

27. Ibid., February 1, 1808.

28. Sears, *Jefferson and the Embargo*, pp. 143-96; Nathan Schachner, *Thomas Jefferson* (New York, 1957), 2:870-75; Samuel Flagg Bemis, ed., *The American Secretaries of State and Their Diplomacy* (New York, 1967), 3:133-36.

29. *National Intelligencer*, June 10, 1808.

type."[30] A few days later Jefferson sent an additional printing order: an answer to petitioners supporting the embargo. Jefferson readily admitted the number was "not likely to be so numerous," and ordered only 50.[31]

The repeal of the embargo in 1809 was overshadowed by a much sadder event for Smith: Jefferson's retirement. Smith lost his greatest reason for editing a paper: the support and defense of the person he considered America's greatest living man. By midsummer, 1809, Smith concluded that perhaps even Jefferson's wisdom had failed to prevent a war with Great Britain. He explained that every effort to conciliate differences was tried and rejected. Injuries and insults were heaped on the United States; justice was treated with injustice. Perhaps, Smith wrote, the cannon was the only way of handling the matter; perhaps it was time for the United States to stop being generous. He suggested that the sections of the country unite and show Great Britain a united front. "Our rights are common, our interests are the same; we have a common country, let us then in the name of Heaven defend it!"[32]

Smith never was convinced that Jefferson's embargo failed. Rather, he believed the people, particularly those in New England, failed the embargo and refused to give it a chance to show its effectiveness. As late as 1826, Smith looked back on the embargo and concluded: "If there was error in the opinion of Jefferson, it sprung from no ignoble motive. No man was more sensible to the wrongs inflicted, none more alive to the interests of his country, none more determined in his course when impelled by a clear conviction of duty." Smith contended that the president thought the problem would be of short duration. "He did believe, that the embargo he proposed would teach our enemies justice through their interests. And who will, at this day, say this might not have been the case, had that measure been enforced by the whole nation?"[33]

30. Jefferson to Samuel Harrison Smith, September 9, 1808, and Smith to Jefferson, September 14, 1808, Jefferson Papers, vols. 180 and 181, Library of Congress, Washington, D.C.

31. Jefferson to Samuel Harrison Smith, September 13, 1808, and Smith to Jefferson, September 19, 1808, Jefferson Papers, vol. 181.

32. *National Intelligencer*, August 23, 1809.

33. Samuel Harrison Smith, *Memoir of the life, character and writings of Thomas Jefferson* (Washington, D.C., 1827), p. 20.

Clearly, in Smith's eyes the country was doomed for war once the embargo was repealed,[34] and such attempts as the Macon Bill, passed in 1810,[35] were futile. With this feeling of hopeless resignation, Smith concluded his days on the *Intelligencer.*

Jefferson's retirement did not in itself cause Smith's decision to leave the paper, for the young editor had determined years before to quit the publishing field. Neither he nor his wife ever was happy with their Washington City business, although they had achieved remarkable success and felt at home there. No longer bored with the capital, both found city life far too demanding, and like Jefferson, were eager to retire to the country.

In 1804 the Smiths purchased "Turkey Thicket," a country home and acreage in northeast Washington City, just off the Bladensburg road on land now a part of the campus of Catholic University of America. The family renamed the place "Sidney," and both Mr. and Mrs. Smith hoped some day to live there permanently.[36] Sidney was used largely as a summer home, because business in Washington City usually forced the family to move back to the city during the winter. At Sidney the Smiths entertained some of the nation's leading political figures, including Henry Clay, William Crawford, and John C. Calhoun. Smith himself gardened part of the land during the summers[37] with the help of slaves.[38]

Smith wished to retire from publishing for several reasons; the many annoyances that plagued nearly all editors of that day caused part of his dissatisfaction. He experienced nearly continual fights with the postal department over the failure of subscribers to receive their papers.[39] He also had difficulty

34. *United States Statutes at Large* (Boston, 1845), 4:211-18.

35. Ibid., pp. 305-7.

36. Margaret Bayard Smith Diary, undated entry, Library of Congress, Washington, D.C.; "Samuel Harrison Smith," *Dictionary of American Biography* 17:343-44, 1956; Margaret Brent Downing, "Literary Landmarks," *Columbia Historical Society Records* 19 (1916): 28.

37. For an enthusiastic account of the family's agricultural efforts, see Margaret Bayard Smith Papers, summer months, 1806, Library of Congress, Washington, D.C.

38. For conflicting statements on Smith's ownership of slaves, see "Samuel Harrison Smith," *Dictionary of American Biography* 17:343-44, and Charles Hurd, *Washington Cavalcade* (New York, 1948), p. 36. Proof that Smith owned slaves is found in Mrs. Samuel Harrison Smith, *The First Forty Years of Washington Society* (New York, 1906), p. 338.

39. See *National Intelligencer*, February 9, 1801, for an example.

in collecting subscriptions, for the *Intelligencer's* extensive circulation was spread over a large part of the United States.[40]

More important than these irritations was Smith's disillusionment with the life of a political editor. He was so devoted to Jefferson that even the slightest criticism of his leader was disappointing; and such criticism was bitter during Jefferson's second administration.

But the *Intelligencer's* heavy demand on Smith's time and energy accounted for his main reason for selling. Putting out the paper, nearly singlehandedly on the editorial and business ends, left little time at home. This displeased both Smith and his wife, as she complained in her diary: "My good husband, could give me but a few moments in the day; besides editing the paper he took the debates of congress, which this session were very long & highly interesting."[41]

Therefore, Mrs. Smith had decided by 1803 that she would like her husband in another business. After a short vacation in the country, Mrs. Smith lamented all the more her husband's heavy work schedule. She wrote: "Mr. Smith in the city, was a man of business, in this retreat, he was the fond lover, the enlightened friend, the beloved companion;— Oh why when we are both so much happier in the country, are we doomed to a City-life?"[42]

To gain relief, Smith occasionally stole a day or two of rest by suspending publication.[43] He also discountinued the paper for a brief period in the summer to allow a short vacation and during that time published an abbreviated edition for readers within the city. Subscribers were told the editor needed relief from "the laborious duties of the Editor of a public Print, and from the necessity of recruiting health, unavoidably impaired by a constant devotion to business." He assured readers a special edition would be published in case of any major news event.[44] When Smith was sick the paper continued publication, but nearly all Washington news was omitted.[45]

40. Samuel Harrison Smith to Mary Ann Smith, December 15, 1801, Margaret Bayard Smith Papers, vol. 7.
41. Margaret Bayard Smith Diary, undated entry.
42. Ibid.
43. *National Intelligencer*, January 1, 1801.
44. Ibid., November 16, 1801; see the August 20, 1802, issue for notice of suspension.
45. Ibid., October 19, 1801.

No doubt Smith's heavy schedule did take its toll, and as early as 1803 he began to advertise for a person "well qualified to REPORT THE DEBATES OF CONGRESS." Newspaper publishers who copied the debates from the *Intelligencer* were asked to insert the notice in their papers.[46]

Hiring an unidentified reporter and suspending the paper during certain periods of the year failed to solve the problem of help on the *Intelligencer*. Mrs. Smith still felt her husband was overworked, and behind her complaints was the strong desire to see him rid of the newspaper. She thought publishing was not genteel. Agriculture was a much better pursuit for a gentleman, and even some other business might be preferable to publishing.

By 1807 Mrs. Smith was so disturbed about her husband that she confided to her sister: "It seems impossible that Mr. S can continue such unremitting employment; his health at least will suffer; his business every day increases & he has today added another workman & 9 previous ones. His manners are uniformly mild, kind & cheerful; the most perplexed ... & fatiguing business neither irritates his temper, or ruffles his tranquility."[47]

Subsequently, a notice in the *Intelligencer* announced Smith's offer to sell his establishment, consisting of both the *Intelligencer* and the *Universal Gazette*. He advised: "This disposition will only be made to a person of sound republican principles."[48]

During the summer the political situation between the United States and Great Britain worsened, climaxed by the *Leopard*'s attack on the *Chesapeake* off Hampton Roads, Virginia. The tense situation caused Smith to reconsider his offer to sell his papers and instead to seek some additional help.[49]

Working out an arrangement that would enable him to continue publication, Smith informed his readers he had engaged the services of Joseph Gales, Jr., "an able stenographer, who, with additional aid contemplated by one of the first

46. Ibid., August 3, 1803.
47. Margaret Bayard Smith to Jane Kirkpatrick, January 8, 1807, Margaret Bayard Smith Papers, vol. 8.
48. *National Intelligencer*, issues for May and June, 1807.
49. Ibid., September 7, 1808.

Stenographers in America, Joseph Gales, Sr.[50] will, it is expected be fully competent to presenting a comprehensive and faithful statement of the Debates." Smith further explained that he would devote more time to the mechanical aspects of the paper.[51]

It is impossible to determine just how many publishing duties young Joe Gales assumed, but the format and content of the *Intelligencer* changed little. By January, 1809, Gales evidently had proved his competence, and the publishing firm became Smith and Gales: "THE NATIONAL INTELLIGENCER will henceforth be conducted by SAMUEL H. SMITH AND JOSEPH GALES, JUN. and printed at the Office of the former, to whom subscribers and correspondents are requested still to address themselves."[52]

On August 31, 1810, Smith sold the *National Intelligencer* and the weekly *Universal Gazette* to Gales. Both papers were continued under the new ownership. Gales was surprised when the offer was made to him, although under the terms of the agreement signed when he came to the *Intelligencer* he realized this might eventually happen.[53] Smith's sale was made without consulting the Madison administration, according to Gales's recollection, but Smith's distaste for publishing was widely known.[54]

Although Smith and his wife may have hoped to follow Jefferson's example and to retire to the country to pursue an agricultural life, the couple was disappointed. They left for Sidney following the sale of the paper, but before the transaction was completed, Smith already was engaged in his new line of work: banking. In 1809 he was named a director of the Bank of Washington and the following year became president.[55] The family continued its country life, however, and Mrs. Smith experienced a happiness she never had known as the wife of a political publisher. She wrote her sister: "Oh how I rejoice that we have thrown anchor into the beautiful

50. Joseph Gales, Sr., helped report the debates of Congress during the first session covered by his son.
51. *National Intelligencer*, September 7, 1808.
52. Ibid., January 3, 1809.
53. Ibid., July 30, 1857.
54. Ibid.
55. Margaret Bayard Smith to Susan Smith, October 16, 1809, Margaret Bayard Smith Papers, vol. 9.

haven of private life, where the breath of hasty feuds cannot blast, nor the whim of a man in power wreck our little all. *We now* feel, as if no public place could tempt us from this peaceful security. . . ."[56]

But even with such moments of happiness Smith still maintained a busy schedule of civic and business affairs, so that by July, 1811, Mrs. Smith again lamented the demands on her husband as she confided to her sister: "Mr. Smith I see only at meals. For two weeks he was every day & all day in the city being foreman of the grand jury, and there is not an association of any kind, in which he is not on some committee, so that 3 & 4 times a week he is in the city. . . ."[57]

The country life was disrupted in 1813 when President Madison appointed Smith first commissioner of the revenue of the Treasury Department, a job that demanded much of Smith's time and necessitated a move back to the city, much against the wishes of both Smiths.[58] In 1814 Smith served a short term as secretary of treasury ad interim.[59] In 1828 he became president of the Washington Branch of the Second United States Bank, a position he held until the branch closed in 1836.[60]

In addition to his banking duties, Smith served as director of the Washington Library, as treasurer of the Washington Monument Society, and as a member of educational committees until his death.[61]

Mrs. Smith also continued to be active in Washington City affairs and was considered one of the city's leading hostesses. Rearing four children—Julia, Susan, John, and Anne—[62] took much of her time, but she also achieved some fame as a writer. Two of her novels were published in this country, one of

56. Margaret Bayard Smith to Jane Kirkpatrick, April 7, 1811, Margaret Bayard Smith Papers, vol. 9.

57. Margaret Bayard Smith to Jane Kirkpatrick, July 14, 1811, Margaret Bayard Smith Papers, vol. 9.

58. Samuel Harrison Smith to Jefferson, August 29, 1813, Jefferson Papers, vol. 199.

59. Smith, *First Forty Years*, p. vi.

60. "Samuel Harrison Smith," *Dictionary of American Biography* 17:343-44; Smith, *First Forty Years*, p. vi.

61. "Samuel Harrison Smith," *Dictionary of American Biography* 17:343-44.

62. Gen. Jas. Grant Wilson, "Colonel John Bayard (1738-1807) and the Bayard Family of America," *The New York Geneaological and Biographical Record* (New York, 1885), 16:71.

which also was printed in England and France.[63] Numerous articles authored by her appeared in *Godey's Lady's Book, The Southern Literary Messenger, Peter Parley's Annual,* and *Herring and Longacre's National Portrait Gallery.*[64]

Her more famous novel, *A Winter in Washington,* published in 1824, concerned the social life of the city during her early years there. The central figure is a character patterned after Jefferson, and Mrs. Smith admitted that many descriptions, scenery, and bits of society included in the novel were authentic. The book idealizes moral virtues and attempts to demonstrate the good that can be accomplished through following exemplary lives.[65]

Mrs. Smith's other novel, *What is Gentility?,* published in 1828,[66] also pleaded for moral living. Neither of these writings received any lasting recognition.

The Smiths continued an active interest in politics and applauded the elections of Madison and Monroe. In 1824 they strongly backed Crawford and followed many Republicans into the Whig party in 1834. Both violently opposed Jackson, and Mrs. Smith, especially, was shocked by the conduct of the democratic masses at Jackson's inauguration.[67]

The friendship between Smith and Jefferson continued through correspondence for years after both retired from the Washington City political scene, but evidently the two men did not see one another after 1809. In the early years after Jefferson's retirement, frequent letters contained profuse expressions of admiration. Business or social transactions, rather than a purely personal nature, occasioned most letters. For example, Smith sent Jefferson a copy of a July Fourth oration[68] the former editor gave before the citizens of Wash-

---

63. For arrangements concerning the foreign publishing of this book, see William H. Crawford to U. B. De Constant and Richard Rush, William Crawford Papers, Library of Congress, Washington, D.C.

64. "Margaret Bayard Smith," *Dictionary of American Biography* 17:318-19, 1956; Smith, *First Forty Years,* pp. vi-vii.

65. Margaret Bayard Smith, *A Winter in Washington; or, Memoirs of the Seymour Family,* vols. 1, 2 (New York, 1824). See the introduction of the book for Mrs. Smith's purpose in writing the novel.

66. Margaret Bayard Smith, *What Is Gentility?* (Washington, D.C., 1828).

67. Smith, *First Forty Years,* pp. 290-98.

68. For a copy of the published speech, see Samuel H. Smith, *Oration, pronounced in the city of Washington on Monday, the Fifth of July, 1813* (Washington, D.C., 1813).

ington City,[69] and Jefferson responded that he agreed with much of the speech, though he still felt it dangerous for the United States to attempt to meet Great Britain at sea rather than on land.[70]

After the British destroyed the Library of Congress during the War of 1812, Smith negotiated the purchase of the former president's personal library.[71] Less than a month after the raid, Jefferson wrote he would be glad to offer his library of some nine to ten thousand volumes as the nucleus for the new collection. He offered to sell the volumes at a convenient price but admitted that he intended the government to receive the books after his death.[72]

Smith wrote immediately, thanking Jefferson for the offer, and set the machinery turning for completing the transaction.[73] By October 19, 1814, Congress passed the acts necessary for the purchase,[74] but several months elapsed before Smith quoted Jefferson the price for the library: $23,950. Final arrangements for transferring the volumes were completed by the early summer of 1815.[75]

A letter of introduction to the Marquis de Lafayette occasioned an exchange of correspondence in 1821 in which Jefferson attempted to quiet Smith's concern about the affairs of the country. Jefferson admitted, however, that he saw reason for concern about the possibility of a geographic division within the country over sectional problems, something to be avoided at all costs.[76]

69. Samuel Harrison Smith to Jefferson, August 18, 1813, Jefferson Papers, vol. 199.

70. Jefferson to Samuel Harrison Smith, August 23, 1813, Jefferson Papers, vol. 199.

71. Wilhelmus Bogart Bryan, *A History of the National Capital, 1790-1884* (New York, 1914), 1:636.

72. Jefferson to Samuel Harrison Smith, September 21, 1814, Jefferson Papers, vol. 202.

73. Samuel Harrison Smith to Jefferson, October 7, 1814, Jefferson Papers, vol. 202.

74. Samuel Harrison Smith to Jefferson, October 19, 1814, Jefferson Papers, vol. 202.

75. Samuel Harrison Smith to Jefferson, June 11, 1815, Jefferson Papers, vol. 203. For other letters pertaining to the details of the transaction, see: Jefferson to Smith, October 11 and 29, 1814, and February 27, 1815; and Smith to Jefferson, October 7, 14, and 21, 1814, and January 30, February 15, March 11, and March 21, all in 1815, Jefferson Papers, vols. 202 and 203.

76. Samuel Harrison Smith to Jefferson, April 6, 1821, and Jefferson to Smith, April 12, 1821, Jefferson Papers, vol. 220.

In the last known correspondence between the two, Smith turned for political guidance to the man who had played such an important role in his life. Smith was uncertain whom he should support in the election of 1824, and he was equally disturbed by the "great distortion of truth" that permeated the campaign. He admitted, however, that he generally favored Crawford, a close friend of the Smith family. Political rumors hinted that Jefferson supported Jackson. Smith felt Jefferson would be more inclined to favor Crawford and wanted to use the former president's name in supporting the secretary of the treasury.[77] Jefferson refused to be drawn into the campaign and assured Smith that the peace of retirement was an advantage of old age: ". . . there is a time when it is a duty to leave the government of the world to their existing generation."[78]

The answer did not discourage Smith completely, and a few months later he again requested permission to disclose Jefferson's refusal to support any candidate. Jefferson's views, Smith contended, were being flagrantly misrepresented.[79] The former president's reply left no doubt of his sentiment: "Do not for the world, my dear Sir, suffer my letter of Aug. 2 to get before the public, nor to get out of your own hands or to be copied." Jefferson cherished retirement too much to have it broken by political feuds, although he hoped some good Republican would be elected.[80]

Mrs. Smith died on June 7, 1844, and her husband on November 1, 1845. He was buried in Rock Creek Cemetery in Washington City. Their deaths received only slight notice in the *Daily Intelligencer*, with no mention of the fact that Smith and his young bride had founded what was for years Washington's largest and most influential newspaper.[81]

Smith's tenure as editor marked some important contributions to the role of the political editor in American politics

77. Samuel Harrison Smith to Jefferson, July 22, 1823, Jefferson Papers, vol. 224.

78. Jefferson to Samuel Harrison Smith, August 2, 1823, Jefferson Papers, vol. 224.

79. Samuel Harrison Smith to Jefferson, December 13, 1823, Jefferson Papers, vol. 225.

80. Jefferson to Samuel Harrison Smith, December 19, 1823, Jefferson Papers, vol. 225.

81. *Daily National Intelligencer*, June 8, 1844, and November 3, 1845.

during the early decades of the nineteenth century. No newspaper published before the *National Intelligencer* was as intimately identified with a political party and a national administration as was Smith's journal. Cobbett and Fenno served various factions of the Federalist party well and certainly expressed strong sympathies with the Federalist administrations, but no single newspaper spoke for Presidents Washington or Adams.

President Jefferson was a more political being than his predecessors in the presidency. He understood the desirability, even necessity, of political parties in this country. Jefferson had succeeded to a remarkable degree in directing various institutions, mechanisms, and methods toward the aim of gaining the support of the electorate and "perpetuating the political power of the party."[82]

One of the factors contributing to his success was his use of the press to serve party purposes, and at the center of the information-disseminating machinery was the *National Intelligencer*. He used it not only to inform the citizenry about the general issues facing the nation but also to lead the nationally based party, to try out ideas before deciding policy on issues, and to relay information to Congress without having to be identified personally with the point of view.

In all these areas it was Jefferson who was the innovator rather than Smith. But in serving Jefferson and the Republicans Smith performed well.

Smith personally contributed to the journalism of his day. During the ten years he owned and published the newspaper, he laid down the format and many of the policies the paper followed throughout its existence. He established a newspaper that supported liberal policies in a conservative manner. But as important as any of the other characteristics of the *Intelligencer* under Smith was its reputation for fairness, accuracy, and honesty, a tribute to a conscientious and devoted man who established one of the important cornerstones of Washington journalism.

82. Noble E. Cunningham, Jr., *The Jeffersonian Republicans in Power: Party Operations, 1801-1809* (Chapel Hill, N.C., 1963), p. 300.

CHAPTER 5

From Sheffield
to Washington City

Joseph Gales, Jr.,[1] a young North Carolinian only twenty-one years old when he joined Smith on the staff of the *Intelligencer* in 1807, already was an experienced journalist. Neither his personality nor his appearance was particularly imposing, although his alertness and shrewdness commanded respect. Smith's new associate was not tall; indeed, although he was slightly below average height, reaching not more than five feet, two inches,[2] his body was well proportioned. What struck acquaintances was Joseph's large head, broad face, and thick hair.[3] Although his general complexion was dark, his

1. In order to avoid confusion, Joseph Gales, Jr., will be referred to as Joseph throughout this chapter, and his father, Joseph Gales, Sr., will be called Mr. Gales.

2. Allen C. Clark, "Joseph Gales, Junior, Editor and Mayor," *Columbia Historical Society Records* 23 (1920): 136.

3. Oliver Hampton Smith, *Early Indiana Trials: and Sketches* (Cincinnati, Ohio, 1858), p. 464.

face was pale and was dominated by keen black eyes. Ann Royal, a perceptive observer, described Gales as "affable and easy," gracious, and exceedingly polite.[4] This was the man who for the next fifty-three years played a significant—if not the dominant—role in the affairs of the *Intelligencer.*

Joseph's background was both interesting and complex. He sprang from a family of newspapermen and authors. His father, son of a village artisan, had begun his publishing career years earlier in England, where he was born at Eckington on February 4, 1761.[5] His mother published her first novel, *Lady Julia Seaton,* at the age of seventeen,[6] and two other works of fiction followed, *The History of Emma Melcombe and Her Family*[7] and *Matilda Berkeley.*[8] The latter was published by her husband in 1804[9] and was said to be the first novel written by a resident North Carolinian and printed in North Carolina.[10]

After attending village school at Eckington, Mr. Gales moved to Manchester, where he eventually was apprenticed to Prescott's Book and Stationery Store, a local printing concern. He remained in Manchester until a quarrel with his employer's wife caused him to sue successfully for release from his indenture papers.[11]

4. Description by Ann Royal as given in Allen C. Clark, "Colonel William Winston Seaton and His Mayoralty," *Columbia Historical Society Records* 29-30 (1928): 8.

5. Winifred and Joseph Gales, Gales' Recollections, Gales Family Papers, Southern Historical Collection, University of North Carolina, Chapel Hill, N.C., p. 136.

6. Willis G. Briggs, "Two Pioneer Journalists," *National Republic* 18 (October, 1930): 18-19, 47.

7. A search of the Library of Congress, British Museum, and North Carolina archives has failed to locate copies of either *Lady Julia Seaton* or *The History of Emma Melcombe and Her Family.*

8. The Library of Congress has a copy of Mrs. Winifred (Marshall) Gales, *Matilda Berkeley, or Family Anecdotes* (Raleigh, N.C., 1804).

9. Richard Walser, "The Mysterious Case of George Higby Throop (1818-1896)," *The North Carolina Historical Review* 33 (January, 1956): 12; Guion Griffis Johnson, *Ante-Bellum North Carolina: A Social History* (Chapel Hill, N.C., 1937), p. 814.

10. Mrs. J. R. Chamberlain, "Two Wake County Editors Whose Work Has Influenced the World," *North Carolina Historical Commission Publications,* bulletin 30 (Raleigh, N.C., 1924), p. 47. See also Roger Powell Marshall, "A Mythical Mayflower Competition: North Carolina Literature in the Half Century Following the Revolution," *The North Carolina Historical Review* 27 (April, 1950): 185.

11. Robert Neal Elliott, Jr., *The Raleigh Register, 1799-1863,* James Sprunt Studies in History and Political Science (Chapel Hill, N.C., 1955), 36:5.

From Manchester Mr. Gales moved to Newark, where he completed his apprenticeship under J. Tomlinson, a printer and bookseller. Here Mr. Gales met and married on May 4, 1784, Miss Winifred Marshall, daughter of a prominent local citizen.[12] Following his marriage Mr. Gales decided to go into business for himself, and, although the date is uncertain, he moved to Sheffield, England, and began a printing and stationery store.[13]

The young printer by this time was interested in the liberal movements affecting both religion and politics in eighteenth-century England. As a religious liberal he joined the Unitarian church, and as a political liberal he read much of Thomas Paine and joined a constitutional reform movement then underway.[14] His activities with reform movements convinced Mr. Gales of the need for a liberal paper in Sheffield, and in 1787 he began publishing the *Register*.[15] This paper espoused the cause of the workers in this northern English industrial center and as a result was solidly supported by labor. By 1793 the *Register*'s weekly circulation was 1,468.[16]

Championing the laboring classes and advocating constitutional reform were unpopular causes in England at that time, largely because of reaction to the excesses of the French Revolution. Nevertheless Mr. Gales continued to publish articles advocating reforms and went so far as to circulate a petition, signed by some eight thousand persons, calling for reapportionment of representation in the House of Commons. The petition was rejected.[17] Mr. Gales further raised the ire of the more conservative element by disapproving of the war between Britain and France. In addition, he openly advocated the cause of the Unitarian church. All these factors brought him into bitter conflict with a newly founded rival paper, the Sheffield *Courant*, dedicated to supporting government and church.[18]

12. Gales' Recollections, p. 27.
13. For an account of Mr. Gales's early activities and the move to Sheffield, see P. J. Wallis, "A Further Note on Joseph Gales of Newark, Sheffield, and Raleigh," *The North Carolina Historical Review* 30 (October, 1953): 561-63.
14. Elliott, *Raleigh Register*, p. 6.
15. Ibid.; Gales' Recollections, p. 28; W. H. G. Armytage, "The Editorial Experience of Joseph Gales, 1786-1794," *The North Carolina Historical Review* 28 (July, 1951): 334.
16. Elliott, *Raleigh Register*, p. 8.
17. Armytage, "Editorial Experience of Joseph Gales," p. 346.
18. Elliott, *Raleigh Register*, p. 8.

Specific acts alienated Mr. Gales more and more from the British government. One of the chief offenses was his publication of a series of liberal pamplets the government had suppressed, including Locke's *Treatise on Civil Government* and Paine's *Rights of Men* and *Address to the Addressors.*[19]

In May, 1795, events moved toward a climax when Thomas Hardy, secretary of the London Corresponding Society, a reform organization, was arrested, and a note incriminating Mr. Gales was found among Hardy's possessions.[20] The note, written by Richard Davison, a *Register* employee, mentioned that members of the reform group in Sheffield were considering arming themselves for protection. Davison claimed Mr. Gales had arranged with a local cutler to make "some specimens of a pike," and Hardy was asked whether or not the London group intended to take similar defense measures.[21]

The Sheffield society continued to work for reform and issued a declaration stating that "the People ought to demand as a right, not petition as a favour for, universal representation." Mr. Gales contended that not more than fifty of the fifty thousand people in the Sheffield had the right to vote.[22] The declaration for universal representation brought immediate action, and the writ of habeas corpus was suspended.[23]

Mr. Gales's activities incurred the wrath of the government, and luckily he was not in Sheffield when agents arrived to arrest him. Fearful of returning, he hid in a neighboring town and continued to write for the paper, which his wife and James Montgomery continued to publish. Montgomery was Mr. Gales's assistant editor and later gained considerable note as a poet.[24]

While Mr. Gales was hiding, a House of Commons investigation into the Sheffield activities forced him to flee England.

19. Ibid., pp. 7, 9; Gales' Recollections, p. 40.
20. Elliott, *Raleigh Register*, p. 9; Gales' Recollections, p. 53; Armytage, "Editorial Experience of Joseph Gales," p. 358.
21. Elliott, *Raleigh Register*, p. 9.
22. *Raleigh Register and North-Carolina State Gazette*, December 10, 1804. Hereafter this newspaper will be referred to as the *Raleigh Register.*
23. Gales' Recollections, pp. 53-54.
24. "James Montgomery," *Dictionary of National Biography* 38:317-20, 1894; see also James Holland and James Everett, *Memoirs of the Life and Writings of James Montgomery*, 5 vols. (London, 1854).

He escaped to the continent, while his wife remained to publish the paper and to determine a future course of action. After she decided to sell the *Register* and leave England, she experienced some difficulty in arranging a sale, but Montgomery finally managed to purchase the paper. Mrs. Gales and her four children joined her husband in Altoona, Denmark, then Schleswig-Holstein.[25]

The Galeses had discussed coming to the United States before they left England, and in Altoona they again considered the plan. In England the family had met Thomas Digges, an American visiting the Duke of Norfolk. A friendship developed, and Mrs. Gales credited Digges with introducing the idea of their coming to America: "We were delighted with his manners and conversation—they were both new to us, or rather modified somewhat differently, though both were frank, manly, and polished."[26]

But Mr. Gales did not surrender completely the idea of returning to England and to his Sheffield *Register*. He felt a certain loyalty to his native country, and he made sure his return was impossible before he undertook the difficult voyage to the United States. He wrote to friends in Sheffield about his desires: "I . . . expressed by Letter my Willingness to return to my native Land, if it were thought by my Frds. to be safe and eligible. A Meeting was therefore held by my Frds. at Sheffield to consult upon the Eligibility and Safety of this Step, when it was concluded that it was not safe for me to return to England whilst the Suspension of the Habeas Corpus Act was continued, or the System of Persecution for political Practices continued."[27]

The Gales's situation was serious. They lived in a strange land without a source of income, and Mrs. Gales was ill during much of their stay in Altoona.[28] Friends in England raised sufficient money to pay for the Gales's voyage to America, as well as for the purchase of English printing equipment to be

25. Gales' Recollections, p. 60.
26. Ibid., p. 40.
27. Joseph Gales, Sr., Diary, undated entry, Department of Archives and History, Raleigh, N.C. The diary was published in *The North Carolina Historical Review* 26 (July, 1949): 335-47. Mr. Gales's diary is a small notebook filled with comments on his family life in Denmark and the trip to the United States. The pages are unnumbered, and most entries are undated.
28. Ibid., undated entry.

shipped to Philadelphia. They sent seventy pounds, partly as a gift and partly as a loan, and offered to raise three hundred pounds for payment of the equipment.[29]

In booking passage to America Mr. Gales sought a ship sailing either to Philadelphia or to New York.[30] Possibly he anticipated that his publishing background and his knowledge of shorthand, a skill little known in the United States at that time, might be useful at the nation's capital, then located in Philadelphia.

On July 30, 1795, the Galeses arrived in the City of Brotherly Love with no job, little money, and no hope that the printing materials ordered would arrive before the next spring. Until that time, Mrs. Gales admitted, she "had never visibly regretted" her change of station.[31]

Within a short time Mr. Gales secured employment as a journeyman at one of the leading publishing houses in the nation, Dunlap and Claypoole. John Dunlap and David C. Claypoole, owners of the first successful daily newspaper in the United States,[32] both had illustrious publishing careers. Their paper in 1795 was *Dunlap and Claypoole's American Daily Advertiser*, a continuation of the *Pennsylvania Packet; and the General Advertiser*, a weekly Dunlap started October 28, 1771.[33] Claypoole took over the paper on January 1, 1796, dropped the Dunlap name from the title, and continued to publish the newspaper until 1800.[34]

Grateful as she was for the money, Mrs. Gales found her husband's menial job as a printer difficult to accept.[35] When Dunlap and Claypoole learned of Mr. Gales's shorthand knowledge, however, they hired him to take the congressional debates for twenty-five dollars a week—a job that gave him the chance to meet some of the nation's leading political figures. He continued to report for Claypoole even after the

29. Ibid.
30. Ibid.
31. Gales' Recollections, pp. 142-43.
32. Clarence Brigham, *History and Bibliography of American Newspapers, 1690-1820* (Worcester, Mass., 1947), 2:942; Frank Luther Mott, *American Journalism: A History of Newspapers in the United States through 250 Years, 1690-1940* (New York, 1950), p. 116; Edwin Emery and Henry Ladd Smith, *The Press and America* (New York, 1954), p. 173.
33. Brigham, *American Newspapers*, p. 942.
34. Ibid., p. 896.
35. Gales' Recollections, pp. 139-40.

printing equipment arrived from England, and according to his wife's recollections, the publishers "were very proud of employing the best Stenographer in the Union."[36]

After he received his printing equipment, Mr. Gales purchased the *Independent Gazetteer* from the widow of Eleazer Oswald, who had founded the newspaper on April 13, 1782.[37] Publication frequency of the *Gazetteer* changed several times during its life; it became a semiweekly after Mr. Gales's purchase. He changed the title to *Gales's Independent Gazetteer*, and his first issue appeared September 16, 1796.[38]

Gales's Gazetteer professed a nonpolitical stand. Shortly after Mr. Gales began publication, however, his liberal views were evident; he favored France rather than England, and he easily chose the Republican rather than the Federalist party.[39]

After publishing the *Gazetteer* just less than a year, Mr. Gales ended his Philadelphia publishing career when he sold the paper to Samuel Harrison Smith on November 16, 1797.[40] The decision was influenced partially by the yellow fever epidemics that plagued Philadelphia at this time and sent families to the countryside for relief.[41]

The family was unable to locate a new position immediately and remained in Philadelphia for another two years while Mr. Gales continued his printing work. Here the family renewed its acquaintance with Dr. Joseph Priestley, whom they had known in England. The famous English scientist, educator, author, and theologian was jailed in England for his liberal political ideas, and after his release from prison sought asylum in the United States, where he spent the remainder of his life.[42] The Gales family and Dr. Priestley supported the Unitarian church of Philadelphia, and Mr.

36. Ibid.
37. Brigham, *American Newspapers*, p. 919.
38. Ibid., p. 910.
39. Elliott, *Raleigh Register*, p. 15.
40. Ibid., p. 16; Brigham, *American Newspapers*, p. 910.
41. For a detailed account of yellow fever in Philadelphia, see J. H. Powell, *Bring Out Your Dead* (Philadelphia, 1949). Powell deals only briefly with yellow fever epidemics after 1793.
42. For details of Dr. Priestley's life, see John Graham Gillam, *The Crucible: The Story of Joseph Priestley, LL.D., F.R.S.* (London, 1931); Anne Holt, *A Life of Joseph Priestley* (London, 1931); and Edgar F. Smith, *Priestley in America, 1794-1804* (Philadelphia, 1920).

Gales is credited with being the first lay reader of the church.[43] The Gales felt at home in the Unitarian church and especially liked the individual freedom the church allowed. Their children were encouraged to be individualists in action and belief, and the parents made concerted efforts to refrain from imposing their religious beliefs on the children.[44]

Although the family prospered in Philadelphia, the Gales were not happy. In 1798 the dreaded yellow fever struck again,[45] this time afflicting Mrs. Gales. The family moved to Bucks County, Pennsylvania, where Mrs. Gales recovered, and returned to the city after the plague passed.[46]

Fortunately for the Galeses, a Republican group from North Carolina was interested in beginning a newspaper in Raleigh, the state's capital. Nathaniel Macon, North Carolina congressman and a leading Republican in the House, and Richard Stanford, North Carolina congressman representing the Raleigh district, were included in the group. Mr. Gales's journalistic work so impressed the North Carolinians that they made him such an attractive offer that he was induced to leave plague-ridden Philadelphia. A trip to Raleigh in the summer of 1799 convinced him that great opportunity existed there for him.[47]

Whether the Alien and Sedition laws affected Mr. Gales's decision to leave Philadelphia is not clear. He, as an alien and a journalist, was subject to both laws, and in Philadelphia the two acts were fairly strictly enforced. Even if Mr. Gales experienced no personal conflict with the laws, he undoubtedly felt his activities and publishing would be under less careful scrutiny in North Carolina, away from the Federalist-dominated national capital.[48]

After completing arrangements for the move, the Gales family, which included seven children, traveled by boat and

43. Clark, "Joseph Gales, Junior," p. 93.
44. Gales' Recollections, p. 170.
45. Powell, Bring Out Your Dead, pp. 282-83.
46. Elliott, Raleigh Register, pp. 15-16.
47. Ibid., p. 16.
48. For details of the enforcement of the Alien and Sedition Acts, see James Morton Smith, Freedom's Fetters: The Alien and Sedition Laws and American Civil Liberties (Ithaca, N.Y., 1956) and John C. Miller, Crisis in Freedom: The Alien and Sedition Acts (Boston, 1951).

carriage from Philadelphia to Raleigh. During the boat trip between Philadelphia and Norfolk, the youngest daughter died and was buried at sea.[49]

The newly laid-out town of Raleigh which greeted the family in 1799 had been established only seven years before and had a population of about 669. A capitol, built five years before, dominated the town from its site on Union Square, with a few stores and homes clustered around it.[50] The Galeses took a temporary residence until their permanent home on Fayetteville Street was vacated by officers of the provisional army.[51]

The printing equipment arrived from Philadelphia about a month after the family, and on October 22, 1799, the first issue of the *Raleigh Register and North Carolina Weekly Advertiser* appeared.[52] The *Register* continued its initial name until December 2, 1800, when the title was changed to the *Raleigh Register and North-Carolina State Gazette.* On December 27, 1811, after the state printing contracts were surrendered, the paper became the *Raleigh Register and North-Carolina Gazette.*[53]

In Raleigh Mr. Gales found an ideal spot for a political newspaper. The Republican party, there as well as nationally, was fighting to control the government, and a Republican printer stood a good chance of gaining the profitable state printing contracts. The *Register*'s rival for the job was the *Minerva*, established by two strong Federalist supporters, Abraham Hodge and William Boylan.

Hodge, a New Yorker, started his first North Carolina paper in 1786 at New Bern, where he was employed as state printer. Later he published at Edenton and Halifax before moving to Fayetteville. In 1796 Boylan, Hodge's nephew, joined the firm, and together they edited one of the strongest Federalist journals in the state.[54] The two started the *North-Carolina Minerva* on March 24, 1796, in Fayetteville, where they published until May 7, 1799, when the first issue was

49. Gales' Recollections, p. 139.

50. Federal Writers' Project, *North Carolina: A Guide to the Old North State* (Chapel Hill, N.C., 1939), p. 234.

51. Gales' Recollections, p. 142.

52. *Raleigh Register*, October 22, 1799.

53. Brigham, *American Newspapers*, pp. 774-75.

54. H. W. Wagstaff, ed., "The Papers of John Steele," *North Carolina Historical Commission Publications* (Raleigh, N.C., 1924), 1:187n.

printed at Raleigh.[55] The *Minerva* continued under Hodge and Boylan until 1803, when Hodge retired from the paper. Boylan sold his interest on November 29, 1810.[56] Undoubtedly the desire for state printing played an important role in the move from Fayetteville to Raleigh, and Hodge and Boylan did not welcome the presence of any rival paper.

The Republicans were not quite strong enough in 1799 to secure the printing for the *Register*, and Hodge and Boylan continued as state printers.[57] The North Carolina Federalists, however, realized the Republicans' intent, and as the campaign developed at the 1800 session to get Mr. Gales elected printer, one Federalist member worried about Gales's background. The Federalist wrote: "Great expectations are making by Mr. Baker, Blount, Macon[58] and a few others to have Gales elected public printer in place of our friend Hodge. The *gentleman Gales* is said to be by birth an Irishman, but it is certain that he lately conducted a weekly publication in Sheffield in England and came to America because he did not behave peaceably at home. It is certain that he was invited from Philadelphia to Raleigh by party men for party purposes."[59]

The Republican move succeeded, and the following legislature elected Mr. Gales official printer for North Carolina, a position he held ten consecutive years.[60] The state printer received around $1,200 a year, a sizable sum in 1800.[61]

During this time Mr. Gales built his paper into the most widely circulated Republican journal in the state, a tribute to his "aggressiveness and ability." The *Register* was credited with helping the Republicans win a long dominance in the state.[62]

---

55. Brigham, *American Newspapers*, pp. 764, 774.
56. Ibid., p. 773.
57. Mary Lindsay Thornton, "Public Printing in North Carolina, 1749-1815," *The North Carolina Historical Review* 21 (July, 1944): 196-97.
58. Mr. Baker probably was Blake Baker, attorney general of North Carolina from 1793 to 1802, Macon was Nathaniel Macon, North Carolina congressman, and Blount refers to Thomas Blount, also a congressman. See Wagstaff, "Papers of John Steele," 1-2: 416-86, for more complete identification.
59. Charles W. Harris to Robert Harris, August 29, 1800, in Thornton, "Public Printing in North Carolina," p. 197.
60. Ibid.
61. *Raleigh Star*, November 29, 1810, quoted in Elliott, *Raleigh Register*, p. 25.
62. Wagstaff, "Papers of John Steel," p. 191n.

Mr. Gales patterned his Raleigh newspaper after the journal he had edited in Sheffield, England. The same format included front-page advertising, small label headlines, exchange news, and editorial opinions. The paper was not attractive in appearance, but editorial exchanges with competitors provided lively reading material.[63]

Keen competition for state printing continued, and in nearly every legislative session Boylan sought to replace Mr. Gales by attacking the *Register* editor on several points. Boylan thought Mr. Gales overcharged the state for the work done, and the *Minerva* editor promised he would be pleased to do the printing at a considerable discount and at the same time improve the quality of printing. In addition to criticizing Mr. Gales's printing, Boylan chided the *Register* editor for his English background and questioned whether a foreigner ought to receive such strong support from the state.[64]

During the autumn of 1804 the conflict between the two publishers intensified, and Boylan's famous temper became more and more unruly.[65] Mr. Gales, who usually refused to answer Boylan's charges concerning his political activities in England, finally exploded: "If it be criminal to have been born in England or to have exerted himself as the Editor of a popular Newspaper whilst living there, to obtain a reform of the corruptions of government, he is verily guilty."[66] Partisans in the legislature stood up and cheered their respective candidates.[67]

Boylan's temper was whipped to a frenzy, and in December he attacked Mr. Gales with a cane on the steps of the state capitol, inflicting injuries that forced the *Register* editor to suspend publication for one issue.[68] On resuming publication Mr. Gales told his readers that at last Boylan had showed himself for what he really was, a "cold-blooded assassinator of private character," a "butcher of good names," a "secret

---

63. The North Carolina State Library, Raleigh, has a nearly complete file of the *Raleigh Register*.

64. *Minerva*, December 7, 1802; Thornton, "Public Printing in North Carolina," pp. 197-99.

65. Thornton, "Public Printing in North Carolina," pp. 197-99.

66. *Raleigh Register*, September 17, 1804.

67. See Joseph Pearson to John Steele, quoted in Wagstaff, "Papers of John Steele," pp. 440-42.

68. *Raleigh Register*, December 10, 1804.

plotter against his neighbor's fame," and a "scientific desperado."[69]

Mr. Gales went still further and insinuated that Boylan was responsible for a fire that destroyed the *Register* in February, 1804. Mr. Gales sued Boylan for assault and collected a hundred pounds following a trial in the Hillsboro Superior Court.[70] The *Register* editor donated the sum, less legal fees, to the Raleigh Academy, which he strongly supported.[71]

The fight for state printing patronage continued on a less dramatic basis until 1810, when the legislature reduced the salary from $1,200 to $900 a year. The *Register* resigned the position the following year.[72] By this time Mr. Gales also owned a paper mill and a stationery store and was less dependent on the state for support.[73] Later he added a plantation and much city property to his holdings.[74]

The Galeses prospered in Raleigh and became one of the best known and most influential families in the city and state. Mr. Gales served as mayor of the city from 1819 until he retired from the newspaper in 1833.[75] He was elected commissioner and treasurer of the town[76] and served as director of the State Bank.[77] He also was secretary of the Raleigh Auxiliary Society for Colonizing the Free People of Colour of the United States,[78] of the Agricultural Society of North-Carolina,[79] of the Wake Agricultural Society,[80] and of the convention in North Carolina favoring John Quincy Adams's reelection.[81]

In Raleigh the Galeses did much to promote the Unitarian

69. Ibid.

70. Elliott, *Raleigh Register*, p. 26.

71. Ibid. For an account of Mr. Gales's relationship to the academy, see Johnson, *Ante-Bellum North Carolina*, p. 286.

72. Thornton, "Public Printing in North Carolina," pp. 198-99; Elliott, *Raleigh Register*, p. 26.

73. Louis Martin Sears, *Jefferson and the Embargo* (Durham, N.C., 1927), p. 235; Elliott, *Raleigh Register*, p. 27; Johnson, *Ante-Bellum North Carolina*, pp. 765-66.

74. Gales's will, office of Clerk of Superior Court, Wake County Court House, Raleigh, N.C.

75. Elliott, *Raleigh Register*, p. 36; "Joseph Gales, Sr.," *Dictionary of American Biography* 7:99-100, 1956.

76. Elliott, *Raleigh Register*, p. 36.

77. *Raleigh Register*, December 10, 1819, and June 21, 1811.

78. Ibid., June 18, 1819; Johnson, *Ante-Bellum North Carolina*, p. 569.

79. *Raleigh Register*, December 18, 1818.

80. Ibid., May 9, 1823.

81. Ibid., December 25, 1827.

church in the South. One of their friends was Jared Sparks, famed Unitarian minister, historian, and president of Harvard University, who carried on a lengthy correspondence with both Mr. and Mrs. Gales on religious as well as on personal topics.[82] During a visit Sparks made to Raleigh in 1826, he enjoyed the hospitality of the Gales's home.[83]

In 1833 Mr. Gales retired from the *Register* and turned over the paper to his youngest son, Weston, who was born April 28, 1802, in Raleigh. Weston continued to publish the paper until he died in 1848,[84] and his son, Seaton, took over until the paper was sold in 1856.[85]

It is not surprising that Mr. and Mrs. Gales produced children of outstanding character and ability, such as their son Joseph. He was born in Eckington, England, April 10, 1786, and was less than ten years old when his family fled England. His education, begun in the classics before leaving England, was continued in Altoona and Philadelphia and completed in North Carolina.[86] Mr. Gales wanted Joseph and Weston to receive academic education, in addition to training as printers,[87] and sought to give them the best university education available. He was disappointed in both cases.

Joseph entered the University of North Carolina in the autumn of 1800. Scholastic work gave him no difficulties; he excelled in composition, and one instructor went so far as to describe him a "genius" in his writing ability.[88] Joseph encountered his troubles outside the classroom.

82. Much of the Gales collection of papers at the North Carolina Department of Archives and History, Raleigh, is composed of photostats of the Gales-Sparks correspondence taken from the Sparks collection in the Massachusetts Historical Society.

83. Herbert B. Adams, *The Life and Writings of Jared Sparks* (Boston, 1893), 1:443, 449.

84. Edgar Estes Folk, "W. W. Holden and the North Carolina Standard, 1843-1848," *The North Carolina Historical Review* 19 (January, 1942): 45.

85. Elliott, *Raleigh Register*, p. vi.

86. Gales' Recollections, pp. 19-20.

87. A third son, Thomas, never engaged in the newspaper business. He studied law in Raleigh and then moved to Louisiana, where he served as a voluntary aide-de-camp to General Andrew Jackson in the New Orleans campaign. Thomas died while engaged in military activities in the Louisiana area, and little mention is made of him in the Gales family writings and letters. See John Spencer Bassett, ed., *Correspondence of Andrew Jackson* (Washington, D.C., 1927), 2:98; Henry Thomas Shanks, ed., *Papers of Willie P. Mangum* (Raleigh, N.C., 1950), 1:2n.

88. University of North Carolina Student Records, 1795-1809, May Term, 1801, University of North Carolina Library, Chapel Hill, N.C.

The University of North Carolina was divided into two literary groups, the Dialectic and the Philanthropic societies, and admission to one was practically essential to matriculation.[89] Accordingly, on April 16, 1801, Joseph joined the Dialectic Society.[90] His tenure of membership in good standing was short-lived, for on July 16, 1801, he was fined for neglect of duty, and sterner action against him was begun: "The Censor Morum informed the Society that there were articles of impeachment on the table against Mr. Joseph Gales." He was accused of being "malicious in his disposition, having acted improperly on some former occasions . . . and being generally trifling and loose in his manners." A letter from a former member, Adlai Osborn, informed the group that he had decided "with some difficulty" to report on Joseph because Osborn felt the society had been injured and "justice ought to be had on the delinquent." Joseph was accused of saying that Osborn had quit the society because four members refused him a diploma. "Besides this absolute infringement of the law, the character of Mr. Gales as to veracity is such as to disgrace your body, which many of your members can prove," said the correspondent. The letter was signed "A. Osborn."[91] Action on the charges against young Gales came on August 15, 1801, when the body voted Joseph guilty as charged and "determined by ballot that he should be totally and finally expelled. The President . . . in an eloquent but pertinent speech informed him of his fate."[92]

The college education of Joseph Gales, Jr., ended after just thirteen months. His brother Weston spent even less time pursuing higher education. He was sent to Yale on Jared Sparks's recommendation in order to avoid the "loose habits of the young men of Raleigh."[93] Weston was expelled for engaging in a fight with another southern youth, but he was little to blame, according to his parents.[94]

89. R. D. W. Connor, ed., *A Documentary History of the University of North Carolina* (Chapel Hill, N.C., 1953), 1:477-79.

90. Minutes of the Dialectic Society, University of North Carolina, 1798-1804, University of North Carolina Library, Chapel Hill, N.C.

91. Dialectic Society Papers, 1782-1808, University of North Carolina Library, Chapel Hill, N.C.

92. Ibid.

93. Joseph Gales, Sr., to Jared Sparks, February 18, 1820, Gales Papers, North Carolina Department of Archives and History, Raleigh, N.C.

94. Ibid., January 28, 1821.

Joseph, after expulsion from the University of North Carolina, returned to Raleigh and entered the newspaper business with his father. Here he improved his shorthand skills and his knowledge of printing. When the *Register* plant was burned in 1804 before the printing for the state had been completed, Joseph went to Warrenton, where a friend, Richard Davison, furnished the type and presses for completing the job. Joseph handled most of the work, an indication that he possessed an extensive knowledge of the printing field at an early age.[95]

Joseph's training on the *Register*, however, did not satisfy his father, who felt his son needed greater experience than could be gained in Raleigh. He therefore sent Joseph to Philadelphia, where under the supervision of William Young Birch, printer and close friend of Mr. Gales, Joseph was given the desired training.[96] On completion of his work, he received a diploma from the Typographical Society of Philadelphia certifying him a finished printer and member of the society.[97]

Joseph was working in Philadelphia in 1807 when Samuel Harrison Smith's advertisement offered the *Intelligencer* for sale. Mr. Gales did not know Smith well and had not seen him since he bought the *Universal Gazette* before the Gales moved to Raleigh. The only news of Smith had been through the *Intelligencer*, which indicated that Smith had done well in Washington. Mr. Gales was surprised that the paper was for sale, as he considered "it to be one of the most desirable situations both for usefulness and profit in the Country."[98]

The *Intelligencer* interested Mr. Gales. He might have bought the paper had not his family so recently settled in Raleigh.[99] But he wrote that if Smith would accept a partner, he thought his son Joseph would be interested. Mr. Gales suggested that although his son would in time make an "acceptable editor," he lacked the experience necessary for taking over the *Intelligencer*.[100]

Smith answered that there was no one to whom he would

95. Clark, "Joseph Gales, Junior," p. 94.
96. Gales' Recollections, p. 155.
97. *National Intelligencer*, January 7, 1829.
98. Gales' Recollections, p. 155.
99. Ibid., pp. 155-56.
100. Ibid.

rather sell the paper than Mr. Gales, but that he was not interested in acquiring a partner. The *Intelligencer* editor, tired and dissatisfied with the newspaper business and politics, wanted to leave both. He explained, however, that if he failed to receive a better offer, he might write later about the partnership.[101]

At that time British-American relations reached a critical stage, largely because of the *Chesapeake-Leopard* affair. Smith decided his political leaders needed all possible support, and thus he decided to continue as publisher until some less crucial time. After he reached his decision, he wrote the Galeses, asking that Joseph come to Washington City to make some arrangement for joining the *Intelligencer* staff. The two Galeses, Smith, and Birch, the Gales's friend from Philadelphia, met in Washington, and arrangements were completed.

Plans called for Joseph to work on salary for two years, and then if Smith found his partner competent, Joseph would assume full authority. Mr. Gales promised to help his son report the congressional debates during the 1807-8 session. The elder Gales was sure that by the end of the session his son would become "an able Reporter."[102]

Smith was not completely satisfied with the arrangement, but he was relieved of some of the publishing load. His wife particularly looked forward to the additional help. She confided to her husband's sister: "My heart is quite brightened by the thought that my dear husbands labours are lightened; For his health was so much injured last winter, that I was seriously alarmed." Joseph was to live with the Smith family.[103]

Joseph's lodging at the Smith home soon became a source of complaint to Mrs. Smith. She was prominent in Washington City society, and she had forgotten her early irritations concerning a lack of proper companionship. President Jefferson and Smith were on social as well as business terms, and congressmen frequently dined at the Smith home. Competent as Joseph might have been as a reporter, Mrs. Smith, unlike

101. Ibid.
102. Ibid.
103. Margaret Bayard Smith to Mary Ann Smith, August 28, 1807, Margaret Bayard Smith Papers, vol. 8, Library of Congress, Washington, D.C.

Ann Royal, regarded him as rather a "country bumpkin." After all, he came from North Carolina and was trained primarily as a printer. Less than a year after her expression of pleasure that Joseph was joining the paper, she critically observed:

You will perceive by the paper that Mr. Gales is taken into partnership & that he will be a member of our family for some years at least—My endeavours to soften & polish his manner proving ineffectual, last winter, I have given up the manners I assumed for the purpose—I am civil & kind to him, but pay him no particular attention; he consequently never comes in the parlour except to meals, or when some acquaintance of his, is there, I find it much the best method & his manners are much more mild and genteel than they were.—He continues kind to the children & attentive to me, much more respectful & civil towards Mr. S & extremely polite to Betsy—but as I observed we meet only at meals, & all familiarity avoided.[104]

On August 31, 1810, the masthead of the *Intelligencer* listed Joseph Gales, Jr., as sole publisher. Smith explained that he had remained in the publishing field longer than intended, but now he was surrendering his paper to a highly qualified man. In Joseph's hands the *Intelligencer* would receive "the best guarantee for an adherence to that purity and fidelity with which it has been my unremitted effort to conduct it."[105]

Joseph pledged his devotion to Smith's policies and assured his readers of his "firm purpose to maintain, and to preserve inviolate the independence of the print now committed into my hands." He further acknowledged his devotion to a Republican form of government and to Republican administrations "which so happily unite the American people. . . ." Joseph also promised that no expense would be spared to bring the readers a paper worthy of their patronage.[106]

The editorial marked the end of the Smith period for the *Intelligencer* and the beginning of fifty years of ownership under Joseph Gales, Jr.

---

104. Margaret Bayard Smith to Susan B. Smith, December 4, 1808, Margaret Bayard Smith Papers, vol. 9.
105. *National Intelligencer*, August 31, 1810.
106. Ibid.

CHAPTER 6

The War of 1812

Joseph Gales's[1] position in 1810 was challenging, to say the least. At twenty-four he owned one of the nation's largest and most influential papers, which had the added distinction of serving as the president's semiofficial organ. The next five years marked a tremendously important period for the young publisher, for he took a lifetime business partner, married a young Virginia lady, and strongly supported the war with Great Britain.

Gales's business partner, a young Virginian named William Winston Seaton, was associated with Gales on the *Intelligencer* for the next forty-eight years. Plans to take Seaton into partnership began during the winter of 1812, when the pressures of publishing the *Intelligencer* confined Gales to his bed most of the season. His father responded to the call for help and came from North Carolina to report the congressional session.[2]

1. Joseph Gales, Jr., hereafter will be referred to as Gales. His father will continue to be called Mr. Gales.
2. Joseph Gales, Sr., to Wood Jones Hamlin, April 9, 1812, Hamlin Papers, North Carolina Department of Archives and History, Raleigh, N.C.

As father and son talked over the problems of the *Intelligencer*, the two hit upon a plan to secure a partner. At that time the senior Gales had as his associate on the *Raleigh Register* his son-in-law, Seaton, whom Mr. Gales felt might fill the *Intelligencer* demands. When Mr. Gales returned to Raleigh, he took up the matter with Seaton, and "being pleased with the offer, the fall of that year, 1812, Mr. Seaton and his family removed to Washington."[3]

Seaton's addition to the staff was necessitated not only by the demands of publishing the triweekly *Intelligencer* and the *Universal Gazette*, but also by plans to start a daily edition of the *Intelligencer*. The first daily appeared January 1, 1813, under the name of Gales and Seaton.[4]

Seaton, twenty-seven years old when he joined the *Intelligencer*, presented a more imposing physical appearance than his partner. According to Ann Royal, he was tall, stout, and "well made." His complexion was fair, his face round, and his features regular and handsome. Two "penetrative blue eyes" dominated his face. In general he looked strongly masculine and dignified, and he talked and acted decisively.[5]

Seaton's entire background was southern. He was born in King William County, Virginia, in 1785, son of Augustine and Mary (Winston) Seaton, members of a prominent Virginia family which immigrated to this country from Scotland in 1690 during the unsuccessful attempt to bring a Stuart back to the Scottish throne,[6] a cause the Seaton family supported.

Seaton's father directed his son's early schooling, and young Seaton reputedly early developed scholarly interests. He also was tutored by a man known as Ogilvie, earl of Finlater, a "Scotch gentleman then living as a refugee in Virginia. . . ." who ran an academy in Richmond.[7]

Seaton began working on the *Virginia Patriot*, Richmond, when he was seventeen. Thomas Ritchie, who later published

3. Winifred and Joseph Gales, Gales' Recollections, Gales Family Papers, Southern Historical Collection, University of North Carolina, Chapel Hill, N.C., pp. 156-57.

4. *Daily National Intelligencer*, January 1, 1813.

5. Description by Ann Royal in Allen C. Clark, "Colonel William Winston Seaton and His Mayoralty," *Columbia Historical Society Records* 29-30 (1928): 8.

6. For a more detailed discussion, see George Macaulay Trevelyan, *England Under the Stuarts* (New York, 1946).

7. *Smithsonian Miscellaneous Collections* (Washington, D.C., 1880), 18:310.

the *Richmond Enquirer* and the *Union*, a Washington City newspaper, also was employed on the *Patriot* at the time Seaton was there. From Richmond Seaton moved to Petersburg, Virginia, where he edited the *Republican* and gained considerable reputation as a political editor.[8] In 1806 the young Virginian moved to Raleigh to assist William Boylan on the *Minerva*.[9] The following year Seaton went to Halifax, North Carolina, where he published the *North Carolina Journal*, another paper with a strong Republican slant.[10]

When Seaton became editor of the Halifax paper, Republicans and Federalists in that part of the state were engaged in a bitter political struggle. Seaton hesitated to take the editorship because of his youth, but he accepted it and performed well. One writer claimed of Seaton that it was "mainly through his well directed exertions the reign of federalism was subverted in that part of the State. . . ."[11]

While in Raleigh, Seaton met Sarah Gales, daughter of Joseph Gales, Sr., and the two were married March 30, 1809. On January 5 of that year the *Raleigh Register* carried this note: "J. Gales . . . admitted into a share of his Printing Business, Mr. William W. Seaton, (late Editor of the Halifax Journal,) . . . ."[12]

This Raleigh firm of Gales and Seaton continued until October, 1812, when Seaton joined young Gales in Washington City on the *Intelligencer*. Business arrangements are not known, but a contract drawn up in 1816 indicates Seaton held only a third interest in the paper. A formal 1816 agreement called for Seaton to pay $5,000 for one-third of all "goods, merchandise, chattels, stock, & utensils in trade belonging to said Joseph Gales, Junior, and situate in the Printing office and appartments belong attached thereto. . . ."[13]

The partnership covered all book debts and outstanding accounts except overpaid wages and mechanical equipment. Seaton was to receive one-third of the newspaper and print-

8. Josephine Seaton, *William Winston Seaton of the "National Intelligencer"* (Boston, 1871), p. 16.

9. Gales' Recollections, p. 156.

10. Seaton, *William Winston Seaton*, pp. 17-18.

11. *Smithsonian Miscellaneous Collections*, p. 311.

12. *Raleigh Register*, January 5, 1809.

13. Contract between Gales and Seaton, November 24, 1816, Gales and Seaton Papers, Library of Congress, Washington, D.C.

ing profits and was to pay one-third of the expenses. Dividends were to be divided at the first of each month, and not less than $500 cash was to be kept on hand. Money was to be borrowed jointly and was to be provided in proportion to the shares in the business. Checks were to be withdrawn only in a checkbook prepared for the purpose, and none was to be drawn for business except the regular monthly payments. In case either Gales or Seaton died within five years, the surviving member was to have the option of buying the *Intelligencer* under terms to be decided upon by referees, including Mr. Gales and Weston Gales.[14]

The year after completing his business partnership, Gales successfully wooed a young Virginia lady, Sarah Juliana Maria Lee, daughter of Theodorick Lee and niece of "Light Horse Harry" Lee of Revolutionary fame. The wedding was performed at Winchester, Virginia, on December 14, 1813.[15]

Before assuming ownership of the paper, Gales had been just a reporter, skilled in taking shorthand and competent in printing and journalistic work. On becoming editor, he assumed control over the most vital communication link between government and the people.

The *Intelligencer* was the channel through which the federal administration carried its message to the people. Both in the United States and in foreign countries, the *Intelligencer* was looked to for an indication of what policies the Madison administration would follow. This did not necessarily mean that the president and his cabinet dictated the *Intelligencer*'s content. However, if the newspaper was viewed as the official organ, the editor was expected to have sufficient understanding of the administration policy to lend intelligent support. With the tense relations with both England and France, Gales soon realized the responsibilities he faced were indeed weighty for a twenty-four-year-old.

Shortly after taking over the editorship, Gales met with Secretary of State Robert Smith for a conference on the delicate negotiations being pursued with France in an effort to get France to repeal its trade restrictions against the United

14. Ibid.
15. *Raleigh Register*, December 24, 1813; "Joseph Gales, Jr.," *Dictionary of American Biography* 7:100-101.

States. Smith pointedly reminded Gales of the official character of his position as an editor, and although Gales resented
Smith's attempt to school him, he left fully realizing that his
was not a job for taking independent positions on issues but
rather that of serving as a pliant instrument.[16]

Although Gales took over publication of the newspaper
during the summer, not until October 17 did he see Madison.
The president was cordial enough, but he must have hesitated
somewhat to place his confidence in an editor so young and
relatively inexperienced. The interview with Madison dealt
mainly with the possibility of the French revoking trade restrictions and the threat of British expansion in South
America and Florida. Gales left feeling awe both for the president and for the position of *Intelligencer* editor.[17] Shortly after
this Gales attended his first drawing room at the White
House; he noted that Madison seemed cordial enough but
thought Mrs. Madison was a bit cool.

If Gales's role of speaking for an administration with which
he was barely acquainted did not make his early days difficult
enough, the nation's editors added further problems. By the
end of October much was being made of the fact that Gales
had been born in England and that a foreign editor was writing the material designed by the Madison administration to
prepare members of Congress for the coming session.[18]

Such criticisms may have bothered Gales, but his position
allowed little time for answering or for concerning himself
with such accusations. He was busy meeting and becoming
acquainted with cabinet members, attending dinners at the
White House, where he had long conversations with Madison
and Secretary Albert Gallatin, and learning from the leading
figures of the nation that all was not peace and harmony
within the administration.[19]

Gales was bothered that he had not been taken into the
administration's confidence enough so that he was aware that
Secretary of State Smith was about to resign from the cabinet,
to be replaced by James Monroe. It also bothered him, when

16. For Gales's account of the early days, see excerpts from his diary published
in the *National Intelligencer* on July 30, 1857.
17. Ibid.
18. *New York Evening Post*, October 27, 1810.
19. *National Intelligencer*, July 30, 1857.

Monroe took office, to realize that Monroe and Madison had different views concerning how relations with France might be worked out.[20] He was somewhat annoyed and embarrassed when both Mr. and Mrs. Gallatin lectured him for an article on the Smith resignation that appeared to offer more praise than criticism. Gales, unaware that the Madison administration sought the resignation, claimed he merely wrote the article to express appreciation for Smith's services.[21]

Gales learned quickly from Secretary Monroe that any freedom to speak on foreign policy issues would be earned. Shortly after taking office, Monroe summoned Gales to his office, notifying him politely but firmly that anything from the State Department would be issued directly by Secretary Monroe if the *National Intelligencer* were to continue as the official organ. Gales accepted the terms.

Within a relatively few months Gales's position was fairly well defined. He had gained the administration's confidence and his paper continued as the government's official organ. In return, he realized he had relatively little freedom to express his own views or to criticize the administration's course. He further realized that Secretary Monroe had not placed full confidence in the *Intelligencer*, as demonstrated by a letter criticizing the paper, which Gales suspected had originated with the secretary of state. Gales reacted to the criticism by avoiding the government offices for two weeks.[22]

Gales's differences with Monroe arose over the policy toward Great Britain. The editor agreed with Madison's policy of going to war as soon as public opinion allowed while Monroe favored a more cautious course of utilizing all possible conciliation before resorting to war. Britain's threatening position during the summer of 1811 ended the divided opinion between the president and his chief cabinet officer and also saw the *Intelligencer* take on a more warlike spirit. By the end of 1811, Gales had Monroe's confidence as the newspaper moved to create a climate of opinion necessary for a declaration of war.[23]

With early differences past, Gales and Monroe pursued a

20. Ibid., August 8, 1857.
21. Ibid.
22. Ibid.
23. Ibid., September 12, 1857.

common policy as the *National Intelligencer* encouraged the move toward war. During the spring of 1812 one student of the *Intelligencer* during this period concluded that so intimately was the paper in tune with the administration that it was difficult to tell who was writing the editorials.[24] Monroe sent frequent notes outlining policy to Gales.[25] The variety of writing styles appearing in the *Intelligencer* during the early months of 1812 also may be accounted for by the illness that plagued Gales during most of the winter. Since Mr. Gales came from Raleigh to assist, he may have done some of the writing.

Although Gales had criticized Congress for its lack of action in the 1811 session,[26] he now courted the members and encouraged them to stand behind the administration. His writing indicated that the executive branch had done all it could and that now it was up to the legislative branch to determine the final verdict for the country.

Federalist congressmen, seldom praised by the *Intelligencer*, were complimented for their conduct in helping prepare for war, and the editorial writer wondered if at last unity of purpose were attained.[27] The *Intelligencer* registered none of the suspicion held by some Republicans that the Federalist cooperation was only an attempt to lure the United States into a disastrous war for which the Republicans could be blamed. Greater concern was registered among the Republicans, however, for their own recalcitrants, led by Samuel Smith of Maryland and William Giles and John Randolph, Jr. of Virginia.[28] *Niles' Register* was so confused by Randolph's political affiliation that it abandoned its usual policy of printing Republican names in italics and Federalist ones in Roman letters. It printed Randolph's half in italics and half in Roman.[29]

During the month of April the *Intelligencer* carried several pleas for a break with Great Britain, contending that all hope

24. Howard Mahan, "Joseph Gales and the War of 1812" (Ph.D. thesis, Columbia University, 1957), pp. 148-56.

25. Monroe to Joseph Gales, Jr., April 3, 1812, Monroe Papers, New York Public Library, New York.

26. *National Intelligencer*, March 21, 1811.

27. Ibid., March 7, 1812.

28. Julius W. Pratt, *Expansionists of 1812* (New York, 1949), pp. 127-33.

29. Francis F. Beirne, *The War of 1812* (New York, 1949), p. 64.

was abandoned that either Britain or France would repeal trade restrictions. The ninety-day embargo, Gales sensed, pushed the United States a step nearer actual hostilities. He wrote: "We should be blind to the evidence of the most striking and important facts if we did not perceive and acknowledge this great truth. . . . It has been forced on us by the voice of the whole American people, who, deeply incensed at these wrongs, have called on their government, for redress." The choice faced by the United States between "submission to these wrongs" and a "manly assertion of their rights" was not difficult for Gales: it was time to fight.[30]

Whether Gales actually believed the country was united and ready for war is difficult to ascertain. At any rate, his paper, as the administrative organ, carried the heavy responsibility of readying the reluctant sections of the country for conflict. He reviewed the list of grievances the country had suffered at the hands of the British, along with the efforts of the United States through embargoes and trade restrictions to maintain peace. But Britain had insisted on her antagonistic policy, which proved to Gales that England sought control of the ocean, and the United States had to submit to such control or to fight.

On April 14 Gales wrote: "In their operation they violate the rights, and wound deeply the best interests, of the whole American people. If we yield to them, at this time, the cause may be considered as abandoned."[31] This editorial, one of the most urgent pleas, later was credited to Secretary Monroe,[32] as was the famous War Manifesto, which for years was thought to have been the work of John C. Calhoun, the man who delivered the document to Congress.[33]

The *Intelligencer* editorials during the late spring of 1812 were among the most spirited ever written for the journal, for the editor keenly sensed his duty of arousing Congress and the nation to support the administration's war policy. In Gales's view, the push for war came only after a conference between Madison, Clay, Calhoun, and a delegation from Con-

30. *National Intelligencer,* April 9, 1812.
31. Ibid., April 14, 1812.
32. Irving Brant, *Madison the President, 1809-1812* (Indianapolis, 1961), 5: chap. 27.
33. See Gaillard Hunt, ed., "Joseph Gales on the War Manifesto of 1812," *American Historical Review* 13 (January, 1908): 309-10.

gress at which it was decided that a majority of the legislative body now favored the war.[34] His friends, the War Hawks, were becoming successful.[35]

War was declared June 18, 1812, but the *Intelligencer* did not carry the story until two days later. Gales was satisfied with the declaration: "Its adoption . . . stamps reality on what was before mere inference and conjecture."[36]

The myth that the country was united in the war effort soon was exposed, however. The *Columbia Centinel* hailed the declaration as the worst possible news: "THE overwhelming calamity so much dreaded by man—so little expected by the community at large—but so long considered inevitable by a few—has befallen OUR COUNTRY." The *Boston Repertory* reacted similarly, and Gales realized that winning New England's support would be difficult.[37]

Gales may have been bothered by these attacks on the administration, as well as on the *Intelligencer*, but he was convinced that freedom to speak out had to be continued. At no time did he favor the passage of any laws making such criticisms of the government seditious. On only one occasion did temper rather than calm reasoning dominate an answer to New England's criticism.

This display of annoyance came after the famous meeting in Boston's Faneuil Hall, at which time the *Intelligencer* was severely criticized for its role in bringing about the war. Gales was absent from Washington attempting to recover his health in Virginia when the notice of the meeting appeared. On returning he wrote what was probably his most bitter attack on the opposition.[38]

By the summer of 1813 the *Intelligencer* editors joined others in the mid-Atlantic area in attempts to trace the actions of a

34. Ibid.
35. For a description of the ideas and work of the War Hawks, see Carl Schurz, *Life of Henry Clay* (Boston, 1887), 1: chaps. 5-6; Gaillard Hunt, *The Life of James Madison* (New York, 1902), chaps. 21-24; Bernard Mayo, *Henry Clay* (Boston, 1937), 1: chaps. 9-13; Charles M. Wiltse, *John C. Calhoun, Nationalist, 1782-1828* (Indianapolis, 1944), 1: chaps. 4-7; William E. Dodd, *The Life of Nathaniel Macon* (Raleigh, N.C., 1903), chap. 16. Beirne, *War of 1812*, has a good brief discussion of the role of the War Hawks.
36. *National Intelligencer*, June 20, 1812.
37. Ibid., August 4, 1812.
38. For an interesting reminiscence of Gales on the incident, see *National Intelligencer*, January 8, 1847.

British fleet as it ranged down the Eastern coast, particularly in the Chesapeake Bay and Potomac River areas. Military action before that time had failed to excite Gales and Seaton. Detroit's fall and military reverses received calm treatment in the *Intelligencer*—they were distant. Northern border battles brought forth pleas for support, but nothing more.

A British fleet, however, appeared to be at the doors of Washington City.[39] As the fleet moved south, citizens of the capital became concerned, and by July both Gales and Seaton had volunteered for service in the District of Columbia militia. Seven workmen from the shop also joined, and subscribers were asked to understand if the paper were not the best and if mistakes were more numerous than usual.[40] Five days later only two pressmen were left to publish the paper, and the illness of one made the task especially difficult.[41]

Mrs. Seaton and a sister visiting in Washington City moved to Samuel Harrison Smith's home while Gales and Seaton were stationed at Warburton. Although this helped excite the fears of Mrs. Smith's family, she felt no great danger. "It is generally believed impossible," she said, "for the English to reach the city, not so much from our force at Warburton, Tho' that is very large, as from the natural impediments. . . ."[42]

Mrs. Seaton also felt little fear from the threatened invasion: "Joseph assures us most solemnly that he does not believe they will dare attempt to land or pass the numerous and brave force of volunteers and regulars who are assembled, and positively believes that there will be no fighting."[43]

Gales and Seaton alternated in returning to the city to supervise the *Intelligencer*, but the paper's content suffered from their absence. Friends urged the editors to remain with their paper, since "the continual direction of the public record printed in the office" meant more than individual military

39. For a discussion of the Chesapeake campaign of 1813, see Beirne, *War of 1812*, pp. 168-82.
40. *National Intelligencer*, July 12, 1813.
41. Sarah Gales Seaton to unnamed correspondent, July 22, 1813, quoted in Seaton, *William Winston Seaton*, pp. 111-12.
42. Margaret Bayard Smith to Jane Kirkpatrick, July 20, 1813, Margaret Bayard Smith Papers, vol. 9, Library of Congress, Washington, D.C.
43. Sarah Gales Seaton to unnamed correspondent, July 20, 1813, quoted in Seaton, *William Winston Seaton*, p. 110.

contributions. But Gales, particularly, felt he had to fight. His sister Mrs. Seaton wrote: "Joseph would more naturally incur the imputation of disinclination to defend his country from enemies than William, from the accident of being a foreigner, and therefore I should like him to prove the contrary, if he has indeed a political enemy who would be so ungenerous as to asperse his actions and motives."[44]

Suspense of the threatened British invasion was climaxed July 24 when rumors circulated that the British had landed. The reports were untrue, and the threat quickly passed. By July 27 the volunteers were discharged, and Gales and Seaton were back at the *Intelligencer*.[45]

The following year, a momentous one for the young publishers, was ushered in amid rumors of an armistice proposed by Russia.[46] Gales and Seaton hoped the stories were true, for the editors sensed that the citizens of the country were restless because of the lack of success or decisiveness of action in the war. Impatience with the War Department became more noticeable, and even the *Intelligencer* offered only mild defense by saying delay was part of the "strategy."[47]

As far as peace was concerned, Gales and Seaton were willing to accept any honorable conditions that might be proposed. But "war was preferred to an ignoble peace, by a nation conscious of its rights and able and willing to support them. On the recognition of those rights, peace will be restored to us. . . ."[48] On January 20 the *Intelligencer* readers were told that the peace delegation had sailed for Europe.[49]

The editors continued their party forays by passing out compliments to the Republican party for supporting the war efforts.[50] Gales and Seaton warned against the Federalist outbursts opposing the war carried by Federalist prints: "This is the season for bravado."[51]

Early spring brought news of victories over the Indians in

44. Ibid., July 22, 1813, quoted in Seaton, *William Winston Seaton*, p. 111.
45. *National Intelligencer*, July 27, 1813.
46. Samuel Flagg Bemis, ed., *A Diplomatic History of the United States* (New York, 1965), pp. 161-66.
47. *National Intelligencer*, January 8, 1814.
48. Ibid., January 11, 1814.
49. Ibid., January 20, 1814; Bemis, *Diplomatic History*, pp. 161-63.
50. *National Intelligencer*, January 18, 1814; Beirne, *War of 1812*, pp. 168-69 and 322-34, has a description of New England's action.
51. *National Intelligencer*, January 20, 1814.

the South by General Andrew Jackson and his men.[52] The editors defended Jackson against charges of cruelty and claimed the type war he fought was necessary because of the enemy with which he dealt. This was one of the few times the *Intelligencer* actively supported Jackson.[53]

In early summer, amid rumors that Napoleon had fallen in Europe,[54] the *Intelligencer* reported that a British fleet was approaching.[55] The editors assured their readers that the force mustered by the United States could handle any British invasion.[56] Two days later the *Intelligencer* warned that the enemy had landed on the Patuxent River. Gales and Seaton urged the citizens to stop fighting the federal government and turn instead to the British, warning that the country was in real danger.[57]

July was a busy month for Gales and Seaton. Nearly every issue of the *Intelligencer* carried an account of preparations made against a British attack. The editors also were busy helping prepare for the capital's defense.

On July 26 the *Intelligencer* published one of the most bitter attacks written against Gales's native land. The editors claimed the ambition guiding the British was desire for power to rule the seas and that the country would use every method to gain this end. Particularly odious to Gales and Seaton was what they termed England's use of Indians to slaughter Americans.[58]

The editors' ire had been raised, and attacks on the British appeared with every new issue of the paper. The United States' conduct of the war also was criticized. General James Wilkinson's handling of the northern campaign, previously defended, was questioned. The war became more real as the British fleet approached Washington City.[59]

---

52. Marquis James, *Andrew Jackson: Portrait of a President* (Indianapolis, 1937), chaps. 20-22; and James, *Andrew Jackson: The Border Captain* (Indianapolis, 1933), chaps. 10-11.
53. *National Intelligencer*, April 30, 1814.
54. Bemis, *Diplomatic History*, p. 163; *National Intelligencer*, May 19, 1814.
55. For a detailed account of the British military movements against the United States, see A. T. Mahan, *Sea Power in Its Relations to the War of 1812* (Boston, 1905), 2:329-54.
56. *National Intelligencer*, June 21, 1814.
57. Ibid., June 23, 1814.
58. Ibid., July 26, 1814.
59. Ibid., August 4, 1814.

Perhaps Gales and Seaton failed to realize that the preparations made for defending the capital against the British were completely inadequate. Military and civil leaders disagreed concerning where the British attack would be made—against Baltimore, Annapolis, or Washington City—and as a result few defenses were prepared. The defending forces, sizable on paper, were much smaller in reality and were inadequately trained and conditioned. The long list of tragic mistakes and blunders that accompanied the American attempt to defend the capital city was more characteristic of a comic opera than of a military campaign.[60]

Each day the situation grew more serious. Some time after the middle of August Gales took his wife and sister, Mrs. Seaton, to Raleigh, out of danger at the family home.[61]

As the British troops moved nearer Washington City, all workmen employed at the *Intelligencer* were called into service, forcing the paper's suspension. Seaton interceded with the secretary of war, pointing out that the *Intelligencer* was the only source of news from Washington City, and a few workmen were relieved temporarily for work duty.[62]

Seaton had just gone to bed the morning of August 24 after the day's issue was printed when he was awakened and informed that the post office was closed and no papers could be sent from the city. He then realized the futility of publishing the paper, so he dismissed his workmen and joined his company to defend the city.[63]

The British made short work of the hastily assembled defenses surrounding the capital, and by August 25 they had set fire to most public and some private buildings in Washington City.

Admiral George Cockburn's torch brought more than humiliation to Gales and Seaton, for the *Intelligencer's* equipment and supplies were destroyed during the raid. As the admiral rode down the street with his troops, he reportedly

60. For the best descriptions of the invasion of Washington City, see Major General George C. Cullum, "The Attack on Washington City in 1814," *American Historical Association Papers* (New York, 1887), 2:54-68; Beirne, *War of 1812*, pp. 264-88; Charles Burr Todd, *The Story of Washington* (New York, 1889), pp. 67-95; John S. Williams, *History of the Invasion and Capture of Washington* (New York, 1857).

61. Seaton, *William Winston Seaton*, p. 115; Gales' Recollections, pp. 20-21.

62. Williams, *History of the Invasion*, pp. 263-64.

63. Ibid., p. 264.

stopped in front of the *Intelligencer* office and ordered its destruction. Mrs. Samuel Harrison Smith gave one of the most graphic accounts of the incident: "When he went to burn Mr. Gales's office, whom he called his 'dear Josey'; Mrs. Brush, Mrs. Stelle & a few citizens remonstrated with him, assuring him that it would occasion the loss of all the buildings in the row. 'Well,' said he, 'good people I do not wish to injure you, but I am really afraid my friend Josey will be affronted with me, if after burning Jemmy's [Madison's] palace, I do not pay him the same compliment,—so my lads, take your axes, pull down the house, & burn the papers in the street.' This was accordingly done."[64] The admiral also reportedly ordered all *C*'s in the type cases destroyed so that the editors could not vilify his name.[65]

The September 2 issue of the *Raleigh Register* carried news of the *Intelligencer*'s destruction: "And though private property was generally respected, the office of the National Intelligencer was exultingly torn to pieces, under the direction of some of the principal officers." Mr. Gales explained that his son was absent from the city at the time the enemy took possession and "so *valiantly* destroyed the office of the Intelligencer, along with all public property of the city, thereby honorably distinguishing its Editors from the rest of their fellow citizens."[66]

Gales got word of the burning when he reached Richmond, Virginia, and placed a card in newspapers that cared to publish it:

The Senior Editor of the National Intelligencer, having been unfortunately absent from the city of Washington at the time the enemy obtained possession of it . . . takes this means of informing the numerous patrons of that paper, that he is proceeding with all possible dispatch to the present seat of Government, at or near which he proposes immediately to issue such a paper as his means will enable him, as a vehicle of authentic news at a moment so interesting.—No pains will be spared to reestablish as soon as possi-

64. Margaret Bayard Smith, "Washington in the Hands of the British, from the diaries and family letters of Mrs. Samuel Harrison Smith (Margaret Bayard)," ed. Gaillard Hunt, *Scribner's Magazine* 40 (July-December, 1906): 433; for other descriptions, see Anne Hollingsworth Wharton, *Social Life in the Early Republic* (Philadelphia, 1902), p. 162; Todd, *Story of Washington*, p. 86; Beirne, *War of 1812*, pp. 286-87.

65. Beirne, *War of 1812*, p. 287.

66. *Raleigh Register*, September 2, 1814.

ble, the regular publication of that paper, which has been so unfortunately interrupted. . . ."[67]

Mr. Gales, writing years after the destruction, explained that the paper was singled out for burning "under the barefaced pretext that it was a *Governmental* Office. Cockburn, however repeatedly said it was because the Editors took so decided a part in favor of America against Britain."[68]

The *Intelligencer*, smaller in size and obviously hurriedly edited, resumed publication on August 31, 1814. The printing was handled in an unidentified print shop.[69] Reduction in size was necessary until supplies could be sent from Philadelphia, and the smaller size prohibited editorials and allowed little news.[70]

Loss of the entire physical plant of the *Intelligencer* was a terrific blow which took years to overcome. The editors' only method of making a living was destroyed, and replacing the equipment left them in serious financial straits. Friends, realizing their position, offered donations to get the paper on its feet again. The editors politely refused such aid and assured the offerers that "they cannot accept . . . assistance of this description." Rather, the losses incurred would have to be replaced by "the labor of their own hands, without accepting of that gratuitous aid so generously proffered, of which, unfortunately, but too many of their fellow citizens have much greater need than they."[71]

Family recollections carry estimates of the loans and gifts offered as reaching "20,000 or 30,000$. But they invariably but gratefully declined any pecuniary aid, other than what should accrue from extended patronage."[72]

British destruction of the *Intelligencer* meant more than just the loss of printing equipment. Circulation lists, books containing records of debts, and all the early correspondence of the paper were gone. This lack of records plagued the editors for years. For example, in 1821 Madison wrote to Gales, asking him to locate a series of papers John Jay had written.

67. Ibid.
68. Gales' Recollections, pp. 20-21.
69. Ibid., p. 21.
70. *National Intelligencer*, September 10, 1814.
71. Ibid., September 6, 1814.
72. Gales' Recollections, p. 21.

Gales replied: "I much regret, that it is wholly out of my power to oblige Mr. Jay. Admiral Cockburn, when he paid his respects to us, took care to leave us no spare copies of the National Intelligencer—having burnt them, with the few books I had at that time collected."[73]

The *Intelligencer's* misfortune was viewed as less than a calamity by some of the Federalist press that had felt the bitter sting of its editorial barbs. The Salem (Massachusetts) *Essex Register* thought the incident might be retribution for comments the *Intelligencer* had made when the *Federal Republican* offices were destroyed earlier by a Baltimore mob.[74] Such sentiments, Gales and Seaton wrote, were unthinkable, for never had they expressed "glee" at the destruction of other papers.[75] Some New England newspapers, such as the *Columbia Centinel*, merely reported the incident without expressing regret or pleasure.[76]

By September 26th, a normal-sized *Intelligencer* was restored to its usual form. This joyful occasion prompted Gales and Seaton to reaffirm their reliance on the public and their devotion to "the cause of Truth, Justice and the Country," and their opposition to "the malevolence of Faction, as against the violence of the national enemy—both of which have been of late most magnanimously exerted, the one in the destruction of their property, the other in pitiful assaults on the reputation of the paper and its Editors." The efforts, commented the editors, all had been "impotent."[77]

Despite the stress of the war and their personal involvement, Gales and Seaton noted a poem written during the firing on Ft. McHenry. Though not realizing the work would become the national anthem, the editors thought "Whoever is the author of those lines . . . did equal honor to his principles and his talents."[78] They referred, of course, to Francis Scott Key, author of the "Star-Spangled Banner."

Two points irritated Gales and Seaton during the fall of

73. Joseph Gales, Jr., to Madison, June 22, 1821, Madison Papers, vol. 49, Library of Congress, Washington, D.C.

74. Henry Adams, *History of the United States of America* (New York, 1931), 6:406-7.

75. *National Intelligencer*, September 10, 1814.

76. *Columbia Centinel*, September 3, 1814.

77. *National Intelligencer*, September 26, 1814.

78. Ibid.

1814. First, they concluded the war could be ended only by an all-out attack on Canada.[79] But even more irritating was the political rebellion in New England, which was climaxed in the Hartford Convention.[80] Gales and Seaton placed little faith in the first rumors of the New England meeting, for they reasoned the area would become a pauper if it left the United States.[81]

The *Intelligencer* editors were shocked when New England papers urged withdrawal from the federal union. The *Columbia Centinel*, on the other hand, thought nothing of the United States remained and that New England would be destroyed unless it left the union. The army and navy were gone, wrote the editor, and little was left but a president moaning over the ashes of a destroyed capital.[82]

Gales and Seaton responded bitterly: "A virtuous and charitable people could scarcely credit the fact that there existed in their bosom a nest of reptiles brooding over schemes of dismemberment, and waiting only for a moment when they might without endangering their necks light up the torch of civil war."[83]

Gales and Seaton contended that the very men who caused the disastrous situation through lack of support of the war advocated the disunion plan. Indeed, the whole move was nothing more than an attempt of Federalist politicians to "vault" into power, and, fortunately, the editors agreed, the whole plan failed. In response to the manifesto issued by convention delegates, Gales and Seaton replied: "Neither the manifesto or their subsequent efforts redeemed the party from the disgrace into which it was precipitated by the preposterous measure, which made all thinking people look about them, and argue . . . what such a party would do if it were in power."[84]

Turning from the Hartford convention, Gales and Seaton

79. Ibid., November 24, 1814.
80. For a discussion of the Hartford convention, see Adams, *History of the United States*, 8:225-38, 287-310; Samuel Eliot Morison, *The Life and Letters of Harrison Gray Otis, Federalist, 1765-1848* (Boston, 1913); and Theodore Dwight, *History of the Hartford Convention* (New York, 1833).
81. *National Intelligencer*, October 22, 1814.
82. *Columbia Centinel*, September 10, 1814.
83. *National Intelligencer*, December 1, 1814.
84. Ibid., January 14 and November 4, 1815.

lashed out again at Great Britain. The editors were impatient with those who contended that the United States was wrong in attacking Britain. Just because England was at war in Europe did not mean the United States could not seek redress of wrongs. Indeed, it behooved all countries to prevent Britain from controlling the waterways of the world, according to the editors.[85]

Perhaps, the editors reasoned, if Great Britain experienced the sufferings of war she would not be so ready to rush into conflicts. Since the British Isles never felt the ravages of conflict, claimed the *Intelligencer*, the British "continue to nourish that passion for war and dominion, which, if uncontrolled, may in the end be fatal to herself, and must in the meantime be a calamity to the rest of the world."[86]

Bitterness turned into joy in the winter of 1815. First came the great victory of Jackson at New Orleans. Then in February came news of the treaty ending the war. The agreement between the United States and Great Britain was signed at Ghent on December 24, 1814, and delivered in the United States February 15, 1815.[87] The *Intelligencer* story fairly screamed relief: "The Peace. Americans! Rejoice! Republicans, rejoice! Federalists, rejoice! Rejoice, all men, of whatever party ye be!"[88]

The desire to bring Great Britain to her knees either was forgotten or mistakenly thought to have been achieved as far as Gales and Seaton were concerned. The message the paper carried did not hail a great victory but welcomed peace. There was no bravado, no wild claims, no disillusionment with the terms: "The general principle of the treaty, is a restitution and recognition of the rights and possessions of each party, as they stood before the war; with adequate provisions to settle all the disputed points of boundary. . . ."[89]

The end of the War of 1812 in some ways marked a trial period for the firm of Gales and Seaton, and particularly for Gales. He had taken over the *Intelligencer* in the period preceding the war as a young and largely untried editor who shoul-

85. Ibid., January 5, 1815.
86. Ibid., January 17, 1815.
87. For a history of the negotiations, see Bemis, *John Quincy Adams and the Foundations of American Foreign Policy* (New York, 1949), pp. 196-220.
88. *National Intelligencer*, February 16, 1815.
89. Ibid.

dered heavy responsibilities. He had earned the respect and confidence of the Madison administration during this period and had played a vital role in providing a communications link and channel that helped hold the nation together until some settlement of the disastrous conflict could be worked out. Five years before he had faced serious uncertainties concerning how he could be accepted by President Madison and his cabinet members and whether the *Intelligencer* would be the medium these officers would use to rally the nation to the cause of the war. During this five-year period, in the opinion of most, he had performed well and had secured an important position for himself closely related to the policy-making levels of the federal government.

In addition, Gales had acquired during this period a wife, a partner, and a daily newspaper, as well as earning for himself a position, both social and professional, in Washington City's society. Probably there was no greater testimony to this fact than the place Gales occupied at the joint celebration of the end of the war and Washington's birthday. It was Gales who was chosen to accompany Dolly Madison as she entered the hall, radiant and happy in the peace that had come to the nation.

To a Federalist critic, the sight of the president's wife on Gales's arm was offensive. Harrison Gray Otis, an old-line Federalist, described the entry and confided to his wife that Gales, with a face and manner similar to a Malay, on entry had stared around the room with ineffable self-complacency and impudence: "He acts I suppose as manager, but then she should have gone into the room as a private lady." If she were to be announced "queen of peace," Otis was certain she should have selected an escort different from that "dirty editor."[90]

But the end to the era was marked in other ways. During the war Gales and Seaton had played a role as agents of the government, not as commentators or critics or policy makers. That too was to change, for Gales and Seaton, Gales particularly, were too independent to be satisfied with such a position. They had earned a position of respect; it remained for them to earn a strong position of independence.

90. Harrison Gray Otis to his wife, February 24, 1815, quoted in Morison, *Harrison Gray Otis*, 2:63-64.

CHAPTER 7

The Era
of Good Feeling

Gales and Seaton welcomed the calm that blessed the United States following the War of 1812. The young publishers then had a chance to appraise the progress of their first years of owning the *Intelligencer* and to attempt to establish themselves more securely in the social, business, and political circles of Washington City.

During the period 1815-24, known as the Era of Good Feeling, the Seatons, particularly, became prominent in the highest social groups of Washington City, and their home was known as one of the capital's social centers. Financially the young publishers did not fare as well; Gales and Seaton were more heavily in debt by the early 1820s than at the end of the War of 1812. Politically these years were not exciting for Gales and Seaton, but the period was important, for the *Intelligencer*'s general attitude was defined toward the tariff, slavery, internal improvements, foreign policy, and the Second Bank of the United States.

The Seatons attracted much attention in Washington City society, due largely to the charm, grace, and energy of Seaton's young wife, Sarah Gales, who had inherited many of her mother's characteristics. Sarah was thrilled at the idea of moving from Raleigh to the nation's capital. Shortly after arriving there she was presented at the White House to President and Mrs. Madison,[1] and with this important step the Seatons entered an area in which they presided for more than fifty years.

Sarah's family letters read like a social calendar of the city; she mentioned the president's drawing rooms,[2] cabinet ministers' dances,[3] foreign ministers' social functions,[4] and personal visits from Mrs. Madison.[5] Her talents made her equally at home playing a waltz for Mrs. Madison or helping her husband transcribe his shorthand notes of congressional speeches.[6]

By 1815 Sarah was not only well established socially but had become somewhat critical of the shortcomings of Washington City's social circle. During that year the hero of New Orleans, Andrew Jackson, and his wife visited Washington City, and dinners, plays, and balls throughout the District honored the Tennessean. Thus the editor's wife saw much of the general: "He is not striking in appearance; his features are hard-favored (as our Carolinians say), his complexion sallow, and his person small. Mrs. Jackson is a totally uninformed woman in mind and manners, but extremely civil, in her way. . . . I suppose there have never been in the city so many plain women, in every sense of the word, as are now here among the families of official personages. I have always heard it asserted without contradiction, that nothing was easier than to learn to be a fine lady; but I begin to think

---

1. Sarah Gales Seaton to her parents, November 12, 1812, quoted in Josephine Seaton, *William Winston Seaton of the "National Intelligencer"* (Boston, 1871), p. 84.

2. Ibid., March 5, 1813, p. 98.

3. Ibid., January 2, 1813, p. 90.

4. Ibid., May, 1819, p. 143.

5. Ibid., March 5, 1813, p. 98.

6. Helen Nicolay, *Our Capital on the Potomac* (New York, 1924), p. 84.

differently, being morally certain that many among the new-comers will never achieve that distinction."[7] These were strange words coming from the sister of Joseph Gales, who just eight years before had been considered by Mrs. Samuel Harrison Smith to be nearly totally lacking in social graces.

The Seatons were on cordial terms with President Madison's family;[8] at a ball in Annapolis in 1816 Sarah recalled that Mrs. Madison was "very polite, expressing herself surprised and delighted at our arrival, introducing me very handsomely to . . . Governor and Mrs. Ridgely, of Maryland, and other notabilities, which, in a strange land, was very kind and acceptable."[9]

Two of Sarah's closest friends were Mrs. William Crawford,[10] wife of the secretary of the treasury under President Monroe, and Mrs. John C. Calhoun, wife of the South Carolina representative who became secretary of war. Mrs. Crawford was one of the most "amiable and refined" of her acquaintances,[11] wrote Sarah. Her friendship with Mrs. Calhoun developed after the South Carolinians moved into a house in the Seaton neighborhood. Mrs. Calhoun, who frequently spent from "nine in the morning" until "ten at night" at the publisher's home, was described as a "devoted mother, tender wife, industrious, cheerful, intelligent, with the most perfectly equable temper." Calhoun was equally impressive, according to Sarah. In addition to being a "profound statesman" and "elegant scholar," she found him "endearing, as well as captivating," and thought it as impossible "not to love him" as it would have been to "refuse your admiration of his oratorical powers."[12]

7. Sarah Gales Seaton to her parents, November, 1815, quoted in Seaton, *William Winston Seaton*, p. 132.

8. For a description of the social life in Washington during the Madison administration, see Katharine Susan Anthony, *Dolly Madison, Her Life and Times*, (New York, 1949), pp. 183-257; Anne Hollingsworth Wharton, *Social Life in the Early Republic* (Philadelphia, 1920), pp. 131-60; Mrs. Samuel Harrison Smith, *The First Forty Years of Washington Society* (New York, 1906).

9. Sarah Gales Seaton to her parents, May, 1816, quoted in Seaton, *William Winston Seaton*, p. 133.

10. Margaret Bayard Smith, also an intimate of Mrs. Crawford's, gave an excellent description of the social circle in which Mrs. Seaton moved in *The First Forty Years of Washington Society*.

11. Sarah Gales Seaton to her parents, November, 1815, quoted in Seaton, *William Winston Seaton*, pp. 131-32.

12. Ibid., March, 1818, p. 135.

But, though Seaton's wife was impressed with her southern friends, she felt much less warmly toward such New Englanders as Mr. and Mrs. John Quincy Adams. Regarding the New Englanders' lack of social success, Sarah wrote: "Mrs. Adams . . . *invited* a large party, which we attended, at which there were not more than three ladies. In a familiar, pleasing manner, the sprightly hostess made known to each of her visitors that every Tuesday evening during the winter, when they had nothing better to do with themselves, it would give her great pleasure to receive them. The evening arrived, and with it two other guests besides her sisters!"[13]

Sarah also criticized White House social activities after Mrs. Monroe sharply curtailed the personal visiting customs and attempted to create a more formal atmosphere in Washington City social centers. Neither move pleased Mrs. Seaton.[14]

Even the social events Mrs. Monroe organized were not of the standard Sarah expected. After one such function she reported to her parents: "The drawing-room of the President was opened last night to a 'beggarly row of empty chairs.' Only five females attended, three of whom were foreigners."[15]

The Seatons built their commodious brick residence on the south side of E Street N., midway between Seventh and Eighth Streets W., in 1823.[16] The house was about forty feet square, with a ground floor that contained three wine cellars and in the southwest corner a kitchen measuring about twenty feet square. A living room, two drawing rooms, dining room, and pantry were on the second, or main, floor. Four bedrooms were on the third floor and two more on the top story of the house. Across the back of the house was a large piazza, and a separate structure housed a library and a general utility room. A conservatory and a smokehouse were also on the lot. The Seatons were known for their fruit trees, including a pear tree given them by Calhoun, and a large garden

13. Ibid., December, 1819, p. 144.
14. Sarah Gales Seaton to unnamed correspondent, March, 1818, quoted in Seaton, *William Winston Seaton*, p. 136.
15. Sarah Gales Seaton to her parents, December, 1819, quoted in Seaton, *William Winston Seaton*, p. 144.
16. Henry E. Davis, "The Seaton Mansion," *Columbia Historical Society Records* 29-30 (1928): 293.

they raised between Fifth and Sixth and L and M streets.[17]

One of the first social functions held in the new home was a reception for General Lafayette during his visit to the United States in 1824.[18] Both Seaton and his wife served on local committees arranging the Washington visit.[19]

Gales, following his marriage in 1813, lived with his bride at E and Ninth Streets N.W. in a house that was built for Dr. John I. Crocker and identified with his name during this period.[20] After 1829 the Gales moved to the fashionable Lafayette Square area where they occupied the brownstone house next to St. John's Church, later known as the Ashburton house, the residence of the British diplomat during his residency here in the 1840s.[21]

The Gales did not participate in the city's social life as fully as the Seatons, for neither Gales nor his wife was as gregarious or as outgoing as the junior partner and his wife. Mrs. Gales was considered a lady of great dignity but more content in her home than at social gatherings.

Although the homes in which Gales and Seaton lived might indicate that the publishing business returned large profits, this was not the case. The *Intelligencer*'s loss during Admiral Cockburn's raid on the city amounted to several thousand dollars,[22] a deficit that was increased rather than reduced during this period. Only a short time after the Second United States Bank opened, Gales and Seaton started borrowing,[23] and by 1818 Gales gave a deed of trust to the Bank of the United States for debts amounting to $6,500. The deed made Seaton a surety for the amount and covered the *Intelligencer* property on Pennsylvania Avenue and "all the types,

17. Ibid., pp. 291-94.
18. Sarah Gales Seaton to her parents, December 16, 1824, quoted in Seaton, *William Winston Seaton*, p. 170.
19. Seaton, *William Winston Seaton*, pp. 166-67.
20. Washington Topham, "The Benning McGuire House, E Street and Neighborhood," *Columbia Historical Society Records* 33-34 (1932): 87-130.
21. Gist Blair, "Lafayette Square," *Columbia Historical Society Records* 28 (1926): 133-73; see also Fremont Rider, *Rider's Washington* (New York, 1924), p. 100.
22. John S. Williams, *History of the Invasion and Capture of Washington* (New York, 1857), pp. 265-66.
23. Note signed by Gales and Seaton for $664 on September 27, 1816, United States Bank, collection of papers relating mainly to the First Bank of the United States, Box 4, Library of Congress, Washington, D.C.

materials and Stock" in the printing office, as well as debts due the paper and future profits.[24] One witness to the deed was Thomas Donohoe,[25] who served as business manager during most of Gales's and Seaton's editorship. About this time the *Intelligencer* office was moved from Pennsylvania Avenue to a leased building at Seventh and D Streets, which became the permanent home for Gales's and Seaton's business.[26]

In addition to the bank debts, money was owed to private individuals, a situation Gales and Seaton admitted existed because they failed to collect debts due them, amounts the editors contended "exceeded belief."[27] In response to a request made by James Ronaldson for payment of a note due him, Gales and Seaton said: "We observe by your letter of the 16th you are of opinion you have been ill-used by us, in respect to our note. We are not of that opinion. We would have paid our note long ago, would others have paid us. We have debts of 80 or an hundred thousand dollars due to us, but cannot at this moment realize. We are now doing our best to do so; and rest assured, your demand shall not remain unpaid a moment longer than we can help."[28]

Reasons for the financial troubles are not clear. The newspaper venture was a complete success, with the combined circulation of the daily and triweekly standing at around six thousand by 1823.[29]

With the awarding of the government printing contracts to Gales and Seaton in 1819 there was a strong possibility that the publishers' financial problems might be over. Between 1804 and 1819 the printing contracts for the Senate and House of Representatives had been let by the secretary and clerk, respectively, of the two bodies. Terms of the 1804 joint resolution had demanded that the contracts be let to the lowest bidder, and under this system, no newspaper publisher was

24. Deed of Trust between Joseph Gales and Richard Smith, United States Bank, dated September 11, 1818, Office of the Recorder of Deeds, District of Columbia.

25. Ibid.

26. *National Intelligencer*, November 14, 1818; Wilhelmus Bogart Bryan, *A History of the National Capital, 1790-1884* (New York, 1914), 2:175.

27. *National Intelligencer*, October 19, 1822.

28. Gales and Seaton to James Ronaldson, September 19, 1820, Gales and Seaton Papers, Historical Society of Pennsylvania, Philadelphia.

29. *National Intelligencer*, December 11, 1823.

able to underbid the proprietors of the local printing houses.

Dissatisfaction with this system grew as frequent changes of printer after 1814 meant the use of inexperienced help, which accounted for long and costly delays in delivering bills to Congress. Letting the contracts to the lowest bidder developed a system whereby the printers bid below what was necessary to yield a profit, knowing that it would be possible to go to Congress later with the plea that an increase would be necessary to complete the work. Congress had helped printers in these circumstances but was becoming annoyed with the situation.[30]

Also, congressmen criticized the quality of the printing, alleging that the contracts were being awarded to printers incapable of turning out the needed printing in the specified time and who therefore printed a product of inadequate quality under the pressure exerted.

The joint committee meeting in 1819 considered three alternatives. The first was a continuation of the 1804 system, but committee members concluded that the low prices prevented the care and attention necessary for neatness and accuracy. Members also reported they were unable to find a printer in the District who would undertake the printing at the low prices Congress demanded.[31]

The second alternative was the establishment of a national printing office, a plan the committee actually favored but because of expense deemed unadvisable in 1819.[32]

The third plan was to set up a tariff of prices on all printing required by the two bodies and for each house to elect a printer to execute the contract. The set prices, the committee concluded, would be adequate "to perform the work expeditiously, and to ensure such care and attention as shall give it such a degree of accuracy and elegance, as shall not dishonor the literature and typography of the country."[33]

The committee recommended the third plan, which both houses adopted, but political more than monetary considera-

---

30. For a discussion of the problems with the 1804 system, see *United States House Report 754*, Twenty-Ninth Congress, First Session.
31. *United States Senate Document 99*, Fifteenth Congress, Second Session.
32. Ibid.
33. Ibid.

tions dictated the choice. In fact, the plan was proposed with Gales and Seaton in mind. Already aspirants were looking toward the election of 1824 and hoping the *National Intelligencer* might lend support to a particular aspirant's candidacy. One of the chief contenders for the office was Henry Clay, and primarily through his guidance the bill was pushed through Congress. Clay, a politician well aware of the necessity to operate from a base of power in order to achieve political office, undoubtedly sought to obtain ties to Congress as well as to the executive branch of government from the capital's leading political newspaper. In fashioning this new method of awarding printing, Clay had put together one of the richest patronage schemes the country yet had seen, and the editors of the *National Intelligencer* held a virtual monopoly of these rich contracts for nearly ten years.[34]

This patronage act, which gave printing to the newspapers for the next thirty years, had great impact on the *National Intelligencer* publishers. First, it provided a source of income other than the newspaper that would enable Gales and Seaton to alleviate the debts that had accumulated during their early years. Second, the demands of the congressional contracts made it necessary for Gales and Seaton to build up one of the nation's largest printing plants—an asset during the years when the editors were awarded the printing contracts and a liability during the drought periods when the political opposition controlled Congress.

But in 1819 there was no political opposition, for Gales and Seaton shared the confidence of the Republican party. During the first five years the *Intelligencer* editors held the contracts, the total sum yielded for carrying out this work was $158,-186.14,[35] a startling sum of money when compared with printing wages, which were $10 a week for a competent printer and no overtime, and paper cost $5 to $6 a single ream. Later investigations of printing patronage showed the profits for the congressional printer were about 55 percent for this period.[36]

34. For an account of the debate on the measure, see *Annals of Congress*, Fifteenth Congress, Second Session (Washington, D.C., 1855), 33:367, 386, 416, 418, 435, 436.
35. *United States House Document 83*, Twenty-Ninth Congress, First Session.
36. See *United States House Report 298*, Twenty-Sixth Congress, First Session; also *United States Senate Report* 18, Fifty-Second Congress, First Session.

One of the most obvious results of the new system of letting printing contracts was the increased costs, which arose immediately and were contributed to by a number of forces. More documents than usual were printed, and larger runs of selected reports were made. For the House of Representatives the printing more than doubled for the first five years after the adoption of the new procedure in comparison to the five years between 1814 and 1818.[37]

But though these sums were large, they did not give a true indication of the net returns to Gales and Seaton during the first two years under the new contract. Before 1819 the *Intelligencer* plant had not been equipped to handle the large printing orders, and the new contractual obligations necessitated a heavy investment on the part of Gales and Seaton to fill the requirements. Returns from the first session under the new plan did not cover the debts incurred in outfitting the new plant; and the second session, which produced a much smaller volume and printing for the *Intelligencer* despite the fact that a full force of printers was kept on hand, actually brought a loss to the plant. After these first two sessions, however, Gales and Seaton admitted they made a "fair profit."[38] Despite their admission of a fair profit, the congressional printing did not yield enough to see the publishers free from debts, but rather the financial difficulties that had plagued them from the beginning continued to mount. After March 3, 1819, Gales and Seaton monopolized congressional printing for eight years.[39]

Although congressional printing kept the *Intelligencer* in business, congressional reporting filled the paper and accounted for most of Gales's and Seaton's work during the period following the War of 1812. Since the editors shared Smith's enthusiasm for lengthy accounts of congressional proceedings, the format of the paper continued much the same, with news of Congress carried on at least two and

37. *United States House Report 754*, Twenty-Ninth Congress, First Session.
38. *United States House Report 298*, Twenty-Sixth Congress, First Session. It was difficult for the editors to estimate accurately what profit the printing yielded since they did not keep accounts separate from their general business expenses.
39. For the letting of the contracts, see *Annals of Congress*, Fifteenth Congress, Second Session, 34:1441; *Annals of Congress*, Sixteenth Congress, Second Session (Washington, D.C., 1855), 37:403 and 1292; *Annals of Congress*, Seventeenth Congress, Second Session (Washington, D.C., 1855), 40:277 and 1097.

frequently all four pages. The same news and opinion columns that Smith started on pages one and three were continued under the new publishers. Gales and Seaton did a major share of the congressional reporting and supposedly shared the snuff boxes with the presiding officers of the House and Senate—Seaton in the House and Gales in the Senate.[40]

Pressures of writing, editing, and publishing a triweekly and daily newspaper made systematic coverage of the Senate impossible until 1818. The editors regretted lack of coverage before that time but shared Smith's feeling that the Senate was not as responsive to the voters as the House and therefore of less interest.[41] After 1818, however, the Senate was given nearly as much news space as the House.

The *Intelligencer*, as Washington City's only major newspaper during part of this period, was copied by almost six hundred papers because of its detailed congressional accounts and because it was considered the semiofficial organ of the federal government.[42] The view expressed by the *Intelligencer* was considered that of the administration in power, and in some instances this was the proper assumption. For example, Monroe, when Secretary of State, told of writing an article for the *Intelligencer* to convey the sentiments of the government.[43] Adams also gave evidence that cabinet members wrote reports of meetings for the *Intelligencer* in order to convey the official stand.[44]

Being the official organ of the government meant more than reflecting official opinion. Proclamations, advertisements for bids, and other notices were run in the *Intelligencer* and paid for by the federal government. Official docu-

40. Charles Lanman, "The National Intelligencer and Its Editors," *The Atlantic Monthly* 6 (October, 1860): 476-80; Seaton, *William Winston Seaton*, p. 151.

41. *National Intelligencer*, March 12, 1818.

42. Elizabeth Gregory McPherson, "The History of Reporting the Debates and Proceedings of Congress" (Ph.D. thesis, University of North Carolina, 1940), p. 32; Frederic B. Marbut, "The History of Washington Newspaper Correspondence to 1861" (Ph.D. thesis, Harvard University, 1950), pp. 7 and 11.

43. Monroe to unnamed correspondent, undated letter, Monroe Papers, vol. 20, Library of Congress, Washington, D.C.; Monroe to Joseph Gales, Jr., July 21, 1815, Monroe Papers, New York Public Library, New York.

44. Adams's diary, July 24, 1818, quoted in *Memoirs of John Quincy Adams, comprising portions of his diary from 1795-1848*, ed. Charles Francis Adams (Philadelphia, 1875), 4:116.

ments such as treaties and proclamations were published first in the *Intelligencer* and then copied by other papers, which enhanced the *Intelligencer's* importance as a news source.

Some newspapers throughout the country openly criticized the *Intelligencer's* relationship to the presidents. The *Cincinnati Literary Cadet* nicknamed the *Intelligencer* the "court paper."[45] The *National Advocate* of New York thought the *Intelligencer* lacked independence. The editor was sure that Gales and Seaton always took their " 'cue' from somebody or other in Washington." Gales and Seaton denied this: "We stretch our views abroad over the nation, speak truly what we think its interest dictates, support the measures which appear to us to contribute to it, and oppose those which appear to be opposed to it."[46]

On occasion the *Intelligencer* editors were embarrassed when their views were taken as those of the president. The editors attempted to explain: "We understand that an editorial remark of ours . . . has been taken literally, and regarded as an expression not only of our personal view but of those of the Executive on that point." Gales and Seaton thought a serious mistake had been made: "We have no knowledge of the views of the Executive on that subject; and our occasional speculations, on this or any other subject, are regarded as of vastly too much weight, if they are supposed to be impressed with executive sanction. Nothing would be more wide of the fact than such a supposition."[47]

The editor of *Niles' Register*, friendly to the editors of the *Intelligencer* in spite of frequent editorial fights, liked to chide Gales and Seaton for their relationship to the national administrations. In 1823 when rumors were circulated that Samuel L. Southard was to be appointed secretary of the navy, Gales and Seaton at first denied but later confirmed the appointment. Niles commented: "Take the 'whole together,' it is an affair 'sui generis' and must lead to the conclusion, that Messrs. Gales & Seaton were neither *advised* of, nor had *consented* to, the appointment of Mr. Southard, in the recess of the Senate."[48]

45. *National Intelligencer*, November 8, 1820.
46. Ibid., August 17, 1822.
47. Ibid., March 28, 1828.
48. *Niles' Register*, September 20, 1823, p. 627.

Papers generally appreciated the *Intelligencer* editors' work. Typical of this view is an excerpt from the *Baltimore Federal Republican,* which was copied in the *Intelligencer*: "The public have long been indebted to the National Intelligencer for the debates of Congress. That they have been at all published in the comprehensive manner in which they have appeared, we presume has arisen from the capacity and personal exertions of the editors than induced by the pecuniary remuneration yielded through the distinction it has given to their paper."[49] The article continued by announcing that a qualified man was being added to the staff of the *Intelligencer* to help with the debates: "This must be a subject of general gratification among the editorial fraternity, who largely partake of it, if they do not exclusively depend upon what they thus obtain without either cost or trouble. Such is the Tribute justly due to the National Intelligencer."[50]

The two editors were disappointed in the amount of their debates used by other papers. Gales and Seaton thought nothing of omitting nearly all other news for the sake of the debates and at times even omitted advertisements.[51] Proximity to the national legislature undoubtedly caused Gales and Seaton to exaggerate the importance of the proceedings, and the editors complained:

It has given us some pain, for more important reasons than that our labors are thrown away, or undervalued, to find, that so small a portion of the debates of Congress find their way into the newspapers dispersed over the country. If from this circumstance the public taste is inferred, we fear we have proved wretched caterers. We feel it our duty, however, to present to our readers everything we have been able to collect and preserve, of any interest whatever . . . and, if it really be acceptable to them, can only regret, that, in so doing, we are obliged to consult what we believe to be the public interest, rather than the public appetite.[52]

Probably lack of interest rather than suspicion of accuracy of the *Intelligencer*'s accounts prompted most papers to run only small amounts of the debates. Few editors found the long

49. *Federal Republican,* quoted in *National Intelligencer,* November 21, 1821.
50. Ibid. The identity of the reporter could not be determined.
51. *National Intelligencer,* April 16, 1818.
52. Ibid., June 9, 1818.

verbatim accounts of speeches of sufficient interest, and brief summaries would have suited most publishers.

Disappointment at the reception of their reports was even more keen because Gales and Seaton found the job of covering the debates unpleasant. Although they seldom complained about their lot as newspaper editors, Gales and Seaton confessed they thought the job of reporting the debates was odious, "for it is a task such as condemned criminals might be put to, and no man of sensibility would willingly resort to, who can gain a decent living in any other way."[53]

They complained that the situation in the House of Representatives especially was bad, and in 1822 they worked to get a table placed in front of the Speaker's chair so the proceedings could be covered more conveniently.[54] Their request was turned over to a House committee, an action the *Intelligencer* editors termed unnecessary since the Speaker of the House had the right to let reporters sit where they wished—a point Samuel Harrison Smith had argued twenty-two years earlier. Further, Gales and Seaton contended, the Speaker was well aware of the problems of hearing the debates since he, too, had difficulty at times understanding the speakers.[55]

Gales and Seaton opposed the committee's voting on their request since they believed a majority of the group felt the *Intelligencer* personnel were not reporting the debates fully enough. The editors thought committee members failed to realize that if a more advantageous point from which to report were granted then the debates would be reported more fully. The request brought no improvement in the reporter's position.[56]

Gales and Seaton experienced another annoyance in obtaining accounts of speeches that satisfied the congressmen. To insure accurate reporting, the editors, where possible, submitted the speeches to the authors for corrections before publication. This policy began as early as 1813 and may even have been used during the Smith period. First evidence of this

53. Ibid., April 25, 1822.
54. Ibid.
55. Ibid., May 3, 1822.
56. Ibid.

practice is found in a letter from Langdon Cheves, representative from South Carolina and a War Hawk, who returned a corrected speech with the comment that the report was a faithful if not a literal summary of his speech. He assured Gales and Seaton he altered "a little the phraseology that part which you sent me."[57]

Contemporary public officials generally commented favorably on the accuracy of the *Intelligencer* debates. Timothy Pitkin, Connecticut congressman, in response to the *New York Post*'s criticism of the *Intelligencer* reporting, said he had not observed any faulty reporting of an incident in question. In general, he felt the *Intelligencer* gave both sides, was much more complete, and was more impartial than most other papers.[58]

Peter Force, later editor of the *National Journal*, considered starting a paper in 1818 and wrote to several officials to check on the reliability of the *Intelligencer* debates. Alexander Smyth, Georgia, responded that he deemed "the reports of that paper essentially correct although there may be occasionally typographical, & perhaps verbal errors." He hastened to point out that Smyth was misspelled in Force's letter.[59]

Not all congressmen were as impressed with the accuracy of the *Intelligencer* reporting. Probably the most outspoken was John Randolph, Jr., of Virginia. Never noted for his sunny disposition or his tact, Randolph used some of his sharpest barbs on the *Intelligencer* and its editors. Randolph realized the role the paper played in furnishing debates to papers throughout the country, and he wanted his speeches published, and published correctly.

One of the bitterest attacks on the *Intelligencer* by Randolph came early in the 1816 congressional session when Randolph wrote Gales and Seaton:

Mr. Randolph takes the Liberty to inform the editors of the National Intelligencer that he finds his sentiments as well as his language very much misapprehended & consequently misrepresented

57. Langdon Cheves to Joseph Gales, Jr., April 30, 1813, Gales and Seaton Papers, Library of Congress, Washington, D.C.
58. Timothy Pitkin to Gales and Seaton, December 31, 1817, Miscellaneous Collection, New York Public Library, New York.
59. Alexander Smyth to Peter Force, February 2, 1818, Peter Force Papers, vol. 1, Library of Congress, Washington, D.C.

in the Debates published this morning—as that paper is (in this particular) copied by all the rest throughout the Union Mr. R. conceives that an impression very disadvantageous to him may be & most probably will be made on the American Publick. Mr. Randolph's ambition to appear before the Publick is very limited; but he should be very sorry that they should misconceive the nature of his opinions in whatever language they may be.[60]

But Randolph's feelings were not shared only with Gales and Seaton, for he did not hesitate to tell his contemporaries of his criticism of the *Intelligencer* and its editors: "Let me apprise you that there is no report of my speeches or any one of them that has the least resemblance to the Truth. Gales who alone can take them is prevented: both by indolence & party spirit from doing it. His own patrons complain of his invincible laziness. What then have I to expect?"[61]

Yet Randolph continued to seek to have his speeches published in the *Intelligencer*, and evidently Gales and Seaton followed the policy of having him check his speeches before publication to limit friction. In February, 1817, Randolph returned a speech to the editors with corrections he had made —inserting different words or phrases in two places and whole paragraphs in two other sections.[62]

Sometimes when he thought he was about to give an important speech he requested that Gales report the event, since he did not trust others on the *Intelligencer* staff. On April 15, 1824, he wrote, "Mr. Randolph specifically requests Mr. Gales to report him today."[63]

Randolph's criticisms of the *Intelligencer*, however, were not always based on omission of his remarks; sometimes, in the Virginian's opinion, the paper included too much. The question of whether the House should adjourn for the funeral of Commodore Stephen Decatur brought the *Intelligencer* and Randolph into another conflict. Decatur was killed in a duel when the general sentiment of the country was against such defenses of honor, and the *Intelligencer* was outspoken against

60. Randolph, Jr., to Gales and Seaton, January 6, 1816, Randolph Papers, Library of Congress, Washington, D.C.

61. Randolph, Jr., to H. Bleecher, February 4, 1816, Randolph Papers.

62. Randolph, Jr., to Gales and Seaton, February, 1817, Randolph Papers.

63. Randolph, Jr., to Gales, Jr., April 15, 1824, Randolph Papers.

the duel as a method of settling arguments. Randolph thought the House should adjourn and spoke at length on the subject. No *Intelligencer* reporter was allowed to be present, but the editors obtained and printed the speech. Randolph felt such remarks should have been kept out of the papers and was so angered that he formally proposed that Gales and Seaton be expelled from the House. What actually happened during the debate is unknown, but the proposal was turned down.[64]

The proceedings Gales and Seaton covered during the Era of Good Feeling were important but lacked the dramatic and explosive qualities that characterized congressional debates of later periods. The country was developing the background and institutions for later hostilities. The rise of the West took place at a vastly accelerated pace. The Second Bank of the United States received its charter; Congress accepted the protective tariff; and Jackson's New Orleans and Florida victories brought him much attention in administrative and congressional circles. The debate over the admission of Missouri to the union brought the controversial issue of slavery to the floor of Congress. On the foreign affairs scene, considerable debate took place as to whether several Latin American countries in revolt against Spain should receive diplomatic recognition, and the famous Monroe Doctrine was proclaimed.

The growth of the West had a sharp impact on the nation, but Gales and Seaton little understood this rising force. The editors failed to realize that with the millions of new people in the West came a sharply revised attitude toward the right of an individual to govern. At the same time, the rise of the West also impaired the feeling of national unity predominant during most of the first quarter of the nineteenth century. Economic divisions split the country into pockets of regional interests. The age of nationalism and the illusory concept of pride in the young country were gone with the Panic of 1819, which did so much to bring an end to the Era of Good Feeling.[65]

The panic had begun to fade by the time James Monroe

64. *Annals of Congress*, Sixteenth Congress, First Session (Washington, D.C., 1855), 36:1694-95; *National Intelligencer*, March 29, 1820.
65. See George Dangerfield, *The Era of Good Feelings* (New York, 1952), for insight into this period.

began his second presidential term, but in his final years in office Congress dealt with many of the issues that surrounded the panic.

One institution Gales and Seaton thought had helped to stabilize the country during the panic was the Second United States Bank. As early as 1814 the *Intelligencer* editors encouraged congressional support for rechartering such an institution. They supported the measure to avoid "evils resulting from the issuance of paper money" by state banks. Specifically Gales and Seaton wanted to guard "against the confusion which must ensue from the diversity of paper which the Pennsylvania *litter* of Banks will put into circulation, in addition to that already afloat."[66] To these publishers there was no doubt of the constitutional right to establish a national financial agency. As loyal Washingtonians, however, they thought the bank should be located in the nation's capital rather than in Philadelphia.[67]

The national bank issue saw Gales and Seaton a bit at odds with President Madison, although there was no open conflict. The *Intelligencer* editors did not condemn his veto in 1815, although they did write that the disagreement between the president and Congress continued a "great national evil."[68] A year later when Congress passed and Madison signed the bank bill,[69] Gales and Seaton congratulated the country on this important step toward relieving existing financial confusion.[70]

Rechartering the bank kept it from becoming a major issue in shattering the illusion of national harmony that prevailed in the first half of the 1820s. The first major issue symbolizing the split was the debate over the admission of Missouri to the union. It was more than just a question of abolition, for at that time the North cared little about freeing the slaves. The important issue was who controlled the new West across the Mississippi River. The South also had a deep interest, for here the planter had placed capital in land and slaves and the new

66. *National Intelligencer*, March 26, 1814.
67. Ibid., March 29, 1814.
68. Ibid., February 1, 1815.
69. *Annals of Congress*, Fourteenth Congress, First Session (Washington, D.C., 1854), 29:280-81.
70. *National Intelligencer*, April 6 and April 11, 1816.

West was essential to his economic expansion. Slaveholders were angered by the contention that slavery was incompatible with the democratic way of life, terrified by the thought they were losing control of the Republican party, and unable to conceal their simple desire to rule the West.[71]

Gales and Seaton showed great interest in the debate concerning the admission of Missouri to the Union but registered little editorial opinion. Their position was simply stated: Should this territory have restrictions placed on its admission which were not imposed on such states as Alabama and Louisiana? "Of the merits of this question we do not propose to speak. Enough of it has been said in the newspapers. . . ."[72]

This was part of the *Intelligencer*'s policy of not commenting on slavery for fear of agitating the issue. Mrs. Seaton, however, in her correspondence, gave an idea of the sentiments of the editors toward the issue as she wrote of the excitement of the occasion: "Congress has been occupied during three weeks in the discussion of the Missouri bill,—the right to prohibit the admission of slaves in the new State of Missouri. . . ." She thought the question should more aptly be stated: "Shall Missouri be a State, or not? for it is well understood that she does not wish to enter the confederation, except on an equal footing with other States. . . . The excitement during this protracted debate has been intense."[73]

Sarah worried what effect the debate would have on the Negroes who paid close attention to what was being said. "They hear all, but understand much less than half." They realized it was a question of servitude or freedom but "imagine that the result will immediately affect their condition." She worried about what might happen when the slaves of southerners returned home with exaggerated accounts of what they had heard: "I fear that many deluded creatures will fall sacrifices to their misapprehension of the question."[74]

Gales and Seaton so greatly feared discussing slavery that they would not comment or carry letters that dealt in any way

71. Dangerfield, *Era of Good Feelings*, p. 223.
72. *National Intelligencer*, December 21, 1819.
73. Sarah Gales Seaton to her parents, February 1820, quoted in Seaton, *William Winston Seaton*, p. 145.
74. Ibid., pp. 145-46.

with the subject. This policy continued until the middle 1840s, when politics and slavery were so fused that slavery could no longer be ignored.

Even sharper demonstration of the sectional division came in the debates on the tariff in 1820 and 1824. The votes on these issues showed the dramatic change in sentiment that was taking place concerning this issue as the North and Northwest gave nearly solid support against the near-solid opposition of the South and Southeast. Where the North saw the tariff as protection of the rising industries, citizens of the South began to view the tariff as a tax imposed at the expense of the South, solely to protect the northern interests.

The stand Gales and Seaton took during this period was one they supported throughout their lives. The editors felt a tariff should protect infant industries but should not be used as a revenue-raising measure. Although they commented little editorially on the tariffs before 1820, they supported the tariff of 1816, hoping it indicated agreement between agricultural and manufacturing interests.[75]

By 1821 the *Intelligencer* again was filled with the debates on the tariff issue as a new attempt to revise the tariff faced the nation. The editors feared the conflict between agriculture and manufacturing interests was increasing rather than decreasing. Perhaps, they wrote, agricultural interests were becoming too powerful for the good of the manufacturing interests and they feared a swing away from protection. Regarding the agricultural bloc, Gales and Seaton wrote: ". . . jealousy has been unwisely cultivated between it and the manufacturing interest, by the railings and denunciations of the writers for newspapers, which is unfavorable to the further encouragement of manufacturers, and will be felt whenever this question comes up."[76]

Although Gales and Seaton said little about the tariff revision proposed in 1824, Henry Clay accused the "official paper" of opposing the revision. Clay was annoyed, he contended, that a paper supported by the "purse of the House

---

75. For a discussion of the tariff of 1816, see Harry J. Carman, *Social and Economic History of the United States* (Boston, 1934), 2:29-31; Edward Channing, *A History of the United States* (New York, 1936), 5:315.

76. *National Intelligencer*, August 18, 1821.

and of the Government" should be used against the best interests of both.[77]

Gales and Seaton replied that if Clay had read the *Intelligencer* he would not have so "widely misunderstood" its stand. The editors were not opposed to a moderate revision but opposed any tariff so high that it became prohibitory. Really, Gales and Seaton wrote, they were not "positively or negatively" inclined toward the tariff.[78] Their main desire was to settle the matter so the manufacturing interests in the country could plan with a little certainty what foreign competition to expect.[79] Following passage of the Tariff of 1824, Gales and Seaton wrote that the tariff "approached so nearly to the beau ideal of a 'judicious' one" that they hoped it would be untouched for years.[80]

To the South, this was no judicious tariff, and politicians of the area noted with alarm that the areas favoring the tariff had gained twenty-eight seats in Congress since the passage of the tariff of 1816. The sections that were divided or opposed to the tariff had gained only six. In these figures there was a serious forecast of trouble.[81]

On the major domestic issues, Gales and Seaton had taken an unquestionable stand. They favored internal improvements as a means of binding the country together. Money expended for better transportation would bind the agricultural regions to the manufacturing and thus benefit the entire country. By this period the *National Intelligencer* was well committed to the main tenants of Clay's American System, and for the next decades would not deviate in supporting this proposal.

On the foreign-policy issues facing the country, the *Intelligencer* also took several important stands. The editors opposed Clay's move in 1818 to give diplomatic recognition to Latin American countries that were throwing off the yoke of Spanish domination.[82] Gales and Seaton, always great believ-

77. Ibid., April 1, 1824.
78. Ibid.
79. Ibid., May 20, 1824.
80. Ibid.
81. Charles Wiltse, *John C. Calhoun, Nationalist, 1782-1828* (New York, 1944), p. 287.
82. For a detailed discussion of the problem, see Samuel F. Bemis, *The Latin American Policy of the United States* (New York, 1943), pp. 40-42.

ers in avoiding involvement in the affairs of foreign countries, instead urged a slow and cautious path in dealing with the former Spanish colonies. The editors felt diplomatic recognition should come only when the country was well established.[83] Above all, Gales and Seaton warned, the United States was wrong to attempt to interfere in the internal affairs of any of the newly founded republics.[84] "We wish those people well," they said; "we shall rejoice in their success—but we cannot consent to embroil ourselves in their quarrels. We interfere in the internal concerns of no nations, as we suffer none to interfere with us."[85]

As late as December, 1821, the editors still urged caution in dealing with the new republics to the south.[86]

Gales and Seaton failed to specifically note the Monroe Doctrine when it was declared on December 2, 1823. The following issue of the *Intelligencer* reported the president had given a message to Congress of considerable importance. But Gales and Seaton told their readers they had not sufficiently digested the message to comment on it immediately.[87] A few days later the editors reported they had decided to withhold comment on the message, but they published numerous favorable comments from newspapers around the country.[88]

The editors did admit that the message, because of its enunciation of United States policy toward protecting the western hemisphere from further outside colonization, had "created a sensation." About 35,000 copies of the message were distributed, some 6,000 through the regular editions of the *Intelligencer* and 10,000 more through the *Intelligencer* extras. The remainder was distributed through government printing orders and other newspapers.[89]

Another thorny foreign-policy problem during the years following the War of 1812 concerned the Floridas and the United States designs on these lands. The climax in 1818

---

83. *National Intelligencer,* June 15, 1818.
84. Ibid., July 21, 1818.
85. Ibid., June 20, 1821.
86. Diplomatic recognition was given the first of the Latin Americas in 1822; see Samuel F. Bemis, *A Diplomatic History of the United States* (New York, 1936), pp. 200-201.
87. *National Intelligencer,* December 4, 1823.
88. Ibid., December 8, 1823.
89. Ibid., December 11, 1823.

involved many factions of the country in bitter controversy. General Jackson made his famous march into the Floridas that year, seized Spanish forts, and won a victory over the Indians. Jackson's action caused a great furor within the Monroe cabinet as members considered the desirability of holding the Spanish forts despite Spanish protests.[90] Calhoun, secretary of war, and Crawford, secretary of the treasury, both felt Jackson acted without authority in seizing the forts.[91] Adams, secretary of state, defended Jackson, while President Monroe wavered but eventually sided with Calhoun and Crawford.[92]

Gales and Seaton trod a narrow and dangerous path on the subject. They were annoyed by the great debate that took place in the press of the country concerning the controversy and thought far too much criticism was made of Jackson's action. But the editors recommended an investigation of the affair before any decision was made. At first glance, Jackson's actions in court martialing and executing the British subjects, Arbuthnot and Ambrister, for their actions in inciting the Indians against the United States, seemed justified. After all, concluded Gales and Seaton, General Jackson approved the executions, and his "humanity as well as his valor has often been tested."[93]

Returning the forts to Spain was a question that only President Monroe could decide, an *Intelligencer* editorial contended. Gales and Seaton were certain he would do right by the country[94] and approved the president's decision to return the forts. The editors pointed out, however, that in their opinion neither Monroe nor Jackson had committed any wrong with regard to Florida.[95] Jackson as a military leader always was respected by the *Intelligencer* editors.

With all these issues facing the nation, it was ironic that

90. Marquis James, *Andrew Jackson: The Border Captain* (New York, 1933), pp. 316-26.

91. For the Jackson letters relating to the controversy, see John Spencer Bassett, ed., *Correspondence of Andrew Jackson* (Washington, D.C., 1927) 2:382-87, 389-91, and 398.

92. John Quincy Adams's diary gives an excellent account of the debate within the cabinet on Jackson's action in Florida. See *Memoirs of John Quincy Adams*, 4:105-20.

93. *National Intelligencer*, June 20, 1818.

94. Ibid., July 14, 1818.

95. Ibid., July 28, 1818.

the 1824 election, which terminated the Era of Good Feeling, was fought primarily on personality issues. The National Republican party was breaking up, and political traditions that had developed in the country, such as the congressional caucus, had not gained sufficient acceptance to survive. Then, too, the depth of the divisions within the nation was not fully realized, and even such key political observers as Gales and Seaton failed to note that a new political alignment was taking place. The editors soon would become the voice of the conservative party in the nation's capital rather than of the liberal party.

CHAPTER 8

The Loss of Executive Patronage

The year 1825 marked the end of an era for Gales and Seaton. John Quincy Adams's election meant the *Intelligencer* was replaced by the *National Journal* as the semiofficial spokesman for the president of the United States—a position the *Intelligencer* had held since its founding in 1800. But the presidential election was important also for the preview it gave of the changing political situation in the United States and the effects this change would have on the *Intelligencer*.[1]

The *Intelligencer* was remarkably free of serious competition from 1800 until after 1820. Numerous papers started publication during that period, but except for the *Washington Federalist* and the Georgetown *Federal Republican*, none provided strong competition. The absence of an effective Federalist

1. For an account of the Washington press in the election, see Samuel Dean Olson, "The Capital Press in the 1824 Election" (Master's thesis, University of Washington, 1962).

party probably contributed to this situation, but government patronage, controlled by the Republicans, undoubtedly was the chief factor. Without this support the *Intelligencer* most likely would have met the same fate as many other newspaper ventures in Washington City.

In return for the patronage, the *Intelligencer* strongly supported the Republican party, which had united solidly behind James Madison in 1808 and 1812 and prevented any factionalizing of its ranks. In 1816 a brief flurry of excitement surrounding the choice of the congressional caucus candidate for president was short-lived. James Monroe was the obvious candidate, and the *Intelligencer* early backed him.[2] Although other Republicans aspired to the office, none betrayed great interest except William Crawford, then secretary of war.[3]

Before 1824 Gales and Seaton had not been forced to choose a candidate, for there had been no opposition to the candidates nominated by the congressional caucus. Members of Congress met, nominated a candidate, and the country accepted him. In 1824, however, no one candidate stood out above the rest but rather five candidates sought the office, several of whom might have been supported by the *National Intelligencer*.

Gales and Seaton faced a difficult situation, for it meant redefining their position. In what ways were they the semiofficial government spokesman? During Gales's early days of editing the *Intelligencer* he had submitted quite freely to the advice and counsel of President James Madison and his secretary of state, James Monroe. In bold terms Secretary Monroe had traced out the course that led toward war, and the *Intelligencer* was the vehicle he had used. The paper had continued in this role in the years following the war, but now its position was not as clear. Was its allegiance to President Monroe as a man, or was it to the government? True, the *Intelligencer* had differed with the presidents, but only on minor points, and clearly the newspaper was considered the voice of the executive branch.

In the past the *Intelligencer*'s position had been partially

2. *National Intelligencer*, January 26, 1816.
3. For an account of a Crawford supporter's view of the congressional caucus of 1816, see J. E. D. Shipp, *Giant Days; or, The Life and Times of William H. Crawford* (Americus, Ga., 1909), pp. 141-44.

determined by the president. The man the president supported also had been supported by the caucus, and thus the *Intelligencer* faced no choice. But in 1824 President Monroe indicated no successor and the office was thrown to an open field, raising a most perplexing problem for Gales and Seaton.

One candidate who logically might have expected the *Intelligencer's* support was William H. Crawford, secretary of the treasury. Many considered Crawford, from Georgia, to have the necessary background and characteristics to allow him to continue the aristocratic tradition that had developed in Washington City under the administrations of Jefferson, Madison, and Monroe. He had served in the government since 1807, both in Congress and in the cabinets of Madison and Monroe. He also had acted as minister to France during the War of 1812. In Washington City he was an intimate part of the aristocratic social circle that had developed within the capital and also made astute use of the political patronage that went with his cabinet position. He had a considerable following both within the city and outside, and his most ardent supporters frequently cited his strong showing in the 1816 congressional caucus as evidence of his being the logical candidate. Despite his withdrawal that year, Crawford received only eleven votes less than Monroe.[4]

Crawford's political ambitions were not pushed forward without attracting several powerful enemies: Andrew Jackson, John Quincy Adams, and John C. Calhoun. These men generally viewed Crawford as politically corrupt and unfit for the presidency. Jackson wrote that he hated Crawford so much that he would support the devil before Crawford for the presidency.[5] Calhoun described Crawford as "a worm preying upon the vitals of the Administration,"[6] and on another occasion contended there never had been a man "who had risen so high, of so corrupt a character or upon so slender a basis of service."[7] Carl Schurz, Clay's biographer, described

4. *National Intelligencer*, March 18, 1816.

5. John Spencer Bassett, *The Life of Andrew Jackson* (Garden City, N.Y., 1911), p. 327.

6. *Memoirs of John Quincy Adams, comprising portions of his diary from 1795-1848*, ed. Charles Francis Adams (Philadelphia, 1875), 5:315.

7. Allan Nevins, ed., *The Diary of John Quincy Adams, 1794-1845* (New York, 1928), p. 278.

Crawford as a "man with a reputation for a reputation."[8]

Crawford had little support from within the Monroe cabinet, and even the mild-mannered president had waved a pair of fire tongs and chased Crawford from the White House. Crawford ignited the explosion by threatening President Monroe with a cane and calling him a "damned, infernal, old scoundrel!"[9] From 1820 on Crawford seemed bent on alienating the administration as he constantly criticized Calhoun and on repeated occasions argued with Adams, thus earning his undying hatred. He was especially critical of Jackson's Florida campaign, which may account for the general's strong negative feelings.

Despite all this, rumors circulated that Gales and Seaton favored Crawford. Examination of Crawford's political policies made such a position all the more unlikely. During this period he veered away from his strong nationalist position. On most of the issues in which Gales and Seaton were interested, Crawford had moved away from the nationalist position and raised constitutional issues concerning the tariff and internal improvements. As to the power of the central government, he believed the South with slavery would not be able to remain within the union.[10]

To support his claim to the presidency, Crawford had his own paper in Washington City backed by patronage from the Treasury Department. Although the *Washington City Gazette* did not openly support Crawford until after the caucus vote in 1824, the treasury secretary had good reason to know of the paper's sympathies. The *Gazette* was founded in 1813 by Jonathan Elliot, an English adventurer who had served with Simon Bolivar in the liberating army in South America.[11] The *Gazette* was converted to a daily in 1817 with the aid of the Treasury Department printing contracts. Before 1822 the paper generally had followed a policy of "tearing down" other contenders rather than openly supporting Crawford. Elliot made certain he did not completely

8. J. P. Gordy, *Political History of the United States* (New York, 1902), 2:514.
9. Bennett Champ Clark, *John Quincy Adams: "Old Man Eloquent"* (Boston, 1932), p. 178.
10. Shipp, *Giant Days*, pp. 168-69.
11. "Jonathan Elliot," *Dictionary of American Biography* 6:92-93, 1931.

alienate any of the candidates, but overtures of friendship from the editor were viewed with suspicion by Adams at least.[12]

Elliot's vacillation can best be explained by the noncommittal policy followed by the *National Intelligencer* during the years leading to the election of 1824. If the *Intelligencer*, as it was rumored, also supported Crawford, it was possible the much sought-after printing patronage might go to that prestigious paper and not to the *Gazette*, and as a result, Elliot kept slender bridges built to several candidates. Also, the *Gazette* editor changed positions several times on important issues, such as the congressional caucus, internal improvements, and the tariff.[13]

Why the *National Intelligencer* leaned toward such a candidate as Crawford is difficult to understand without placing the editors' sentiments on a personal rather than a political basis. Crawford was a close friend, a warm individual popular in Washington society. Both *Intelligencer* editors were young and much taken by the man, Gales more than Seaton. Rumors that Seaton actually opposed Crawford received such wide circulation during 1824 that Gales had to reassure the candidate. Crawford was relieved and assured Gales that he "never believed that Mr. S. was ever unfriendly to him either individually or politically; although frequent intimations of the latter . . . were given him."[14]

Despite their leaning toward Crawford, Gales and Seaton considered supporting other candidates. The editors and their wives had known Secretary of State Adams for years, and in 1823 the Seatons visited New England and were introduced by their "good friend John Quincy Adams" to his father, then living at Quincy.[15] The visit, which Sarah described as the "most interesting" she ever had, erased the

12. John Quincy Adams to Louisa Catherine Adams, September 2, 1822, *The Writings of John Quincy Adams*, ed. Worthington Chauncey Ford (New York, 1917), 7:299-300.

13. See *Washington City Gazette*, August 9, 1820; May 2, 1823; and January 25, 1824.

14. Crawford to Gales and Seaton, March 14, 1824, Miscellaneous Collection, New York Public Library, New York.

15. Sarah Gales Seaton to unnamed correspondent, 1823, quoted in Josephine Seaton, *William Winston Seaton of the "National Intelligencer"* (Boston, 1871), p. 158.

impression of "hauteur" that Sarah had associated with former President John Adams.[16]

On the basis of personal friendship, Gales and Seaton might have supported either Calhoun or Clay. Calhoun especially was an intimate of the Seaton family. Historian George Bancroft claimed the editors thought the South Carolinian too young. Seaton supposedly asked Calhoun: " 'At the end of your second term you will be still in the prime of manhood. What would you do?' And Calhoun answered, 'I would retire and write my memoirs.' "[17]

For even more compelling reasons the *Intelligencer* might have supported Henry Clay. He had led the fight for passage of the printing contract bill in 1819 under which the *National Intelligencer* had received all congressional printing contracts after that date. Despite this Clay evidently knew he could expect no support from the *Intelligencer*, and this may have occasioned his attack on the newspaper during the debate over the tariff of 1824. At the time of this debate Sarah confided to her parents that "Mr. Clay spares neither of the editors of the 'Intelligencer' as such, nor the men personally. . . ." She expected her husband and brother to "teach this Western Hotspur that *they* control public opinion and the 'most sweet voices' he is so anxious to win."[18]

The editors opposed the fifth candidate in the field, Andrew Jackson, because of his military background. Sarah, at least, found him acceptable as a human being. She wrote her parents: "He is, indeed, a polished and perfect courtier in female society, and polite to all. He will, however, if our President, have a most warlike cabinet, I presume, and will send his Message to Congress by the Secretary of War, flanked by Orderly Sergeants. A more despotic sovereign would not reign in Europe. . . ."[19]

As early as 1822 Gales and Seaton complained that friends were trying to pressure them into supporting a candidate. Political maneuvering for the office and the lack of respect shown President Monroe annoyed many, including Sarah.

16. Sarah Gales Seaton to her parents, undated, quoted in Seaton, *William Winston Seaton*, p. 137.

17. Seaton, *William Winston Seaton*, p. 162.

18. Sarah Gales Seaton to her parents, December, 1823, quoted in Seaton, *William Winston Seaton*, pp. 160-61.

19. Ibid., p. 161.

She saw humor, however, in the proposal of one Washingtonian, who thought a committee should be appointed to ask the president to resign so the office seekers would not have to wait.[20]

Both Adams and Calhoun realized by 1822 that they would not receive the *Intelligencer* support. Adams, at least, assumed that Gales and Seaton supported Crawford primarily in the belief that he would be successful and would secure for them the much-sought printing contract.[21] On a carriage ride home from a White House party, Adams and Calhoun talked over the political situation, particularly with respect to the capital's newspapers. Calhoun thought both the *Intelligencer* and the *Gazette* were growing unfriendly to the Monroe administration, and he blamed Crawford and Clay. The *Gazette*, known to have been under Crawford's influence, was especially cool to Calhoun and, Adams admitted, it was "cautiously" unfriendly to him. Calhoun thought little more could be expected from the *Intelligencer*. Adams gave this account of Calhoun's views:

The National Intelligencer is also in subjection both to Clay and Crawford, by the Act of Congress which Clay carried through, under which the printers of Congressional documents for every Congress are chosen by the preceding Congress. Calhoun thinks that this gave the Speaker of the House absolute control over the National Intelligencer newspaper, both as a rod over the heads and a sop for the mouths of its editors; and he has no doubt it was Clay's object in carrying the law. By making them dependent upon Congress, it palsied them at least, as supporters of the Executive. They incline also from other motives towards Crawford, and, although uncertain which will be the strongest side, and therefore wishing to keep themselves neutral as much as possible, they will, while endeavoring to avoid direct commitment of themselves, lean as much as they can in favor both of Crawford and of Clay.[22]

Calhoun received his support from the *Washington Republic*, a paper founded by Thomas L. McKenney. A superintendent of the Indian trade, McKenney was reputed to have a fiery disposition. Calhoun, certain of McKenney's support, termed

20. Sarah Gales Seaton to her parents, 1822, quoted in Seaton, *William Winston Seaton*, p. 155.
21. Adams's diary, September 9, 1822, *Memoirs of John Quincy Adams*, 6:61.
22. Ibid., July 28, 1822, p. 47.

the *Republican* a truly independent paper of great service to the country. Adams, who was less certain, confided to his diary: "I think it [the *Republican*] originated in the War Office, and will be Mr. Calhoun's official gazette, as long as it lasts."[23]

The *Republican* began publication on August 7, 1822,[24] and almost immediately there was constant quarreling with the *Gazette*.[25] Ridicule, satire, and sharp political barbs were the daily fare of the *Republican*, with Crawford the object of most attacks.[26] During the first years of McKenney's publishing, editorial exchanges with the *Intelligencer* were mild. Undoubtedly Gales and Seaton resented the fact that the War Department patronage was taken from the *Intelligencer* and given to the *Republican*.

Although the *Gazette* generally was considered to be Crawford's organ, Elliot was shrewd enough not to show his hand too prominently and attempted to offer his paper to either Crawford or Adams, whoever would give the best printing patronage. Adams told the editor he wanted no support purchased that way.[27] The *Gazette* editor was not long in flying his colors after this conversation, and Crawford was hailed as the man for the presidency.[28]

Adams was disturbed by the incident, for he was certain to be the political target for both the *Gazette* and the *Republican*. He gained a defender when a year later Peter Force's *National Journal* appeared.[29] Adams claimed to be surprised by the *Journal*'s support of his candidacy.[30]

Force became one of the city's more famous journalists and early historians. He came to Washington City from New York as a printer and was associated in business with William A. Davis, also a printer. Force later served a term as mayor of the city.[31]

23. Ibid., p. 48.

24. Winifred Gregory, ed., *American Newspapers, 1821-1936* (New York, 1937), p. 90.

25. William Montgomery Meigs, *The Life of John Caldwell Calhoun* (New York, 1917), 1:293-94.

26. The Library of Congress has the most complete file of the *Republican*, although scattered issues are missing.

27. Adams's diary, August 26, 1822, *Memoirs of John Quincy Adams*, 6:56.

28. *Washington Gazette*, August 26, 1822.

29. *National Intelligencer*, August 9, 1823.

30. Adams's diary, August 9, 1824, *Memoirs of John Quincy Adams*, 6:407-8.

31. Wilhelmus Bogart Bryan, *A History of the National Capital, 1790-1884* (New York, 1916), 2:170; "Peter Force," *Dictionary of American Biography* 6:512-13, 1931; A. R. Spofford, *Columbia Historical Society Records* 2 (1899): 218-33.

After the *Journal* appeared, only Clay and Jackson were without newspaper support in the national capital. A prospectus for the *American Mercury*, a paper to champion Clay's cause, was printed in June, 1824, but the paper never was published.[32] Jackson did not have a supporting paper in Washington City until after the 1824 election.

Although both the *Republican* and the *Journal* favored a particular candidate, their primary aim was to defeat Crawford. By 1823 most political observers were certain Gales and Seaton would support Crawford, and therefore the *Intelligencer* as well as the *Gazette* was a fair political target. During all the political bickering between the papers of the city, the *Intelligencer* remained dignified and rather withdrawn. Until the summer of 1824 it treated all candidates courteously and appeared to be more of an unconcerned observer than an actual participant. The *Intelligencer's* was a high level of political comment as the editors sought to keep themselves from being involved in the political maneuvers taking place.

The editors were not allowed to continue such a high-level operation, however. On January 20, 1823, the *Republican* began printing a series of letters signed "A.B.," which directly involved the integrity of the *Intelligencer* and jarred it from its lofty position. The letters criticized some printing done by Gales and Seaton for the Treasury Department and accused Secretary Crawford of incompetence in his work and irregularity in his procedures.[33]

The January 20 letters, addressed to Gales and Seaton, claimed that the editors had willfully suppressed part of certain Treasury Department documents. The deletions showed Secretary Crawford was guilty of malpractice in the deposit of the funds, the author charged.[34] This letter precipitated the most significant controversy in the 1824 campaign. Gales and Seaton responded quickly, claiming the charges were false. A congressional investigation,[35] demanded by the editors and completed ten days later, completely absolved the *Intel-*

32. Bryan, *History of the National Capital*, 2:171.

33. *Daily Washington Republican*, January 20, 1823. *The Daily Republican* carried the letters on January 20, 21, 23, 27, and 29, February 3, 6, 10, 17, and 24, and March 3. Letters in the semiweekly edition were seen on March 5, 26, and 29 and April 2 and 9.

34. *Washington Republican*, January 20, 1823.

35. *Annals of Congress*, Seventeenth Congress, Second Session (Washington, D.C., 1855), 40:652.

ligencer of any blame for the deletions,[36] basing the conclusion on the fact that the deleted parts had been bracketed for omission before the *Intelligencer* received the work.[37]

In the same issue Gales and Seaton explained to their readers that the real purpose behind the "A.B." letters was an attack on Crawford. The House investigation had not cleared Crawford, who had admitted before the committee that he had marked all the deletions except one. Such deletions, he explained, were routine for handling "irrelevant" material in published documents. This paragraph, marked by an unknown person, referred to Crawford's having followed an unorthodox procedure in dealing with a bank in Steubenville, Ohio. Crawford had transferred to Steubenville a larger amount of money than was requested by the bank, and a bank official questioned the action in the deleted paragraph. The committee could name no one who was responsible for the deletion.[38]

A second committee began investigation and in March issued the second report, which exonerated Crawford.[39] Still many questions were unanswered, and as yet the name of the writer had not been learned and the person who had marked the deletion had not been named. Crawford felt certain by the middle of February that he knew, although he made no public accusation. He suspected Ninian Edwards, former chief justice of the Kentucky Court of Appeals and a former governor of the territory of Illinois. Edwards was a close friend of Calhoun, the candidate of the *Republican* in which the letters appeared.[40] The Calhoun camp felt positive the "A.B." letters did much to hurt the Crawford campaign.[41]

Matters rested for nearly a year while the *Intelligencer* continued to avoid taking a stand for any candidate. By this time Gales's and Seaton's plan of operation was clear. The editors would wait for the congressional caucus, which was expected

36. Ibid., pp. 735-39.

37. *National Intelligencer*, January 31, 1823.

38. Ibid.

39. Ibid., March 4, 1823.

40. Crawford to Charles Tait, February 16, 1823, as quoted in Shipp, *Giant Days*, p. 236.

41. S. D. Ingham to Ninian Edwards, August 20, 1823, as quoted in Ninian W. Edwards, *History of Illinois, from 1778 to 1833; and Life and Times of Ninian Edwards* (Springfield, Ill., 1870), pp. 497-98.

to nominate Crawford. This way they could argue they were following past precedent and would not, they hoped, alienate the other candidates.

Early in 1824 the campaign to select a candidate moved toward a climax as the congressional caucus approached. As the *Republican* and *Intelligencer* strongly supported the institution, it became obvious that a large part of the electorate was not satisfied with this means of selecting a candidate. Particularly in the Southwest the caucus was unpopular, where opponents charged it violated the Constitution,[42] opposed the will of the people,[43] took the election out of the hands of the people,[44] and was not truly indicative of the proportional support of Crawford.[45] Caucus opponents argued that Crawford had much more strength in Congress than he did in the country at large.

The *Intelligencer* made no real attempt to defend the caucus. Some opponents felt the states should take over a more prominent part in nominating candidates.[46] This suggestion brought a varied response. A resolution passed by the Tennessee legislature urging Congress to do away with the caucus also was approved by South Carolina. The New York legislature expressed dissatisfaction with the congressional caucus and urged some uniform method of nominating candidates. It was not in favor of state nominations, however.[47] One meeting in Philadelphia advocated continuing the caucus, while a group of Pennsylvania Democrats favored state conventions to select the candidates for president and vice-president.[48]

A letter to the *Intelligencer* urged a constitutional amendment that would leave the choice of candidates to the people, either through an electoral system or a direct vote.[49] Gales and Seaton agreed that a procedure allowing for direct nomination of the president and vice-president by the people in congressional districts would be best. The editors favored an

42. *National Journal*, January 7, 1824.
43. *Washington Republican*, January 19, 1824.
44. *National Journal*, December 17, 1823.
45. *Washington Republican*, January 4, 1823.
46. *National Intelligencer*, January 1, 1824.
47. Ibid., January 13, 1824.
48. Ibid., January 15, 1824.
49. Ibid., January 22, 1824.

amendment to the Constitution to allow this, but, they argued, until this passed, the congressional caucus should be continued.[50]

By that time it was evident that the old Republican party, the party of Crawford and Madison, favored the caucus. A new party faction, led by Jackson, opposed the method. The *Intelligencer*, long the official organ of the older party interests, was willing to go along with the caucus one more time. Opposition papers soon criticized the *Intelligencer* and accused it of blind party loyalty. Gales and Seaton denied this, and again they asserted that they supported the system only until one that represented every congressional district as well as Congress did could be passed.[51]

But Gales and Seaton did want Crawford to win the presidency, and the caucus was an important factor. Adams saw the situation clearly: "The caucus is the forlorn-hope of Mr. Crawford. His friends have hitherto been confident that in a general meeting of the Republican members they would outnumber the votes of any one competitor, and thus obtain a final majority in his favor. The other candidates and their friends are averse to a caucus, on various grounds. . . ."[52]

On February 7, 1824, the *Intelligencer* carried a notice: "The DEMOCRATIC MEMBERS OF CONGRESS are invited to meet in the Representatives chamber, at the capitol, on the Evening of the 14th of February, at 7 o'clock, to recommend candidates to the People of the United States for the Offices of President and Vice President of the United States."[53]

The reaction was immediate. Calhoun called his friends together and urged them to stay away from the caucus.[54] In Congress twenty-four signed a petition to cancel the caucus,[55] and a notice of their opposition appeared in the same issue of the *Intelligencer* that carried the notice of the meeting.[56] Pressures were brought to make certain that a majority of the Republican members avoided the meeting. The *Intel-*

50. Ibid., January 24, 1824.
51. Ibid., February 5, 1824.
52. Adams's diary, January 28, 1824, *Memoirs of John Quincy Adams*, 6:240.
53. *National Intelligencer*, February 7, 1824.
54. Adams's diary, January 24, 1824, *Memoirs of John Quincy Adams*, 6:235.
55. *Washington City Gazette*, February 7, 1824.
56. *National Intelligencer*, February 7, 1824.

ligencer editors, however, were inclined to believe that opponents to the meeting were in the minority and that enough senators and representatives would attend the caucus to make it valid.

Despite their favoring the caucus, Gales and Seaton set forth a policy to serve both sides in the controversy: "Whatever may be offered for publication on the subject, from responsible sources, whether for or against our opinion, shall be laid before our readers, to such extent as is consistent with the demands of matter of a different description."[57]

The February 17 issue of the *Intelligencer* reported the caucus nomination of Crawford for president and Gallatin for vice-president. Although they admitted attendance was not large, the editors were pleased with the results.[58]

The caucus nomination was no great boost to the Crawford candidacy, however, for the boycott of the session clearly demonstrated strong opposition to the ambitious Georgian. His supporters could not allow themselves to be discouraged even by such a hollow victory.[59]

Gales and Seaton were unwilling to separate themselves from the sham caucus and thus weakened their political position. They were tied to old institutions which were out of step with rising new political forces.

Adams was among those most annoyed by the *Intelligencer*'s role in the election. He wrote:

The editors of that print were, indeed, giving great dissatisfaction, probably to a majority of Congress, by the disingenuous course they were pursuing in regard to the Presidential election. But they still kept within bounds reconcilable to any of the candidates who might succeed, other than their own; and whenever the election of printers to Congress should come on, the destruction of their establishment by the British in 1814 would be remembered in their favor. And, after all, the question will remain, whether Congress can expect to gain anything by a change. An establishment which should report the debates in Congress even as well as they do could not easily be formed.[60]

57. Ibid., February 10, 1824.
58. Ibid., February 17, 1824.
59. Raymond Walters, Jr., *Albert Gallatin: Jeffersonian Financier and Diplomat* (New York, 1957), pp. 320-24.
60. Adams's diary, April 13, 1824, *Memoirs of John Quincy Adams*, 6:291.

During the spring of 1824 the "A.B." plot again dominated the political scene. The Crawford supporters, smarting under the criticism of the letters, sought the identity of the author and eventually pointed an accusing finger at Edwards, who had just been nominated as minister to Mexico. Crawford's followers viewed the Mexican appointment as compensation for writing the "A.B." letters. Accordingly, just after Edwards left Washington City for his new post, a report from Crawford's Treasury Department was sent to Congress that questioned the veracity of the new minister and reopened the "A.B." incident.

Edwards returned to Washington City and repeated the charges he had made the previous year. Another committee was appointed to investigate the charges and met well into June before upholding the charges against Crawford but absolving him of any intentional wrongdoing. Edwards agreed that he saw no evil intentions on Crawford's part but claimed he had alleged only incompetency. In many ways the committee agreed.[61]

A bewildered President Monroe turned to his cabinet for counsel concerning what should be done with Edwards. This meant three of the main contenders for the presidency were involved in the decision. Although Edwards had support within the cabinet, most members felt his effectiveness as a minister was seriously damaged. Edwards therefore was advised to resign the post, which he did.[62]

Gales and Seaton had not as yet come out in support of any candidate and dared express no opinion concerning the incident. Their sympathies undoubtedly were with Crawford. The *Intelligencer* was not much longer to enjoy the privilege of remaining aloof to such political squabbles. Adams's impatience with the Edwards case may have been partially responsible for his determination to force the *Intelligencer* to disclose its political choice.

As secretary of state Adams had used the *Intelligencer* as the medium for publishing the official State Department docu-

---

61. Edwards, *Life and Times of Ninian Edwards*, pp. 153-54.

62. Edwards to Monroe, June 22, 1824, as quoted in Ninian Edwards, *The Edwards Papers*, ed. E. B. Washburne (Chicago, 1884), 3:224-29; Adams's diary, June 21 and 22, 1824, *Memoirs of John Quincy Adams*, 6:389-94; Edwards, *Life and Times of Ninian Edwards*, pp. 135-54; Charles M. Wiltse, *John C. Calhoun, Nationalist, 1782-1828* (Indianapolis, 1944), p. 293.

ments. During the spring of 1824 Adams devoted a good deal of attention to obtaining support for an agreement with Great Britain to suppress the slave trade. The plan met considerable opposition in the Senate, and Adams sought support by having the appropriate documents published in the *Intelligencer*.[63]

Adams contended the published documents were garbled and incomplete and pointed this out to Seaton when the two met at church the following Sunday. The secretary of state was greatly irritated by the situation, probably because the *Washington Gazette*, the Crawford paper, charged Adams with personally suppressing some of the documents.[64]

Adams reported his annoyance with the *Intelligencer* to President Monroe and threatened to have the documents republished in Force's *National Journal*, with a notice that the *Intelligencer* account was incomplete. Seaton's apology and explanation received little consideration from Adams.[65]

The story of Adams's dissatisfaction with the *Intelligencer* spread, and Calhoun's political organ, the *Republican*, vigorously entered the attack on Gales and Seaton. The *Republican* claimed many governmental officials, including the president, Calhoun, and Edwards, now preferred the *Republican* to the *Intelligencer* for official announcements. In fact, the editor continued, " 'the *Intelligencer* was no longer considered the administration paper.' " Gales and Seaton had no comment.[66]

A week later the *Intelligencer* editors formally announced their support of Crawford for president: "We consider Mr. CRAWFORD *the* candidate, in preference to every other that could be named, because, at the close of the period of ten years, preceding, following and including the late war with Great Britain, during which period every publicman was tried as with fire, he was considered by the Republicans, without exception, as the only competitor with the last of the Revolutionary sages for the highest office in the government. . . ."[67]

63. *National Intelligencer*, May 29, 1824; see also Adams's diary, May 30, 1824, *Memoirs of John Quincy Adams*, 6:367-68.
64. *Washington Gazette*, May 29, 1824.
65. Adams's diary, May 30, 1824, *Memoirs of John Quincy Adams*, 6:368.
66. *National Intelligencer*, June 10, 1824.
67. Ibid., June 17, 1824.

Undoubtedly Adams's withdrawal of the State Department patronage was a factor in the *Intelligencer*'s announcement at that time. Gales and Seaton had lost in their fight to keep Adams's patronage without supporting him for the presidency. Gales and Seaton placed the entire blame with Adams.[68]

On July 3 the *Washington Republican* again asserted that Adams no longer considered the *Intelligencer* the official publication of the government. State Department documents now would be run in the *Republican*, the editorial explained.[69] In the same week the *Intelligencer* editors assured their readers they had done all possible to rectify any errors they had committed.[70]

The *Intelligencer*'s lofty position was shaken, and a third Washington City paper was brought into the fight when Force and his *National Journal* supported Adams's charges. Force contended the *Intelligencer* editors omitted "all parts of them as they pleased to think immaterial. . . ." The *Journal* thought this was particularly bad since other papers copied their official news from the *Intelligencer*.[71]

In this same issue Force announced that his *National Journal*, at Adams's request, carried the official documents in full, along with other State Department business.[72] Force served notice that his paper and not the *Republican* was the new official journal of at least the State Department.

The *Intelligencer* editors pleaded innocent on all counts. In answer to the *Journal* editorial, Gales and Seaton wrote:

A candid and dispassionate review of this matter leaves us yet in utter astonishment that the Secretary of State—this elevated officer, this self poised, enlightened, and experienced Statesman, should, for a cause this trivial—for an error, if it were one, rectified as soon as known, have taken mortal offense, and deliberately resolved to withdraw his confidence and countenance from a print which has from its beginning foundation stood by its country and its Republican administration, through evil and through good report, and has

68. Ibid., July 1, 1824.
69. *Washington Republican*, July 3, 1824.
70. *National Intelligencer*, July 10, 1824.
71. *National Journal*, July 8, 1824.
72. Ibid.

enjoyed the unwavering confidence of a JEFFERSON, a MADI-
SON, and a MONROE, for four and twenty years![73]

Gales and Seaton must have been a bit pleased when in the
midst of the fight the *Republican*, the paper which had brought
the fight into the press, ceased publication and was purchased
by the *Journal*. In announcing the end of the *Republican*, the
Intelligencer editors were "sorry to say, to the last moment, it
had not the least symptom of penance for its manifold trans-
gressions. . . ."[74]

The controversy between Adams and the *Intelligencer* continued as Gales and Seaton criticized Adams for writing
editorials for the *Journal*.[75] They claimed only Adams could
have written the note that stated that Gales and Seaton had
attacked Adams with "a stab under the fifth rib, with the
salutation of 'Art thou in health, my brother?' "[76]

The *Intelligencer* replied:

In conclusion, let us rejoice that the stab under the fifth rib, which
the Secretary supposes himself to have received from us, hath not
shed out the bowels of our brother, as Amason forced by Joad's
hand, at the great stone which is in Gideon. This mortal purpose,
the reader has already discovered, was altogether in the imagination
of the honorable Secretary. His valuable life, may Heaven be
praised, is yet preserved to his country, and long may it be! The
weapon which he thought to be felt was but a "dagger of the
mind," the point, it seems, instead of the handle presented towards
him. Honest heads and open hands are the worst danger the Secretary has to encounter from us. We parry his blows without returning them. We scarcely resist him. We retreat before him. He follows
us up, and drives us against the wall. We ask a truce, and it is
refused. Still we ward off his blows without attempting to return
them.[77]

Gales and Seaton frankly admitted the fight with Adams had
not helped them. It was the "most unwelcome" controversy
in which they had been involved.[78] The most telling blow

73. *National Intelligencer*, July 10, 1824.
74. Ibid., July 14, 1824.
75. Adams's diary, July 13, 1824, *Memoirs of John Quincy Adams*, 6:400.
76. *National Intelligencer*, July 17, 1824.
77. Ibid.
78. Ibid., July 22, 1824.

came when Gales called at the president's office. Monroe was upset by the course the *Intelligencer* had pursued, he informed Gales, and proceeded to lecture the editor with great severity.[79]

The fight between the federal executive branch and the *Intelligencer* was an occasion for which many editors had long waited, for they envied the paper's relations with the presidents. Now there were signs that this relationship was destroyed; even the president was dissatisfied.[80]

The *Baltimore Patriot* was delighted with the break. Gales and Seaton were annoyed by the enthusiasm with which the *Patriot* editor received the "war which has commenced against the *Intelligencer*. Has he received the signal to rouse the clans against us?"[81]

The *Boston Patriot* joined the attack on the *Intelligencer* by saying that not only had the editors refused to publish the documents on slave trade as requested but that Gales and Seaton had led the opposition against Monroe. The Washington City editors countered by explaining that although they did not support Monroe on all matters, they still strongly favored the administration.[82] The *Alexandria Herald* was sure the *Intelligencer* suffered great loss of advertising because of the fight.[83]

All this meant little, Gales and Seaton contended. What mattered were the attacks on the *Intelligencer* because its editors openly favored a particular candidate for president. Gales and Seaton now played fully on the theme that they were abused because they supported Crawford. They disagreed with the idea that the president was to choose his successor. Further, ". . . we deny the duty, on the part of a national politician, to approve every measure of an administration, whether of the President, or either of his Secretaries, or all of them collectively. We maintain the inalienable right to freedom of opinion and of speech."[84]

79. Adams's diary, July 22, 1824, *Memoirs of John Quincy Adams*, 6:402.
80. For Adams's view on the subject, see editor's note, Adams's diary, *Memoirs of John Quincy Adams*, 6:396.
81. *National Intelligencer*, July 14, 1824.
82. Ibid., July 31, 1824.
83. *Alexandria Herald*, quoted in the *National Intelligencer*, August 3, 1824.
84. *National Intelligencer*, August 3, 1824.

As far as the loss of executive support was concerned, "the *pecuniary* patronage of the Executive Departments" amounted to little or nothing, Gales and Seaton contended. The editors further explained that they had relied on the scanty profits of the *Intelligencer* until a few sessions ago when they had been appointed by Congress to print its documents.[85] Gales and Seaton probably were minimizing the returns they had received as the official printer and spokesman for the executive departments.

Undoubtedly the break with the executive branch lost Gales and Seaton some subscribers, although probably not too many. J. H. Doe, of Fredericksburg, Virginia, complained to Force, *National Journal* editor, that both the *Intelligencer* and *Gazette* had extensive circulation in his area, and Doe felt people gained false impressions from these journals concerning the presidency. He subscribed to the *Journal* to help overcome the faults "imbibed from reading of such papers as I have named."[86] Another Force correspondent paid for a subscription for a friend and noted: "He wanted the Intelligencer; but when I told him you now was the govt. paper, the thing was soon settled."[87]

The effects of the "A.B." affair still were felt throughout the city, and not even the celebration of the nation's founding escaped being touched by the conflict. In preparing for the Fourth of July celebration, General John P. Van Ness, a prominent citizen of Washington, vindictively acted to bar Edwards from the celebration. Cabinet members quickly retaliated, and with the exception of Crawford all refused to attend the celebration. Gales, as chairman of the arrangement committee, received notice of the boycott and realized that the pettiness of Van Ness's move had done little to help their candidate.[88]

Although it is probable that no one gained much in the way of support from the "A.B." incident, certainly Crawford suffered most from the attack. Doubts were raised about his

---

85. Ibid.

86. J. H. Doe to Peter Force, July 23, 1824, Force Papers, vol. 2, Library of Congress, Washington, D.C.

87. Sam H. Davis to Peter Force, March 22, 1825, Force Papers, vol. 2.

88. For an account of the charge in official papers, see Adams's diary, *Memoirs of John Quincy Adams*, 6:396-97.

competence and his personal attributes, and these, coupled with a more serious problem, caused many voters to support other candidates.

The more serious problem was Crawford's health. In November, 1823, the secretary of the treasury suffered an illness that so disabled him that he was without speech and sight for a time, and much of his body was paralyzed.[89] Between November and June Crawford improved, although he still was severely disabled. Before June, 1824, the papers opposing Crawford were reserved in their comments on his health, but during the summer open speculation concerning the seriousness and nature of the attack became frequent and rumor spread that he was expected to withdraw from the race.[90]

The *Intelligencer*, giving the most optimistic interpretation to the situation, informed readers that Crawford had not fully recovered but assured them that he would overcome the illness.[91] In honesty, the *Intelligencer* editors could go no further.

Yet for many Crawford supporters the *Intelligencer* was too mild in its approach to the campaign. There was dissatisfaction. To the south one of the greatest allies was Thomas Ritchie, editor of the *Richmond Enquirer*, who was to become an arch rival of Gales and Seaton and a strong supporter of Andrew Jackson. Ritchie wanted the Washington editors to be "bold, firm, active" so that there would be no danger of lack of success. He warned them: "I assure you, in confidence, that all parties here think the *N. Intelligencer* is too mild. Your enemies here are chuckling at your late appearance of giving up to Mr. Adams." Ritchie begged to be excused for his suggestions and admitted he should consider them "impertinent and officious if the good of the country were not at stake."[92]

Crawford forces in New York, a crucial state in the election,[93] were commanded by Martin Van Buren, the energetic

89. Shipp, *Giant Days*, p. 174.
90. *Washington Republican*, June 3, 1824.
91. *National Intelligencer*, August 7, 1824.
92. Ritchie to Seaton, July 15, 1824, quoted in Seaton, *William Winston Seaton*, pp. 161-62.
93. For a description of the complex political debate in New York during the election, see Olson, "Capital Press in the 1824 Election," pp. 145-64.

little New Yorker who eventually became president of the United States.[94] Gales and Van Buren worked closely together and supplied each other with information on how the campaign was going. Van Buren was concerned about Crawford's health, and Gales assured the New Yorker that health was not an important consideration but that it would take a great deal of patience to get this message to the people.[95] Less than two weeks later Gales again assured Van Buren that Crawford was "in every respect competent for any description of Executive business." Gales admitted, however, that the candidate's speech and limbs still were quite afflicted.[96]

Another problem that required Van Buren's and Gales's attention was the vice-presidential position. Gallatin's foreign birth again was criticized, and rumors circulated that he would resign from the ticket.[97] Gales wanted Van Buren to find out the decision on the matter so that the campaign could be waged in the proper light.[98]

Gallatin withdrew,[99] and Gales figured the nomination should go to Clay—"not that he is preferred by our friends to all others, but that it is supposed he will be more acceptable to the People than Mr. Gallatin, or than any other who can be now named." Gales recognized that Clay might decline the nomination, but the editor thought such an announcement would come too late to affect the election.[100] Gales admitted, however, that the vice-presidency did not particularly worry him.[101]

Throughout the campaign Gales liberally praised Van Buren's political maneuvering: "Whatever may happen with you, it is very well understood that, through the whole of this

94. For an account of Van Buren's activities during this election, see "The Autobiography of Martin Van Buren," *American Historical Association Reports*, vol. 2, ed. John C. Fitzpatrick (Washington, D.C., 1920).

95. Gales and Seaton to Van Buren, September 3, 1824, Van Buren Papers, vol. 6, Library of Congress, Washington, D.C.

96. Ibid., September 15, 1824.

97. Walters, *Albert Gallatin*, p. 323.

98. Gales and Seaton to Van Buren, October 14, 1824, Van Buren Papers, vol. 6.

99. Walters, *Albert Gallatin*, p. 324.

100. Gales and Seaton to James Barbour, October 17, 1824, Barbour Collection, New York Public Library, New York.

101. Gales to Van Buren, November 22, 1824, Van Buren Papers, vol. 6.

trying crisis, you have been almost the only firm, steady, consistent, and cool man at Albany. . . ."[102] This admiration, however, was tempered a bit by some misgivings. Gales thought the New Yorker placed far too much confidence in party discipline, and the *Intelligencer* editor rebelled against this: "For my self, I must be allowed to follow . . . the dictates of my own judgement, with respect & deference to the opinion of others, but obedience to none." Gales accurately foresaw a time when he and Van Buren would be opposed in political choices.[103]

Although Thurlow Weed, Albany journalist and later a politician, reported that Gales went to Albany to help Van Buren fight the Crawford cause there,[104] this report seems doubtful since Gales supposedly visited there on November 15 and none of the Van Buren–Gales correspondence concerned such a visit.

By late November the election remained as much in doubt as ever, and the decision lay with the House of Representatives. Gales had decided that should Crawford lose, the editor would throw his support to Clay rather than to Adams. His feelings against Adams remained bitter politically, but evidently social lives were not as affected. Sarah answered her family's inquiry regarding the effects of politics on society by saying there was no change in the relationship: "No individual could have had more enjoyment, or been treated with more attentive politeness . . . than I, at Mr. Adams's ball."[105]

At a party given for General Lafayette all the cabinet attended except Crawford, who still was ill. President Monroe was not invited. "Mr. J. Q. Adams and family," said Sarah, "seemed to enjoy themselves as much as our other friends, notwithstanding our wordy war. . . ."[106] She thought the candidates vying for the presidency seemed fairly good-natured despite the inner tensions: "Mrs. Adams came to see me this morning, being the first visit without invitation which has been exchanged since that unlucky stab under the fifth rib.

---

102. Ibid., November 11, 1824.
103. Ibid., October 17, 1824.
104. Thurlow Weed to Editors of the *National Journal*, November 15, 1824, Weed Papers, Library of Congress, Washington, D.C.
105. Sarah Gales Seaton to her parents, October, 1824, *William Winston Seaton*, pp. 168-69.
106. Ibid., December 16, 1884, p. 170.

They are all very courteous just now; but should Mrs. A. be Presidentess, . . . she, perhaps, will not forget that her husband was foiled in combat with us even with his own weapon,—the pen. . . ."[107]

The "stab under the fifth rib" was not forgotten, even though the heated exchange between Adams and Gales and Seaton was not mentioned prominently during the campaign. Many politicians still thought the *Intelligencer* had received its "comeuppance"—that it had betrayed its trust by openly supporting a candidate. Gales and Seaton disagreed: "From those who hold this belief, we beg leave to differ. The National Intelligencer was, it is true, the organ for the promulgation of the acts of Congress, and of the Executive." But, reasoned the *Intelligencer* editors, when the secretaries of the president were vying for the presidency, "they voluntarily cast off the official mantle, and stand before the people in their personal character, on the same footing with any other individual." Those who did not realize this, Gales and Seaton contended, did not understand the "genius of this government and the principle of equality which is at the foundation of it."[108]

Gales and Seaton had hoped during the election in the House of Representatives that Crawford might have a chance. By February 24, however, the House decision was final, and Adams was president.[109] Sarah wrote her parents: "The city is thronged with strangers, and *Yankees* swarm like the locusts of Egypt in our houses, our beds, and our kneading-troughs! Mr. and Mrs. Adams are perfectly *comme il faut.—he* is a little more gay and polite. . . ." She told of attending a drawing room immediately after Gales and Seaton again had been elected by the House and Senate as official printer for the next two years: "We were congratulated on every side, and passed a pleasant evening. The powers that be, did *not* congratulate us; probably we had omitted the same ceremony in regard to them on a similar occasion."[110]

The importance of the 1824 election as far as Gales and

107. Sarah Gales Seaton to her mother, January, 1825, quoted in Seaton, *William Winston Seaton*, p. 172.
108. *National Intelligencer*, December 18, 1824.
109. For a graphic description of the election of Adams to the presidency, see Samuel F. Bemis, *John Quincy Adams and the Union* (New York, 1956), pp. 32-54.
110. Sarah Gales Seaton to her parents, February 24, 1825, quoted in Seaton, *William Winston Seaton*, p. 176.

Seaton were concerned was not Crawford's defeat or even Adams's election. Instead, the rise of Jackson as a leading political contender was far more significant. By the time the House election was over, Gales and Seaton were not as disappointed at Crawford's defeat as they were pleased to have escaped Jackson as president. But they also realized that Jackson's strong showing meant the Tennessean was bound to be important in politics in the years ahead.

CHAPTER 9

A Period of Transition

John Quincy Adams's administration provided an important transitional period for Gales and Seaton. In 1825 the *Intelligencer* editors lost their position as spokesman for the president of the United States; before the administration ended in 1829 they had lost the very life blood of their publishing firm: the congressional printing contracts. The man responsible for this change in fortune was not the president, but the man who took over the office in 1829, Andrew Jackson.

But in other ways the period could be characterized by gains for the *Intelligencer*. Its most important acquisition was a position few political newspapers ever experienced: independence. The *Intelligencer* had moved a far distance from the Madison administration when it operated nearly completely at the will of the executive officers. With the loss of the official position during Adams's administration came a new freedom to criticize and to suggest alternative policies; with the loss of the printing contracts a similar situation developed in relation to Congress.

151

The *Intelligencer* editors were by no means free of obligations during this period, and it was some years before they achieved a high level of independence; and in some ways the commitments to the president and Congress were replaced with ties to a master that became as strong and as demanding: the Second United States Bank.

From almost any observation point the families of Gales and Seaton during this period were considered among the elite of the city—active in social affairs, owners of large, beautiful homes, and presumably among the most successful business owners of the city. In many ways, however, this was an uncertain period for the two families. Washington City under Adams's administration was not as active socially, and the activities of the editors were not as demanding as during the *Intelligencer*'s official period. Sarah's lack of participation may have been caused partially by grief over the loss of a six-year-old son, who was dragged to death by his pony when his foot caught in a stirrup.[1] Sarah, to help overcome the tragic loss, undertook the serious study of the Spanish language and mastered it so well that she could translate Spanish documents for the paper.[2] In addition, she undoubtedly was busy with the demands of her large family, which by this time numbered eleven: Augustine, Julia, Altoona, Joseph Gales, William, Ann Eliza, Virginia, Josephine, Carolina, Malcolm, and Arthur. The Gales had no children of their own but adopted a niece of Mrs. Gales, Juliana.[3]

From all appearances the business Gales and Seaton had built was large and flourishing. The triweekly and daily newspaper, coupled with the congressional printing contracts, required a large manpower force and a sizable printing plant. By 1827 the *Intelligencer* employed a hundred persons;[4] weekly wages and paper costs were about $800 each.[5]

1. Anne Hollingsworth Wharton, *Social Life in the Early Republic* (Philadelphia, 1902), p. 231; Josephine Seaton, *William Winston Seaton of the "National Intelligencer"* (Boston, 1871), p. 197.

2. Sarah Gales Seaton to her parents, March, 1827, quoted in Seaton, *William Winston Seaton*, p. 194.

3. Winifred and Joseph Gales, Gales' Recollections, Gales Family Papers, Southern Historical Collection, University of North Carolina Library, pp. 168-69.

4. *Niles' Register*, January 13, 1827, p. 305.

5. *National Intelligencer*, January 29, 1828.

The income from the newspapers was small, however, compared to funds received from the congressional printing contracts. Between 1819 and 1829 Gales and Seaton received a total of $299,622.78 for the Senate and House printing, an amazing income for any business during that period.[6]

The reason why the congressional printing contracts failed to make Gales and Seaton free from debt is not clear. Printers who held the contracts before 1819 freely admitted that they had made handsome profits and indeed became wealthy from the printing. Such printers were unable to understand why Gales and Seaton had not attained a similar position. Undoubtedly part of the cause was poor management policies on the part of the *Intelligencer* editors, for neither centered his attention on the printing end of the establishment. They felt their main duties rested with the *Intelligencer*, and the printing contracts were a convenient means of supporting the newspaper.[7]

The congressional printing contracts, however, did not allow for the most efficient use of the labor force. The great bulk of the work came during the congressional sessions when jobs had to be turned out promptly. Then, during the congressional recess the editors were left with a large force and little work. This uneven distribution undoubtedly was partially responsible for a publishing venture Gales and Seaton undertook in 1824. Before that time there was no published record of congressional proceedings except that which appeared in the newspapers, particularly in the *Intelligencer*. The editors reasoned that publishing congressional reports from their newspaper in book form would provide a permanent record of congressional proceedings and at the same time would furnish summer work for their printers.[8] Gales and Seaton also hoped that a national subscription to the volumes might bring needed money to their coffers.[9]

The first issue of the *Register of Debates in Congress*, the name

---

6. *United States Senate Document 11*, Twenty-Fourth Congress, First Session.

7. *United States House Report 298*, Twenty-Sixth Congress, First Session.

8. Elizabeth Gregory McPherson, "The History of Reporting the Debates and Proceedings of Congress" (Ph.D. thesis, University of North Carolina, 1940), p. 96.

9. A sample of the prospectus for the proposed publication was printed in the *Raleigh Register*, November 12, 1824.

given the new publication, appeared on September 24, 1825.[10] In this issue Gales and Seaton explained that they long had considered the necessity for such a publication and were surprised that the need had not been fulfilled before. They proposed to present a year-to-year "History of the Legislation of the Government of the United States." The editors admitted debates were not always literally reported but were as accurate as possible. In addition to the debates, presidential messages and important executive documents were included. If the work had merit, Gales and Seaton were sure it resulted from the lack of bias and distortion with which it was prepared.[11]

Contemporaries acclaimed the *Register* as the first successful attempt to record permanently each congressional session.[12] Undoubtedly many years elapsed before the true value of this contribution was realized and before Gales and Seaton received just praise for the publication. Records do not indicate whether Gales and Seaton received any sizable income from the *Register of Debates*, but congressional subscription to the volumes[13] no doubt helped the editors realize some return.

Despite this new source of income, the *Intelligencer* editors' precarious financial situation continued, and little if any headway was made in erasing the debts owed the Second Bank of the United States. On January 6, 1826, Gales and Seaton signed another deed of trust to the bank, which covered both their personal and business debts and assigned as security their homes and the lot and building of the *Intelligencer*. The deed gave the bank officials the right to advertise and sell any of the property if the debts were not met within sixty days after demand. Until such a sale took place, Gales and Seaton would be allowed to "possess, occupy and enjoy the same. . . ."[14]

10. McPherson, "History of Reporting," p. 96.

11. *Register of Debates in Congress*, Eighteenth Congress, Second Session (Washington, D.C., 1825), 1: preface.

12. McPherson, "History of Reporting," p. 96.

13. *Register of Debates in Congress*, Nineteenth Congress, Second Session (Washington, D.C., 1829), 3:1531.

14. A Trust By and Between Joseph Gales and William W. Seaton, Grantors, and Richard Smith, Grantee, dated the 6th day of January, 1826, and recorded on the 7th day of January, 1826, Office of the Recorder of Deeds, District of Columbia.

The editors' only hope of paying off these debts lay in the continuance of the congressional printing contracts, and to secure these contracts Gales and Seaton needed support from a majority in each congressional house. The political tides seemed to favor the rise of Jackson, and Gales and Seaton opposed this man.

As members of the Crawford party, the editors were free to move into either the Adams or the Jackson camps following 1824, but Gales and Seaton refused to commit themselves.[15] The *Intelligencer* was friendly to Adams, perhaps hoping to regain the executive patronage, even though Gales and Seaton contended this yielded little financial return. They did receive many of the official papers for publication but without remuneration.[16] Peter Force, of the *National Journal*, called on the president to receive the official reports,[17] and Force sent out advance copies of his paper to editors throughout the nation. These were the duties that brought payment.[18] Gales and Seaton were paid for some legal publications during the first few months of the Adams administration,[19] and as the term progressed at least one cabinet member, James Barbour, secretary of war, used the *Intelligencer* for part of his official notices.[20] Clay's refusal to use the *Intelligencer* for his State Department notices was a sore point between him and the editors.[21]

The friendship demonstrated by the *Intelligencer* editors toward Adams was not viewed favorably by the Jackson supporters. Furthermore, Gales and Seaton had taken a major step in opposing Jackson when they refused to put any faith in the charges of a "corrupt Bargain" that grew out of Clay's support for Adams in the House election that gave Adams the victory. Clay's appointment as secretary of state proved to the Jackson followers that a bargain was made to keep Jackson out of office. Gales and Seaton could see nothing wrong with

15. J. M. Johnston to John McLean, May 4, 1827, McLean Papers, vol. 1, Library of Congress, Washington, D.C.

16. *National Intelligencer*, March 20, 1826.

17. Adams's diary, December 2, 1825, *Memoirs of John Quincy Adams, comprising portions of his diary from 1795-1848*, ed. Charles Francis Adams (Philadelphia, 1875), 7:67.

18. Ibid., December 4, 1827, p. 367.

19. Ibid., December 15, 1825, p. 81.

20. Ibid., November 25, 1826, p. 186.

21. *Niles' Register*, April 28, 1827, p. 815.

what had happened in the House. The method of selecting a president was outlined clearly in the Constitution and had been followed, as far as the editors could see.[22]

Former Crawford men who had gone over to the Jackson camp were annoyed by such stands taken by the *Intelligencer*. By 1826 Gales and Seaton had broken with both Thomas Ritchie, editor of the *Richmond Enquirer*, and Martin Van Buren, the ambitious New York senator. Ritchie especially was inclined to criticize any support the *Intelligencer* gave Adams, although the Virginia editor did not declare himself for Jackson until 1827.[23] In response to Ritchie's charge that the *Intelligencer* had surrendered to Adams, Gales and Seaton wrote: "If we have discovered no ground on which to arraign this Administration, so we cannot rail, in concert with the Enquirer, at the Administration . . . ," must their honesty be impugned?[24]

The relationship between Van Buren and Gales suffered a sharp break. Small differences between the two men became exaggerated, and by 1826 they were quibbling over a chance remark Mrs. Gales made concerning Van Buren. Gales explained: "I have heard that you have taken seriously some . . . haphazard remark of my Lady, as supposing them to be derived from me. What she told you herself on that head, you may rely upon. I have nothing to say in your disparagement, and, if I had, should not be likely to say it in my family, where politics are never or very superficially introduced."[25]

The *Intelligencer*'s general attitude toward Jackson before 1827 was cool but not hostile. No doubt the editors were concerned to see so many of their friends move over into the Jackson camp, but they displayed no inclination to support the general. Such Jackson supporters as Calhoun, however, still found the pages of the *Intelligencer* open to them, and Calhoun used the Gales and Seaton paper for his "Onslow" letters attacking Adams in 1826.[26]

Socially the editors tried to be friendly with Jackson, for

22. *National Intelligencer*, March 17, 1825.
23. Charles Henry Ambler, *Thomas Ritchie* (Richmond, Va., 1913), pp. 107-9.
24. *National Intelligencer*, November 14, 1826.
25. Gales, Jr., to Van Buren, January 15, 1826, Van Buren Papers, vol. 7, Library of Congress, Washington, D.C.
26. Charles M. Wiltse, *John C. Calhoun: Nationalist, 1782-1828* (Indianapolis, 1944), p. 334.

Sarah, at least, found the general very likable.[27] Dinner invitations from the Galeses were extended to Jackson even though on at least one occasion he refused. Jackson replied: "Genl. Jackson returns his compliments to Mr. Gales Jr. and informs him that he is prevented from the pleasure of dining with him on Saturday next being previously engaged to dine with a friend on that day."[28]

It was unlikely that Jackson supporters ever had any idea that the *Intelligencer* might support their candidate, and after 1826 their actions showed clearly that they had given up all hope of making the *Intelligencer* a Jackson organ. The Tennessean had no newspaper support in Washington City during the 1824 election, but on February 6, 1826, a group of Jackson men[29] purchased the old Crawford paper, the *Washington Gazette*, and began issuing it under the title of the *United States Telegraph*.[30] There was no doubt to whom the newspaper was devoted, and Adams could not help but note that the prime policy of the paper was opposition to his administration. He also saw in the print a "sample of bad English peculiar to Calhoun. . . ."[31] Adams's observance was shrewd.

For a short time the *Telegraph* was edited by John S. Meehan, but in the fall of 1826 the man who brought fame to the paper took over. He was Duff Green,[32] a man tied to Calhoun both by political and family ties.[33]

Green frankly admitted he was a political editor, something other Washington publishers never would have done. Green, thirty-five years old when he took over the paper, had a background of varied experience. He had served as a medical student, school teacher, surgeon, merchant, surveyor, lawyer, member of the Missouri constitutional convention, legislator,

27. Sarah Gales Seaton to her parents, March, 1827, quoted in Seaton, *William Winston Seaton*, pp. 195-96; Arthur M. Schlesinger, Jr., *The Age of Jackson* (Boston, 1945), p. 38.

28. Jackson to Gales, Jr., March 17, 1824, Jackson Papers, New York Public Library, New York.

29. For a list of those lending money, see John Spencer Bassett, ed., *Correspondence of Andrew Jackson* (Washington, D.C., 1928), 3:301-2.

30. Wiltse, *John C. Calhoun*, p. 328; Wilhelmus Bogart Bryan, *A History of the National Capital, 1790-1884* (New York, 1916), 2:173; Winifred Gregory, ed., *American Newspapers, 1821-1936* (New York, 1937), p. 93.

31. Adams's diary, February 7, 1926, *Memoirs of John Quincy Adams*, 7:113.

32. For a short biography, see "Duff Green," *Dictionary of American Biography* 7:540-42, 1931.

33. Green's son married Calhoun's daughter.

mail contractor, writer, engineer, and Indian fighter.[34] He became a journalist in 1824 when he began editing the *St. Louis Enquirer*, a paper that supported Clay for a time but switched to Calhoun because of the tariff issue. Green dedicated the *Telegraph* to showing that Adams's administration was one of "bargain, intrigue and corruption," and his readers were fed a strong diet of these accusations.[35]

Feuds between the *Intelligencer* and the *Telegraph* were inevitable, although the *Telegraph* more frequently criticized the *Journal*, Adams's official organ.[36] Green, always more devoted to Calhoun than to Jackson, remained the leading Democratic editor in Washington more by default than by choice. Loyal Jacksonians were aware of Green's leanings and would have preferred a southern editor less suspect, but Ritchie and others refused to invade the treacherous publishing area of Washington.[37]

Green, as *Telegraph* editor, had another purpose nearly as obvious as his support of Jackson and Calhoun. He wanted to wrest the congressional printing contracts from the *Intelligencer*, and to do this he needed the backing of the Jackson supporters. Gales and Seaton saw dramatic evidence of the well-organized Jackson forces in Congress during the closing hours of the congressional session in 1827. The balloting for printer to the House for the next session saw Gales and Seaton victorious by a sizable margin.[38] Following this, the editors wrote Representative Stephen Van Rensselaer, of New York, thanking him for nominating them and assuring him they would endeavor to "faithfully" discharge their duties.[39]

In the Senate, however, where the Jackson forces were stronger and where Calhoun presided, the election was quite different. Balloting began on March 1, and the most support Green could gain was twenty-three votes, one shy of the

34. Fletcher M. Green, "Duff Green, Militant Journalist of the Old School," *American Historical Review* 52 (January, 1947): 247.

35. For particularly strong attacks on Adams and Clay, see *United States Telegraph*, February 6 and April 20, 1826.

36. See *National Journal*, June 18, 1827, for Force's appraisal of the *Telegraph*.

37. Wiltse, *John C. Calhoun*, p. 350.

38. *Register of Debates in Congress*, Nineteenth Congress, Second Session, (Washington, D.C., 1829), 3:1266-67.

39. Gales and Seaton to Van Rensselaer, February 20, 1827, Simon Gratz Collection, Historical Society of Pennsylvania, Philadelphia.

necessary majority. After numerous ballots on which neither Gales and Seaton nor Green received the majority, the voting was stopped for that session, and no announcement of the official printer was made. It was widely understood, however, that Green would be elected in preference to Gales and Seaton. When this news reached Raleigh, Mr. Gales was deeply concerned and by no means conceded his son was defeated.[40]

But when the following congressional session opened, another vote was taken, and Green was named Senate printer.[41] Thus, for the first time since 1819 Gales and Seaton were deprived of that vital source of income. Equally important was the political rebuke implied. The adverse vote meant the *Intelligencer*, because of its relationship to Adams, had lost the confidence of the Senate, and with this loss another tie was cut between Gales and Seaton and the federal government.

Before 1827 the printing contracts were not involved in any heated political debates, but now the printing patronage clearly was marked as part of the spoils for the victorious party. Gales and Seaton saw that they were part of a bitter political rivalry, and the impact of defeat stunned them. Some whom they had considered friends voted against them. Sarah wrote her parents of her hurt: "You will perceive that the Senate election has gone against us, and that some of our *old friends* have deserted us in our hour of need. . . . Van Buren of New York is the master spring of all the mischief, though working entirely under ground. Party spirit is now fiery hot, and will increase every day. We have never been so much aware of it, not even in war and embargo time, as it has severed the most intimate links of friendship and good-will."[42]

Daniel Webster, who before that time had not emerged as a great friend of Gales and Seaton, was "mortified and angry" by the Senate vote and sought some action to punish those who voted against the *Intelligencer*, but nothing came of

---

40. *Raleigh Register*, March 20, 1827.
41. *Register of Debates in Congress*, Twentieth Congress, First Session (Washington, D.C., 1828), 4:2.
42. Sarah Gales Seaton to her parents, March, 1827, quoted in Seaton, *William Winston Seaton*, pp. 194-95.

this. Sarah was certain all the trouble could be laid to the Jackson supporters.[43]

But Gales and Seaton were not without means of political combat. Sarah hinted that her husband and brother intended to use the paper against those who had deserted the *Intelligencer*. She wrote: "This morning the line is distinctly drawn for the first time in the Intelligencer, and was unavoidable. It will make some of the Senators a *leetle* [*sic*] uneasy in their relative journeys home; but you have no conception to what lengths they went in other things, as well as the sacrifice of old friends."[44]

Jackson supporters were not satisfied with the Senate victory, and the following session they began a move to discredit Gales and Seaton as printer for the House. A committee on retrenchment started an investigation of the printing handled by the *Intelligencer* editors on the grounds that Gales and Seaton were using larger type than necessary and printing on smaller pages than the law required. The editors wrote the committee, citing evidence that their method of printing actually saved the government considerable money. They quoted letters from other printers, Andrew Way and R. C. Weightman, to back their contention.[45]

The committee, split along partisan lines, recommended a study of Gales's and Seaton's printing, and a bill calling for investigation was introduced and passed by the House.[46] The committee found Gales and Seaton guilty of having used pages and type sizes different from that specified in the 1819 regulation, a situation critics of the *Intelligencer* contended had cost the country considerable money. The editors argued that any deviations they made from the 1819 regulations were approved by the clerk of the House and the secretary of the Senate. This defense undoubtedly contributed to the failure of Congress to issue more than a warning to the publishers.[47] At the following session a resolution calling for the

43. Ibid., p. 194.
44. Ibid., p. 195.
45. *National Intelligencer*, May 24, 1828.
46. *Register of Debates*, Twentieth Congress, First Session, 4:2752-53. See p. 808 for a brief consideration of this action by the Senate.
47. *United States House Document 111*, Twenty-Sixth Congress, First Session, 4; *United States House Document 92*, Twenty-Seventh Congress, Third Session.

investigation of methods to reduce printing costs was passed.[48]

Strangely enough, the most bitter clash between the *Intelligencer* and Green involved the reporting of debates rather than the congressional printing. Gales and Seaton were deeply disturbed by an incident involving one of their reporters and Green, but at the center of the controversy stood the *Intelligencer's* most frequent critic—John Randolph, bitterly anti-Adams and spoiling for a fight. The Virginian, who spoke almost daily in Congress, was annoyed by the *Intelligencer's* report of one of his speeches. He wrote the editors: "Mr. Randolph requests Messrs. Gales and Seaton to publish in their paper that the Reporters of the National Intelligencer have widely mistaken &, consequently, mistated, not only his language but, in several instances, his meaning, in the Debate of yesterday—e.g. 'East' for west—'tides' for tithes—with many others too long for insertion here. Neither is this the first instance of the sort. Mr. R. makes no allegation against the Natl. Intelligencer, but for the information of his friends & constituents, states a fact."[49]

Green interceded on Randolph's behalf and personally accused the *Intelligencer* reporter, Edward V. Sparhawk, of maliciously misquoting the *Telegraph's* report of Randolph's speech. Sparhawk was warned not to repeat such action. On January 25, 1828, the two men met in the rooms of the Senate Committee on Claims, and Green physically attacked the *Intelligencer* reporter. Sparhawk claimed Green was armed with a "bludgeon" and gouged eyes and pulled hair during the combat. Green denied this and said Sparhawk's "nose was wrung, and his ears, both of them, pulled," but nothing more happened. Green claimed he had no desire to injure Sparhawk but wanted only to disgrace him.[50]

The fight riled Gales and Seaton and probably was at least partially responsible for their short but bitter leader against

48. *Register of Debates in Congress*, Twentieth Congress, Second Session (Washington, D.C., 1830), 5:125.
49. John Randolph to Gales and Seaton, January 8, 1828, Randolph Papers, Library of Congress, Washington, D.C.
50. Accounts of the fight are given in the *Telegraph*, February 1 and February 11, 1828, and in Green, "Duff Green," p. 251. No mention of the attack was noted in the *Intelligencer*.

Randolph: "We have not quite arrived at the conclusion, (though we are not far from it) . . . never again to publish a line of any thing that may be reported of his [Randolph's] speeches; but we are determined never again, during this generation of Congress at least, to write one line in defence of our Reporters against his unjust imputations."[51] In defending this action, Gales and Seaton informed their readers that Randolph was given the opportunity to see and correct nearly all his speeches before publication, but his corrections were not returned to the *Intelligencer*.[52]

It hardly seemed necessary for Gales and Seaton to announce on August 18, 1827, that their print would support Adams rather than Jackson for president in 1828, but it was the first time they attempted to make a case against Jackson. The editors reiterated that Jackson had an excellent military record but again denied he was qualified for the presidency. They believed that Jackson himself felt he was neither mentally nor temperamentally suited for the office.[53] Gales and Seaton further contended that Jackson had "an impetuous and arbitrary temper" which ill-qualified him for the nation's top post. In addition, he made his own will and pleasure the "sole rule and guide of all his actions" and could not be trusted with presidential powers. But even worse, the *Intelligencer* editorial read, he was inclined to favor war. He could not understand plain expressions of law and would in a crisis "convert the whole country into one great camp, and would reduce almost every thing under military law."[54]

Jackson's "military mind" was Gales's and Seaton's major point of opposition to the Tennessean. To illustrate their point the editors went back more than a decade to revive two incidents that reflected unfavorably on Jackson: the executions of Arbuthnot and Ambrister in Florida and of the six militiamen in Alabama during the Indian wars. Since Gales and Seaton were opposed to Jackson's military leaning, they sincerely believed these two events were an important key to Jackson's character.

51. *National Intelligencer*, March 13, 1828.
52. Ibid. For other defenses against Randolph, see January 29, 1828, and February 19, 1828.
53. Ibid., August 18, 1827.
54. Ibid., August 28, 1827.

Reference to these stories brought accusations that Gales and Seaton were enemies of the "distinguished warrior." The editors responded that they thought the contrary was true: "We are his friends—more truly so than those who seek to force him, against the whole bent of his mind, into the highest civil office under the Government. But we cannot approve of everything that he has ever done. We did not approve of the manner of the trial and execution of Arbuthnot and Ambrister. But much less can we approve of the deliberate shooting half a dozen militia-men at a time, for insubordination, manifested under the belief of their rights being invaded."[55]

Gales and Seaton requested Jackson supporters "to publish an exact transcript of the record of each of these six cases" of the executed militia in order to "ascertain where the security of the life of a citizen ends, and where the right of a court martial to dispose begins."[56] Jackson's explanation of his actions in connection with the executions was printed in full in the *Intelligencer*, with the editorial comment that the people would have to decide whether the general was guilty of improper action. Gales and Seaton admired the courage of Jackson in revealing the facts in the case.[57]

The editors stirred up a hornet's nest in again bringing up the case of the six militiamen and Jackson's military career. As frequently happens, a hero tends to take on saintly characteristics, and to criticize him becomes heretical. Jackson's supporters felt Gales and Seaton had committed an unpardonable offense in questioning the general.

Many Jackson advocates considered the *Intelligencer* the core of opposition to their candidate, and Gales and Seaton were credited with attacks on Jackson they did not make. For instance, a Nashville paper accused the *Intelligencer* of making charges concerning Jackson's personal life, an accusation that was not true. The editors regretted the appearance of personal attacks in the newspapers: "We do not ourselves consider it necessary to follow Gen. JACKSON into the shades of domestic life, or down the long stream of his private concerns

55. Ibid., May 17, 1827. For a copy of the famous coffin handbill, see Marquis James, *Andrew Jackson: Portrait of a President* (Indianapolis, 1937), insert between pp. 158-59. See p. 159 for details.
56. *National Intelligencer*, May 17, 1827.
57. Ibid., June 16, 1827.

or conflicts to establish the prior eligibility of Mr. ADAMS to the presidency." Gales and Seaton admitted that such delving into the life of a man might tell much about his character and temper, but they contended they knew enough of Jackson without resorting to such methods.[58]

Since more space was given to tearing Jackson down than to building Adams up, the *Intelligencer* editors probably waged their most negative campaign to date in 1828 and came closest to dealing in petty personal fights. Over and over the theme of Jackson's being unfit to serve as president was struck. Only the personal characteristics Gales and Seaton felt were important to a president were analyzed and pointed out to *Intelligencer* readers, however, and compared to a number of the country's newspapers, the *Intelligencer* conducted a relatively high-level campaign.

In many ways the rise of Jackson, coupled with the emergence of sectional interests, confused Gales and Seaton. For the first time a man from a western state was strong enough to achieve the presidency. The editors were not products of the West, and they were not familiar or in sympathy with the conditions, traditions, views, or feelings of this rising western tide. Though professing national views and favoring a strong national government, Gales and Seaton really represented the Middle Atlantic section of the country. Probably the West was the section of the country least understood by the editors at that time, for the West they knew was the West of Clay.

Although in many ways there were no more knowledgeable men in the country concerning politics than Gales and Seaton, the campaign that was shaping up for 1828 confused and disturbed them. To them, something of a political revolution appeared to be taking place as they watched various political factions realign themselves in preparation for the election. But most perplexing of all was the vigor with which the Jackson forces set about organizing the country and carrying on the anti-Adams campaign. Gone were the dignity and gentlemanly manner that characterized the elections between 1804 and 1824. Gales and Seaton were disturbed and amazed at the network of Jackson newspapers that was assembled quickly and with purpose throughout most of the country.

58. Ibid., July 26, 1827.

Green had become not only their chief rival in Washington but appeared to be leading a vast army of anti-Adams mouthpieces across the country.[59]

Gales and Seaton viewed the Jackson party's organization and systematic opposition to the Adams's administration as something almost un-American, and unfair at the very least. The rising Democratic press was somewhat suspect to the two *Intelligencer* editors, who had somehow considered themselves above narrow partisan battles and undeserving of any serious opposition newspaper rival in Washington City. Yet the *Intelligencer* editors accepted the financial support the Republican leaders fed to the party newspapers and attempted to wage a vigorous campaign against Jackson with as much dignity as possible.[60]

Gales and Seaton were suspicious of Jackson's political stand on all the issues they considered important: the tariff, internal improvements, states' rights, and the United States Bank. They found it difficult, however, to use any of these issues against Jackson since no one was quite sure just where he stood. For a time they were hopeful the Tariff of 1828 might expose a vulnerable point in the general's armor. The editors favored the protective tariff, not as a money-raising measure but as a benefit to the manufacturing interests of the country.[61] Their criticism of the 1828 measure was mild, even though they felt too many party considerations had gone into the bill to make it favorable to anyone.[62] Undoubtedly they hoped that somehow Jackson would become tied to the southern protest against the measure and thus lose support in the manufacturing centers of the country. Jackson failed to accept the bait.

Closely related to the Tariff of 1828 was the rising issue of states' rights, and on this subject the *Intelligencer* editors held their greatest hope of halting Jackson's increasing popularity. Gales and Seaton viewed with distaste the threats of disunion in South Carolina[63] and laid the blame at Jackson's door. They

59. Robert V. Remini, *The Election of Andrew Jackson* (Philadelphia, 1963), pp. 76-80.

60. Ibid., p. 128, for an account of the role of the Republican newspapers in the campaign of 1828.

61. *National Intelligencer*, April 17, 1828.

62. Ibid., May 17, 1828.

63. Wiltse, *John C. Calhoun*, pp. 375-86; Margaret L. Coit, *John C. Calhoun* (Boston, 1950), pp. 175-91.

admitted that the general probably did not support South
Carolina's action, but he did allow his followers to use opposition to the tariff as a political issue against Adams.[64]

Gales and Seaton worked hard to make states' rights an
important issue. They were uncertain where Jackson stood
on the question, but they did know the position of Calhoun,
considered one of Jackson's leading supporters. They also
knew that Adams was above suspicion on the question. The
real threat the editors saw in the issue of states' rights was
the fact that a segment of the population was willing to recognize no law except that favorable to its interests. This group,
Gales and Seaton contended, was among Jackson's most ardent supporters. The editors saw in these men "a violence of
temper, and a recklessness of consequences" which they also
had seen in General Jackson. Because of this, Gales and Seaton wrote, they were "induced . . . to oppose, with all our
slender means, his elevation to an office for which he was
never designed by nature, and has not been trained by education."[65]

Although Gales and Seaton fell short of their goal of discre-
diting Jackson with the issue of states' rights, they succeeded
in causing some consternation within the Jackson party.
Ritchie, of the *Richmond Enquirer*, noted the *Intelligencer*'s
speculations on this subject and urged that Jackson issue a
strong denial.[66]

Actually the charges against Jackson had no effect on the
tide of popularity on which he rode at that time. By the time
the votes were counted it was Jackson over Adams, 647,276
to 508,064. The electoral college count stood 178 to 83 in favor
of Jackson.[67]

Jackson's election confronted Gales and Seaton with one
of the most trying and also one of the most challenging periods of their publishing lives. In two successive elections their
candidates for president were defeated. Now a man they
strongly feared had been elected, and the editors moved into
what was to be a long period of opposing federal administrations.

64. *National Intelligencer*, July 17, 1828.
65. Ibid., June 20, 1828.
66. *Richmond Enquirer*, August 15, 1828.
67. James, *Andrew Jackson*, p. 163.

Gales and Seaton were dismayed. Indeed, they admitted their confidence in "the durability of this government has been more impaired" by Jackson's election than by "any other event which has occurred since its existence."[68] The editors confessed they were unable to understand why Jackson should triumph over "the upright, virtuous, and unostentatious Republican, Adams." They reasoned that Jackson's military reputation had helped considerably and that he was aided by "geographical feelings of a range of Western States to prostrate an administration, whose principles barred their access to power." Nothing could be done but submit to the duly elected president, wrote Gales and Seaton: "However inclined to doubt its wisdoms, who shall dare to resist its force!"[69]

Gales and Seaton tried to continue friendly relations with the executive branch of the federal government in much the same way as before Jackson's election. A request forwarded to Andrew Jackson Donelson, nephew and secretary to Jackson, recalled that the *Intelligencer* had received advance copies of the presidents' inaugural addresses since Jefferson. The editors hoped this policy would continue.[70] The request was not granted.

Between the election and the inauguration the *Intelligencer*'s attacks on Jackson ceased. Undoubtedly Gales and Seaton sat back and wondered what their position during the years ahead would be. They had opposed Adams also—but in the end they were among his strongest supporters. Jackson was different. Never had they really objected to Adams because of his political views; they opposed him because they preferred another. They were against Jackson politically, and in many ways, personally.

The *Intelligencer* devoted little space to Jackson's inauguration, except a comment that the celebration had passed and the crowds had subsided. Gales and Seaton noted that no serious occurrence had marred the assembly and that there had been no disturbance of the peace. "At the mansion of the President, the Sovereign People were a little uproarious, in-

68. *National Intelligencer*, November 18, 1828.
69. Ibid., December 2, 1828.
70. Gales and Seaton to Andrew Jackson Donelson, December 4, 1829, Donelson Papers, vol. 3, Library of Congress, Washington, D.C.

deed, but it was anything but a malicious spirit."[71]

Mrs. Samuel Harrison Smith was less charitable and more vivid in her description of the inauguration, an event that horrified and depressed her. Although she was violently anti-Jackson, she was interested in the man and spent a good portion of March 4, 1829, watching the inaugural events from a safe distance: "The halls were filled with a disorderly rabble of negroes, boys, women and children, scrambling for the refreshments designed for the drawing rooms! the people forcing their way into the saloons, mingling with the foreigners and citizens surrounding the President." Dishes were broken, costing several thousand dollars, Mrs. Smith wrote, in the struggle to get at the "ices and cakes, though punch and other drinkables had been carried out in tubs and buckets to the people; . . . who claimed equality in all things." Mrs. Smith continued: "At one moment the President who had retreated until he was pressed against the wall of the apartment, could only be secured against serious danger by a number of gentlemen linking arms and forming themselves into a barrier. It was then that the windows were thrown open and the living torrent found an outlet." This pioneer in Washington society seemed to see all her efforts killed in one day. But then, she rationalized, "It was the People's day, the People's President, and the People would rule."[72]

Gales and Seaton did not talk about "the People" as Mrs. Smith did, and perhaps they failed to realize that a new force had burst onto the American political scene. Jackson had been constitutionally elected, however, and the legal way as far as Gales and Seaton were concerned. They were cautious men, and they sat back to wait and see the results of the new administration before drawing any conclusions.

71. *National Intelligencer*, March 7, 1829.
72. Mrs. Samuel Harrison Smith, *The First Forty Years of Washington Society* (New York, 1906), pp. 290-98.

CHAPTER 10

Watchful Waiting

Washington City in March of 1829 was a study in contrasts —exceedingly gloomy or excitingly glad—depending on whether one belonged to those taking office or to those leaving. Jackson's election shook Washington society as it had not been shaken since 1800, and his coming made great inroads on the social aristocracy that had developed in the city since the days of Jefferson. Carriages entering the city brought the joyous victors celebrating Jackson's rise to power, and coaches leaving carried the defeated, the displaced cabinet members, and other long-time Washington residents who saw no hope of favor from the new administration.

Margaret Bayard Smith compared the scene to a great stage. One drama was just finished, the curtain dropped, and she saw behind the stage the "disappointed, exhausted, worn out, retiring with broken fortunes and broken constitutions and hearts rankling with barbed arrows." In contrast, the new actions had the "freshness and vigour of unexhausted strength, with the exhileration of hopes undaunted by fear, of spirits intoxicated with success, with the aspirations of towering ambition. . . ." Time, she allowed, would provide the answer to these hopes. She thought, however, that "most probably, they in their turn will drink the cup of honor to the bottom and find its dregs nauseous and bitter."[1]

Even the Unitarian minister of Washington City, the Reverend Robert Little, decried from the pulpit the great tragedy he felt had befallen the country when he used as his preinauguration sermon title, "When Christ Drew Near the City He Wept Over It." Seaton, for one, agreed, for he saw much to weep over.[2]

Mrs. Smith was no more bitter or despairing than Gales and Seaton, the editors who replaced her husband on the *Intelligencer*. The prosperous publishing firm they had built seemed to be falling into fragments, and they appeared helpless to stay the momentum of the powerful force. Few held any hope that the *Intelligencer* could survive the rise of the Jackson forces, and Mrs. Smith was certain that Gales and Seaton were ruined.[3]

Probably only the editors of the *Intelligencer* fully realized the desperateness of their situation. The most obvious of the difficulties was the loss of congressional printing contracts. The Senate contract went to Duff Green in 1827,[4] and in the closing days of the 1829 session the House printing also was taken from the *Intelligencer* and given to Green. This left Gales and Seaton with only their daily and triweekly issues of the *Intelligencer*, the *Register of Debates*, and such miscellaneous printing jobs as they could obtain.[5]

Had they been debt-free, the editors' position would not have been as hopeless, but Gales and Seaton feared their entire establishment might have to be surrendered to pay for the huge debts that had built up over the years. The indebtedness to the Second United States Bank was large, but immediately after the November election, when it was obvious Jackson would be the next president, Gales was startled to hear

1. Mrs. Samuel Harrison Smith, *The First Forty Years of Washington Society* (New York, 1906), p. 280.

2. Josephine Seaton, *William Winston Seaton of the "National Intelligencer"* (Boston, 1871), p. 210.

3. Smith, *First Forty Years*, p. 290.

4. R. W. Kerr, *History of the Government Printing Office* (Lancaster, Pa., 1881), p. 20.

5. *Niles' Register*, January 13, 1827, p. 305.

that even Nicholas Biddle, president of the bank, was rumored to have supported Jackson. Were this the case, the *Intelligencer* opposition to the president-elect might serve to close even the doors of the bank to the editors, an event that would have guaranteed the end of the newspaper. Gales wrote Biddle, expressing some surprise at the rumor that Biddle leaned toward Jackson rather than Adams: "I think it proper to say, that my belief was, until otherwise informed, that if you had inclined to either side, it was in favor of the present Administration." Gales betrayed his worry concerning Biddle's reaction to the *Intelligencer's* preference for Adams, and Biddle was asked not to take too seriously views against Jackson that Gales had expressed to the head of the bank some time earlier. Gales admitted, however, that Biddle would have to decide for himself whether the editor was "as violent or as bad a man as my political enemies would make me out to be."[6]

Gales, in his note to Biddle, did not refer to the paper's indebtedness to the bank, nor did he mention the fact that Biddle recently had refused an additional loan of $15,000 to the *Intelligencer* editors. Webster, who had registered much indignation when Gales and Seaton lost the Senate printing contract, interceded with the bank president in an attempt to secure the loan for the editors. Biddle responded that he was favorably disposed toward Gales and Seaton and would do all within propriety to assist the editors. He could only consider a loan in the light of simple business principles, however. Biddle realized the *Intelligencer* was important to the bank, but he dared not help a paper that could exist only by bank support, and the bank could not go "out of its way in order to sustain any newspaper. . . ." Biddle did not feel another loan to the *Intelligencer* would be sound since the editors then owed the bank a little more than $50,000, undoubtedly more than the *Intelligencer* would have brought had it been offered for sale. The bank head added, "For this the Bank has . . . just enough & no more to make the debt secure,

6. Gales to Biddle, November 24, 1828, quoted in Reginald C. McGrane, ed., *The Correspondence of Nicholas Biddle, 1807-1844* (Boston, 1919), pp. 55-56. See also Biddle to Gales, December 24, 1827, Miscellaneous Collection, New York Public Library, New York, for an early note Biddle wrote in response to flattering comments from Gales.

& all the other means of the parties are already pledged for other debts."[7]

Biddle added that if there were any chance Gales and Seaton might receive the printing for the next session of Congress, the bank could lend up to $15,000. He saw little hope of this and concluded his letter to Webster: "I am so very sorry that we were obliged to decline but really saw no other course, unless we were ready in all impartiality, to furnish the means for a newspaper under the new administration. I have written thus freely because I thought it would interest you to know the fate of his [Gales's] application & the reason for it."[8]

Biddle attempted to play a nonpartisan role and to wait until he knew where Jackson really stood before committing himself. Before long, however, Biddle gladly showed favors to Gales and was exceedingly pleased to have the *Intelligencer*'s support.

Biddle's refusal to lend more money to the editors provided them more long months of worry, and in June matters turned still worse when, under terms of the 1826 Deed of Trust,[9] the United States Bank purchased the building housing the *Intelligencer*, and Gales and Seaton were once more publishers in a rented building. Ironically, Samuel Harrison Smith, acting for the bank, purchased the *Intelligencer* building on June 11, 1829.[10]

By midsummer rumors circulated that Gales and Seaton would be forced to sell their paper because of the dire financial situation. The *New York Courier*, which at this time supported Jackson, was pleased to suggest that perhaps the *Intelligencer* would be returned to sound Republican principles and again would become the administration organ.[11]

Gales and Seaton denied the rumor. "Seriously, the Editors of the National Intelligencer, do not mean to part with the

7. Biddle to Webster, December 2, 1828, quoted in McGrane, *Correspondence of Nicholas Biddle*, pp. 58-59.
8. Ibid.
9. A Trust By and Between Joseph Gales, et. al, Grantors, and Richard Smith, Grantee, Dated the 6th Day of January, 1826, and Recorded on the 7th Day of January, 1826, in Liber. No. W. B. 15, Folio 222, Office of the Recorder, District of Columbia.
10. *National Intelligencer*, September 12, 1837.
11. *New York Courier*, quoted in the *National Intelligencer*, July 18, 1829.

National Intelligencer, the sole reliance of their families for support, till death do them part."[12]

Gales's and Seaton's hope of continuing the *Intelligencer* lay in a publishing plan for which they had issued proposals in March, 1829: the *American State Papers*.[13] The proposed publication, referred to as "A Compilation of the Executive Documents, and of the Legislative Records of Congress, of date anterior to the third session of the thirteenth Congress," if approved by Congress, would provide Gales and Seaton with a publishing job worth as much as the printing contracts for several congressional sessions.

In their proposal Gales and Seaton pointed out the advantages of such a project. Many official records of the United States were lost during the British raid on Washington City in 1814 and never could be replaced. Those still extant had to be preserved. In addition, manuscript copies, through use, became mutilated and in time would be lost.[14]

The 1829 Congress, which had taken all congressional printing from Gales and Seaton, was not waiting anxiously to underwrite any such extensive publishing program for the *Intelligencer* editors' benefit. The proposal was referred to a Joint Library Committee, where, no doubt, many Jackson supporters hoped the proposal would die. Complaints were registered that the price Gales and Seaton intended to charge, the same per document as that received for congressional printing, was too high, and the Library Committee investigated to determine if the charges were correct.

But Gales and Seaton were willing to fight for the job of publishing the documents and moved to counteract the attempt. The committee wrote to printers in various sections of the country to obtain estimates for the printing proposal, a move Gales and Seaton termed "violent opposition and dirty manoeuvering of our unforgiving enemies in the Senate and out of it."[15] The editors asked such men as Jared Sparks to secure the aid of publishers to help ascertain that the price the *Intelligencer* publishers were asking was not excessive.

12. *National Intelligencer*, July 18, 1829.
13. Clarence E. Carter, "The United States and Documentary Historical Publication," *The Mississippi Valley Historical Review* 25 (June, 1938): 7.
14. Ibid., pp. 7-8.
15. Gales and Seaton to Jared Sparks, February 6, 1830, Gales Papers, North Carolina Department of Archives and History, Raleigh, N.C.

Gales and Seaton explained to Sparks that the Library Committee had received the proposal for the printing through the work of Jackson supporters. The committee, the editors contended, contained two-thirds of "our bitterest antagonists."[16] Gales and Seaton asked Sparks to contact the firm of Hilliard and Gray,[17] Boston publishers, and to explain to these men the amount of work involved in collecting and publishing the material so the Boston publishers would better understand the job before submitting an opinion about the price.[18]

A favorable report was made to Congress by the committee, however, which called for congressional subscription to 750 each of the completed volumes.[19] The Senate discussed the resolution authorizing the subscription during the 1830 session, but no action was taken.[20]

The failure of Congress to approve the plan for the *American State Papers* delayed for at least another year any hope Gales and Seaton had of being rescued from their financial situation. Their total debt to the bank in January of 1830 was between $11,000 and $12,000, in contrast to more than $50,000 the previous year. The sale of some undisclosed property, probably the *Intelligencer* building, had lowered the debt. Biddle admitted that the *Intelligencer* debt was about the same as that of Duff Green, editor of the administration organ.[21]

The retirement of much of this bank debt, however, did not lessen Gales's and Seaton's urgent need for money, and on June 26, 1830, Gales wrote a desperate plea to Richard Smith, of the Washington Branch of the United States Bank: "When I called at your office yesterday, I had not matured any proposition to you concerning money. But the fact is, we must have 399 dollars today at the *hazard of stopping . . .* the newspaper." Gales vainly had hoped the mail would bring him $500 to $600 from an agent in Natchez. He wanted to borrow on

16. Ibid.
17. William Hilliard and Harrison Gray were associated together at this time. For reference, see Madeleine B. Stern, *Imprints on History: Book Publishers and American Frontiers* (Bloomington, Ind., 1956), pp. 24-44.
18. Ibid.
19. Carter, "Documentary Historical Publication," pp. 8-9.
20. *Register of Debates in Congress,* Twenty-First Congress, First Session (Washington, D.C., 1820), 6:94.
21. Biddle to John Potter, Esq., January 9, 1830, quoted in McGrane, *Correspondence of Nicholas Biddle,* pp. 95-96.

a $600 order of printing and assured Smith similar discounts had been given by a Mr. Bradley, to whom Gales would have gone had Bradley not been out of town. Gales's next remark shows his desperateness: "If you do this for me today, I will not say a word to you about money again for three months."[22]

Evidently, despite their acute financial situation, Gales and Seaton hesitated to borrow from political friends. Gales told Smith that if the bank could not lend the money, Gales would be forced to ask Smith to discount a draft on Clay at three days after sight for $250. "This last step I would not take without extreme reluctance," he said. "He and D. W. [Daniel Webster] are the only two public men from whom I would accept any services. At present I owe neither of them a farthing, and would not if I could help it."[23] Gales felt he could better borrow from the bank and be relieved of obligations of political support.

Earlier, however, in 1818 Clay and the *Intelligencer* editors had been involved in financial dealings. Clay signed with Gales and Seaton to borrow $500 on a sixty-day loan.[24] Later he was pressed to repay the money when the editors failed to pay the loan in the allotted time.[25]

And while Gales sought money from the Washington branch of the bank, he sought advice and direction from the president of the bank at Philadelphia. A man in desperate financial straits probably could have had no better ally than Biddle, and Gales may have been conscious of this as he wrote Biddle: "I understand the Bank subject myself, I think pretty well: but I want *particular* knowledge, and original views on it: and I want time (from the necessary attention to the fiscal affairs of our own office) to acquire the knowledge and to prepare my views on paper." Gales thought Biddle was the best-informed man on the bank subject and asked him to answer a reader's questions. Evidently Biddle had done this before, and Biddle was assured by Gales he would like to continue to rely on Biddle's "practical knowledge & eloquent

---

22. Gales to Richard Smith, June 26, 1830, Miscellaneous Collection.
23. Ibid.
24. Note signed by Gales and Clay, September 14, 1818, Clay Papers, vol. 3, Library of Congress, Washington, D.C.
25. J. W. Hart to Clay, December 14, 1818, Clay Papers, vol. 3.

pen."[26] Biddle replied he would meet Gales's request and that he was pleased with Gales's good feeling toward the bank.[27]

Gales's and Seaton's financial situation received a boost during the congressional session of 1831. The resolution for printing the *American State Papers* again was introduced and passed on March 2, 1831, despite strong opposition by a majority of Jacksonian Democrats. Edward Everett of Massachusetts, chairman of the Library Committee, strongly supported the measure and probably was chiefly responsible for the bill's passage. Leading the House opposition were two Southern Democrats, Jesse Speight of North Carolina, and James K. Polk of Tennessee. Speight termed the resolution the most "obnoxious pension" measure considered by the House and warned, "You are about pensioning two printers in this city, whom you have heretofore discarded from your confidence." The $50,000 or $60,000 the printing of the *State Papers* would cost equalled congressional printing contracts for ten years, Speight contended, and why should Gales and Seaton receive such a favor? "Is it because they have and are daily vomiting forth pollution or abuse of Andrew Jackson and his administration?"[28]

The final vote of 98-93 favored the resolution, with such political renegades as David Crockett of Tennessee crossing party lines to vote for Gales and Seaton.[29] Crockett's support of the editors was not surprising, for evidently the colorful Tennessean had been the object of a concerted effort at times to win his vote away from the Jackson camp.

Crockett particularly worried members of the Tennessee delegation in Congress by his unwillingness to support the party line on the Tennessee land bill of 1829.[30] Polk, at this time a congressman from Tennessee, distrusted Crockett and had little faith he could resist the flattery of politicians op-

26. Gales to Biddle, August 16, 1830, Biddle Papers, Library of Congress, Washington, D.C.

27. Biddle to Gales, August 18, 1830, Biddle Letterbooks, no. 3, Library of Congress, Washington, D.C.

28. *Register of Debates in Congress*, Twenty-First Congress, Second Session (Washington, D.C., 1831) 7:815-20.

29. Ibid., p. 820.

30. For the views of Crockett and Polk on the Tennessee land bill, see *Register of Debates*, Twenty-First Congress, First Session, 6:480-81.

posed to Jackson. Because of this Polk was sure Crockett was being used to discredit Jackson, and Gales was among those Polk suspected of attempting to persuade Crockett. Polk wrote: "Gales and some of the Adamsites during the whole discussion, were nursing him, and dressing up and reporting speeches for him, which he never delivered as reported, & which all who know him, know he never did. . . . he can be and has been opperated [*sic*] upon by our enemies." Polk further explained that it was "whispered" that Crockett was inclined to vote for Gales and Seaton for government printers and against Green, the administration's candidate.[31]

Polk was not the only Jackson supporter who mistrusted Crockett and who had evidence that he was not always true to the party line. J. C. Mitchell gave even more concrete evidence that Crockett was courted by the *Intelligencer* editors to the extent where speeches were rewritten to flatter Crockett and show him in the most favorable light possible. Mitchell reported an incident to Polk where Crockett attempted to show his speech to Mitchell:

I told him that he need be at no trouble upon that head for I had heard him deliver it in the house. But he replied, I know that—I want to show how it is in the paper, continuing, I like Gales *prime* for he has made me a much better speech than I made in the house or ever could make & I will get . . . 1000 or 1500 and send them home to my people and they will think I have made a great speech or words to that effect—I observed that Gales had nothing to do with the matter; it was Mr. Stansbury[32] the reporter for Gales' paper who made him the *fine speech.* Colonel Crockett replied "that he knew it was somebody about that paper."[33]

The accusation against the *Intelligencer* editors and reporters certainly was damning, and if true, would do much to discredit the reporting of the *Intelligencer* personnel. Published accounts of Crockett's speech evidently appeared only in the *Intelligencer,* so no check can be made on whether the accusations were true.

The Senate debate on the *State Papers* proposal was charac-

31. Polk to D. M. McMillan, January 16, 1829, Biddle Letterbooks, no. 3, Library of Congress, Washington, D.C.
32. Arthur J. Stansbury. For a short biography, see *Appleton's Cyclopaedia of American Biography* 5:647, 1888.
33. J. C. Mitchell to Polk, February 17, 1829, Polk Papers, vol. 4.

terized by a number of attempts on the part of Jacksonian Democrats to amend the resolution to deprive Gales and Seaton of much of the benefit they hoped to obtain from the printing. Moves to send the resolution back to the Library Committee, to cut down the number of copies Congress would purchase, and to reduce the price all were defeated, and the Senate voted 24-19 to subscribe to the proposed publication.[34]

With this vote Gales and Seaton received permission to begin what has been termed "the high-water-mark of historical publication up to the period of the Civil War," and "perhaps for the entire history of the United States."[35] The *State Papers*, thirty-eight volumes covering the period before 1832, included important documents dealing with foreign relations, Indian affairs, finances, commerce and navigation, military affairs, naval affairs, the Post Office Department, public lands, claims, and miscellaneous matters.

Gales and Seaton have received much credit for this first major historical work carried out by the United States under a consistent plan. But both men claimed their only responsibility, at least for the first issues of the series, was as printers and not as editors. The selection of documents and the organization was the work of Walter Lowrie, Senate secretary, and M. St. Clair Clarke, House clerk, and in the first report of progress Gales and Seaton made to Congress in 1832 these men were credited for their work.[36] The first volumes in the series were delivered on January 4, 1832, and approval of additional volumes was passed March 2, 1833.[37]

In many ways the *American State Papers* represent as important, if not the most important, publishing contribution Gales and Seaton made. They conceived the plan and through their personal prestige secured sanction for the publication from a politically opposed Congress. The project, which carried through 1861, also was praised for the general quality of the volumes. Clarence Carter, editor of the territorial papers for the United States, came to the following conclusion regarding

34. *Register of Debates,* Twenty-First Congress, Second Session, 7:325-27.
35. Carter, "Documentary Historical Publications," p. 7.
36. *Register of Debates in Congress,* Twenty-Second Congress, First Session (Washington, D.C., 1833), 8:41-45.
37. Congressional Document 16, Twenty-Second Congress, First Session; Senate Report 18, Fifty-Second Congress, First Session.

the accuracy of the *American State Papers*: "There are imperfections in these printed versions of the textual matter, to be sure, as a comparison with the original manuscripts discloses, and an organization of the documents which is sometimes provoking; nevertheless it is probably more dependably accurate than any other work of its kind in the era in which it was published."[38]

Although passage of the *American State Papers* resolution gave hope that the *Intelligencer* could be saved, financial returns from the project were delayed until the first volumes were completed, and no sizable returns were realized for more than two years. Meanwhile, the *Intelligencer* dependence on loans from the Second United States Bank continued, but the congressional publishing project gave some assurance that even should Jackson be reelected in 1832, the *Intelligencer* still would be able to continue as a publishing firm.

Gales and Seaton well realized that the solution to their financial problems was tied to the political sphere of the nation. Any security for which they could hope was tied to the defeat of President Jackson. The editors tried to take a neutral stand toward Jackson during the early days of his administration, and attacks on him disappeared from the *Intelligencer* for a time after 1828. To some the olive branch Gales and Seaton extended was viewed as a flag of truce waved in the hope of winning presidential favor. The editor of the *American Sentinel*, Philadelphia, accused the *Intelligencer* of political inconsistency and was confused by what he thought was a change from violent opposition to mild acceptance of Jackson.[39]

Even a note written by Gales and Seaton expressing the hope that rumors of Jackson's ill health were unfounded brought criticism. The editors said they hoped the country never would face the situation in which a president-elect died before taking office, and for these sentiments the publishers were accused of trying to become friendly with Jackson. Gales and Seaton were startled. "We opposed the election of the General, it is true," they said, "but we hope never to see any casualty which shall defeat the constitutionally expressed will of the majority of the People—which is only

38. Carter, "Documentary Historical Publication," pp. 9-10.
39. *American Sentinel*, quoted in the *National Intelligencer*, January 10, 1829.

another word, among Republicans, *for the Law.* . . ."[40]

Undoubtedly Gales and Seaton were sincere in this expression at the time it was written. Before Jackson's two terms expired, however, the editors' constitutional ideals as well as their views on presidential mortality faced some trying periods. If Gales and Seaton were making overtures of friendship toward the Jackson men, the president-elect's followers were unwilling to accept the friendship. The *Intelligencer's* stand during the campaign of 1828 against the great hero of the West had marked the newspaper and its editors as enemies forever.

One of Gales's and Seaton's foremost worries, because it affected many of their friends, was Jackson's policies on political appointments. The editors had criticized such Jackson supporters as Van Buren for his views on party discipline, but where would Jackson stand? How much of the New York state system was to be moved into the federal government? Long-time friends of Gales and Seaton had filled top governmental offices during most of the editors' term of publishing the *Intelligencer.*

Papers supporting Jackson early agitated for the removal of Adams's men holding appointive offices so that Jackson supporters could be moved in. Gales and Seaton found a statement on the use of the appointive power Jackson had made at the time of Monroe's election. Jackson had cautioned Monroe to avoid party feeling and to "consult no party in your choice." Not above using a bit of flattery, Gales and Seaton explained to Jackson that in their eyes these words were of greater consequence than all his military successes.[41]

Jackson's appointees started taking office, and Gales and Seaton early realized that new faces in the Washington offices would mean a difference in the treatment of the *Intelligencer* personnel. One of the earliest indications came from a man who was an adversary of the highest rank for the next twelve years. Amos Kendall was appointed to the office of fourth auditor, and only three days after taking office he cancelled the office subscription to the *Intelligencer*, saying the

40. *National Intelligencer*, February 8, 1829.
41. Ibid., January 8, 1829.

action resulted from a retrenchment program the administration was starting.[42]

Other appointments and removals from office followed quickly. A clerk in the Navy Department was relieved of his office, much to Gales's and Seaton's dismay. Such a policy of removal would handicap the functioning of the government, they thought: "The removal of Clerks in public offices, upon change of Administration, is, as far as we know, a circumstance unknown in any other government in the world."[43]

Gales and Seaton played on the sympathies of their subscribers in the campaign against removals from office. The publishers told their readers in dramatic terms about eleven men being removed in the customs house at Baltimore, and not as part of a retrenchment program because all were replaced. Some of them had been in their jobs since the days of Washington, the editors related.[44]

The publishers did not argue against the removal on legal grounds. They "could conceive . . . that the power of removal may exist, even in regard to appointments limited to four years; but it must be *for a good cause*. This power cannot be arbitrarily exercised. . . ." Following Jackson's policy on removals would make elections "a mere squabble for office, for the reward of friends and punishment of enemies." This was one of the system's most odious features.[45]

Even Thomas Ritchie, editor of the Richmond *Enquirer*, was appalled by Jackson's removals and appointments. Within three weeks after the general took office, Ritchie wrote Van Buren, urging a moderate program of patronage appointments. The Virginia editor confessed: "We are sorry to see the personal friends of the President appointed. We lament to see so many of the Editorial Corps favored with the patronage of the Administration." Ritchie agreed that perhaps some reforms were needed in the civil service corps Jackson inherited. But what was this reform to be? "Is it," he asked, "to turn out of office all those who voted against him, or who decently preferred Mr. Adams? . . . It surely is

42. Ibid., March 28, 1829.
43. Ibid., April 4, 1829.
44. Ibid., April 21, 1829.
45. Ibid., April 1, 1830.

not to put out a good and experienced officer, because he was a decent friend of J. Q. Adams, *in order* to put in a heated partizan of the election of Gen. Jackson. . . ."[46]

Most Jacksonians probably reacted much as Samuel Houston did to the removals. Houston, remembering the promises of the Jackson men in 1828 to "clean the Augean stables," that is, remove the incompetents from public office, was pleased with Jackson's early removals: "I am rejoiced that you have cleaned the stalls of Washington, as well as others! Get rid of all the *wolves* and the barking of Puppies can never destroy the *fold!* It amuses me to see the leaden pointed arrows shot at you by Gales and Co."[47]

Much of the writing Gales and Seaton did on the subject of removals probably was party propaganda. Modern researchers indicate that only between a fifth and a tenth of all federal officeholders was dismissed during Jackson's eight years, a proportion no larger than that removed by Jefferson.[48]

Early in their campaign against the removals Gales and Seaton reset a theme they had played before. It was not the president who was to blame, "except for the facility with which he may have listened to bad advisors."[49] The editors continued to hammer on this idea during Jackson's eight years in office. What was later called the "Kitchen Cabinet" early was recognized and criticized.

But the real villain behind all this, in the eyes of Gales and Seaton, was the party—a party controlled by "King Caucus." The party organization subjected "all the patronage, and all the interests, of the Government, to the schemes of the mere demagogues for their personal aggrandisement." Such ambition could not be too indignantly condemned. "Nothing so hateful has ever heretofore been seen in this government, as the operation of that system of party discipline, of espionage, of denunciation, of cruel calumny, which has, of late, influenced the prescription of good and honored men, to make room for mere partisans. . . ." Gales

---

46. Ritchie to Van Buren, March 27, 1829, quoted in John Spencer Bassett, ed., *Correspondence of Andrew Jackson* (Washington, D.C., 1929), 4:17n-18n.
47. Houston to Jackson, September 19, 1829, quoted in Bassett, *Correspondence of Andrew Jackson*, p. 75.
48. Arthur M. Schlesinger, Jr., *The Age of Jackson* (Boston, 1945), p. 47.
49. *National Intelligencer*, April 18, 1829.

and Seaton thought most job-seekers hardly had the merit of having been on Jackson's side before the election.[50]

Despite the political disagreements many of the Washington City aristocracy had with this "President of the People," Jackson was accepted into the tight social circles that had formed in the nearly thirty years since the move from Philadelphia. But those surrounding him were not cloaked in the office of the presidency and lacked the gentility to move in the aristocratic circles of which Gales and Seaton were members. Washington became divided along party lines in social as well as political matters. Josephine Seaton, Seaton's daughter, described the period: "It was indeed a dark era in the hitherto aristocratic circles of the capital, which had been characterized by elegance of manners and the charm of high-breeding: but now came upon the astonished and exclusive citizens the reign of the 'masses.' "[51]

She, too, recalled that Jackson was not quite like the others around him: "Notwithstanding, however, the extreme bitterness of party spirit ruling political and social events during this 'reign of terror,' General Jackson himself had the power of appreciating the talent, dignity of character, or individual influence to be found in the ranks of the opposition . . . ." As proof of this, he appointed Seaton to a visitation committee to West Point, wrote Miss Seaton.[52]

Gales's and Seaton's aristocratic position was of little help in facing vigorous competition in the news field from the Jacksonian press in the the nation's capital.[53] The *United States' Telegraph*, the official journal of the administration until 1831, was at odds with the *Intelligencer* editors on most issues, but the exchanges between the two papers never were particularly violent.

Internal division in the Jackson cabinet and the divided loyalty of the editor, Duff Green, prevented the *Telegraph* from being a strong party organ of the president. Green's first loyalty was to Calhoun and then to Jackson. This hampered his effectiveness as an editor, particularly after

50. Ibid., May 14, 1829.
51. Seaton, *William Winston Seaton*, p. 209.
52. Ibid., pp. 209-10.
53. For a detailed description of the Washington press during this period, see Culver Haygood Smith, "The Washington Press During the Jackson Period" (Ph.D. thesis, Duke University, 1931).

1830.[54] Green naturally opposed the *Intelligencer* as a competitor for printing patronage and as an outspoken newspaper against his political leader. He waged a spirited campaign to defeat Gales's and Seaton's attempt to get congressional backing of the *American State Papers*.[55]

Green was not above making editorial use of the *Intelligencer*'s financial dilemma, but he probably was not as well informed on the matter as later editors. He related one incident concerning Gales and Seaton and the Post Office Department. Green explained to his readers that Gales and Seaton presented a $3,000 draft to postal officials for postal advertisements and notices the *Intelligencer* editors hoped to run. The postal officials decided not to use the *Intelligencer* for such advertising and therefore refused to pay the draft. This, Green explained, made Gales and Seaton critical of the postal department. The *Intelligencer* editors denied this as the reason for their criticism, but they did not deny the facts.[56]

Green's failure to perform satisfactory service to all segments of Jacksonian supporters—particularly those who made up the Van Buren wing of the Jackson party—spelled doom for the *Telegraph* as the Jackson journal. As Van Buren's influence increased in the Jackson administration, more and more support was withheld from the *Telegraph*.[57]

By 1830 open talk circulated about starting a new paper in Washington to supplement the *Telegraph* and not to supplant it, supporters said. By the fall of that year the man to handle the job was found: Francis Preston Blair, Frankfort, Kentucky, lawyer and contributor to the *Argus of the Western World*, published at Frankfort. Blair was thoroughly a Jackson man except on one issue, internal improvements, and on this point he was converted. The *Argus* had given yeoman service during the campaign of 1828, and Blair's shrewd thinking and vigorous pen were needed in Washington to help support the president.[58]

Blair was not imposing physically; he measured only about

54. Marquis James, *Andrew Jackson: Portrait of a President* (Indianapolis, 1937), p. 266.
55. *National Intelligencer*, February 4, 1830.
56. Ibid., October 17, 1829.
57. William Ernest Smith, *The Francis Preston Blair Family in Politics* (New York, 1933), 1:57.
58. Ibid., pp. 60-61.

five feet, two inches in height and weighed not more than 108 pounds. His face was narrow, even hatchet-like, his complexion fair, his hair sandy, and his eyes blue. His countenance was mild,[59] but he was dynamic.

Kendall, Treasury Department auditor and close friend of Blair's in Kentucky, particularly was active in getting Blair to Washington, and Jackson joined in the enthusiastic "summons." Blair was nearly penniless when he arrived in the capital, but he was almost immediately taken into the president's confidence, and there was little doubt but that Blair would support the administration as Green never had.[60]

The first issue of the *Globe*, Blair's paper, came out on December 7, 1830,[61] but the *Intelligencer* took no particular notice of the new publication until January 18, 1831. Gales and Seaton told their readers of the new paper under the "respected" editorship of Blair and praised the talents of this gentleman from Kentucky. They regretted, however, that he was working under the "particular auspices and protection of the personal friends of the President of the United States." The *Intelligencer* editors further informed their readers that serious discontent with the *Telegraph* had resulted because of Green's closeness to Calhoun.[62]

Shortly after the start of the *Globe* the split in the Jackson ranks became more apparent when the Peggy O'Neil Eaton affair[63] precipitated a crisis that saw Jackson's entire cabinet resign, either willingly or under force. Gales and Seaton expressed no opinion about Peggy Eaton, the tavernkeeper's daughter who had taken John H. Eaton, Jackson's secretary of war, for her second husband;[64] but members of their social circle were shocked and highly scornful of this young lady.[65]

Gales and Seaton briefly noted the breakup of the Jackson

---

59. Description given by John Rives, Blair's business partner in the *Globe*, June 23, 1856, quoted in Smith, *Francis Preston Blair Family*, p. 62.

60. Smith, *Francis Preston Blair Family*, pp. 63-67.

61. Ibid., p. 64.

62. *National Intelligencer*, January 18, 1831.

63. For an excellent picture of the Peggy Eaton affair, see Bassett, *Correspondence of Andrew Jackson*, vol. 4. A sizable portion of this volume deals with the subject. See also James, *Andrew Jackson*, pp. 202-13, 266-82.

64. *National Intelligencer*, October 17, 1829.

65. For a view of the older social circle of Washington regarding the Peggy Eaton affair, see Mrs. Samuel Harrison Smith, pp. 320-21.

cabinet, and the editors registered no surprise, although they admitted such mass resignations were unusual.[66] They gloated a few days later when they explained to their readers that they thought the disruption of the cabinet meant the end of the Jackson party. The factions headed by Calhoun and Van Buren could not be welded into a single party again, the editors wrote: "They have quarreled over the spoils, and are tearing one another to pieces."[67]

Actually the break in the party had come sooner than the cabinet resignations. The disclosure of Calhoun's criticism of Jackson's Florida campaign of 1818 brought the split between Jackson and Calhoun. The *Globe* emerged as the only administration organ, and Green's *Telegraph* became what it always had been: Calhoun's newspaper. Gales and Seaton watched the action, saw the *Globe* and the *Telegraph* hurl unflattering names at each other, and concluded it was a "spicy" affair.[68]

The day following the *Globe*'s elevation to official organ, the *Telegraph* announced that "Amos Kendall & Company have discontinued their subscription to the *Telegraph*. Ahem!"[69] Gales and Seaton knew what Green meant, for two years earlier the same act had signified that the *Intelligencer* was completely dropped from any official relationship to the Jackson administration.

With this severance, the *Telegraph* moved toward a closer alliance with the political forces Gales and Seaton supported, but there is little to indicate any change in relationship between the editors of the *Intelligencer* and the *Telegraph*. On the other hand, the *Globe* and the *Intelligencer* were nearly daily engaged in charges and countercharges on subjects ranging from politics to journalistic practices. Shortly after beginning publication, Blair accused Gales and Seaton of inaccuracy. The *Intelligencer* editors politely admitted that perhaps they had erred, because "as to our editorial articles, generally, they are neither studied nor labored, and we consider it no reproach to be reminded by our neighbor that they are sometimes imperfect. We believe that they are often so."[70]

66. *National Intelligencer*, April 21, 1831.
67. Ibid., April 26, 1831.
68. Ibid., March 31, 1831.
69. *Telegraph*, April 1, 1831.
70. *National Intelligencer*, February 12, 1831.

The second charge the *Globe* made against the *Intelligencer* editors was defamation of President Jackson. Again Gales and Seaton calmly explained that they had "always acceded to him great merit of a certain description whilst questioning his qualification for high civil employment. We have never treated him otherwise than as a gentleman," and since he was president they had not lost sight of the respect due the office. "If to doubt his infallibility be to defame him, then . . . we plead guilty to this arraignment."[71]

Much space in the *Intelligencer* formerly devoted to news now was given to attacks or defenses—usually defenses—involving the *Globe*. Gales and Seaton entered a new type of journalism—one neither liked nor fully understood. This was not the journalism for which they were trained. This was not political reporting, in their eyes, but political bickering.

At first Gales and Seaton were bewildered by this journalistic bundle of energy and nerves called Blair. The *Globe* did not seem dignified to the *Intelligencer* editors, and what was worse, it did not respect the dignity of the *Intelligencer*. Blair made fun of the opposition paper's short, staid editorials and said he was unable to grasp much from these writings. For this reason he called Gales "Joseph Surface"—meaning there was nothing under that which was immediately apparent.[72] The *Globe* always attacked Gales alone and never the two publishers. Blair's biographer contends that Blair would not attack Seaton, even though the *Intelligencer* editor was a political enemy.[73] The fact that Gales did most of the political writing also may account for this.

Even the *Intelligencer* took to belittling the reporting of its opposition. Gales and Seaton contended the *Globe* never gave but one side of an issue and completely biased the news to Blair's way of thinking: "We have already pointed out this vicious habit of suppressing one side of everything, so far as *The Debates* were concerned. The Official now appears to go farther still, and official documents are suppressed, if it dislike them."[74] Blair readily admitted he ran only the speeches of the Jacksonian Democrats.[75]

71. Ibid., February 19, 1831.
72. Smith, *Francis Preston Blair Family*, p. 80.
73. Ibid., p. 77.
74. *National Intelligencer*, May 1, 1832.
75. Smith, *Francis Preston Blair Family*, p. 80.

The newspaper situation in Washington confused many, and with the split between Calhoun and President Jackson subscribers became even more baffled. One subscriber wrote: "I took the National Intelligencer for thirteen years but when Gales and Seaton fastened their harness to the complicated machinery of Clay and Adams I unhitched mine from them and hitched them fast to Duff. . . ." Now what was he to do? the subscriber asked Blair.[76]

Not all Jackson supporters always approved of Blair's policies. An irate Irishman's tirade against Blair and the *Globe* would have been a good circulation builder for the *Intelligencer*. "For the Lord's sake can't Genl. J. get some other Editor than Blair in this hour of trial? Can't you manage, by hook or by crook, but buy up Gales & Seaton? If you do no better send to Europe & import some decent & talented man. There are a great many friends of the Administration, who wish to take a Government paper—but can't stand Blair. Some time ago, I offered a redhot Jackson man my Globe for his Intelligencer, & . . . he asked me $3 to boot!!!"[77]

Any attempts at empathy Gales and Seaton made during the first years of Jackson's administration gave way to tempered anger after 1830. This feeling intensified as such issues as the attack on the Bank of the United States and a plan of distribution of surplus profits were added.

As nearly as Gales and Seaton could tell from Jackson's messages, his main objects were to put down and replace the Bank of the United States with a government bank, "founded on public credit and revenues. . . ." Then, he would stop all expenditures for internal improvement for fear they might induce the continuance of a protective tariff. Further, he planned to distribute the treasury surplus among the states according to their representation in Congress. Last, he would "withdraw protection from Manufacturers lest it should produce a revenue which might induce a continuance of Internal Improvement—thus making the Tariff and Internal Improvement re-act upon each other. What a glorious system!"[78]

76. Tandy Collins to Francis P. Blair, July 17, 1831, Blair and Rives Papers, Washington, D.C.
77. Spencer O'Brien to unnamed correspondent, undated letter, Willie P. Mangum Papers, vol. 4, Library of Congress, Washington, D.C.
78. *National Intelligencer*, June 19, 1830.

These were the major differences between the editors and the president after two years of Jackson's administration. Gales and Seaton had taken a stand on all these points long before Jackson became president, so the editors could not be accused of opposing merely for the sake of opposition.

The subject of internal improvements was important to Gales and Seaton. The editors wrote and worked hard for more federal money to build up the country's transportation system. Jackson's veto of the bill for the Maysville Turnpike Road and the Rockville and Frederick Road gave Gales and Seaton ample evidence of where Jackson stood on the subject. They disagreed with Jackson that these projects were not national in character and resented Jackson's resort to the use of the veto. Further, they disliked the tone of the veto, which seemed to be aimed at the voters rather than at Congress. Was it just a campaign speech, they asked?[79]

The general's use of the veto further angered the editors. The veto seldom had been used in the history of the country, they claimed, and it should not be brought into action on the grounds of expediency—particularly in money matters. Why, even the King of England had not used his veto power for years, argued Gales and Seaton.[80] The reference to the King of England was the first time such a comparison between Jackson and despotism seems to have been made in the *Intelligencer*, but it was not the last. "King Andrew" became a familiar term to Gales and Seaton.

On one issue, however, Gales and Seaton could find no ground to criticize the president: nullification. The question, one on which Gales and Seaton had been suspicious of the president before election, became more and more debated and discussed as the nation moved into the early 1830s, and during this period one of the most famous debates on the state of the union took place: the Webster-Hayne debate. Gales and Seaton were tremendously impressed by Webster's words on this occasion, and Gales particularly felt a sense of personal participation in the great oratorical event.

Webster, after determining that he would answer the speech of Senator Hayne, sent a request for Gales personally to report the speech. Gales did, and his shorthand notes of

79. Ibid.
80. Ibid.

the debate are preserved at the Boston Public Library. The speech, as taken by Gales, was copied off by his wife and then revised by Webster, so the published form differs in several aspects from the message delivered in Congress.[81]

Gales and Seaton were so impressed with Webster's patriotic and nationalistic sentiments that shortly after the speech was published they chose the most famous lines, "Liberty and union, now and forever, one and inseparable," and placed them across their page-three editorial column, a practice continued through the period during which Gales and Seaton owned the *Intelligencer.*

But this moment of glory Gales shared with Webster was offset by the numerous disappointments Gales and Seaton experienced at the hands of the Jackson administration. On nearly all political subjects the editors found themselves in disagreement, but they looked forward to 1832, for with that election perhaps the country could be returned to a more desirable political path. But a strong issue was needed on which to battle Jackson. By late 1831 the point of opposition was determined, but it was one on which Gales and Seaton and their political cohorts were to suffer one of their most bitter political defeats.

---

81. Charles Lanman, *The Private Life of Daniel Webster* (New York, 1852), p. 145; Claude Moore Fuess, *Daniel Webster* (Boston, 1930), 1:383. Gales's notes are in a bound volume in the Boston Public Library. Fuess concluded that the speech as delivered and the one later published vary considerably because of Webster's extensive editing.

CHAPTER 11

The Bank War Begins

In the years immediately following 1831 Gales and Seaton were nearly obsessed with one great desire: to defeat and destroy Jackson politically. They felt Jackson was responsible not only for the political difficulties of the United States but for their personal misfortunes as well. Gales and Seaton agreed with Clay that one issue—the United States Bank—offered the greatest chance of defeating Jackson, and on this point they attempted to rally the diverse elements opposing the president. And on this subject, in many ways, the *Intelligencer* editors suffered their most humiliating defeat.

Gales and Seaton early made two important decisions concerning the election of 1832. They first resolved not to support Jackson, an action they probably never seriously considered. Their second conclusion was to support Clay. Responding to a query from Senator J. S. Johnston of Pennsylvania, Gales and Seaton unqualifiedly answered where the *Intelligencer* support would be placed: "We are, and have been, and as far as we know, ever shall be, for Mr. Clay, *and for no one else!* that is, not for McLean, or Calhoun, or any body now

191

named. If Mr. Clay's chances of election should be, by the artfulness of the antimasons, come to be desperate, it will be time enough for you & us to ask 'where shall we go?' "[1]

Their choice of Clay was extremely logical for Gales and Seaton, for by this time the editors supported Clay's American System nearly as strongly as its author. His views on the tariff, on internal improvements, on federal land policies, on nullification, and on sectional conflicts coincided with Gales's and Seaton's ideas, and in addition, the editors and the Kentucky politician agreed that the United States Bank was essential to the country's economic development.

The neutral role the United States Bank's president, Nicholas Biddle, attempted to play in the hopes of winning Jackson's support for the institution was being sorely tested by 1831.[2] Biddle greatly feared the bank might become a political issue, a fear supported by Clay.[3] But, by November of 1831 Clay had decided to push for an immediate application for a new charter. Following the National Republican party convention in December, 1831, there was little question that the bank would be the political issue in the 1832 campaign, and Biddle had only to decide how and when the bank would become the rallying point.[4]

Gales and Seaton did not occupy a strategy-planning role in relation to the bank but rather executed the policies arrived at by Biddle and political supporters of the bank. What they had done for Madison during the War of 1812, Gales and Seaton now attempted to do for Biddle and the bank. The editors watched Jackson's action in relation to the bank,[5] but in their own course they took no stand without Biddle's approval. It is difficult to ascertain how much their financial dependence on the bank determined this policy.

Both Gales and Seaton early decided that since they were

1. Gales and Seaton to J. S. Johnston, September 10, 1831, Johnston Papers, Historical Society of Pennsylvania, Philadelphia.

2. For an account of Biddle's views during the first years of Jackson's administration, see Ralph C. H. Catterall, *The Second Bank of the United States* (Chicago, 1903), pp. 186-214.

3. For Clay's views, see Clay to Francis Brooke, May 23, 1830, quoted in Calvin Colton, ed., *Works of Henry Clay* (New York, 1897), 4:270-71.

4. Catterall, *Second Bank*, pp. 215-23.

5. For a discussion of Jackson's feeling toward the bank, see Marquis James, *Andrew Jackson: Portrait of a President* (Indianapolis, 1937), pp. 350-85; Arthur M. Schlesinger, Jr., *The Age of Jackson* (Boston, 1945), pp. 74-114.

heavily indebted to the institution and since the United States Bank owned the building occupied by the *Intelligencer*, their safest policy was to avoid editorial comment on the subject. Only when Biddle personally approved the publication of material did the editors include it in their paper.[6]

This policy probably was wise, because as early as September 20, 1830, Green's *Telegraph* carried strong insinuations about the *Intelligencer's* tie to the bank. Green, who after his break with the Jackson administration supported the bank and borrowed frequently from it, was certain the bank financed the *Intelligencer* editors to the point where Gales's home, Eckington, was built from these funds. Green wrote: "Is the Intelligencer a free press? Could it live one single week, if it were not fed by the Bank of the United States? Has not the senior editor retired into the country to a splendid house *built* for him by the Bank? Is not the office in which the Intelligencer is printed the property of the Bank? Can such a press be free?"[7]

Although Biddle had not determined definitely in 1831 when he would seek recharter of the bank, he had decided that any such effort would need strong propaganda support from leading newspapers. To win this backing Biddle granted favors, and Gales and Seaton were among the recipients. First, they were allowed to continue borrowing money, but in order to prevent the Jacksonians from being too aware of this relationship, all financial dealings between the editors and the bank were supposed to be carried out through the main office in Philadelphia. Biddle cautioned Gales and Seaton that they had been warned to make "your negotiation with the Bank *here*, so that it need not necessarily pass [through] any other channels." The editors had not complied. "This you prevent by your note received this morning, which is in fact a *check* by you on the Bank, not a *promise*. Believing it more agreeable to you to have the loan with us than elsewhere, I annex that form for that purpose. . . ."[8]

Fortunately for Gales and Seaton, Biddle believed the public support for the bank could be won through an educational

6. R. D. Smith to Biddle, February 12, 1831, Biddle Letterbooks, no. 3, Library of Congress, Washington, D.C.

7. *Telegraph*, September 20, 1830.

8. Biddle to Gales and Seaton, June 11, 1831, Biddle Letterbooks, no. 3.

program carried out in the newspapers and through pamphlets and other published documents. Biddle held firm to the view that if people were told the truth, the bank would triumph: "I believe that nine tenths of the errors of men arise from their ignorance, and that the great security of all our institutions is in the power, the irresistible power, of truth."[9]

Gales, too, had faith in the power of newspapers, especially his own, but he disdained the general intelligence of subscribers. Responding to a compliment from Biddle about a piece of writing in the *Intelligencer*, Gales explained he was intentionally obscure. "We used such language as would be likely to catch the attention of those who do not reflect—being nine-tenths of readers generally, and one-half perhaps of the readers of the Intelligencer."[10]

This propaganda campaign which Biddle began early in 1831 provided an important source of income for Gales and Seaton but also gave the bank's enemies a potent charge against the institution. Thousands of extra copies of the *Intelligencer*, sent throughout the country at bank expense, stressed the importance of the bank to the economic structure of the United States. At first some pretense was made that the extras sent out by the bank contained information on both sides of the issue. The first *Intelligencer* extra contained not only an article supporting the bank but also an attack on it by Thomas Hart Benton, the antibank senator from Missouri. Gales and Seaton confided to Biddle that they were sure Benton's speech never would be read. The bank paid the *Intelligencer* $500 for 10,000 copies of this issue.[11]

At the same time Gales compiled a mailing list for the bank, made up primarily of the *Intelligencer*'s subscription roster but also including names of leading men in various states. Gales was impressed with his paper's circulation and mentioned his pleasure to Biddle: "It is a curiosity, even to myself to look over. The most remarkable thing in it is the number of Insurance and Bank Companies, Athenaeums Reading Rooms (besides that every village Printing office is a Reading Room)

9. Biddle to Gales, Jr., March 2, 1831, Miscellaneous Collection, New York Public Library, New York.

10. Gales, Jr., to Biddle, March 31, 1831, Biddle Papers, vol. 26, Library of Congress, Washington, D.C.

11. Gales and Seaton to Biddle, February 13, 1831, Biddle Papers, vol. 26.

which it contains: And the best is, that the lowest number of copies sent into any one State of the union is 18 (Rh. Island). Perhaps no periodical in the world ever had so effective a circulation."[12] Gales cautioned Biddle to keep the list confidential and also informed him that the bank would be billed for $50 to cover the work of preparing the list.[13] Biddle failed to understand Gales's bill for the circulation list and protested that he was overcharged. At the same time Biddle acknowledged a $1,000 printing job the *Intelligencer* editors were completing.[14]

Gales explained that the additional charges were for compiling the subscription list, a task that had taken a good deal of time. Gales agreed that the keen interest of the *Intelligencer* editors in the bank issue probably should have compelled them to furnish the list for nothing, but the paper needed money too badly to allow this.[15]

By June the *Intelligencer* editors printed another order for the bank: 25,000 copies sent primarily to Missouri and New Hampshire.[16] The largest printing for the bank handled by Gales and Seaton evidently was an order for 50,000 extras printed in 1834.[17] By then the price for 100 pamphlets was raised to six dollars, and competition for the printing was keen among the newspapers supporting the bank.[18]

J. G. Watmough, Pennsylvania representative and agent for the bank who placed many of the printing orders, was not sure the results of the large printings justified the expenditure. He felt printers were " 'pretty much all alike—let them handle the money, *au diable*, the rest.' "[19] Watmough continued, however, to approve the orders and sought earnestly to keep peace between the printers fighting for the bank's printing orders.[20]

Green, especially, was jealous of the amount of bank printing Gales and Seaton received. Since the *Telegraph's* support

12. Gales, Jr., to Biddle, March 18, 1831, Biddle Papers, vol. 26.
13. Ibid.
14. Biddle to Gales, Jr., March 29, 1831, Biddle Letterbooks, no. 3.
15. Gales, Jr., to Biddle, March 31, 1831, Biddle Papers, vol. 26.
16. Gales, Jr., to Biddle, June 23, 1831, Biddle Papers, vol. 27.
17. Gales and Seaton to Biddle, April 11, 1834, Biddle Papers, vol. 48.
18. Gales and Seaton to J. G. Watmough, January 15, 1834, Biddle Papers, vol. 45.
19. J. G. Watmough to Biddle, February 7, 1834, quoted in Catterall, *Second Bank*, p. 267.
20. J. G. Watmough to Biddle, January 15, 1834, Biddle Papers, vol. 45.

also was important, Biddle was disturbed by the rumors of dissatisfaction and immediately placed a sizable printing order with Green. Biddle admitted he wanted no ill will among the persons whom "we all esteem so much."[21]

Watmough thought Biddle placed too high a premium on Green's support and wrote accordingly: "It is a great assistance to Green, to be sure. He is at best however but a *mauvais sujet*, and scarcely worth what has already been done for him."[22]

The distribution of extras had its humorous aspects. On at least one occasion Gales succeeded in publishing an extra containing mostly speeches highly favorable to the bank with only one speech in opposition. The extras were sent out under the frank of a "good Jackson-man in Congress," so Gales was sure that a good many Jacksonians were reading the *Intelligencer* for the first time.[23]

Biddle's program of distributing extras was criticized severely both by Jackson supporters and by friends of the bank. Mathew Carey, writer and economist of the first half of the nineteenth century, thought most pamphlets and printings were nearly worthless as far as winning bank support was concerned.[24]

The "Government Bank Directors" reached much the same conclusion and issued a report condemning the huge amounts of money spent by the bank for such printing. Among the bills cited in the director's critical report were several paid to Gales and Seaton. One for $1,300 the *Intelligencer* editors received for distributing Albert Gallatin's *Consideration on the Currency and Banking System of the United States*, published in 1831, was noted. Also mentioned was another $1,176 paid to Gales and Seaton for two thousand copies of an unnamed pamphlet and another $800 for printing a committee report.[25]

21. Biddle to Watmough, January 15, 1834, Biddle Letterbooks, no. 5.
22. Watmough to Biddle, February 7, 1834, quoted in Catterall, *Second Bank*, p. 267.
23. Gales, Jr., to William McIlVaine, May 19, 1832, Miscellaneous Collection, New York Public Library.
24. M. Carey to directors of the Bank of the United States, March 28, 1834, quoted in Catterall, *Second Bank*, p. 266.
25. The Government Bank Directors to Jackson, August 19, 1833, quoted in John Spencer Bassett, ed., *Correspondence of Andrew Jackson* (Washington, D.C., 1931), 5: 162-63.

Jackson was sure that such expenditures on the part of the bank were illegal on grounds that "one fifth of these funds belonged to the Treasury of the U. States, and could not be legally appropriated by the Bank to such purposes."[26] Jackson's editor, Blair, claimed the bank had spent enough money on printing by Gales and Seaton and Green and on mailing these articles to "have paid off the Post office Debt."[27]

Complaints concerning the printing Gales and Seaton did for the bank were among the least of the troubles the editors faced with regard to the bank during the period from 1831 to 1835, for the political battle the editors waged to save the institution probably was one of the most trying of their lives. At about the same time that Gales and Seaton started to receive the printing orders from Biddle they began their editorial campaign for renewal of the bank charter.[28] They waged a subtle campaign at the beginning, attempting to show the economic chaos that would result if the charter were not renewed. In the eyes of the editors this was "the strongest ground to take. . . ." More could be accomplished for the bank by pointing out the "hideousness of the features of the political engines professed as a substitute for it, which you well know would be the Trojan horse admitted into the citadel of the Republic. This stand would be particularly good with . . . men of intelligence and experience in business."[29]

By the fall of 1831 the strategy for defending the bank took shape, and short skirmishes started between opponents and supporters. Biddle attempted to lure the *Globe* editors into publishing an account of Monroe's appraisal of the bank which then could be copied in the *Intelligencer* as an example of the *Globe*'s inconsistency on the subject. The *Globe* editors failed to comply, and Biddle secretly asked Gales to publish the letter. "You will not, however," he added, "say or write any thing about the circumstance, which you will have the goodness to confine to yourself."[30]

Gales agreed and commented in a letter to Biddle that Mon-

26. Jackson's Charges Against the Bank, September, 1833, quoted in Bassett, *Correspondence of Andrew Jackson*, 5:175.
27. Francis P. Blair to Jackson, August 18, 1834, quoted in Bassett, *Correspondence of Andrew Jackson*, p. 284.
28. *National Intelligencer*, March 12, 1831.
29. Gales, Jr., to Biddle, March 31, 1831, Biddle Papers, vol. 26.
30. Biddle to Gales, Jr., September 12, 1831, Biddle Letterbooks, no. 4.

roe's letter was a noble document and would have important influence if "truth or reason had any influence over our public men, or, I might almost add, over our people; but that would be treason against the maxim of Republics, *Vox populi vox dei.*"[31] Gales was sure Jackson could be defeated and the bank saved if the "People" could be reached with the truth. But the press was closed, the editor said. The *Intelligencer*, however, rather than losing circulation, was gaining "without any exertion or solicitation direct or indirect. . . ."[32]

By late 1831 Clay and his followers were pushing hard for recharter.[33] Clay hoped to create a situation in which he could trap Jackson no matter which way he turned. Clay felt certain sufficient support existed to pass the measure over Jackson's veto. However, if bank supporters waited until Jackson was reelected before trying for the recharter, matters would be different.

Biddle's mind was not made up as yet on pushing the recharter, and if there had been a chance of Jackson's accepting a modified charter for the bank, Biddle would not have minded robbing Clay of this important political issue. Jackson, however, showed no such willingness, and by January 6 Biddle set the congressional machinery in motion to attempt to push through a recharter.[34]

The *Intelligencer* editors immediately took the cue and began strong agitation for the recharter. At the same time Gales and Seaton also attempted to create a situation whereby it would be difficult for Jackson to veto the measure should it pass Congress. Thomas Ritchie, of the *Richmond Enquirer*, one of the oldest and most active sparring partners of Gales and Seaton, was sure that Jackson would veto the recharter measure. Gales and Seaton feigned disbelief: "Now we desire to know, explicitly, whether, if a bill for a Bank shall pass both Houses, the President of the United States will disregard such an expression of *the public will, clearly ascertained . . .* and oppose his sole will to that of the People of the United States?"[35]

The ties between Gales and Seaton and the bank became stronger as the editors continued to borrow to meet publish-

31. Gales, Jr., to Biddle, September 31, 1831, Biddle Papers, vol. 26.
32. Ibid.
33. Clay to Biddle, December 15, 1831, Biddle Papers, vol. 27.
34. Catterall, *Second Bank*, pp. 219-21.
35. *National Intelligencer*, January 5, 1832.

ing expenses until the *American State Papers* paid dividends. While the move for recharter was getting underway Gales pleaded for more credit from Biddle. The editor apologized for having to resort to frequent borrowing, but he had to have $2,000 on January 11, for which he promised "we shall apply for no additional accommodation." Gales explained that if the bank did not provide the money he would have to borrow from political friends, which he could not do without "sacrificing the political independence to which our paper owes all its influence." Gales emphasized to Biddle that the *Intelligencer* had taken its stand on the bank issue "before you had rendered us any favor, and is not to be affected by circumstances."[36]

By April Biddle and Gales were somewhat concerned by possible investigations concerning the bank's conduct in relation to the newspapers. Biddle assured Gales the bank's report gave only that information "deemed proper in order to prevent any misconception of the subject."[37] But even the portent of such investigations did not stop Gales and Seaton from resorting to the bank for money, despite their promise in January that a loan then would remove the necessity for further borrowing. On May 17 Gales attempted to reassure Biddle that the *American State Papers* publishing would yield enough to cover the debts incurred, and Gales added that Webster felt Congress would increase the number of volumes it was expected to purchase. Gales thought his firm would realize a profit of "between five & ten-fold" on the $10,000 they had invested. All this preceded Gales's real purpose in writing: the need for $6,000. Biddle was assured that at least one note with the bank would be retired within sixty days.[38]

A week later Gales and Seaton wrote the bank requesting a three-month extension of a $10,000 loan. The note was due on June 4, but the editors explained that this date had been arbitrarily set and that a renewal was needed.[39]

These loans and extensions were not sufficient to keep the *Intelligencer* editors in business, and on June 4 Gales again

36. Gales, Jr., to Biddle, January 11, 1832, Biddle Papers, vol. 30.
37. Biddle to Gales, Jr., April 19, 1832, Biddle Letterbooks, No. 4.
38. Gales, Jr., to Biddle, May 17, 1832, Simon Gratz Collection, Historical Society of Pennsylvania, Philadelphia.
39. Gales and Seaton to J. Andrews, May 24, 1832, Dreere Collection, Bank of the United States, Historical Society of Pennsylvania, Philadelphia.

wrote Biddle for an additional loan of $3,000 for ten months which was necessary for "paying off arrears of wages & making fair weather with the paper-makers." Gales also warned Biddle that the number of extra papers sent out should be watched, for the editor feared a protest from the postal department.[40]

In addition, Gales informed Biddle that the identity of another of Jackson's close confidantes in relation to the bank was becoming less and less secret. Gales was certain that a good portion of the public statements Jackson had made on the bank was written by Nicholas P. Trist, son-in-law of Jefferson and a Jacksonian partisan. Trist was brought into the State Department by Clay and then later adopted by Jackson. Gales was sure Trist "has been found very useful to the President —besides that, being bred & married a *Jeffersonian*, he is good authority to the old gentleman for what his letters . . . contain, & he can *sign his name* to them without distrust of their orthodox 'Jeffersonian Republicanism.' "[41]

The battle for the recharter of the bank continued during the early part of the summer, with the Senate passing the recharter measure on June 11 by a 28-20 vote.[42] On July 3 the House approved it by a 107-85 vote.[43] On July 10 President Jackson issued his veto of the bank measure and thus assured Clay and the National Republicans that the bank was the central campaign issue in 1832. Jackson's attack criticized both the financial dealings of the bank as well as its constitutionality, much to the bitter resentment of the institution's supporters. The *Intelligencer* editors wrote: ". . . upon a survey of the whole of the message, we discover that, in fact, the bill is considered unconstitutional, mainly because the President has not, instead of Congress, been allowed to mould its features and to make the law."[44] Gales and Seaton failed to mention that Biddle was quite willing to incorporate some of Jackson's ideas if it meant saving the bank.[45]

40. Gales, Jr., to Biddle, June 4, 1832, Biddle Papers, vol. 27.
41. Ibid.
42. *Senate Journal*, Twenty-Second Congress, First Session (Washington, D.C., 1832), p. 345.
43. *House Journal*, Twenty-Second Congress, First Session (Washington, D.C., 1832), p. 1074.
44. *National Intelligencer*, July 14, 1832.
45. Catterall, *Second Bank*, pp. 233-38.

These were dark times, indeed, for Gales and Seaton. Their financial problems remained, and the editors struggled to continue publishing. Then, to make matters worse, the *Globe* began a series in July accusing the *Intelligencer* of being merely a tool of the bank.[46] On August 4 Blair stepped up his attacks in response to a charge that Gales made that many of the extras printed by the *Globe* were paid for by the Jackson administration. Blair responded: "We have no faith in the Intelligencer's Bank patriotism, although we will not insist that his EXTRAS are paid by the Bank, directly, yet the editors know too much about its course, to suppose that it will allow their coffers to be emptied in its cause, without remuneration." Blair also confided to his readers that he recently learned the *Intelligencer* debt to the bank was increased to $40,000.[47]

Gales and Seaton thought the *Globe*'s accusations were unfair: "The Editor of the Official seeks to escape defeat in public controversy on public questions by the vulgar resort to allusions to the personal affairs of his opponents. We should think he might find enough to do in his own private affairs, without intruding himself into ours." Although the *Intelligencer* editors claimed the allegations were false,[48] they were not.

Even while contending that their relations to the bank were only those of any ordinary client, Gales wrote—indeed, pleaded—with Biddle not to cut off credit. The *Intelligencer* editor realized the relations between the paper and the bank were under close scrutiny. "We are fully aware that our account with you is full; but, believe me, who knows better than any body else, that you have not a better debt of the same amount." But, Gales continued, they needed more money. Their firm had taken in between $30,000 and $40,000, but that money had paid off "the first purposes of the trust. . . ." This referred to old debts, back pay, and paper debts. Gales was desperate. He would have come to Philadelphia to talk to Biddle in person, but Seaton was absent from town. "What can be done?" he asked. "Is it in your power to aid us without committing yourself or the cause? If we had resolutely de-

46. See *Globe*, July 21, July 30, August 7, and August 9, 1832.
47. Ibid., August 4, 1832.
48. *National Intelligencer*, August 7, 1832.

clined paying off old debts at present, we should be in no
difficulty, as it is, 5000 dollars will put us beyond difficulty." He expected more than that amount would be erased
before Christmas.[49]

While Gales pleaded for support the *Globe* continued its
attack by alleging that the bank owned the *Intelligencer* and
that Gales and Seaton had no control over the editorial policy
regarding the bank—that policy was dictated by the bank.
Gales and Seaton strongly denied the charge but admitted
they owed the bank. The debt, however, was no more than
their business called for, they said, and the loans were made
on business principles. In making the loans "the Bank is doing a good business . . ." and received proper security with
interest paid promptly. The editors assured their readers that
"we are doing no wrong, moral or legal, in borrowing from
it; and that, whoever impeaches our motives in that particular, or asserts that we are influenced in our opposition to the
detestable principles of the Veto by our dealings with the
Bank, is guilty of an unqualified truth."[50]

Although requests for funds from the bank were eased by
September of 1832, correspondence between Biddle and
Gales and Seaton continued. Evidently Biddle regarded the
Intelligencer editorials highly, or was not above flattery to insure the continued support of the paper. Concerning the
writer of a letter, Biddle remarked, "His greatest merit in my
eyes is that he subscribes to the Intelligencer, for nothing can
be more crude than his notions about banking, except perhaps
his speculation about politics."[51]

Gales and Seaton had welcomed the bank issue in the campaign of 1832 as the one point on which Jackson might be
defeated. The editors believed during that spring that Jackson
was doomed for defeat, and they probably never were more
inaccurate than when they thought the general might be willing to be somewhat conciliatory toward his strongest opposition—even the *Intelligencer*. Gales wrote Biddle: "The good
old General, I believe, is in great trouble at the present state
of things, and you will be surprised to hear that I believe he
would, after *all our* opposition to the mad measures of his

49. Gales, Jr., to Biddle, August 8, 1832, Simon Gratz Collection.
50. *National Intelligencer*, September 18, 1832.
51. Biddle to Gales, Jr., September 20, 1832, Biddle Letterbooks, no. 4.

Admn., be glad even now to lean upon us for support if we would *let* him. The richmond enquirer is in the wind, all sail fluttering. If it were not for *antimasonary*, our success would be beyond doubt; and even as it is I hardly doubt it."[52]

The anti-Masonic note referred to another of the key issues in the 1832 campaign. The anti-Masonic group drew important votes away from Clay, himself a Mason, and in New England, particularly, divided the National Republican party. Gales and Seaton wanted to give unqualified support to Clay, but at the same time they could not afford to alienate the Anti-Masons opposing Clay.

A personal problem was involved. Seaton was a Mason; Gales was not. Seaton and Clay had worked together in the Masonic Lodge as early as 1822 in publishing a pamphlet on lodge activities.[53] Therefore the *Intelligencer* editors did not agree on the stand to take regarding the Masonic issue. Gales and Seaton ignored the subject as much as possible, and never did the editorial columns of the *Intelligencer* contain an opinion on the subject.

Both Gales and Seaton regretted the insertion of the highly inflammable subject of Masonry into the campaign, for even the vital issue of the United States Bank was affected by the attack on the fraternal organization. Gales commiserated with Biddle on the disastrous possibilities that could result.[54]

Gales had no real sympathy with the Masonic Lodge, and not being sure of Biddle's sentiments, the editor guarded his language fairly closely. Gales, however, was completely out of sympathy with men who made a fanatic defense of the fraternal organization to the point where Gales considered them mentally deranged. Gales continued by expressing the belief that without the "anti-masonic excitement I have no doubt that we should now carry even your State: for truly the Administration is 'in a blaze of glory'—aye, a confusing blaze."[55]

Gales worked closely with Clay in trying to gloss over and

52. Gales, Jr., to Biddle, June 4, 1832, Biddle Papers, vol. 27.
53. Masonry Pamphlet, Clay Papers, vol. 3, Library of Congress, Washington, D.C.
54. Gales, Jr., to Biddle, June 23, 1831, Biddle Papers, vol. 27.
55. Ibid.

play down the candidate's Masonic activities. Gales reminded Clay that the editor was not a Mason, "though not fool enough to be an Antimason."[56]

The *Globe* played on the known differences between Gales and Seaton regarding the Masonic Lodge. The *Globe* wondered how Gales would "accommodate himself to the double aspect of his party. Like Mr. Clay, the Seaton Editor, the man who *issues* the Intelligencer, is a full blown mason. But ground is taken by his writing partner in an editorial as 'an ANTI-MASON,' GALES rubs down his brother SEATON, the mason. And the latter leans to the curry-comb, as if he expected to thrive by it."[57]

Gales and Seaton carried their policy of evading the Masonic issue to the point of refusing articles on the subject from such esteemed men as John Quincy Adams. They reminded Adams that they had published one of his letters on the subject[58] and would publish no more. They advised him to send the letter to another reputable paper engaged in the conflict, because they felt they had not entered this fray.[59] After months of debate, however, the *Intelligencer* editors gave in to Adams's request and published the letter.[60]

Politics during this period manifested itself in many ways and the *Intelligencer*'s perennial object of criticism, the postal department, received special attention from Gales and Seaton during the campaign of 1832. The *Intelligencer* editors wrote that complaints from all quarters of the country contended the *Intelligencer* was received irregularly while there was a deluge of "extra" *Globes*. Gales and Seaton thought it was time to start complaining about such abuses lest the circulation of independent papers be stopped altogether: "We hear from New York and New Hampshire that many of the country post offices are in such a state, that if our subscribers get one-half of their papers they consider themselves well off."[61]

56. Gales, Jr., to Clay, August 27, 1831, Clay Papers, vol. 17.

57. *Globe*, June 14, 1831.

58. John Quincy Adams's diary, April 9, 1833, *Memoirs of John Quincy Adams, comprising portions of his diary from 1795-1848*, ed. Charles Francis Adams (Philadelphia, 1875), 8:539.

59. *National Intelligencer*, April 30, 1833.

60. *National Intelligencer*, September 11, 1833.

61. Ibid., August 30, 1832.

Gales and Seaton accused the Jackson postmasters of delaying or destroying the *Intelligencer*, and similar complaints were made on the opposite side. S. E. Parker of Northampton County, Virginia, complained that though he subscribed to the *Intelligencer*, he opposed the political leanings of the paper. Regarding delivery, he thought it strange "that the Intelligencer should arrive here regularly, & the Globe always fail. . . . There are certainly some Anti-Jackson P. Masters in the mail route from Washington to this place." And to make things worse, Parker continued, the *Intelligencer* editors printed only the news they chose, thus giving their readers a distorted picture of happenings in Washington.[62] The accusations were not new and typified the charges made by partisans on both sides.

Gales and Seaton made little of any issue in the campaign except the bank. They favored Jackson's policy on nullification, both before the election of 1832 and in the months immediately following. Nullification, which had raised its head in South Carolina in 1832, again received strong support from the dominant party in that state in response to the new tariff. Gales and Seaton were impatient with the South Carolina demands for lowering the tariff, and before the passage of the 1832 measure the editors announced their stand: "We do not expect or wish Congress to pursue any course so suicidal as to sacrifice *the principle of protection*, as demanded by the unanimous resolution of the South Carolina Convention,[63] though we have no hope of satisfying the leaders of that party short of it."[64] Gales and Seaton compared the temper of South Carolina to widespread delusion and advised it be treated like "all mental disorders," with sympathy rather than harshness.[65]

By July 14 the tariff bill had passed both houses and was lauded by Gales and Seaton despite the fact that the new bill still contained many sections odious to the antitariff segments rising in the South. The *Intelligencer* editors praised the bill as a great compromise and thought the action redeemed a

62. S. E. Parker to Editor of the *Globe*, September 7, 1832, Blair and Rives Papers, Library of Congress, Washington, D.C.
63. Charles M. Wiltse, *John C. Calhoun, Nullifier, 1829-1839* (Indianapolis, 1949), pp. 143-53.
64. *National Intelligencer*, April 14, 1832.
65. Ibid.

Congress that had done little during the session. "Great and meritorious, and patriotic, have been the concessions to alleged suffering in one part of the country, by their brethren in another. May their extent be appreciated!"[66]

The tariff, of course, was not viewed by the Nullifiers as a compromise, and loud cries of mistreatment and the flag of nullification were raised by the latter part of July. Gales and Seaton reacted impatiently. How could Calhoun have changed so much in his views between 1816 and 1832? They were annoyed that their southern friends could not support Clay for the presidency because of the Kentuckian's view on slavery.[67]

The tariff and nullification issues were not settled until after the election, and Gales and Seaton momentarily forgot their vehement party views against Jackson and strongly supported his Proclamation and Force Bill actions.[68] His opening message to Congress was termed "subdued and not undignified," nearly extravagant praise for Jackson as far as Gales and Seaton were concerned. Jackson's Proclamation against the Nullifiers of South Carolina was described as a "powerful composition" which "cannot fail to produce a great sensation; whether for good or for evil we have some doubt—for we cannot permit ourselves to doubt that it originated in the best intentions."[69]

Gales and Seaton had little to say about the Force bill, which occupied Congress during February, 1833, nor did they write many leaders about the compromise tariff bill Clay introduced. The editors were relieved, however, when the compromise passed. They wrote: "Thus ends a much vexed and trying question, if it shall so end."[70] Their stand on nullification did result in loss of southern subscribers and the bulk of their circulation was in that area.[71]

But, it was neither the anti-Masonic movement nor nullification that was of major concern to the editors during the campaign of 1832. It was the bank, and the editors at least professed to believe that here they had a winning issue. With-

66. Ibid, July 31, 1832.
67. Ibid.
68. James, *Andrew Jackson*, pp. 320-24.
69. *National Intelligencer*, December 11, 1832.
70. Ibid., February 27, 1833.
71. Ibid., March 23, 1839, and November 6, 1839.

out the Masonic subject, it would have been a certainty, they wrote. But even if Clay were defeated, perhaps there would be sufficient support to carry the bank through. Gales wrote: "We begin to believe that we have nothing to fear from the Cause but the treachery of . . . friends. . . ."[72]

The November decision clearly went to Jackson, and Gales and Seaton must have cringed at how wrong their political calculations had been. The Jackson victory was a great defeat to Clay and Biddle, as well as to the *Intelligencer* editors. But the charter did not expire for four years, and Gales and Seaton and other bank supporters took solace from that fact.

---

72. Gales and Seaton to J. S. Johnston, October 12, 1832, Johnston Papers.

CHAPTER 12

The Bank's Demise

In the spring of 1832 Gales and Seaton faced an uncertain political future, and they worried about what the next four years under Jackson might bring. Fortunately their financial situation had improved since 1828, for publication of the *American State Papers* had eased the extreme financial pressures that had plagued them during much of Jackson's first term. The editors still possessed, however, a nearly consuming desire to destroy Jackson politically and to prevent him from ruining the nation economically by closing the United States Bank.

Gales and Seaton realized that Jackson's defeat would require strong leadership. They wondered where they could find a man who possessed the qualities necessary to weld the diverse elements opposing Jackson into a solid unit. The *Intelligencer* was devoted to Clay's American System, but the 1832 election clearly indicated that Clay was not powerful enough to defeat the Jacksonian party. Webster, a strong ally of the bank, was the next most logical choice for Gales and Seaton. But somehow neither the *Intelligencer* nor the nation could get a strong movement underway for the New Englander. Calhoun, friendly to the editors while he served in the Monroe cabinet, was completely unacceptable because of his nullification views, although his forceful opposition to Jackson was needed.

The Whig party, which emerged from the diverse elements opposed to Jackson, was a strange political body. As members of the party, Gales and Seaton found themselves associated with elements that opposed the editors' entire political and economic program: a national bank, protective tariff, internal improvements, and a strong federal government. The unwieldy body had no recognized leader, and like Gales and Seaton, could do little more than negate the program of the hated Jackson.

Although the elements were diverse, one common element besides opposition to Jackson bound them together: they looked backward to the maintenance of a society that had existed, rather than forward to a newly constructed social system. Whig leaders represented the factions that had played important roles in shaping the United States of 1833. These factions were not ready to surrender or change their social values. As one writer has characterized this philosophy: "The Whiggish view looked back to a society embodying the Lockean liberalism of the eighteenth century. In it, all affairs, political or otherwise, moved under the effective control of sagacious men, each within his own locality sufficiently preeminent economically, intellectually, and socially to transcend immediate popular control even if the franchise were widely distributed."[1]

Gales and Seaton, while taking a more national view than many of the leaders of the Whig party, nevertheless had much in common with the "locally based, socially secure, political leadership" that characterized much of the Whig party.[2] The nation's capital rather than an individual state provided the basis of operation for the *Intelligencer* editors, but they had assumed the same type of aristocratic position that many Whig leaders held in other sections of the nation.

The *Intelligencer* editors sensed little of the movement for

1. Lynn L. Marshall, "The Strange Stillbirth of the Whig Party," *American Historical Review* 72 (January, 1967): 462.
2. Ibid., pp. 463-64.

change that had helped the Jacksonians to handily win the elections of 1828 and 1832. No better examples of the Whig philosophy could be found than in Clay's American System and the Second United States Bank. Both were designed to benefit the whole of society from a national center, while at the same time being closely tied to local social establishments.[3] Internal improvement and local manufacturing interests were to be the benefactors of the American System. Each of the bank's branches centered in the local area and drew from the aristocracy for its leadership. This old system was found unsatisfactory by many and in the drive for political as well as social perfectability Americans moved on to new experiments, making those who clung to the past seem dated.

Personal financial problems continued to dominate the lives of the *Intelligencer* editors and their strong political defense of their main financial support—the bank—did little to enhance the position of the *Intelligencer* among the Jacksonian supporters between 1832 and 1836. Before the election of 1832 was scarcely over, and despite promises that they would not borrow more money, Gales and Seaton again went to Biddle for financial aid to keep the *Intelligencer* in business. They needed $3,000 to pay a paper bill to a Mr. Craig of New York. They hated to bother Biddle, but since "this is a lean time of the year for newspaper establishments, we cannot, until the income which the sessions of Congress usually bring, place us in funds, raise for him the sum he needs. . . ."[4]

The following month Gales and Seaton realized that accusations the *Globe* made against the *Intelligencer's* relationship with the bank during the campaign of 1832 were not forgotten. Blair made much of the charge that the *Intelligencer* editors were allowed to overdraw their account with the bank. Gales and Seaton labeled this a falsehood "as base and infamous as the publications which the Official paper is engaged in daily making concerning the Bank itself. We can say nothing worse of it."[5]

The bitterest battle with the *Globe* lay ahead, as Blair con-

3. Ibid., p. 464.

4. Gales and Seaton to Biddle, November 22, 1832, Biddle Papers, vol. 36, Library of Congress, Washington, D.C.

5. *National Intelligencer*, December 14, 1832.

tinued to drive home the charge that the bank really owned the *Intelligencer*. People were urged to disregard the *Intelligencer*'s views because Gales and Seaton were nothing but puppets of Biddle. The ideas expressed by Gales and Seaton were Biddle's, the *Globe* editor contended, and the *Intelligencer* editors long since had ceased to speak independently.[6]

Gales and Seaton, of course, denied all this, claiming Biddle never had written anything on the bank or on any other subject for the *Intelligencer*. "It is not true," they said, "that the National Intelligencer is the 'organ' of the Bank. It is worse than untrue that it is 'paid' by the Bank either 'well or ill.' "[7]

Feelings became even more heated before the 1833 congressional session passed. Since 1829 the *Intelligencer* had received no congressional contracts, as Duff Green held a monopoly on this printing. Green was able to remain in Washington and edit his *Telegraph* as the official organ for the nullifiers because of this congressional printing income. His support after 1831, he realized, was not from the Jackson men, for he spoke bitterly of his former leader: "The Jackson policy had been to denounce every one who has had the independence to disapprove of any measure or to condemn any act of the administration—They have organised [*sic*] the press and . . . have so drilled their party that Jackson can make or unmake members of Congress. . . ."[8]

Green felt that he was persecuted by the Jackson men and believed the loss of federal patronage cost him $5,000 yearly. Should he lose the congressional printing, he would be forced to leave Washington unless the South could devise a plan to help him. Green was certain an agreement existed between friends of Clay and Van Buren to split the printing between the *Globe* and the *Intelligencer*, thus forcing out the *Telegraph*.[9]

After 1833 Green stood little chance of receiving a congressional contract. In the Senate, Blair and Rives scored an easy

6. For attacks on the *Intelligencer*'s relations to the bank, see the *Globe* for December 12, 13, and 15, 1832.
7. *National Intelligencer*, January 3, 1833.
8. Green to Richard Cralle, September 16, 1832, Green Letters, Library of Congress, Washington, D.C.
9. Ibid.

victory, but in the House a bitter battle developed. Ten ballots taken on February 14 all resulted in a deadlock between the *Intelligencer* and the *Globe* editors, and four more ballots were taken the following day before Gales and Seaton secured the necessary votes.[10]

Reaction was immediate and violent. Jackson complained that now the *Intelligencer* was being paid to abuse him.[11] The *New York Standard* thought the *Globe* should have received the contract, for the *Intelligencer* had the profitable *American State Papers* publishing.[12] Gales and Seaton replied that there was nothing lucrative about the *State Papers*, for the editors expected the entire job would fall short of what Congress spent on printing for one session.[13] The *Intelligencer* editors sought to prove that they had acted honorably in seeking congressional support. They wrote:

Four years ago under the power of a political combination, uniting too many elements to be withstood, Congress left useless upon our hands a very large and costly establishment just built up for their service. What cannot be cured must be endured. We complained as little as we could help, if at all. We shall not complain now, if Congress shall bestow their work elsewhere. We are ready to execute it, if called to the task. But, should that happen or not, we shall be at least secure of the consciousness of not having sought it by solicitations or compliances on our own part, nor by malignant slanders upon others who compete for it.[14]

Perhaps Gales and Seaton honestly estimated that returns from the *American State Papers* would be less than the sum received for one session of congressional printing. If so, they were sorely mistaken, for disbursement records beginning in 1834 show the *State Papers* cost far exceeded that of a single session of congressional printing.[15]

Failure to receive the House printing contract was, indeed, a blow to Blair and Rives, an action they refused to accept without a struggle. The *Globe* editors eyed the close margin

10. *Register of Debates in Congress*, Twenty-Second Congress, Second Session (Washington, D.C., 1833), 9:1725-26.
11. Jackson to Hugh L. White, March 24, 1833, John Spencer Bassett, ed., *Correspondence of Andrew Jackson* (Washington, D.C., 1931), 5:46-47.
12. *New York Standard*, quoted in *National Intelligencer*, February 12, 1833.
13. *National Intelligencer*, February 12, 1833.
14. Ibid.
15. See n. 62 in this chapter.

of four by which Gales and Seaton had won and attempted to prove that four votes claimed by their opposition actually were cast for the *Globe* editors. Accordingly, Blair and Rives wrote several congressmen about whose vote there was some question, asking them to help clarify the situation. Blair informed the various representatives that he believed they had voted for the *Globe*, but Gales and Seaton, he explained, claimed that four representatives from whom Blair claimed support had actually voted for the *National Intelligencer*. Blair wished to refute this claim since he was "extremely desirous to have it in my power to do exact justice." Would the representative say whether or not Blair was mistaken in relation to his vote?[16]

The replies must have shaken somewhat Blair's positive stand. Most admitted without qualification that they had voted for the *Globe*. Others switched to the *Globe* after early support of Duff Green, and at least one knew for certain that not all the votes claimed by Blair had gone to the *Globe*.[17] Some southern members of the House frankly explained that they could not vote for Blair because of his support of Jackson in the nullification controversy.[18]

Nothing developed from the *Globe*'s attempt to challenge the House vote, except that Blair became more determined than ever to drive the *Intelligencer* editors from the Washington publishing field. Blair fumed that it was all a conspiracy between Clay and Calhoun to harm the *Globe*,[19] and Blair was not one to be hurt without striking back. Pierce Van Voorhis, congressman from New York, as late as the fall of 1833 still was disturbed by the House vote. He hoped that somehow Blair and Rives might again win the printing contracts "instead of N. Biddle."[20] Blair undoubtedly was right in contending that the combination of National Republican, nullifier, and anti-Mason votes—the elements of the Whig party—carried the election for Gales and Seaton.

The House printing contract represented future income to

16. Form letter, March 25, 1833, Blair and Rives Papers, vol. 2, Library of Congress, Washington, D.C.

17. See James Ford to Blair, April 9, 1833, Blair and Rives Papers.

18. See William Alexander to Blair, April 11, 1833, Blair and Rives Papers.

19. *Globe*, February 21, 1833.

20. Pierce Van Voorhis to Blair, November 29, 1833, Blair and Rives Papers, vol. 3.

Gales and Seaton, but during the spring of 1833 they needed money, and once again a deed of trust and power of attorney was granted Richard Smith, an official of the United States Bank. The deed signed over returns from the *American State Papers* to the bank until Gales's and Seaton's debt was retired. The editors received $10,000 under the terms of the deed to enable them to carry out the printing contracts.[21]

Despite the tense situation surrounding the bank during the summer of 1833, less than usual correspondence passed between Biddle and the *Intelligencer* editors. Jackson contended that during the period the two publishers were allowed to overdraw more than $10,000.[22]

By the middle of September Jackson revealed his plan for dealing with the United States Bank as he ordered removal of the government deposits. Following Secretary of the Treasury William Duane's refusal, the secretary was removed from office and replaced by Roger B. Taney, former attorney general. Taney, an advocate of removal, issued the order, and thus the ground was laid not only for the end of the United States Bank but also for the bitter congressional session of 1833-34.

The *Intelligencer*, of course, opposed the removal but made no startling or profound attacks. No plan was offered for combatting Jackson's order, and the editors did little more than assail the president's action.

Gales and Seaton were disappointed by an article in the *Globe* signed by Jackson that defended the removal. The "fact and figures" set forth, according to the editors, were "almost entirely unfounded imputations against the administration of the bank. . . ." The *Intelligencer* editors thought the reasons were not up to the standards anticipated from the "shrewd intellect and practical pen that produced it. . . ." They referred to Kendall, for Gales and Seaton never dropped their contention that Jackson was simply the tool of the Kitchen Cabinet. Indeed, the *Intelligencer* editorial said that the removal

21. A deed of Trust and Power of Attorney By and Between Joseph Gales, Jr., et al., Grantors, and Richard Smith, Grantee, Dated the 4th Day of May, 1833, and Recorded on the 29th Day of May, 1833, in Liber No. W.B. 46, Folio 157, Office of the Recorder, District of Columbia.

22. Charges against the bank by Jackson, presumed to have been written in September, 1833, quoted in Bassett, *Correspondence of Andrew Jackson*, 5:174; see also *Globe*, October 31, 1833.

defense was "the most exceptional document that the President was ever induced to place his signature to."[23] Blair also had made suggestions for the message, but this was not noted by the *Intelligencer*.

By the middle of October Gales and Seaton were campaigning to show that Jackson's action met with "indignant denunciations" from the press throughout the country: "In the South, the papers of all parties have denounced it—those friendly to the administration in more gentle terms, of course, but all disapprove it, Jackson and Anti Jackson, Nullifiers and Union men."[24]

While Gales and Seaton waited for the Jacksonian opposition forces to devise an antidote to the removal, the editors were confronted with a much more serious personal problem. Blair, who played politics seriously, had not forgotten that the *Intelligencer* beat him for the House printing. By the last of October he had completed his research, and he set forth with enthusiasm to discredit Gales's and Seaton's paper by giving the entire world "proof" that the *Intelligencer* was no more than a tool of the bank.

Blair began his lengthy charge against his rival with a bit of the *Intelligencer*'s history. He pointed out that the paper's birth had been legitimate, for it had come into the world as a Republican newspaper. But the prosperity of patronage from the United States government corrupted its editors, and they departed from "the republican faith" and tied themselves to the Bank of the United States.[25] Blair estimated that during the time the *Intelligencer* was the government organ that its editors had received $1,000,000 in patronage. Blair thought "that such an income would have supported moderate and virtuous men without resort to Banks. . . ." The extravagances of Gales and Seaton proved they strayed politically, for what true "republican" would resort to the use of banks, the article asked.[26]

In estimating the amount actually received by Gales and

23. *National Intelligencer*, September 24, 1833.
24. Ibid., October 16, 1833.
25. *Globe*, October 31, 1833.
26. Blair's philosophy here is clearly that of Jackson's, since he abhorred debts of any kind, considering them nearly sinful. For his views on debts, read the numerous letters published in Bassett, *Correspondence of Andrew Jackson*, vol. 5, written to his adopted son, who managed the Hermitage during Jackson's presidency.

Seaton through government printing contracts, Blair grossly exaggerated the sum. Actual amounts disbursed to Gales and Seaton during this period, as shown by later investigations of government printing, were around $320,000, less than one-third of the Blair estimate.[27] Such exaggeration shows that though Blair may have had some facts on which to base his charges, he also was surmising and falling wide of the mark in certain instances.

The *Globe* writer then proceeded to show, printing verbatim from the documents, that in 1826 a deed of trust was given by the *Intelligencer* editors to Richard Smith, cashier of the United States Bank, Washington Branch.[28] The deed covered not only the property on which the *Intelligencer* stood and the building but also equipment, paper, and debts due the editors. Gales and Seaton could not disagree with these facts.

Blair continued that on June 11, 1829, the lots on which the *Intelligencer* stood were purchased by Samuel Harrison Smith, representing the bank. Since that time, the editorial went on, the *Intelligencer* had remained in the hands of Gales and Seaton by mere sufferance, for the bank could have sold the paper whenever it desired. But why should the bank want to sell when it got such good service from the *Intelligencer?*

The *Globe* writer next considered the *Intelligencer*'s income. The move to buy five hundred copies of the *Register of Debates* for each of the two recent sessions should have brought Gales and Seaton $12,500, in addition to that huge bit of charity, the *American State Papers.* Other printers, contended the *Globe*, offered to print the *State Papers* for much less, but the bank friends in Congress carried Gales and Seaton through. The whole set of volumes was unnecessary and unneeded; Gales and Seaton never would have been permitted to publish the *American State Papers* if Calhoun had not taken his support from the administration. The total bill for the *State Papers* was to be $105,000, Blair wrote. Now more than

27. See *United States Senate Document* 11, Twenty-Fourth Congress, First Session.

28. A handwritten copy of this Deed of Trust was found in the Blair and Rives Papers, showing that Blair did have factual information for at least part of his charges against the *Intelligencer.*

$305,000 had been paid; the *Intelligencer* still was borrowing.

In fact, the debt had risen during the period in which Gales and Seaton published the *State Papers*, Blair wrote. In 1829, when the bank bought the *Intelligencer* property, Gales and Seaton owed $5,610. Shortly after the sum was raised by two loans of $785.58 and $500, the Globe writer contended. But by the time the committee investigated in 1832 the following loans had been added:

Borrowed from the Washington Branch	$10,095
A discounted bill of exchange	900
Debts to the Philadelphia Bank	11,375
Debts in the name of Thos. Donohoe	3,000
(clerk of the Intelligencer)	
W. W. Seaton, borrowed separately	10,000
Total	$35,370[29]

But the matter had worsened since 1832, Blair argued. During the fall of 1833 Gales and Seaton allegedly owed the Philadelphia Bank $47,514.81 and the Washington Branch $32,-748.56. In addition, large amounts supposedly had been borrowed in Donohoe's name and were not included in the totals.

Gales and Seaton, the editorial went on, no longer were allowed to borrow money from the Philadelphia Bank. Only the Washington Branch would take their loans. And, asked the editorial, who could blame bank officials for being skeptical about loans? Even $305,000 had failed to make Gales and Seaton solvent. Further, in order to continue work on the *American State Papers*, the *Globe* added, Gales and Seaton had granted a deed of trust to Richard Smith of the bank on May 29, 1833, and had since borrowed $90,000. And despite all this, the bank officials still allowed the editors to overdraw their accounts.[30]

Unfortunately bank records are not extant to prove or disprove the *Globe*'s allegations. Certainly some points the

29. *Globe*, October 31, 1833. Bank records are insufficient to show whether these figures are true. One statement made by Biddle showed the *Intelligencer* debt to be $32,360. The exact time of this debt is not certain but is believed to be around 1837. See Richard C. McGrane, ed., *The Correspondence of Nicholas Biddle Dealing with National Affairs, 1807-1844*, appendix 1 (Boston, 1919).

30. *Globe*, October 31, 1833.

Globe made were true: the deeds of trust and the sale of the *Intelligencer* building, as well as some of the amounts Gales and Seaton received for government printing. The frequency of borrowing probably was correct, but correspondence between Biddle and Gales indicates the amounts borrowed were smaller than Blair contended. Even if Blair exaggerated, however, huge amounts were involved.

Gales's and Seaton's reply was pointed: "The organ of the Kitchen Cabinet has just added another to its established claims to an unenviable reputation, by the publication of a mass of matter, some of it true, much of it false, and all of it impertinent, concerning the private affairs of the Editors of this paper. . . . It cannot be expected of us to descend to the level of pimps and panders who have been employed in this dirty work, by undertaking to dissect the result of their labors."[31]

The *Intelligencer* editors were not alone in fighting the attack. In spite of frequent pen squabbles between the *Intelligencer* and the *Niles' Register*, Hezekiah Niles could not see his old friends and adversaries treated so harshly by the *Globe*. Niles thought the real reason for the attack on Gales and Seaton was their defeat of the *Globe* in the battle for the House printing. Therefore, Blair's publication of Gales's and Seaton's financial records was motivated by the basest of all desires—money. He disagreed that the editors were unable to provide ample security for all their borrowing. The *Intelligencer*'s plant, Niles wrote, was the most extensive printing establishment in the United States, doing an estimated $100,-000 volume of business each year. And, in addition to their physical equipment, Niles noted, Gales and Seaton were acknowledged as the most prompt, faithful, and correct printers in the country. In his view, the public was concerned with Gales and Seaton only as printers, and in this capacity they were unsurpassed.[32]

Niles was understanding on the subject of finances: "I regret my old friends Gales and Seaton are not perfectly at ease, in money matters. They ought to be so—and probably, soon will be so, if fairly dealt with." He felt the adverse publicity

31. *National Intelligencer*, November 2, 1833.
32. *Niles' Register*, January 4, 1834, p. 1163.

had not harmed Gales and Seaton and might have helped them. Their subscriptions were growing rapidly, "and they deserve them all, for there is no parallel to the industry and fidelity, courtesy and fairness of Gales & Seaton in the newspaper press in the United States." These remarks, Niles assured his readers, came from his heart without regard to politics.[33]

Niles later published a letter from Samuel Harrison Smith, president of the United States Bank, Washington Branch, stating that to his knowledge the *Intelligencer* was not owned by the bank. True, it had been pledged in the deed of trust in 1826, but only the building had been sold. Gales and Seaton paid $600 a year rent on the building, Smith wrote.[34]

The *Cincinnati Daily Gazette* also defended Gales and Seaton, commenting that if this were the way the "cabinet" intended to put down the *Intelligencer*, the *Gazette* editor was much opposed. As to the accusation that Gales and Seaton were illegally chosen printers for the House, the *Gazette* commented: ". . . no sort of accusation can be more base than that which mixes truth and falsehood together, giving a false aspect even to that which is true."[35]

Such political feuding was not without its effect on the newspaper's circulation. Even before the election of 1828 but after the paper's declared opposition to Jackson, the *Intelligencer*'s circulation started to climb. During a six-month period in 1827, 467 new readers subscribed to the paper.[36] Whether this rate of increase continued is unknown, and no particular circulation race seems to have developed between the *Intelligencer* and the *Telegraph* when the latter was the Jackson administration organ. Once the *Globe* entered the scene, however, the rivalry intensified and carried over into circulation. By 1832, only about eighteen months after the *Globe* began publishing, rumors circulated that Blair's and Rives's daily circulation exceeded that of the *Intelligencer*. The *Globe*'s growth was phenomenal, for at that time the *Intel-*

---

33. Ibid.
34. Ibid., January 24, 1834, p. 1166.
35. *Cincinnati Daily Gazette*, quoted in the *National Intelligencer*, November 27, 1833.
36. *Raleigh Register*, September 25, 1827.

ligencer editors claimed their paper had one of the largest circulations in the United States.[37] The rumors evidently had sufficient credulity to warrant Gales's and Seaton's denial of the claim, since the editors contended they did not envy the *Globe*'s success but believed that "no newspaper in the United States has a circulation as great as that of the National Intelligencer—nor any one a subscription list more stable or more certainly increasing than ours."[38]

Again in August Gales and Seaton noted claims that the *Globe*'s circulation exceeded the *Intelligencer*'s: "The Official would have it believed that the circulation of 'the Globe' is greater than that of the Intelligencer. We admit that it is greater than it ought to be; but we would not give the Subscription List of the Intelligencer for three such Lists as that of the *Globe*."[39] Such a defense hardly refuted the *Globe*'s contention.

In January, 1833, Gales and Seaton bragged they had added 689 new subscribers during December, a record just 5 short of the same month of the previous year. They contended that both in congressional and noncongressional circulation their paper bested the *Globe*.[40] The *Globe* editors wrote they were unimpressed by the *Intelligencer* figures.[41]

In 1834 the total combined *Intelligencer* circulation for both the daily and triweekly was 7,440. The triweekly accounted for 5,520 subscribers and the daily 1,920. The editor of the *Niles' Register* considered this a "pretty considerable business."[42]

Gales and Seaton did little to promote circulation before the *Globe*'s challenge, but after the *Globe* began its climb, the *Intelligencer* editors made some effort to increase their paper's circulation. "Extras," financed by the Second Bank of the United States, helped somewhat. These were distributed widely among influential individuals, state legislative bodies, and political organizations, and usually invited additional support of the *Intelligencer*.[43]

37. Gales, Jr., to Biddle, March 18, 1831, Biddle Papers, vol. 26.
38. *National Intelligencer*, June 8, 1832.
39. Ibid., August 3, 1832.
40. Ibid., January 19, 1833.
41. *Globe*, January 17, 1833.
42. *Niles' Register*, January 4, 1834, p. 1163.
43. Gales and Seaton to Biddle, February 22, 1831, Biddle Papers, vol. 25.

The subscriber letters Gales and Seaton received during the circulation war with the *Globe* were as spirited as the competition between the two papers. A Jackson supporter contributed ten dollars to the *Intelligencer*, explaining that he had subscribed since the administration attempted to "put down the National Intelligencer" a few years before. He thought by all means it should be continued because he enjoyed the paper and "should be loth to give it up." He went on to say: ". . . in my opinion the Intelligencer is departing from its respectability in noticing the vulgar abuse of the Globe.[44] Such matters are beneath its contempt. I support Andrew Jackson with all my heart: but were the Globe to find its way within my doors, I would thrust it out with tongs, as an unclean thing: I would feel debased were it seen on my table."[45] Another subscriber objected to missing a single issue of the *Intelligencer.* " 'I am exceedingly disappointed when I do not receive your paper. I can't eat my dinner with half so good relish.' "[46]

But it was the bank, and not the *Intelligencer*, which was on trial. When the congressional session opened in December, both the president and the secretary of the treasury defended the September removal order. The *Intelligencer* editors were unconvinced, yet they were uncertain about a counter plan and requested Biddle's help with several articles attacking Jackson's reasons for removal. Gales was convinced that this series might be important in defending both Biddle and the editors.[47] Nothing seems to have developed from this collaboration, and the *Intelligencer* still lacked a plan for attacking Jackson and restoring the bank.

Gales and Seaton, although never giving strong and enthusiastic support, favored Clay's resolutions of censure introduced into the Senate during the 1833 session. The resolutions called for the Senate censure of both Jackson and Taney for their part in ordering the removal.[48]

This completely negative program was aimed at humiliating Jackson and Taney rather than at saving the bank. Per-

44. The writer probably referred to the charges made concerning the relationship between the *Intelligencer* editors and the bank.

45. *National Intelligencer*, January 10, 1833.

46. Ibid., May 25, 1831.

47. Gales to Biddle, December 7, 1833, Biddle Papers, vol. 43.

48. Carl Schurz, *Life of Henry Clay* (Boston, 1887), 2:31-32.

haps for this reason the *Intelligencer* did not enthusiastically support the measures. Regarding the debates in Congress, the editors wrote: "We think it best, in general, to leave them to be answered and commented on where they are spoken." And throughout the debate, this is what the editors did. On March 28 both Clay resolutions were passed,[49] and Gales and Seaton noted the accomplished fact without strong approbation.[50]

By May of 1834 the *Intelligencer* editors and Biddle were alarmed about more than the bank's demise. A resolution introduced into the House called for an investigation of relations between Biddle and the editors. The bank president quickly rallied his forces: "It is the severest imputation upon the honor of the House—coming as it does directly after Jackson's declaration that two thirds of it would have been bribed. I think some notice of it might be taken in the House itself & our friend Gales might break out against it with special cause since there is a resolution for all our correspondence with him and about him. . . ."[51]

Probably Biddle fully realized that any congressional investigation of newspapers could work to the credit of the bank as well as to its discredit, for he was well aware that more money probably had been loaned to those publishers favorable to the Jackson administration than to those who opposed it.[52] Further, the victory over the bank was realized and there was no need to intensify the attack.

But the failure of Congress to save the bank eased the pressure for a complete study of the records and correspondence of the bank, and the *Globe* had exposed as much of the dealings of the bank and Gales and Seaton as the public was to see.

The early months of 1834 brought nothing too severe in the verbal war between the editors of the *Globe* and the *Intelligencer*. Short, sharp jibes continued to flow from Blair's pen.

49. *Register of Debates in Congress*, Twenty-Third Congress, First Session (Washington, D.C., 1834), 10:1187.
50. *National Intelligencer*, March 29, 1834.
51. Biddle to J. G. Watmough, May 2, 1834, Biddle Letterbooks, no. 5, Library of Congress, Washington, D.C.
52. Thomas Payne Govan, *Nicholas Biddle, Nationalist and Public Banker, 1796-1844* (Chicago, 1959), p. 189.

A May 10 *Globe* editorial contended that nothing was so valuable to Gales and Seaton as that "sort of currency which puts all the machinery of their office in motion." A July editorial painted Gales as a ballyhooer for the bank: "While Gales blows the corporation trumpet, Mr. Biddle will never want a windy reknown. The very cheeks of this Boreas of the Bank are inflated like those of the god of the winds, and at the bidding of his majesty Nick, he will send a breeze over 'the Western woods and prairies,' and will swear all credit of it to the 'CALM SUMMER MORNING.' "[53]

The bank charter expired in 1836, but the argument on the financial questions facing the country continued. The bank remained an issue. Gales and Seaton termed the panic of 1837 the natural result of Jackson's action. They wrote: "Whether the measure of transferring the public money from the Bank be regarded as having been a financial error merely, or an act of vindictive malice, it is a matter not susceptible of serious doubt, in the mind of any practical man, that, if the Government had let the Bank alone, instead of striking at and destroying the national character in which it was an aid to the Government and a blessing to the People, the country would not be in the condition in which it now finds itself."[54]

Gales and Seaton reminded their readers that the editors had predicted financial disaster if the bank were destroyed: "Recollecting the occurrences of 1816-17, we foretold this consequence when the Administration opened its battery upon the late Bank of the United States. . . ."[55]

But readers were asked not to misunderstand Gales's and Seaton's devotion to the bank: "We believe . . . it is entirely *possible* to carry on the fiscal concerns of the Government, and the commerce and manufacturers of the country, without bank agency; but not without inconvenience, to both People and Government, so vexatious as to be almost intolerable."[56]

The editors realized the bank had become a fixation with them—something that overshadowed all their other thoughts.

53. *Globe*, July 31, 1834.
54. *National Intelligencer*, April 5, 1837.
55. Ibid., May 11, 1837.
56. Ibid., July 15, 1837.

An *Intelligencer* editorial commented: "It is doing great injustice to the Whigs, however, to cluster them, as a party, around a question so narrow and circumscribed as the question concerning a National Bank. The Whigs have broader and loftier aims."[57]

Gales and Seaton still were sensitive to the charge that the bank owned and controlled the *Intelligencer*. In September of 1837 the *Globe* editors again asserted that the bank owned the *Intelligencer*, and Gales and Seaton sought a final answer to the allegation. The editors accordingly wrote to Richard Smith, cashier of the Washington Branch. Did the United States Bank actually own the " 'office of the National Intelligencer, its types, presses, and profits'. . . ?" Smith answered that as far as he knew, the specified items were not, and never had been, the property of the bank. He confirmed the 1826 deed of trust and the purchase of the *Intelligencer* building in 1829. "But," he added, "the Bank never claimed any ownership of the type, presses nor profits of the establishment, nor exerted any control over it, as far as I have any knowledge of the subject."[58]

Once again, in 1838, the *Globe* attacked the *Intelligencer* for supporting the bank. The incident occurred during the congressional debate over the Treasury Note Bill when Gales and Seaton announced that they were sympathetic with the Whig opposition. The *Globe* editors replied that such a statement could be expected because Gales and Seaton were "journeymen of the bank of the United States." Gales and Seaton replied: "Taken literally, this is no more than a proved misrepresentation. . . . Metaphorically, this epithet, applied to us, is sheer nonsense. So far from our being employed by the bank, the bank is employed *by us*, and well paid, too, for its services. . . ." Gales and Seaton thought a more apt description would be to say they were payers of the bank: "If the bank be not our journeyman, 'it is certainly our annuitant.' "[59]

Gradually the bank issue disappeared from the editorial pages of both the *Globe* and the *Intelligencer*, although the financial issue continued to provide fuel for fiery exchanges.

57. Ibid., September 12, 1837.
58. Ibid.
59. Ibid., May 22, 1838.

Occasionally a United States Bank was suggested as the solution to the financial problems of the late 1830s and early 1840s.

Not until 1842 did Gales and Seaton make final payment on their bank debt. J. Robertson wrote the editors: "I find your account with the said Bank, in your own names as debtors, principal and interest, was paid off in full. The last payment was made on the 27th June 1842." Robertson further explained that this payment ended Gales's and Seaton's indebtedness to the Bank "either as partners or individuals, or drawers or endorsers. . . ."[60]

The bank had provided the center of opposition to Jackson for the *Intelligencer* editors, and at times the fight to save the bank was one of self-preservation to Gales and Seaton. Their preference for sound money and well-regulated currency undoubtedly would have made the *Intelligencer* editors strong supporters of Biddle and his bank, even without their personal involvement. Preservation and protection of the institution became a cause—one on which Gales and Seaton waged a hard-fought battle but lost. They had much right on their side—but they did not have Jackson.

There is little doubt that Biddle exerted a powerful influence on Gales and Seaton during the bank fight. He supplied them with ideas as well as information. The editors and the bank president worked hand-in-hand, planning strategy and executing maneuvers. But the *Intelligencer* editors had spent most of their newspaper days as an organ for some person or cause, and they did the same with Biddle and the bank. Their need for money perhaps only emphasized a belief both editors possessed.

Evidently Gales and Seaton did not borrow from the bank after 1833. The congressional printing for the years between 1833 and 1836 helped ease the financial situation, and once again the *Intelligencer* plant was running at nearly full capacity with 165 persons employed.[61] But even more important was the income being realized from the *American State Papers*. Before July 12, 1834, the income from the *Papers* was $84,-217.93, but between that date and November 24, 1836, exist-

---

60. J. Robertson to Gales and Seaton, December 29, 1848, Gales and Seaton Papers, Library of Congress, Washington, D.C.
61. *Niles' Register*, January 13, 1837, p. 305.

ing Senate disbursement records show the *Intelligencer* editors were paid $219,172.26.[62]

With such an income, the congressional printing contracts were not as important as before. Since the Jacksonian Democrats controlled the House after 1834, there was little surprise when on December 7, 1835, Blair and Rives received that printing contract.[63] The complexion of the Senate differed considerably, and a coalition of nullifiers and the old National Republicans controlled that chamber. Although some doubt existed concerning who would receive the Senate printing, Blair and Rives stood little chance of getting it. Thomas Sellars wrote the *Globe* editors: "By the bye what will be done for Gales & Seaton and Genl Duff by the Senate. Will they divide the printing or will the Nullifier have to yield to his brother Whigs and trust his claims to the sovereign state of South Carolina—"[64]

62. Disbursements during this period were:

American State Papers up to		
	July 12, 1834	$84,217.93
	September 20, 1834	8,110.12
	September 27, 1834	3,339.41
	September 27, 1834	4,702.86
	November 3, 1834	2,834.41
	November 3, 1834	1,013.23
	December 16, 1834	2,086.07
	February 25, 1835	1,842.62
	March 16, 1835	601.86
	May 1, 1835	3,773.10 1/2
	June 1, 1835	2,997.26
	July 1, 1835	2,856.90
	August 1, 1835	3,908.19
	October 1, 1835	4,336.02
	September 1, 1835	3,752.21
	November 2, 1835	3,841.99
	December 1, 1835	1,805.35 2/3
	December 18, 1835	961.03
	February 2, 1836	1,712.59 1/3
	January 4, 1836	414.35
	March 28, 1836	2,407.91
	July 1, 1836	2,829.99
	January 4, 1836	705.07
	November 24, 1836	158,339.71

Taken from Senate Records 19d-21, Sen. 30D-B2, Records of United States Senate, Record Group 46, National Archives, Washington, D.C.

63. *Register of Debates in Congress*, Twenty-Fourth Congress, First Session (Washington, D.C., 1836), 12:1948.

64. Thomas W. Sellars to Blair and Rives, March 3, 1835, Blair and Rives Papers, vol. 3.

An alliance between Gales and Seaton and Green was unthinkable to the *Telegraph* editor. Instead, he speculated concerning whether the *Globe* and the *Intelligencer* editors might not work out some system of dividing the printing, for he believed Gales and Seaton would do anything to gain the congressional contract. He wrote: "Gales and Seaton are preparing to go over to Van Buren under Kendall's auspices. . . . The public printing is too great a boon. They cannot live without the patronage & hence they would sell themselves for the filthy gold."[65] Gales and Seaton received the Senate contract, the first time since 1829.[66]

The *Intelligencer* editors during the mid 1830s had an additional idea for raising income. They were busy preparing a history of the Congresses before 1824—a publishing project they hoped would be subscribed to by Congress and thus make the *Intelligencer* editors even less dependent on the congressional contracts. The idea of publishing the history of the early proceedings occurred to Gales and Seaton shortly after the War of 1812 and by 1818 was sufficiently planned to warrant presenting a memorial to Congress "paying a subscription for such number of copies as may be required for the public institutions of the country."[67]

In 1818 Gales and Seaton also had consulted prominent statesmen of the early Congresses, such as James Madison, who encouraged their venture.[68] He thought such a legislative history should be written and any delay would only make the project more difficult.[69]

Nothing came of the plan then, and Gales and Seaton turned their attention in 1824 to the *Register of Debates* and in 1831 to the *American State Papers*. By 1833, however, the *Annals* plan was revived. Joseph Gales, Sr., retired from the *Raleigh Register*, and at the urging of his son and son-in-law on the *Intelligencer*, he and his wife decided to move to Wash-

65. Green to Richard K. Cralle, October 5, 1835, Green Papers, Library of Congress, Washington, D.C.

66. *Register of Debates in Congress*, Twenty-Third Congress, Second Session (Washington, D.C., 1835), 11:698.

67. *Annals of Congress*, Fifteenth Congress, First Session (Washington, D.C., 1854), 31:267.

68. Gales and Seaton to Madison, January 26, 1818, Madison Papers, vol. 65, Library of Congress, Washington, D.C.

69. Madison to Gales and Seaton, February 2, 1818, Madison Papers, vol. 65.

ington, D.C., where Mr. Gales took over compilation and editing of the *Annals*. The senior Gales both had passed their seventieth birthdays when they left Raleigh in 1833.[70]

Actual compilation of the *Annals* documents started before August, 1833. Mrs. Gales then wrote her friend Jared Sparks that her husband was busy "assisting to compile a History of the early doings on Congress, he having for several years previous to our removal to Raleigh, reported the Debates in Philadelphia. Our sons are about reprinting those Historical Documents, and you all know how . . . their time is occupied in the daily affairs of business."[71]

Gales and Seaton encountered numerous difficulties in their project and once again turned to Madison for help. They wrote: "The Debates . . . were often inavoidably imperfectly reported; & having ourselves only the volumes of Lloyd,[72] and Fenno's Gazette,[73] with the Journals to compile from; it has appeared to us possible that you may have some materials which you would spare to us for the purpose of embodying in this work. . . ." Gales and Seaton explained that they were especially desirous of obtaining information beyond the accounts given in "Fenno, Brown,[74] Dunlap[75] & Duane[76] for the History of the 2d. 3d. 4th & 5th Congresses. Would you have the goodness to advise us to what other sources to apply for these?"[77]

Madison replied that he was pleased Gales and Seaton were undertaking such a project but said that he was unable to help much as his "recollections are very barren." Newspapers were the only sources of information Madison could suggest:

70. Winifred and Joseph Gales, Gales' Recollections, Gales Family Papers, Southern Historical Collection, University of North Carolina Library, Chapel Hill, N.C., p. 173.

71. Winifred Gales to Jared Sparks, August 11, 1833, Gales' Papers, North Carolina Department of Archives and History, Raleigh, N.C.

72. This undoubtedly referred to Thomas Lloyd, publisher of *Congressional Register of Debates of First House (1789-1790)*, vols. 1-8 (Philadelphia, 1792).

73. The reference here was to John Fenno's *Gazette of the United States*, published in Philadelphia.

74. This probably referred to Andrew Brown, Sr., editor of the *Federal Gazette*, published in Philadelphia in the 1790s. See Clarence S. Brigham, *History and Bibliography of American Newspapers, 1690-1820* (Worcester, Mass., 1947), 2:905.

75. Dunlap undoubtedly was John Dunlap of the Dunlap and Claypoole firm.

76. William Duane was the editor of the *Aurora*.

77. Gales and Seaton to Madison, July 29, 1833, Madison Papers, vol. 87.

"I know of no 'debates' during the period of Lloyds, but his, which are very defective, and abound in errors; some of them very gross when the speeches were not revised by the authors. If there be any depositories of what passed, they must be the contemporary newspapers or periodicals. . . ."[78] Madison suggested Fenno as the best source for debates that took place in New York and suggested Philip Freneau's *National Gazette* for the debates in Philadelphia. He added, "If there be any differences between Freneau and Fenno in a speech of mine Freneau gives the correct one." Madison replied that he had none of his own speeches, as he never wrote them out beforehand.[79]

The first two volumes of the *Annals* were published in 1834 and covered the sessions of the first Congress. Gales's and Seaton's hope that Congress would react favorably to the project and purchase a considerable number of the volumes was not immediately realized. Therefore, the editors temporarily held up work on the *Annals*. Mr. Gales was offered the position of treasurer of the American Colonization Society, an agency devoted to helping free Negroes become settled in an African colony. After six years Mr. Gales resigned as a result of criticism of his handling of funds[80] and returned to the *Annals*. Congress by then had reacted favorably to the first volumes of the work.[81] Mr. Gales worked on the *Annals* only briefly, and further labor on the project was dropped until 1849, when Gales and Seaton began publishing the remainder of the forty-two volumes.

While Gales and Seaton printed the *American State Papers* and the *Annals of Congress*, one of their other publications faced serious competition from the *Globe*. In 1834 Blair and Rives began publishing the *Congressional Globe*, a publication similar to the *Register of Debates*. This competition made the *Register* much less desirable than previously, since the Democratic federal administration favored the volumes published by the *Globe*. Without congressional support, little profit could be realized from publishing the proceedings.[82] Accord-

78. Madison to Gales and Seaton, August 5, 1833, Madison Papers, vol. 87.
79. Ibid.
80. "Joseph Gales, Sr.," *Dictionary of American Biography* 7:100, 1956.
81. Gales' Recollections, p. 174.
82. Elizabeth Gregory McPherson, "The History of Reporting the Debates and Proceedings of Congress" (Ph.D. thesis, University of North Carolina, 1940), p. 98.

ingly, both the *Intelligencer* and the *Globe* editors courted the favor of Congress. Under Jackson, the *Globe* had much better chances of succeeding.

The Jacksonians strongly criticized the *Register*, charging that the publication was filled with inaccuracies and was an " 'aphorism' of 'whiggery.' "[83] Although Gales and Seaton were accused of taking their debates only from the *Intelligencer*, they did copy proceedings from the *Globe* and the *Telegraph* also.[84] In addition to using as many sources of debates as possible, Gales and Seaton also went to considerable trouble to insure the accuracy of their published debates. Congressmen were asked to revise speeches before final publication,[85] and in most cases they complied.

Publishing the *Register* also enabled Gales and Seaton to give more complete coverage to speeches than that given by newspapers. The editors never contended that they fully covered congressional proceedings, but they did attempt to obtain copies of important speeches that they had failed to report or could not copy from other sources.[86]

Congressmen were aware that Gales and Seaton copied some debates into the *Register* from other papers, and this caused Theodore Freylenghusen of New Jersey to warn that a report of his speech appearing in another paper erred. He wanted correction made because the other reporter had "put strange words in my mouth. . . . It seems to have been the work, of what is called in your art a printers' devil."[87]

Probably the most bitter attack on the *Register* was made in 1834 in the Senate by Thomas Hart Benton, the violently antibank Missouri senator. Benton accused Gales and Seaton of deliberately omitting some of his speeches. The editors

83. Ibid., p. 99.

84. Ibid.

85. Ibid., p. 98. For letters dealing with revisions, see James Barbour to Gales and Seaton, July 10, 1824, Barbour Collection, New York Public Library, New York; George Bibb to unnamed correspondent, February 22, 1833, American Statesmen Papers, Dreere Collection, Historical Society of Pennsylvania, Philadelphia; Gales and Seaton to Willie P. Mangum, December, 1825, Mangum Papers, vol. 2, Library of Congress, Washington, D.C.

86. For examples, see Gales, Jr., to Willie P. Mangum, June 29, 1836, Mangum Papers, vol. 2; Gales and Seaton to John Leeds Kerr, August, 1833, Bozman and Kerr Papers, Library of Congress, Washington, D.C.

87. Theodore Freylenghusen to Gales and Seaton, January, 1830, Gales and Seaton Papers, Library of Congress.

filed a written protest to the charges, but this defense probably did little to erase the stigma Benton placed on them.[88] Even if Benton's charges were true, one needs only to glance at the *Register* during the 1830s to determine that if not all Benton's speeches were covered certainly much space was devoted to his remarks.

Undoubtedly the Jacksonian party preference for the *Globe* had much to do with Gales's and Seaton's decision to discontinue the *Register* after 1837. The *American State Papers* were yielding profit, and, although the records are not clear, Gales and Seaton probably determined that there was little room for two such publications as the *Register* and the *Congressional Globe* in Washington. At any rate, the *Register* was discontinued with Volume XIV, thus ending one of the most valuable publishing contributions Gales and Seaton made. The *Register* has been praised for having served its purposes remarkably well.[89]

From many standpoints, Gales and Seaton were in a much better position toward the end of Jackson's second term than they had been at the beginning. Despite the political defeats that the *Intelligencer* candidates suffered, the publishing firm itself had weathered the Jackson term amazingly well. Socially the Gales and Seaton families still were among the most prominent of the capital city, and as Mrs. Samuel Harrison Smith aptly expressed it, "with few exceptions all the most respectable and fashionable people" belonged to the opposition party.[90] Jackson had not succeeded in carrying Washington society with him, and the "elite" of the city sat back and waited for salvation from the dark days they had endured under Jackson. They looked forward to the election of 1836 as the great hope.

88. *Register of Debates,* Twenty-Third Congress, Second Session, 11:33-35.

89. McPherson, "History of Reporting," p. 110.

90. Mrs. Samuel Harrison Smith, *The First Forty Years of Washington Society* (New York, 1906), p. 344.

CHAPTER 13

A Whig Triumph

The *Intelligencer* editors had secured a measure of both political independence and economic security when they faced the election of 1836. The *American State Papers* gave the editors economic security, and the diversity of the Whig party was responsible for their political independence. The Whig party, a label attached to the Jacksonian opposition after 1834, failed to give Gales and Seaton a comfortable political home, for they had little sympathy with many elements within the party.

Gales's and Seaton's stand during the campaign was clearly delineated: support of a United States Bank and internal improvements, protection of manufacturing, nonintervention in foreign affairs, salvation of the union at nearly any price, and sound financial principles for dealing with western lands. Some Whig elements opposed all the policies for which Gales and Seaton stood. The editors well realized this weakness, but they also understood that they would be a political voice of no consequence unless they spoke for the Whigs.

The decade of the 1830s marked a period of transition

which made possible the change from a colonial order "into modern industrial America."[1] Politics, particularly the successful politics of the Jacksonian Democrats, was among the first of the nation's institutions to demonstrate organization as a key factor in meeting the new demands of the society that characterized America during the 1830s.

Although many of the politics for which Gales and Seaton stood required the changes that took place during the Jackson period, the *Intelligencer* editors, as well as large segments of the Whig party, were pledged to a social system of the past and preferred consistency of policy to the pragmatism that proved so successful for the Jacksonians.[2]

In Gales's and Seaton's eyes Whig leadership rested in two men: Clay and Webster. Between 1828 and 1848 the editors were so closely tied to these two men that the *Intelligencer* never enthusiastically supported any other Whig candidate. If the editors' opinions differed concerning which candidate was preferred, Gales usually favored Clay, while Seaton advocated Webster's cause.[3]

During the closing years of Jackson's administration, the *Intelligencer* editors played a consistent but not particularly effective role of opposing Jacksonianism. Gales and Seaton, though defeated in most bouts with Jackson, always licked their wounds and returned to battle with spirit and dignity. The editors believed that the longer Jackson remained in office the worse the financial situation would become.[4] They were inclined to agree with a Philadelphia newspaper in 1835 that claimed conditions in the country never were worse— nor had there ever been such despondency over financial matters.[5] The rising labor organizations in the East and the agrarian organizations of the West were suspected and feared by Gales and Seaton. "Locofocoism," a term the editors used for all shades of opposition and which favored destruction of

1. Lynn L. Marhall, "The Strange Stillbirth of the Whig Party," *American Historical Review* 72 (January, 1967): 468.

2. For a discussion of the policies of the Whig party during this period, see E. Malcolm Carroll, *Origins of the Whig Party* (Durham, N.C., 1925), pp. 118-220.

3. For personal letters between Seaton and Webster, see C. H. Van Tyne, ed., *The Letters of Daniel Webster* (New York, 1902), pp. 613-14, 633; Josephine Seaton, *William Winston Seaton of the "National Intelligencer"* (Boston, 1871), pp. 302-10.

4. For a clear account of Jackson's financial policies and problems, see Arthur M. Schlesinger, Jr., *The Age of Jackson* (Boston, 1945), pp. 115-31.

5. *National Intelligencer*, January 3, 1835.

the existing social systems, was the favorite label employed against the opposition during the last half of the 1830s.[6]

At the time the Whig party was formed, Gales and Seaton had not served as the official presidential organ for ten years, during which time they supported John Quincy Adams and Clay for the presidency. They had exercised important leadership during the early period of the Jackson administration but had become more independent than effective political organization allowed.[7] Although still tied to the federal government by printing patronage and to the United States Bank by debt, the *Intelligencer* editors operated a bit more independently than during their official years. They became reluctant to surrender their independence, and their days of giving unqualified support to any political party were gone.

In some ways the *Intelligencer* played a satisfactory role to no element of the Whig party. Certainly the paper was far too outspoken against nullification to receive any consideration from Calhoun. John Quincy Adams, who at times had been close to Gales and Seaton, was disgusted with the general attitude of the *Intelligencer.* He particularly was annoyed during the spring of 1835 when the Senate, under the leadership of Clay and Webster, refused an appropriation asked for by Jackson. The president made the request to meet the threat of war with France resulting from a quarrel over the collection of a French debt to the United States.[8] The *Intelligencer* praised the Senate's refusal to support Jackson and condemned the House's approval of Jackson's action. House criticism of the *Intelligencer* became more frequent and more heated until Adams felt called upon to request a "truce" from Gales and Seaton. The senior editor was annoyed by Adams's remarks and accused the Massachusetts congressman of "undertaking to school" the editors. Adams disclaimed this but "added that he [Gales] might deify the Senate as much as he pleased, if he would only cease to demonize the House."[9] Adams undoubtedly realized that any plan not approved by

6. Ibid., September 9, 1837.

7. Carroll, *Origins of the Whig Party*, pp. 222-23.

8. For an account of this, see Claude G. Bowers, *Party Battles of the Jackson Period* (Boston, 1928), chap. 14.

9. John Quincy Adams's diary, March 17, 1835, *Memoirs of John Quincy Adams, comprising portions of his diary from 1795-1848*, ed. Charles Francis Adams (Philadelphia, 1875), 9:221.

Webster and Clay would receive no support from the *Intelligencer.*

But by the election of 1836 even Webster was dissatisfied with the course Gales and Seaton pursued. Webster wanted the Whig nomination in 1836, and since Clay unsuccessfully carried the banner in 1832, there was good reason for Webster to hope for the nomination. The Massachusetts legislature supported its senator, but backing from other sections of the country did not materialize.[10] The anti-Masons refused their support[11] and the *Intelligencer* lamented that many opposed Webster because he was considered of "too high an order of intellect" to be president.[12]

Webster, however, was not the only candidate in the field. William Henry Harrison received the support of the Pennsylvania Whig convention, and Hugh Lawson White, a conservative Democrat, was nominated by the Tennessee legislature. There was always an element willing to support Clay, a fact that disturbed Webster and caused him to press hard for Gales's and Seaton's backing. The editors waited for Clay to make his move before committing their paper.[13]

By May, 1835, Webster was completely impatient with the anemic policy Gales and Seaton followed. Webster thought the editors should be forced to support a Whig candidate— preferably him. Webster chose Biddle as a man who might persuade the editors. He wrote Biddle that it was lamentable that the *Intelligencer* should be so unwilling to give or take "suggestions on questions most interesting" to the Whig party. Could Biddle do something to overcome this reluctance? He wrote: "If Messrs. G. & S. are not disposed to support, at present, any named Candidate, they might at least, preach the necessity of supporting *a* Whig Candidate— *some* Whig candidate. We are in danger of breaking up, & dividing. Our national field marshall—he that would rally & encourage us, is the leading paper on our side."[14] But to Webster, this "leader" lacked object or aim. If the bank president decided the matter needed attention, he could, better than

10. Claude Moore Fuess, *Daniel Webster* (Boston, 1930), 2:40-42.
11. Carroll, *Origins of the Whig Party*, p. 137.
12. *National Intelligencer*, May 24, 1836.
13. Clay to Biddle, January 6, 1836, Biddle Papers, vol. 57, Library of Congress, Washington, D.C.
14. Webster to Biddle, May 12, 1835, Biddle Papers, vol. 64.

anyone else, "give an availing kick, in the right quarter."[15]

If Webster hoped for dramatic action, he was sorely disappointed, for throughout the 1836 election the *Intelligencer* editors played a strange and aloof role. They battled against Jackson and his chosen successor, Van Buren. They warned against involvement with Texas and greatly feared the United States would become entangled in a war with Mexico unless those ambitious to acquire territory could be restrained.[16] As far as the border problem between the United States and Mexico was concerned, Gales and Seaton felt Mexico's contention was completely right and justified.[17]

But in all the months during which Gales and Seaton struggled against Jackson's Texas policy, less attention than usual was given presidential candidates. Their preferences were not pressed on their readers. Not until August 13, 1836, did Gales and Seaton reveal their hand. They had no hope that a Whig candidate could be elected. Their one chance was for a defeat of the "spoil" candidate, Van Buren, and then the House might decide from among the Whig candidates. Personally, they admitted, they preferred Webster, but the party throughout the country had failed to support that candidate's just claims.[18] Gales and Seaton realized they were fighting an election without a candidate.

Van Buren's victory came as no surprise to the editors, and they pledged full support to the constitutionally chosen president.[19] Jackson did not escape from the presidential office without a final criticism from the *Intelligencer* editors. They looked upon his farewell address not as a legitimate subject for comment but as a matter to be treated with forbearance. After all, they concluded, he had not written the speech.[20] "Considered, however," they said, "as the production of other minds, which he has only *signed*, it presents itself in a different point of view."[21]

Although the campaign itself lacked luster, two new Wash-

15. Ibid.
16. *National Intelligencer*, July 16, 1836.
17. Ibid., August 6, 1836.
18. Ibid., August 13, 1836.
19. Ibid., December 3, 1836.
20. This was part of the *Intelligencer*'s contention that all Jackson's speeches and writings were the work of the Kitchen Cabinet.
21. *National Intelligencer*, April 13, 1837.

ington newspapers, the *Sun* and the *Washington Mirror*, appeared to support candidates. The *Sun* was edited by J. D. Learned and Charles Pickney and supported White. The *Mirror* favored Harrison and was edited by William Dawes.[22]

Other Washington newspapers followed true to form. The *Globe* unqualifiedly supported Van Buren, and the *Telegraph* favored Calhoun, without a hope of his winning the election. Before Van Buren's inauguration, however, the *Sun*, the *Mirror*, and even the *Telegraph* ceased publication. Duff Green turned over the editorial control to Richard K. Crallé, Virginia nullifier and Calhoun supporter,[23] and one of Washington's most colorful editors was gone from the scene.

Green's failure to receive any congressional support spelled the end of his paper, and his other efforts to stay in business also failed. One unsuccessful project was the Washington Institute, a training school for printers which he opened in 1834. Boys between eleven and fourteen years of age were entered in Green's institute, where they were clothed, fed, and after the first year given a small stipend for their work. Girls also were given work in Green's plant under the supervision of the Sisters of Charity.[24]

Rival printers complained of Green's program, and the Columbia Typographical Society labeled the work of the institute as subversive. Street fighting broke out between Green's printers and those from other plants.[25] Printers in Green's shop eventually went on strike against the *Telegraph* editor, preventing journeymen from doing the work of the strikers and causing Green to abandon his training system. The tradesmen undoubtedly feared that a surplus of trained personnel might result, and the incident precipitated one of the first successful printers' strikes.[26]

The end of the *Telegraph* left Washington with only two

22. Wilhelmus Bogart Bryan, *A History of the National Capital, 1790-1884* (New York, 1916), 2:229.

23. Fletcher M. Green, "Duff Green, Militant Journalist of the Old School," *American Historical Review* 52 (January, 1947): 258. For the lengthy correspondence on Crallé's assuming the editorship, see the Duff Green Papers, Library of Congress, Washington, D.C.

24. Green, "Duff Green," p. 262.

25. Ibid., p. 263; *National Intelligencer*, June 19, 1835.

26. Green, "Duff Green," p. 263.

major papers, the *Globe* and the *Intelligencer*. The *Globe* was a readily accepted voice for the Van Buren forces, but the multileadership of the Whig party still found much to complain about the *Intelligencer*. Its support of Webster late in 1836 made him look favorably on the paper. On the other hand, the *Intelligencer's* preference for Webster alienated Clay. By the end of 1837 Clay's dissatisfaction reached the point where he was anxious to start another Whig paper in Washington. Clay wrote Judge Francis Brooke, a Whig friend in Virginia: "They [Whigs] do not propose to establish it, by resorting to the public crib. . . ." Instead, it would be supported by voluntary contributions "raised among an abused and betrayed people. There is no occasion to conceal the object. The Whigs mean to beat the Admin. party, and the Public press will be one of their instruments. The design is to establish a new paper to espouse and advance *the cause* generally, without reference at present to any particular candidate."[27]

Clay saw clearly how the Jackson party had effectively used its press for rallying support and intended to imitate it. Although Clay's newspaper failed to materialize during the Van Buren administration, another important rival for the congressional printing was found. Blair and Rives, because of the Democratic victory, expected the congressional contracts following the 1836 election, and they did receive the Senate printing.[28]

The vote in the House of Representatives, however, proved that all was not harmonious within the Democratic party either. Conservative Democrats, under the leadership of William C. Rives of Virginia and N. P. Talmadge of New York, led a group in Congress who was impatient with Van Buren for following Jackson's financial policy, which began with the species circular and continued on with the independent treasury system. In the summer and fall of 1837 Rives and Talmadge made plans for defeating the Jackson policy and perhaps even taking over leadership of the Democratic party in 1840. The political maneuvering did not escape Andrew Jack-

27. Clay to Brooke, December 19, 1837, Clay Papers, vol. 21, Library of Congress, Washington, D.C.
28. R. W. Kerr, *History of the Government Printing Office* (Lancaster, Pa., 1881), p. 20.

son and his followers, who feared that Rives might hope to secure the Democratic nomination in 1840.[29]

Early in 1837 the conservative Democrats talked of beginning a paper to support their cause, and Rives and Talmadge had found a candidate for the editorship. Thomas Allen, a native of Massachusetts, recently had completed his law training in New York. While in New York he had gained some writing experience by contributing to magazines, and he eventually became editor of *Family Magazine,* a monthly illustrated journal for general reading. While in this position he visited Washington, where he met some of the nation's leading politicians. He found the capital exciting and warmed to the proposal of Rives and Talmadge that he come to the city and start a newspaper to support their cause. When it became obvious during the summer that Van Buren had no plans for deserting the Jackson financial program, Allen was summoned from a visit in Peoria, Illinois, and returned to Washington to issue the first copy of the *Madisonian* on August 16, 1837.[30]

Andrew Jackson, from his comparatively isolated position at the Hermitage, observed more keenly than many of his friends in Washington that the *Madisonian* meant trouble both for the Democratic party and for the *Globe.* The Jacksonian party was being split, and the spoils would have to be divided. To Jackson, the *Madisonian* meant mischief, and the only one to benefit from the new publication would be the hated Whig party.[31]

Within a month after the first issue of the *Madisonian,* Blair realized that Jackson was correct in his appraisal of the situation. In the balloting for the House printing contract, most observers expected a sharp contest between the *Intelligencer* and the *Globe* now that the *Telegraph* was gone from the scene. The battle proceeded along these lines for the first several ballots, after which the new *Madisonian* was offered as an alternative. Many congressman were weary of the fights

29. See Jackson-Blair correspondence for the late summer of 1837 in the Blair Family Papers, Library of Congress, Washington, D.C.
30. House Miscellaneous Document Number 47, Forty-Eighth Congress, First Session. See also "Thomas Allen," *Dictionary of American Biography* 1:206-7, 1958.
31. Jackson to Blair, September 15, 1837, Blair Family Papers.

over the printing patronage and accepted the alternative. The *Globe* and the *Intelligencer* editors were disappointed to see the *Madisonian* receive the profitable House contract less than a month after the paper was founded.[32]

Gales and Seaton hastened to explain Allen's situation to their readers, saying that Allen's establishment lacked time to build up such an office as was required for the business of the House of Representatives: "The printing will therefore be executed for him, for the present at the office attached to the establishment of the National Intelligencer. . . ."[33]

Blair, dissatisfied with this simple explanation, suspected significant political implications and wrote his former chief, Jackson. Blair correctly blamed Allen's election on friends of the bank. Conservative friends of banks had worked throughout the summer, Blair wrote, to woo away strength from the *Globe* editor: "Gales and Seaton, and Thos. Allen, I presume, form but one firm, though they have different signs."[34] Blair was bitter that the bank issue continued to plague him and his party: "It is the curse of our cause that the Banks have our Editors and Statesmen or their Brothers or sons in their debt, and the result is that their politics take the color of the corporation, that feed them. They are Camelions, [sic] that assume the complexion of the substance on which they repose." But the worst part of all, as far as Blair was concerned, "was to see my office-hands (men and women) turned out of employment without knowing how they were to get their bread. It was a gloomy time at the Globe Office, but it will grow bright again."[35]

By October 1 Blair agreed that Jackson had appraised the *Madisonian* correctly. Indeed, Blair was certain that here was a plan hatched to divide the Democrats in such a way as to defeat Van Buren in 1840.[36]

During the remainder of Van Buren's term, the *Globe* continued to receive the Senate printing. On January 30, 1840,

32. See *Register of Debates in Congress*, Twenty-Fifth Congress, First Session (Washington, D.C., 1837), 14:582.

33. *National Intelligencer*, September 9, 1837.

34. Blair to Jackson, September 9, 1837, quoted in John Spencer Bassett, ed., *Correspondence of Andrew Jackson* (Washington, D.C., 1931), 5:509.

35. Ibid., pp. 509-10.

36. Blair to Jackson, October 1, 1837, quoted in Bassett, *Correspondence of Andrew Jackson*, 5:513.

the House contract also went to Blair and Rives.[37] This meant the only income Gales and Seaton received from Congressional contracts during Van Buren's administration came from the printing handled for Allen and the *Madisonian*, but the profitable *American State Papers* contract continued.

Dissatisfaction with the fights over congressional printing contracts had existed for years. Even before Van Buren's election, criticism reached such proportions that a bill was introduced into Congress calling for abolition of the 1819 rate system. The bill proposed awarding the contracts to the lowest bidder and would have prohibited any newspaper publisher from holding the contract. The proposed legislation served as little more than a protest, since no congressional action was taken.[38]

The printing problem again came before the 1839 session of Congress when members complained that the federal government was overcharged for its printing. The congressional committee heard testimony regarding the type and page sizes used by Washington printers and attempted to determine whether the charges were correct.

The committee investigation amounted to little except to occasion a series of bitter editorial exchanges between the *Intelligencer* and the *Globe*. On December 24 the *Globe* carried an editorial that not only criticized the *Intelligencer*'s printing but attacked the editors' basic integrity. Blair argued that the congressional investigation offered "incontestable proof that, by the use of illegal type, making illegal pages and other artifices, the Opposition printers had made illicit profits varying from three to a hundred per cent on different documents and portions of documents."[39]

The next day the *Intelligencer* took issue with the *Globe*'s assertions, contending the returns from the congressional printing were grossly exaggerated: "The Printing of the House of Representatives, for the 16th, 17th, 18th, 19th and 20th Congress . . . was executed . . . by Gales and Seaton as Printers to that body, and the Printing for the last Congress was executed by Thomas Allen at the printing Establishment

37. Kerr, *Government Printing Office*, p. 20.
38. *Register of Debates in Congress*, Twenty-Third Congress, Second Session (Washington, D.C., 1835), 11:278 and 1457.
39. *Globe*, December 24, 1839.

of Gales and Seaton. The *average* amount of the Printing for the House of Representatives, taking *these six Congresses*, was exactly *Thirty-nine Thousand six hundred and twenty-two dollars* for each session of Congress and no more."[40]

Replying to the *Globe's* charges concerning profits, Gales and Seaton wrote that there were times when congressional printers had lost money. The average profit, Gales and Seaton claimed, never could exceed one-third of the total contract.[41]

A few days later Gales and Seaton thought the *Globe* attacks "evidence of nothing but its [the *Globe*] Editor's unhappy temper and propensities. . . ." Gales and Seaton could not understand how Congress ever could support such a miserable newspaper as the *Globe*. The editors concluded they were confident that among members of Congress "there is not one . . . who will say that we have ever done him personal injury which he is justified in revenging in this way. . . ."[42]

The political philosophies of Van Buren's administration were as odious to Gales and Seaton as Jackson's. The editors viewed Van Buren as something of a puppet who continued the rule of King Andrew, and Gales and Seaton took part in the "systematic opposition" with which the Whigs plagued Van Buren throughout his term.[43]

A few weeks after Van Buren's inauguration, Gales and Seaton pointed toward the coming 1840 election as the only hope for relief from the evils afflicting the country: "Nothing, it is certain, but a change of rulers, afford to the People any prospect of relief from the oppressive evils under which they now suffer from the disastrous policy of the Government." Gales and Seaton were certain that the voters realized their mistake in electing Van Buren and thought if he were to run again, he would not carry six states.[44]

Fiscal policies of the country constituted the chief area of difference between Gales and Seaton and Van Buren. Briefly, the *Intelligencer* policy advocated the United States Bank, as similar to the one which expired in 1836 as possible, and

40. *National Intelligencer*, December 25, 1839.
41. Ibid.
42. *National Intelligencer*, December 28, 1839.
43. Glyndon G. Van Deusen, *The Life of Henry Clay* (Boston, 1937), chap. 20, pp. 320-36.
44. *National Intelligencer*, April 5, 1837.

unequivocal opposition to Van Buren's "sub treasury system." Gales and Seaton, of course, blamed the Specie Circular for much of the great depression of 1837 and for other economic worries throughout this period. If the nation were not ruined by such measures, it was due only to Providence and not to the wisdom of the Van Buren administration.[45]

The *Intelligencer* summarized its reaction to the entire Van Buren administration in an editorial in the fall of 1839. All the problems of the United States were traced to the death of the United States Bank: "The Bank was broken down by the force of Executive power and patronage, and its fall was followed by the depression of the national prosperity which was predicted by patriotic and clear-sighted statesmen as the inevitable consequence of it. The evidence of the truth of these predictions is now seen in the wrecks of industry and enterprise which are strewn about us in all directions."[46] Gales and Seaton were certain that every man who had to work for his "daily bread" suffered greatly for the follies of Jackson and Van Buren.[47]

The subtreasury legislation proposed by Van Buren's administration received little but ridicule from Gales and Seaton. They thought an amendment proposed to the 1839 version of the treasury bill was particularly bad. The amendment, dealing with the method of depositing money from revenue collectors, was of no particular consequence. Yet the *Intelligencer* bitterly attacked the proposal: "We cannot conceive of any thing that can more fully illustrate the whole scope, end, and aim, of the Sub-Treasury Scheme. . . . If it does not open the eyes that are yet blind to the odiousness of this project, surely nothing will."[48]

During the remainder of the administration the *Intelligencer* followed the expected path of any Whig journal: opposition to annexing Texas, support of internal improvements, and preservation of the union at all costs.

The *Intelligencer* engaged in the usual battles with the *Globe*, and because of Blair's attacks on Webster and Clay, Gales and Seaton were certain the *Globe* was becoming more

45. Ibid., December 6, 1838.
46. Ibid., October 26, 1839.
47. Ibid.
48. Ibid., February 21, 1839.

degraded as time passed. They wondered at the "increasing ferocity and abandonment of the official journal. . . . From day to day it becomes more rabid, and from day to day reflects more discredit upon the Administration by its less and lessening regard for propriety and conventional decencies."[49]

Despite all this, the 1840 election loomed as a great promise to Gales and Seaton, for they longed for an end to the political drought they had experienced since Jackson's first triumph.[50] The editors hoped the long-frustrated elements of the Whig party would triumph, and Gales and Seaton never were more certain that such a change was needed: "A change is now, indeed, called for to reform the reform of the party in power, which, by a system of the vilest quackery that was ever palmed off on a confiding People, has brought the country to the verge of bankruptcy and ruin. . . ." The editors thought the past twelve years had represented frequent and large depredations "both upon moneyed institutions of the States, and upon the Government. . . ."[51]

Gales and Seaton had stated their program years before, and it was this program they hoped would bring victory for the Whig party. They wanted to "restore the Government to its purity; to recover for the Legislature the powers usurped from it by the Executive; to rescue from the Executive grasp and absolute possession the money of the People; to diminish the extent of Executive patronage; to secure the freedom of election; and, generally, to reform existing abuses."[52]

Gales and Seaton chose Webster as the candidate having the greatest chance of carrying out this program. Webster, too, eyed the presidency with longing and set himself on a plan designed to win support. He toured the western states to gain greater understanding of the problems there. But no great enthusiasm developed, and the press of private affairs and his desire to travel and engage in other activities designed to win political support prompted Webster to consider resigning his Senate seat in 1837.[53]

A note to Gales and Seaton accompanied Webster's retire-

49. Ibid., February 10, 1838.

50. For a full account of the Whig party in the campaign of 1840, see Robert Gray Gunderson, *The Log-Cabin Campaign* (Lexington, Ky., 1957).

51. *National Intelligencer*, May 2, 1840.

52. Ibid., September 12, 1837.

53. Fuess, *Daniel Webster*, 2:59.

ment announcement and explained its purpose. Webster wrote that he wanted to leave the Senate before his term expired, but he hesitated to mention he might wish to return later: "I do not desire that that act would have too much the appearance of retirement."[54] Friends and party members convinced Webster he should remain in the Senate, and he withdrew his resignation.[55]

But although Gales and Seaton hoped that the election of 1840 would release the nation from all its troubles by electing a Whig, they worried about party affairs. The editors realized that their party lacked the exciting quality necessary to capture the public's imagination. They knew a campaign could not be waged on opposition to Van Buren alone. A strong leader had to be chosen if victory were to be realized. Gales and Seaton felt sure that Webster was such a man.

The Massachusetts senator was a more astute politician in this case than either Gales or Seaton. Realizing his slim chance for victory, Webster left for a trip to England and announced there he did not seek the Whig nomination.[56] The *Intelligencer* refused to accept Webster's verdict as final and kept endorsing him editorially. One editorial read: "Although the name of Mr. Webster is withdrawn from the list of candidates for the Presidency, yet we are persuaded that there is no man who possesses a more powerful influence over the minds of the intelligent portion of his country men, and exercises a great control over their opinions on political subjects, than this man."[57] To demonstrate Webster's qualifications, the *Intelligencer* announced it would run a series of articles on the Massachusetts senator.[58]

In some ways the *National Intelligencer* stood apart from the colorful campaign that was waged on behalf of Harrison and Tyler. There was none of the "Tippecanoe and Tyler, too" in the *National Intelligencer*; instead it waged an anti-Van Buren campaign, rather than one that was pro-Harrison.

The *Intelligencer* had little to say at the time of the nomination. Although its comments left hardly any doubt that it

54. Webster to Gales, March 8, 1837, Webster Papers, vol. 5, Library of Congress, Washington, D.C.
55. Fuess, *Daniel Webster*, 2:60.
56. Ibid., p. 81.
57. *National Intelligencer*, July 20, 1839.
58. Ibid.

wished a Whig victory, not much enthusiasm was shown for the ticket the party offered. February's news columns were instead devoted to a lengthy series of articles criticizing the treasury report of the Van Buren administration.

During March and early April the *Intelligencer* carried its most positive endorsement of Harrison: a series of long, well-researched and tedious articles on Harrison's performance during his time in Congress. The series was concluded on April 2 with a ringing endorsement of Harrison—one of the few such enthusiastic statements issued by Gales and Seaton during the campaign: "We place his claim to public office on loftier ground, when we rank him among the most eminent of his fellow citizens, as a man rich in intellectual gifts and rare acquirements, uniting in his character the wisdom of age and the buoyancy of youth, elevation of soul and humility of pretension, a strong sense of justice and a diffusive humanity."[59] This was the *Intelligencer*'s contribution to positive support for Harrison as a person. The other major contribution was a series of articles, typical of Gales's and Seaton's political writing, which in their view brought the salient issues of the campaign to the people. The series included "Hard Money for the Office-Holders and Direct Taxation for the People—The Complicated System,"[60] "General Washington, the Currency, and the Locofocos,"[61] "Excise Laws,"[62] "A Mirror for the Pretended Democracy,"[63] and "Executive Patronage—The Freedom of Elections—Locofocoism and the U.S. Attorney for the Southern District of New York."[64]

Only once did the rum and hard cider of the campaign appear to have affected the *Intelligencer* editors. In their "Last Appeal" Gales and Seaton demonstrated an emotional depth seldom seen in their newspaper. The editors sounded the charge for all Whigs to "unfurl your banners—give them freely to the breeze, and upon their ample folds inscribe not only the names of the brave Harrison and the virtuous Tyler . . . imitate the chivalry of the heroes of the elder time, and

59. *Daily National Intelligencer*, April 2, 1840.
60. Ibid., August 25, 1840.
61. Ibid., August 27, 1840.
62. Ibid., September 1, 1840.
63. Ibid., October 1, 1840.
64. Ibid., October 22 and 24, 1840.

emblazon upon your signs the rallying cry, 'For God and our Country.' "[65]

The most intimate glimpse of the management of the editorial side of the paper is given for a seven-month period during the 1840 campaign. An excerpt from the diary of Phillip Richard Fendall, Washington lawyer and former editor of the *National Journal*,[66] gives strong evidence that not all editorial matter appearing in the *Intelligencer* was the work of Gales and Seaton, although the paper never identified such writers as Fendall. His account further points out that Gales and Seaton still were not financially at ease, although they did not face the danger of bankruptcy as they had earlier in the decade. But probably most important of all, the diary gives a view of the unbusinesslike way in which the *Intelligencer* was conducted.

Fendall, who occasionally wrote for the paper, was contacted by Gales in May of 1840 to write regularly for the *Intelligencer*. Fendall was reluctant to take such a job because of the demands of his law practice, but Gales insisted, offering $1,200 a year. Fendall's duties included writing reviews of articles from the *Richmond Enquirer* on election issues, a job similar to that which Robert Walsh, the Philadelphia editor, also held.[67] As the election progressed, Fendall found his *Intelligencer* duties took up so much time that he was forced to exclude some of his legal clients. Gales, however, assured Fendall that the *Intelligencer* payments would make this worthwhile.[68]

Fendall's entire employment with the *Intelligencer* was unsatisfactory. Gales failed to furnish newspapers and other publications necessary to carry on the work, which inconvenienced Fendall. Another annoyance involved Gales's instructions that Fendall's writing for the paper be kept secret. Fendall claimed he kept his work hidden, yet he wrote that

65. *National Intelligencer*, October 27, 1840.

66. Bryan, *History of the National Capital*, 2:225. For a short sketch of Fendall, see *Appleton's Cyclopaedia of American Biography* 2:429-30, 1888. See also Clay to Fendall, September 10, 1830, Clay Papers.

67. For a short biography of Robert Walsh, see "Robert Walsh," *Dictionary of American Biography* 19:391-92, 1956.

68. Undated excerpts from the diary of Phillip Fendall, Fendall Papers, Flowers Collection, Duke University Library, Durham, N.C.

Seaton went about telling that the lawyer was writing for the paper. Fendall thought secrecy was of no great importance, but it was exasperating to him.[69]

Probably the most annoying aspect of their entire relationship concerned payment. From May until the latter part of December, Fendall claimed, he received only $50 from the *Intelligencer*, despite the fact he had turned away legal clients in order to carry out his editorial duties. On December 21 Fendall asked Gales for $200 to meet personal obligations and was assured the money would be paid the next day. The following day Gales was ill and unable to collect the necessary $200 to pay Fendall. This delay continued for days, Fendall wrote, and he eventually borrowed money from a friend after Gales promised the sum on a certain date. No money was received.[70] Fendall's diary ends before any financial settlement was made, but if his allegations are correct, they help explain the practices that were partly responsible for the *Intelligencer*'s business plight.

The editors failed to understand the new type of ballyhoo that accompanied the campaign of 1840 and in some ways the issue-oriented paper appeared out of date. The publishers stated their opposition to the admission of Texas and carefully avoided Blair's trap in attempting to give the Whig party an antislavery tinge.[71] Except for a few fervent outbursts, the editors were calm and rational. They did not make superclaims for their candidates, nor did they play too hard on the log cabin and frontier background theme. Neither were Gales and Seaton excessively jubilant with the outcome. They were pleased but not ecstatic.

The editors, sensing that the *Intelligencer* might again become the official presidential journal, warmed to Harrison following his election. Though there was little they could say about his politics, Gales and Seaton contended that Harrison was kind and in public life worked hard in "vindicating the rights and the interests of the poorest, the humblest, and most helpless classes of Society." No one had distinguished himself more for "vindicating the claims of the pioneer. . . the private

69. Ibid.
70. Ibid.
71. William E. Smith, *The Francis Preston Blair Family in Politics* (New York, 1933), 1:137.

soldier, the widow, and the orphan."[72] This was hardly a brilliant defense of the newly elected president.

The nearer the inauguration, the more enthusiastic Gales and Seaton became. Newspaper editors from throughout the nation were invited to join the *Intelligencer* editors in Washington to celebrate the "revolution" that had put the United States back on a safe path. And, reasoned Gales and Seaton, who was more entitled to celebrate this great event than the editors of the journals who had worked hard to achieve this revolution of principle which turned the country back on the old "Washington and Madisonian track"?[73] The festival of editors preceding the inauguration was considered a success.[74]

During the early months of 1841 Gales and Seaton were more optimistic than they had been in sixteen years. The government had been restored to a national course—the pendulum at last had swung back in the right direction. Inaugural addresses no longer were something to be attacked; they were to be applauded: "For ourselves, we should be treacherous to the principles which, with unvarying faith, we have upheld and defended, from the early days of Mr. MADISON'S Administration through all changes which have intervened, if we did not most cordially assent to and adopt the principles of this [Harrison's] Address."[75] The *Intelligencer* editors were proud of the humble part they had played in bringing all this about.[76]

Though Harrison had not been their choice, Gales and Seaton decided that since he was to be their political bedfellow they would make every effort to befriend him. The president-elect stayed at Seaton's house until the inauguration,[77] and Seaton made the address at the city's welcoming ceremony.[78] Seaton's role in the inauguration was rather a natural one, for he recently had been elected mayor of Wash-

72. *National Intelligencer*, January 21, 1841.
73. Ibid., February 21, 1841.
74. Ibid., March 2, 1841, and March 11, 1841.
75. Ibid., March 9, 1841.
76. Ibid.
77. Seaton to John Crittenden, November 14, 1848, Crittenden Papers, vol. 12, Library of Congress, Washington, D.C.; Dorothy Burne Goebel, *William Henry Harrison* (Indianapolis, 1926), pp. 370, 373.
78. Seaton, *William Winston Seaton*, p. 292.

ington in an overwhelming Whig victory.[79] Seaton had served on the Board of Aldermen for the city for several terms since 1819.[80]

Also a guest in Seaton's home at that time was Webster, who had just been appointed secretary of state.[81] The famous incident concerning Webster and President Harrison's inaugural speech supposedly took place there. Webster and Clay jockeyed to control Harrison, and Webster claimed the right to edit Harrison's inaugural speech, which was rife with classical quotations and references to Roman history. One evening as Webster returned home, Sarah Seaton asked him if anything interesting had happened during the day. Webster reportedly replied: "You would think that something had happened if you knew what I have done. I have killed *seventeen Roman proconsuls* as dead as smelts, every one of them!"[82]

Undoubtedly Webster's story provided good humor for the gay and festive Whigs gathered at the Seaton home. And probably this same group talked over Seaton's decision to refuse, as mayor, to sign a resolution expressing appreciation to Van Buren for his service as president. The Boards of Aldermen and Common Council passed the resolution and gave it to Seaton for his signature. On February 22 Seaton returned the resolution with his note explaining his refusal to sign: "If the fulfillment of this resolution could be construed as an expression of mere personal good wishes to a gentleman going into retirement, who had filled the office of President of the United States, I should not object to uniting with the two Boards in the ceremony. . . ." However, Seaton argued, no such tribute had been paid to Jefferson, Madison, Monroe, or Adams, and the editor deemed it " 'uncalled for now.' " He continued: "But as the terms of the resolution express a sentiment of high respect for the official course of the President, and as that sentiment would naturally be construed by him into one of approbation, my signature to the

79. *National Intelligencer,* June 2, 1840.
80. Allen C. Clark, "Colonel William Winston Seaton and His Mayoralty," *Columbia Historical Society Records* 29-30 (1928): 14.
81. Fuess, *Daniel Webster,* p. 90.
82. Ibid., p. 91; Benjamin Perley Poore, *Perley's Reminiscences* (Philadelphia, 1886), 1:250; Peter Harvey, *Reminiscences and Anecdotes of Daniel Webster,* ed. G. M. Towle (Boston, 1921), p. 161n.

resolution would not be in unison with my avowed opinions, and would be known to the President himself to be hollow and insincere." Seaton did not wish his refusal to sign to be construed as an "uncivility at the Chief Magistrate of the Union"; but he chose to take the chance of misconstruing rather than sign a document with which he did not agree. The resolution was tabled following Seaton's action.[83]

These were among the final actions Gales and Seaton took against the Democrats before the party retired from the presidential office in 1841. There was something almost petty about Seaton's action, which shows the bitterness that existed between the *Intelligencer* editors and the party of Jackson and Van Buren. But all this had changed, and the Whigs were in power.

83. Clark, "Colonel William Winston Seaton," pp. 21-22.

CHAPTER 14

A Hollow Victory

Washington weather turned brisk and cold for the March 4, 1841, inauguration of President William Henry Harrison, somewhat dampening the enthusiasm of the jubilant Whigs. The president spurned a fine carriage offered by Whigs in Baltimore; instead he rode his favorite mount, Old Whitey, down Pennsylvania Avenue to the capitol steps. A chilly northeast wind nipped the crowd of some fifty thousand gathered to hear this man who ended the twelve-year dominance of the Democratic party.[1]

Obvious reasons, however, made the consolidation of the Whig victory impossible. The tired old general brought out of retirement to head the Whig ticket already was dragged down by the heavy demands of the campaign, the inaugural activities, and the constant entreaties of office seekers. To succeed as president he needed his full strength to face not only Democratic opposition but also to maintain independence from the Whig Party's leaders—Webster and Clay.

1. Freeman Cleaves, *Old Tippecanoe: William Henry Harrison and His Time* (New York, 1939), pp. 336-37.

Both politicians smarted with the disappointment of losing the Whig nomination in 1840, but each buried his feelings and supported Harrison once he became the party's choice. Each hoped to control Harrison, and each succeeded in occupying a strategic position from which to wield such influence. Clay refused the offer of a cabinet position and remained the leading Whig in the Senate, thereby exercising great power over both houses of Congress. Webster was elevated to the key cabinet post of secretary of state, but partisans of Clay made up much of the remainder of the cabinet. Two of Clay's closest political friends, John J. Crittenden, junior senator from Kentucky, and Thomas Ewing of Ohio, were named attorney general and secretary of the treasury. The remainder of the cabinet included John Bell of Tennessee, secretary of war; George C. Badger of North Carolina, secretary of the navy; and Francis Granger of New York, postmaster general. Only Webster and Granger were not considered sympathetic to Clay's political ambitions.[2]

Clay and Webster represented no unified front, for personal ambitions focusing on the Whig nomination of 1844 motivated them. Both politicians represented nationalistic views in contrast to the states' rights view held by many Whigs. Clay, particularly, believed his American System could bring the country economic maturity through a protective tariff, a national bank, internal improvements, and distribution of revenues from sales of federal lands. Since Webster turned his attentions to the nation's diplomatic problems, for the most part Clay's attempt to win legislative control over the executive branch of the government went unchallenged.[3]

Gales and Seaton, along with the rest of the nation, waited to see what changes the Whigs would bring about. The regular congressional session was nearly over by the time the new administration took office, but on March 17 President Harrison issued a call for a special session to meet on May 31.[4] Then, Gales and Seaton hoped, Clay's domestic program would be adopted.

2. Oliver Perry Chitwood, *John Tyler, Champion of the Old South* (New York, 1939), p. 269.
3. Robert J. Morgan, *A Whig Embattled: The Presidency under John Tyler* (Lincoln, Neb., 1954), p. 23.
4. Ibid., p. 29n.

Time remained in the regular session, however, to allow the Whigs to attack one of the party's outspoken critics, vitriolic Francis Preston Blair. Gales and Seaton took pleasure in seeing their strongest opposition lose one of the rich patronage plums. Blair and his partner, Rives, were elected printers to the House in January, 1840.[5] A year later, on February 11, 1841, less than a month before the Whig party gained control of the government, a lame duck Democratic majority gave the Senate printing to Blair's *Globe*. This was not the proper time to let the printing contract, according to the 1819 regulations. On this basis, the Whigs, with Clay leading the attack, sought the removal of Blair and Rives. Thomas Hart Benton, Missouri Democrat, strongly upheld the *Globe's* retaining the contract,[6] but Senator William Rufus King of Alabama was the chief defender of Blair's position. The exchange between Clay and King was so bitter that the Alabaman demanded satisfaction on the dueling field, and only the careful work of close friends averted bloodshed.[7]

Clay's move succeeded,[8] and political forces began to regroup to elect the new printer. Leading Democrats such as William L. Marcy, New York congressman, felt sure Gales and Seaton would win the contract, but the prospect displeased him. Marcy wrote: "This will be doubtless a good job for G & S but not for the universal Whig party. . . ."[9] Undoubtedly the *Intelligencer's* position as Harrison's official organ caused Marcy to suppose Gales and Seaton would be elected.

If Gales and Seaton wanted the contract, they were disappointed. It went to the *Madisonian,* the paper which then served both anti-Jackson Democrats and a wing of the Whig party.[10] Why Gales and Seaton were refused the contract is unclear, but Allen's election showed the diffusion of the Whig party.

5. *The Congressional Globe,* Twenty-Sixth Congress, First Session (Washington, D.C., 1840), 8:157.

6. *The Congressional Globe,* Twenty-Sixth Congress, Second Session (Washington, D.C., 1841), 9:256.

7. George Rawlings Poage, *Henry Clay and the Whig Party* (Chapel Hill, N.C., 1936), pp. 25-26; William L. Marcy to P. M. Wetmore, March 9, 1841, Marcy Papers, vol. 6, Library of Congress, Washington, D.C.

8. *The Congressional Globe,* Twenty-Sixth Congress, Second Session, 9:236-56.

9. Marcy to Wetmore, March 11, 1841, Marcy Papers, vol. 6.

10. *The Congressional Globe,* Twenty-Sixth Congress, Second Session, 9:236-56.

During the closing days of the 1840-41 session another fight in the House indicated the dissatisfaction with the congressional printing contract system. A House committee held extensive hearings into the cost of congressional printing to determine whether or not prices could be lowered from the 1819 schedule. Prime movers for the reduction were Gales and Seaton, who evidently hoped to scare off other contenders for the contracts by making the prices low enough to make them unattractive to other printers. Gales and Seaton argued that the pricing system in effect in 1840 yielded the printer about 24 percent profit. They were willing to reduce prices sufficiently so that only a 4 percent profit would be realized.

Testifying before the House committee, Gales and Seaton defended their move by explaining that their large printing plant, costing some $50,000, had been built exclusively to handle the congressional printing. Without it, much of the plant stood idle and their printers unemployed. A printing plant operating at a 20 percent reduced profit was better than one standing idle, they argued.

In addition, other factors made reducing the price possible. Paper costs, several of the city publishers admitted, had been cut by half between 1819 and 1840. The price of a double ream of paper had dropped from between $10 and $12 to $5. Gales and Seaton also admitted that the cost of labor between 1819 and 1840 had dropped about one-half. More women and children were being used in the plants at a considerable savings. The *Intelligencer* payroll of some $800 a week covered fifty compositors, forty women and girls, twenty boys for press work, and ten or fifteen assistants and superintendents.

Another major saving was created by the improved technology of printing, particularly in the press room. Some press work had been reduced as much as 80 to 90 percent, Washington printers estimated. They admitted, however, that the small number of copies printed of each congressional document did not allow full advantage of the improvements in printing presses.

The strongest testimony opposing the cut in prices advocated by Gales and Seaton came from John C. Rives, business manager of the *Globe*. He thought the profits being received by the Washington, D.C., publishers were not excessive for the risks involved in the printing: the uncertainty of election and reelection; the great rapidity, dispatch, and punctuality required; the illegibility and imperfection of a great portion of the manuscripts sent; the extra wages for work necessarily done at night and on Sunday; the necessity of employing a large number of first-rate journeymen instead of apprentices; and the high percentage of premium demanded for insurance of such establishments.

The committee, despite its interest in reducing the printing costs, largely agreed with Rives when it concluded that 4 percent profit would "induce no intelligent and competent man, unless pinched by extreme necessity, to devote his time and capital to the hazardous and laborious business of Congressional printing." Congress, the committee concluded, was unwilling to take advantage of the "embarrassments of any man, to procure his labor, and the use of his capital, for less than it is really worth. . . ."[11] Fortunately for Gales and Seaton, they won the House contract without any reduction in prices being imposed.[12]

Within Congress, the great divergence of views within the Whig party soon was apparent. President Harrison resented what he considered Clay's attempts to "lecture" him and accordingly wrote Clay on March 13 expressing annoyance at the Kentuckian's dictatorial manners and asserting the right to seek advice from counsels other than Clay.[13]

Clay was humiliated, but General Harrison died before Clay had the opportunity to plan new strategy. Before the various factions of the Whig party had a chance to tear the general apart, his health gave way to his years and to the heavy demands of the campaign, inauguration, and the few weeks in the presidency. On April 4, General Harrison died of pneumonia. Some felt Harrison's death rescued him from a worse fate. Henry A. Wise, conservative Democrat from Virginia, wrote: "Heaven saved him from the fate of Actaeon; for, had he lived until Congress met, he would have been devoured by the divided pack of his own dogs."[14]

11. *United States House Report 298*, Twenty-Sixth Congress, First Session.
12. *The Congressional Globe*, Twenty-Seventh Congress, First Session (Washington, D.C., 1841), 10:44.
13. Cleaves, *Old Tippecanoe*, p. 339; Carl Schurz, *Life of Henry Clay*, American Statesmen Series (Boston, 1887), 2:194-95; Poage, *Henry Clay*, pp. 226-32.
14. Henry A. Wise, *Seven Decades of the Union* (Richmond, Va., 1881), p. 180.

The Whigs, particularly those of the nationalist school headed by Clay, turned their attention toward Tyler and speculated on what kind of president this Virginian would make. Gales and Seaton hurriedly assured their readers that Tyler was a good man, though they knew little about him and his political program. They portrayed him as a man of "honor, of talent, and character. . . ." He supported the same principles as Harrison. The *Intelligencer* editors hastened to reassure the ranks of the badly shaken Whig party: "President Tyler is a Whig—a true Whig; and we risk nothing in expressing our entire confidence that he will fulfill . . . the expectation of the People. . . ."[15]

Not all Gales's and Seaton's friends were as impressed with Tyler, the first vice-president to fill the top executive office as a result of a president's death. Adams, probably the greatest living student of the presidency, confided to his diary: ". . . Tyler is a political sectarian . . . with talents not above mediocrity, and a spirit incapable of expansion to the dimensions of the station upon which he has been cast by the hand of Providence. . . ."[16]

Tyler inherited an unfortunate position. Many were uncertain whether he was really president or only an acting president.[17] Then, too, his political views or leanings were not well known. He played little part in the 1840 campaign and managed to keep his views in the background while supporting the general party line. Tyler was a particularist—a sectionalist—a southerner—a states' rights man. His views sharply contrasted with the nationalist views of Clay and his elements in control of Congress. Tyler was a congenial man who tried to keep harmony within the Whig party—but he was no puppet and in no way subservient to Clay.[18] The new president, rather than facing a crisis during his first days in office, agreed to retain Harrison's cabinet, although he knew the members held loyalties to Clay and Webster rather than to him.

15. *National Intelligencer*, April 7, 1841.

16. John Quincy Adams's diary, April 4, 1841, *Memoirs of John Quincy Adams, comprising portions of his diary from 1795-1848*, ed. Charles Francis Adams (Philadelphia, 1876), 10:456-57.

17. Morgan, *Whig Embattled*, pp. 1-21.

18. For discussions of Tyler's views, ibid., chaps. 1, 2, and 3; Chitwood, *John Tyler*, pp. 217-36.

The second major problem facing the new president was a special session of Congress he neither called nor desired. The Whigs hoped to push through a new charter for a national bank, and Tyler was no bank man. Tyler and the Clay Whigs quarreled over the cabinet and bank issues during the summer of 1841, and by fall all Whigs realized that their victory of 1840 was hollow indeed.

Within weeks after Tyler took office rumors circulated that he had quarreled with members of his staff over fiscal policy, particularly with regard to the constitutionality of a national bank. The *Intelligencer* criticized the *National Gazette* of Philadelphia for printing such stories and labeled them more "feints of the enemy" which good Whigs should guard against. Again the editors reassured their Whig friends: "So far from the above rumors being true, an entire and perfect harmony exists between the President and the Heads of the Departments, and between and among the heads of Departments themselves."[19]

Tyler played a waiting game, refusing to specify what he considered a desirable fiscal agent for the federal government. Clay, on the other hand, knew exactly what he wanted and doggedly sought this end. Both Clay and Tyler agreed to the repeal of the subtreasury act passed during the Van Buren administration, and both agreed the nation needed some type of regulatory fiscal agency. Clay favored a national bank chartered in the District of Columbia with state branches established with or without the consent of the states. Clay's plan further favored giving the national bank the right of discount. Ewing, Tyler's secretary of the treasury, sent a report to Congress favoring the District of Columbia fiscal agent, but denying it the right to establish state branches without the permission of the state involved. As passed by Congress, the bank bill provided that assent should be assumed unless dissent was expressed by the legislature of the state concerned at its next session.[20]

The bill was passed on August 7, 1841, and for the next ten days the inhabitants of the national capital waited for Tyler's action. Those familiar with Tyler's strong states' rights views maintained that the president would never sign a bill that

19. *National Intelligencer*, July 24, 1841.
20. Schurz, *Life of Henry Clay*, pp. 204-6.

placed a time limit on a state's right to deny the establishment of a branch bank. Some hoped for the sake of harmony he might let the bill become law without signing it.[21]

On August 16 the president took dynamic action by issuing a stinging denunciation of the measure. The veto criticized the discount power of the proposed bank, but the main thrust of the message attacked the constitutionality of the measure. Tyler doubted the power of Congress to create a national bank to operate per se over the union. He particularly objected to the provision that assumed consent if the legislature at its first meeting did not expressly declare against the establishment of a branch. Tyler doubted states could act so rapidly on such an important question without holding an election.[22]

The Clay Whigs chafed under the veto, for they considered this a betrayal of the principles on which the election of 1840 was determined. Gales and Seaton expected the veto because of Tyler's states' rights views but probably were as sorely disappointed as any member of the Whig party. The bank meant as much to them as it did to Clay.

Whig reaction came almost immediately from party members in the nation's capital who smarted under the frustration they felt at seeing new obstacles thrown in the way of their program. One Whig partisan was arrested for his Senate outburst against the veto.[23] The arrest failed to quell the rising resentment, and that evening town partisans gathered in small groups to discuss the president's action. Bitter Whigs who gathered at the Log Cabin Tavern finally determined to march on the White House and to complain personally to the president.

Seaton heard of the plan, and as the city's mayor, hurried to the tavern, where he convinced some of the more prominent individuals to withdraw from such public action. He returned home, certain he had stopped the rally. Later that evening, however, a group of about thirty citizens, well fortified with liquor, assembled before the White House. Members of the mob, accompanied by drumbeats and trumpet blares, cheered rousingly for Clay and the bank and strongly con-

21. Chitwood, *John Tyler*, pp. 223-26.
22. Ibid., pp. 226-27.
23. *National Intelligencer*, August 16, 1841; *Madisonian*, August 16, 1841.

demned the veto. The next night the president was burned in effigy near the White House.[24]

On August 19, 1841, Mayor Seaton called a public meeting to condemn the actions of those few "worthless individuals" who had insulted the president. One resolution passed at the meeting praised the president for his work during his days in Congress on behalf of the District. Another action commended Seaton for his attempt to break up the demonstration.[25]

Despite the intensity of Whig feeling toward Tyler, the *Intelligencer's* editorials remained calm and conciliatory. Gales and Seaton opposed but respected Tyler's constitutional views.[26] The close friendship between the editors and Webster undoubtedly influenced the *Intelligencer*, and Webster wanted no break with Tyler yet. Many ideas expressed in an *Intelligencer* editorial were based on a note framed by Webster for the editors' information.[27]

Webster focused his attention on diplomatic relations with Great Britain, and he hoped to remain in the cabinet long enough to carry out successful negotiations. Clay, on the other hand, hoped to win further favor with the Whig party by attacking Tyler rather than carrying out Webster's conciliatory program. For a time the *Intelligencer* followed Webster.

On August 20 the second bank bill of the session was introduced, and presidential intimates were certain he would approve this measure. The bill was similar to the first, except that it called for a bank with the right only to issue, deposit, and exchange, and not to discount. Without the discount function, Webster and other cabinet members believed Tyler would not object to establishing branches without the consent of the states involved. The bill was hurried through Congress and placed on the president's desk by September 3. The bill still did not meet Tyler's constitutional require-

24. Allen C. Clark, "Colonel William Winston Seaton and His Mayoralty," *Columbia Historical Society Records* 29-30 (1928): 27; Wilhelmus Bogart Bryan, *A History of the National Capital, 1790-1884* (New York, 1916), 2:272; Chitwood, *John Tyler*, pp. 228-29.
25. Clark, "Colonel William Winston Seaton," p. 27.
26. *National Intelligencer*, August 17, 1841.
27. A copy of this note is quoted in Fletcher Webster, ed., *The Writings and Speeches of Daniel Webster* (Boston, 1903), 15:135-36.

ments, and on September 9 he vetoed the session's second bank. Whig hopes of a national bank died.[28]

By the time of the veto of the second bank bill, the battle between Clay and Tyler had grown. The real issue became more apparent daily and rested on whether or not Clay could bring the president under control. In order to do this, Clay had to dominate the cabinet, which the Kentucky senator did for the most part. In order to discredit Tyler, Clay attempted to make much of the fact that the president refused to listen to his cabinet's advice, although Washingtonians knew that a break between the president and the Harrison-appointed cabinet was inevitable.[29]

The *Intelligencer* tried to ignore rumors of the entire cabinet's resignation, but by August 17 the story was sufficiently widespread to warrant a denial. Gales and Seaton could see no reason why the cabinet should resign, and at the same time they repudiated any doctrine of executive supremacy over the cabinet. Disagreement between the cabinet and the president was no reason either for resignations or dismissals.[30]

During the debate over the cabinet resignations, Gales and Seaton attempted to steer a difficult path through the pressures exerted by Clay and Webster. Clay favored the mass resignation of the cabinet to repudiate Tyler and his program. If Clay could defeat Tyler in this way, one of the Kentuckian's rivals for the Whig nomination in 1844 would be eliminated. Webster's only hope of achieving the nomination in 1844 was to remain in the cabinet and to negotiate successfully with Great Britain regarding the northern border of the United States.

Undoubtedly the possibility crossed Clay's mind that since Tyler was at odds with both his cabinet and Congress over the bank issue, he might be persuaded to resign from the presidency, and a special election might have brought Clay to office. It seemed much more likely, however, that Tyler would dismiss his cabinet.[31]

No doubt Gales and Seaton fully realized that passage of the second bank bill would bring the cabinet crisis to a climax.

28. Chitwood, *John Tyler*, pp. 244-45.
29. Morgan, *Whig Embattled*, p. 67.
30. *National Intelligencer*, August 17, 1841.
31. Morgan, *Whig Embattled*, p. 71.

Still on August 31 the editors assured their readers that no trouble existed between the president and his cabinet. The editorial has been viewed as a "falsification" to help Clay force Tyler either to accept the bill or to face the humiliation of the breakup of his cabinet.[32]

The passage of the second bank bill made the cabinet disruption inevitable—either through resignations or removal by the president. On September 9 Gales and Seaton admitted that Whig opponents were trying to isolate the president from his cabinet and leaders in the party.[33] That same evening the cabinet members, except Webster, met and decided to resign.[34]

The *Intelligencer* editors still refused to give themselves over completely to an anti-Tyler program. They commented: "Our feelings of regret, mortification, and pain at this breaking up of the Cabinet are too sincere to allow us to trust ourselves to comment . . . either upon the factor or upon the means and instruments whereby the ill-feeling has been brought about which has thus ended in an open rupture."[35]

Tyler lost little time in appointing his new cabinet. By mid-September, 1841, the executive heads, with the exception of Webster, were men much more sympathetic to the president's political views. Gales and Seaton passed a critical eye over the newly appointed officers. Abel P. Upshur, a Virginia judge, was named to the navy post. The attorney general position went to an anti-Calhoun man from South Carolina, Hugh S. Legare. This was taken as notice Tyler was not leaning toward the Nullifier. John C. Spencer, former representative from New York and ardent foe of a national bank, became secretary of war. Walter Forward of Pennsylvania filled the treasury post, and Charles A. Wickliffe, former governor of Kentucky and a political opponent of Clay, headed the Post Office Department. Gales and Seaton were not too displeased with the appointments. They wrote: "Of all the gentlemen appointed to fill the vacancies, except one, we have some personal knowledge. . . ." Though these were not the "best selections" that could have been made, wrote the editors, "we have no hesitation in saying that the appointments

32. Poage, *Henry Clay*, pp. 88-89.
33. *National Intelligencer*, September 9, 1841.
34. Chitwood, *John Tyler*, pp. 272-73.
35. *National Intelligencer*, September 14, 1831.

are upon the whole better than could have been expected."[36]

The breakup of the Whig cabinet forced Gales and Seaton to make a difficult decision. If they continued to support Tyler, they certainly would lose Clay's friendship, for clearly Clay aimed to replace Tyler as the head of the Whig party. On the other hand, if Gales and Seaton supported the cabinet resignations, they politically opposed Webster, a close friend. Clay and Webster each viewed his particular position as the surest way to the Whig nomination in 1844, and the *Intelligencer* editors were torn between the political ambitions of these two men. Tyler's opposition to a national bank determined the decision, and Gales and Seaton declared their opposition to Tyler and indirectly to Webster.

Webster supporters belittled the *Intelligencer*'s actions. One admirer wrote Webster, asserting that Gales and Seaton took their particular stand because "they are very ignorant of the [bank] subject, but principally because they considered that the confidence of the majority of the Whig party in this city, was especially given to Mr. Clay."[37]

The *Intelligencer*'s decision to support the Clay faction brought immediate responses from both Tyler and Webster. The president displaced the *Intelligencer* as the administration's official paper and took his support instead to Thomas Allen's *Madisonian.* Tyler used strong language: "I can no longer tolerate the Intelligencer, as the official paper. Besides assaulting me perpetually, directly and indirectly, it refuses all defensive articles. . . . There is a point beyond which one's patience cannot endure."[38]

The *Madisonian* aptly phrased the break between the *Intelligencer* and Tyler: ". . . the Intelligencer could not have been an Administration organ unless a National Bank had been established, and it can see no good in the workings of any Administration opposed to a Bank. . . ."[39]

Webster wished to avoid any direct break between himself and the *Intelligencer* editors, and immediately following the resignations of other cabinet officers, he wrote his publishing

36. Ibid., September 16, 1841.
37. E. Litell to Webster, September 14, 1841, Webster Papers, vol. 6, Library of Congress, Washington, D.C.
38. Tyler to Webster, quoted in Chitwood, *John Tyler*, pp. 325-26.
39. *Madisonian*, December 29, 1843.

friends. He did not see sufficient reason for dissolving the cabinet, although he agreed that some banking institution was necessary "to aid revenue and financial operations, and to give the country the blessings of a good currency and cheap exchanges." He was sure the president would operate toward this end. He also stressed the importance of "delicate and important affairs now pending" in the foreign relations' field and thought he should complete these if at all possible.[40]

Evidently on the basis of Webster's explanation Gales and Seaton inserted the following paragraph in the next day's *Intelligencer.* "We are requested to say that Mr. Webster will remain at the head of the new organization of the Cabinet, equally in compliance with the wishes of the President and the unanimous recommendations of his [Webster's] private friends."[41]

Webster was highly annoyed. The paragraph did not convey the essence of the note sent to Gales and Seaton, and he assured the editors that the item was not printed at his request.[42]

This incident hastened a cooling in relations between the publishers and the secretary of state; the general tone of the *Intelligencer* criticism eventually so annoyed Webster that he wanted nothing whatsoever to do with its editors. The rupture took place one day when Seaton called at the secretary's office and was received with an "icy and repelling politeness." Seaton left, determined that he would make no advance of friendship toward Webster until the secretary recovered from his hurt feelings. The break was so complete that an embargo placed by both families forbade any social relations, even though friends attempted unsuccessfully to bring Seaton and Webster together again. At last Webster, "preceded by his son Fletcher, as a diplomatic *avant courier*," came to the Seaton house one evening, embraced his editor friend, and ended the quarrel.[43]

Probably it was fortunate for Webster that he made his

40. Webster to Gales and Seaton, September 13, 1841, quoted in Webster, *Writings and Speeches of Daniel Webster*, 16:358.
41. *National Intelligencer*, September 14, 1841.
42. Webster to Gales and Seaton, September 14, 1841, quoted in Webster, *Writings and Speeches of Daniel Webster*, pp. 358-59.
43. Josephine Seaton, *William Winston Seaton of the "National Intelligencer"* (Boston, 1871), pp. 295-96.

peace with the *Intelligencer*, for the paper strongly supported diplomatic negotiations during the months ahead. Seaton particularly was credited with playing an important role in winning support of the Clay Whigs for the Webster-Ashburton treaty, which settled the border problems in the Maine area between this country and Great Britain.[44] The editors favored a peaceful settlement of the issue and strongly condemned the so-called "Aroostock War," which threatened to involve the two countries in hostilities during the Van Buren period. Gales and Seaton felt certain the British were acting fairly in this matter and that the affair needed only calm, rational minds to settle it.[45] The *Globe*, of course, contended the *Intelligencer* was Webster's tool and questioned the secretary's negotiations.[46] Newspapers of the nation widely reprinted the *Intelligencer*'s editorials, and Gales and Seaton have been credited with helping Webster win vital support for the treaty.[47] The *Intelligencer*'s editorials were particularly forceful once the provisions of the treaty were agreed upon by the negotiators. None of the points that might have been considered disadvantageous to the United States was disclosed, and only favorable comment on the treaty was printed by Gales and Seaton.[48] The paper's stand undoubtedly was intended to counteract the contentions of the *New York Courier and Enquirer* that Webster was the dupe of the British minister, a charge that had little effect.[49]

Gales and Seaton were elated at the signing of the treaty on August 9 and its ratification by the Senate.[50] The agree-

44. Richard N. Current, "Webster's Propaganda and the Ashburton Treaty," *Mississippi Valley Historical Review* 34 (September, 1947): 188.

45. See *National Intelligencer*, June 9, July 30, and August 2, 1842, for the views of the editors.

46. *Globe*, June 9, 1842.

47. For an appraisal of the effectiveness of these editorials, see Current, "Webster's Propaganda," pp. 192-93. Current maintains that Webster was accorded many propaganda privileges in the *Intelligencer* during these negotiations, but the proof he offers does not seem sufficient to find the *Intelligencer* editors guilty of intentionally misleading their readers. There is no doubt that Webster did submit material to the *Intelligencer* on this subject. See Webster, *Writings and Speeches of Daniel Webster*, 16:154-55.

48. Current, "Webster's Propaganda," pp. 193-94; see also the *Intelligencer* during the latter part of July and the first part of August, 1842.

49. Current, "Webster's Propaganda," p. 195.

50. For a copy of the treaty, see *United States Statutes at Large* (Boston, 1846), 8:575-77.

ment, the editors wrote, proved that Webster had put his country above strong party feelings. Gales and Seaton wondered whether any "other citizen would have had it in his power to bring the affair to so happy an issue."[51]

Matters more practical than foreign policy and treaties faced Gales and Seaton during the early years of the Tyler administration. The editors still depended on the congressional printing patronage. The 1841 investigation did not answer the growing dissatisfaction with the printing system on the part of both congressmen and printers. Forces underway eventually brought great changes in the system before the decade passed, but during the Tyler period congressional members continued to complain that the prices allowed under the 1819 printing law were too high. Accordingly, at the extra session of the 27th Congress, an amendment attached to an appropriation bill lowered printing prices by 20 percent.[52]

The reduction, instead of solving the printing problem, caused additional friction between Congress and the Washington printers. Publishers were little interested in contracts that failed to produce a reasonable profit.

The cut was short-lived, for at the closing session of Congress in 1843 the House restored the printing prices to the 1819 level after Gales and Seaton complained that their firm was losing money under the reduced schedule.[53] The Senate held firm for a time to the 20 percent reduction, but following Gales's and Seaton's receipt of the Senate contract on December 5, 1843,[54] special legislation was enacted whereby the *Intelligencer* editors received $37,000 to overcome the loss they expected to sustain under the contract. This was the last congressional printing contract Gales and Seaton held. Upon expiration of the House contract, Blair and Rives once again were elected to the position.[55]

Prices accounted for only part of the agitation between Congress and Washington printers during the early 1840s.

51. *National Intelligencer*, August 23, 1842.
52. *United States Statutes at Large* (Boston, 1846), 5:764.
53. *The Congressional Globe*, Twenty-Seventh Congress, Third Session (Washington, D.C., 1842), 12:382.
54. *The Congressional Globe*, Twenty-Eighth Congress, First Session (Washington, D.C., 1843), 13:9, 210.
55. Ibid.

Congressmen never were satisfied with either the accuracy or the completeness of the reporting of congressional proceedings, even during the period when both Gales's and Seaton's *Register of Debates* and Blair's and Rives's *Globe* existed. Beginning in 1837 Congress discussed the desirability of each house hiring its own reporters. These were to include reporters from newspapers representing both major parties, and those hired were to be sworn to report correctly.[56] Such legislation sounded ideal on paper but had little chance of producing the desired effect. Errors usually were due to the clumsy shorthand system, poor reporting conditions in the two houses, or to the incompetence of the reporters. Political leaning probably had little effect in most cases.[57]

Criticism reached a peak during the 1841 congressional session, and a special committee recommended that Congress hire five reporters to insure adequate and accurate coverage.[58] The plan failed to pass in 1841 and was revived again in 1842 with added stipulations. Hired reporters were required to have proceedings for the entire day in the printer's hands within three hours after adjournment of the houses, a feat considered impossible because of the slow shorthand system used.[59]

The entire plan was defeated,[60] but the hearings provided some interesting information on reporting salaries during this period. Gales and Seaton estimated it would cost $1,200 in wages to report a short session. The editors used two different methods of determining wages—a flat weekly rate and a column rate. Henry G. Wheeler, a top reporter, received $75 a week.[61] Arthur J. Stansbury, another able man of their staff, received $5 a column for his reports.[62] The *Intelligencer's* esti-

56. *The Congressional Globe*, Twenty-Sixth Congress, First Session, 8:470-71.

57. For an appraisal of the reporting in Congress during this period, see Elizabeth Gregory McPherson, "The History of Reporting the Debates and Proceedings of Congress" (Ph.D. thesis, University of North Carolina, 1940), p. 130.

58. *The Congressional Globe*, Twenty-Seventh Congress, First Session, 10:145, 441; McPherson, "History of Reporting," p. 130.

59. McPherson, "History of Reporting," p. 130.

60. *The Congressional Globe*, Twenty-Seventh Congress, Second Session (Washington, D.C., 1842), 11:548, 560-61.

61. *United States Senate Document 114*, Twenty-Seventh Congress, First Session.

62. For an appraisal of Stansbury's work, see Adams's diary, February 19, 1832, *Memoirs of John Quincy Adams*, 8:474-75.

mate of reporting costs for a session ran considerably lower than that of Blair and Rives. The *Globe* editors thought reporting costs would go as high as $250 a week, or $2,500 for even a ten-week session.[63]

Congressional criticism of reporting brought no major change in the staid old *Intelligencer*, but technological advancements underway resulted in drastic changes to the field of journalism before the decade passed. Already the new type presses which made faster printing possible brought a new and more lively newswriting style to the New York penny papers. Sensational climbs carried them to undreamed-of circulation heights.[64] All this amazed Gales and Seaton, but they refused to become part of the revolution, noting that their circulation never was more extensive.[65] The only change they made in their publishing schedule was the addition of a weekly edition of the *Intelligencer*.[66] Evidently the weekly worked out well enough to warrant its continued publication, although no evidence shows it as an outstanding success. The weekly edition followed the same format of the daily and triweekly papers. The diet furnished by the *Intelligencer* remained nearly exclusively hard political news, a policy that had not changed from the time Samuel Harrison Smith issued his first copy in 1800.

Still the papers of the two periods differed. Smith edited a paper of support while Gales's and Seaton's paper was given nearly completely to opposition. Tyler's attitudes toward a financial system for the country and his views on annexing Texas provided Gales and Seaton with editorial fuel during the last years of Tyler's administration.

The *Intelligencer* editors saw little hope of the nation achieving financial stability under Tyler. They felt certain the subtreasury system never would work, and the president's narrow views made a national bank impossible. On these points

63. McPherson, "History of Reporting," p. 130.

64. For details of the changes, see Frank Luther Mott, *American Journalism: A History of Newspapers in the United States through 250 Years, 1690-1940* (New York, 1950), pp. 228-52; Edwin Emery and Henry Ladd Smith, *The Press and America* (New York, 1954), pp. 213-42.

65. *National Intelligencer*, January 1, 1842.

66. See Gales and Seaton to Fendall, September 11, 1841, Gales and Seaton Papers, Library of Congress, Washington, D.C., for a discussion of the prospectus for the weekly paper. See also Winifred Gregory, ed., *American Newspapers, 1821-1936* (New York, 1937), p. 89.

the editors concluded that the president was no sounder than Jackson or Van Buren.[67]

Gales and Seaton supported Clay's revenue bill of 1842 which raised the nation's tariffs and provided for an unconditional continuance of distribution of land sales' profits.[68] Tyler's veto proved to the *Intelligencer* editors that the president was not a Whig but rather a Democrat. The bitterness of this feeling crept into the paper: "A mind thus cramped and fettered by prejudice . . . could hardly be in a condition to form a sound judgement upon any measures which it might become the duty of Congress to present to the President."[69]

Financially, Gales and Seaton concluded, Tyler was nothing more than a "locofoco." The editors referred to the radical element of the Democratic party which blamed the nation's economic difficulties on paper money and the credit system.[70] Gales and Seaton broadened the term considerably and included nearly all elements opposed to a national bank and protective tariffs.[71]

Tyler's frequent use of the veto and his adherence to the doctrine of executive power proved nearly as annoying to Gales and Seaton as his financial policies. Tyler, they charged, defied the Constitution and assumed powers never intended for a president, for to them, there was no such thing as the prerogative power he exercised: "This has been our doctrine from the moment that General JACKSON set up his prerogative pretensions—pretensions in no respect less exceptionable at the present day than when we first denounced them during his iron reign."[72]

But Gales and Seaton offered hope of solution to all these problems. The answer lay in electing a true Whig to the presidency in 1844. In the election showdown, Gales and Seaton believed, "these undaunted Whigs will stand shoulder to shoulder . . . and when they move onwards, will do so with

67. *National Intelligencer*, February 24, 1842.
68. Frederick Jackson Turner, *The United States, 1830-1850: The Nation and Its Sections* (New York, 1935), pp. 503-4; Lyon G. Tyler, *The Letters and Times of the Tylers* (Richmond, Va., 1885), 2:166-70, gives a strongly pro-Tyler view.
69. *National Intelligencer*, July 12, 1842.
70. For a discussion of the locofoco movement, see Arthur M. Schlesinger, Jr., *The Age of Jackson* (Boston, 1945), pp. 201-9.
71. *National Intelligencer*, July 12, 1842.
72. Ibid., March 23, 1843.

a force and power that will be absolutely irresistible."[73]

A year later the *Intelligencer* carried the news that Clay, Gales's favorite of many years, had been named the Whig candidate. Gales and Seaton hailed the Kentuckian as the "fittest man for the office" and praised Clay's forty years of experience and observation of federal government. "For this opinion of ours, and our consequent action, Mr. CLAY owes us nothing; nor is the National Intelligencer, on that account, any more his organ, avowedly or in fact."[74]

But Clay's views on the annexation of Texas as published in the so-called Raleigh letters printed in the *National Intelligencer* in the spring of 1844 had considerably dampened the ardor of many Southern supporters. The letters were written during a stop in Raleigh, North Carolina, while Clay was on a tour of the southern states. Clay forwarded the first letter to John Crittenden for insertion in the *Intelligencer*, but both Crittenden and Gales and Seaton opposed publishing the letters on the grounds that such views would lose Clay the southern support he needed. Gales and Seaton delayed publishing the letter until Clay returned to Washington, D.C., but the Kentuckian could not be deterred in his determination to make his views known.[75]

Clay's insistence on the publication of the letter and the subsequent position of Van Buren on the Texas question have led historians to speculate that an agreement existed between the two candidates to keep Texas out of the campaign of 1844. The Raleigh letter is viewed as Clay's attempt to live up to that agreement.[76]

Clay was not the only Whig candidate in the field, for Tyler's supporters within the party, a small and generally leaderless group, met at Baltimore the following month and nominated the president for reelection. The *Intelligencer* termed the entire Tyler convention as farcical; the editors were unable to comprehend why the president would accept such a nomination.[77] Gales and Seaton wondered why Tyler

73. Ibid., April 11, 1843.
74. Ibid., April 13, 1844.
75. *Washington Star*, January 17, 1903.
76. Glyndon Garlock Van Deusen, *The Life of Henry Clay* (Boston, 1937), pp. 364-66.
77. *National Intelligencer*, June 1, 1844; Oscar Doane Lambert, *Presidential Politics in the United States, 1841-1844* (Durham, N.C., 1936), pp. 159-61.

failed to realize that he was a man without a political party and that such a man was dead politically.[78]

The Tyler nomination did little but annoy the Whigs, because the real threat to that party's victory, of course, lay with the Democrats. Gales and Seaton fully expected their archenemy Van Buren once again would carry the Democratic banner during the campaign, but such a belief betrayed their lack of perception concerning what was happening in the Democratic party.

In the eyes of such Democrats as Blair, Thomas Ritchie, and Andrew Jackson, there was only one man for the Democratic nomination: Martin Van Buren. But Van Buren lost the nomination because of his reluctance to advocate an all-out policy of annexation, which made him suspect among many southerners. In addition, Calhoun and other southern Democrats who had supported the Whig party during the Jackson period now returned to their party and were influential in depriving Van Buren of the support he needed for nomination. The expansionists needed a man firmly dedicated to the annexation of Texas and westward expansion. They found such a man in James K. Polk of Tennessee.

Gales and Seaton knew Polk and had opposed him for years, particularly during the defeat of the Second United States Bank. The editors disliked Polk's politics and were surprised at his nomination.[79] He was not a strong candidate, they assured their readers, and the nomination could "be considered as the dying gasp, the last breath of life, of the Democratic party." Gales and Seaton conceded Polk commanded respect as a gentleman but none as a politician.[80]

Polk's nomination clearly indicated that Tyler's financial policies would not dominate the issues in the 1844 campaign. This issue would have to share the campaign spotlight with the annexation of Texas and the question of the border location for the Oregon territory. Expansionist philosophies added an emotional element to the campaign which the Whigs were unable to match in their drive to elect the next president of the United States.

78. Morgan, *Whig Embattled*, pp. 175-77.
79. For a description of the convention, see Lambert, *Presidential Politics*, pp. 145-59.
80. *National Intelligencer*, May 30, 1844.

Texas was not a new subject, for Gales and Seaton and their Whig brothers for years had opposed annexing this territory. The editors cited two main reasons for opposing the Texas annexation. First, they argued, the United States could not annex the republic without violating treaties with Mexico, which might mean war. Gales and Seaton further argued against acquiring any new territory unless the nation could demonstrate a need to extend its boundaries.[81] The *Intelligencer* editors particularly were annoyed with the views of such southern expansionists as Calhoun and argued that the "old south" would lose rather than gain by such a move. Gales and Seaton concluded: "Nothing is more probable than that the 'annexation' of Texas will drain South Carolina of the most valuable part of her population, if it *did* not leave the State comparatively an unpeopled desert."[82]

Polk was nominated at a time when expansionist elements in Congress were pushing hard for annexation, and the cry was heard that unless the United States acted quickly, Texas might become tied to Great Britain or France through treaties that would make it impossible for the United States to annex the territory.[83] Gales reassured his readers that this country had little to fear from British intervention in Texas, but his effort did little more than again raise the charges that the editor was more pro-British than pro-American in his sentiments. Even the mild *Madisonian* mentioned this point. Gales dismissed the idea as mere rudeness on the part of his opponents.[84]

Calhoun probably was most responsible for the defeat of the treaty to annex Texas in June, 1844. The fiery South Carolinian urged annexation to prevent the British from gaining control of the republic and bringing about the complete abolition of slavery in Texas. Such a challenge rallied the antislavery elements to the side of expansion opponents, and the Senate voted 35-16 against annexation.[85]

The Senate's refusal to annex Texas relieved Gales and

81. Ibid., March 16, 1844.
82. Ibid., April 11, 1844.
83. For a description of the Texas maneuvering with regard to Great Britain and France, see Alfred Hoyt Bill, *Rehearsal for Conflict: The War with Mexico, 1846-48* (New York, 1947), pp. 55-58.
84. *National Intelligencer*, March 19, 1844.
85. Bill, *Rehearsal for Conflict*, pp. 26-27.

Seaton. To them, the rejection meant: "We have not . . . been plunged illegally in a war as detestable as that by which, under the pretenses much the same, Russia, Austria and Prussia helped themselves to whatever part of Poland they liked. . . ."[86]

Clay, more through inept political maneuvering than from conviction, became identified as opposed to the annexation of Texas. True, he wanted no immediate annexation, but expansionists were in the mood for no delay. Gales and Seaton underestimated the importance of the issue and by September forecast that Polk would do well to carry seven states.[87]

By November 12 this optimism was replaced by the bitter depression caused by Clay's defeat. Gales and Seaton viewed the election as an indication of coming disaster. Three days after they admitted their loss the editors wrote of a "paralyzing effect on the public confidence and the moneyed affairs of the country." Business, they continued, would suffer because the victorious party was dedicated to unsound economic policies, just as Tyler had been.[88]

Never, in more than thirty years, did the *Intelligencer* express greater disappointment over an election return than at the outcome of this campaign. They scarcely could reconcile themselves to Clay's defeat by such a relatively unknown politician from Tennessee: "The disappointment and pain with which this result of the late animated canvass has filled our breasts it would be mere affectation in us to deny, or to attempt to conceal from our readers. Wholly unexpected, the event took us completely by surprise. Not even for a moment apprehended, the blow came upon us with a staggering force."[89]

Polk's pledge to annex Texas seemed even more dangerous to Gales and Seaton than his opposition to a protective tariff and to a national bank. Following his election, the *Intelligencer* editors urged that if action be taken, let it not "shock the sensibilities of such of our countrymen as yet entertain some respect for the good old Constitution of the United

86. *National Intelligencer*, July 2, 1844.
87. Ibid., September 17, 1844.
88. Ibid., November 16, 1844.
89. Ibid., November 26, 1844.

States—some regard for the character of probity and fairness in all our dealings as a nation. . . ."[90]

But Polk did not decide the Texas annexation issue, for Tyler had one final victory over the party that elected him. Late in 1844 Tyler again revived and successfully concluded the annexation issue.[91] Gales and Seaton were annoyed by Tyler's contention that this move would serve humanity. They answered: "It would have saved us some trouble if the President had had the . . . good taste—had left out of his several Messages at least all about humanity, and fairly confessed that he wanted a province."[92]

It troubled the *Intelligencer* that some contemporaries seemed to think that acquiring Texas was like "a wedding garment which we have but to don. . . . To us, this wedding garment is the shirt of Nessus, coveted in the prospect, but pregnant with disease, dangerous undoubtedly, and possibly fatal, to our political constitution."[93]

This time the Senate responded more favorably, and Texas became a part of the United States. Gales and Seaton accepted the accomplished fact: "Our own efforts, as those of much abler and wiser men, have failed to arrest an act which a few years ago any man would have deemed insane who had seriously proposed it, we must bow to the will of the majority."[94]

The *Intelligencer*'s pessimism deepened. A man they completely opposed occupied the White House, and the only prospect Gales and Seaton saw for the nation was a bloody war, which at the most could gain objectives with which Gales and Seaton were unsympathetic. What a different picture would have prevailed, they thought, if only Clay had been elected.

90. Ibid., December 14, 1844.
91. Nathaniel Wright Stephenson, *Texas and the Mexican War: A Chronicle of the Winning of the Southwest* (New Haven, Conn., 1921), p. 177; Morgan, *Whig Embattled*, p. 145.
92. *National Intelligencer*, December 24, 1844.
93. Ibid., February 1, 1845.
94. Ibid., March 1, 1845.

CHAPTER 15

A War Against
Manifest Destiny

Torrents of rain swept across the capitol grounds on March 4, 1845, as James K. Polk delivered his inaugural address to what has been described as merely a "large assemblage of umbrellas."[1] Two of these umbrellas sheltered Gales and Seaton, and no others in the audience felt less sympathy for the policies the new president outlined than did the *Intelligencer* editors. Never in all the ten inaugurations Joseph Gales had watched had he felt as alienated by a president's message.

Gales and Seaton were disillusioned and discouraged —even bitter. The nation they hoped to see built seemed far away as they listened to Polk's words. They had tried to understand Jackson before they started criticizing, but Polk

1. John Quincy Adams's diary, March 4, 1845, *Memoirs of John Quincy Adams, comprising portions of his diary from 1795-1848*, ed. Charles Francis Adams (Philadelphia, 1877), 12:179-80.

enjoyed no respite from Gales's and Seaton's editorial barbs.

The editors took exception to nearly every point of Polk's address. They felt the new president seemed to be flaunting his differences with Whig philosophies. Gales and Seaton wrote: "The points of the Address to which we particularly object are the eulogy of the odious Veto power; the unnecessary fling at those who endeavored to avert the public and private distress which followed the refusal to renew the charter of the defunct Bank of the United States; all that part of the Address which relates to the Texas question; and the unnecessary introduction into such a document of the Oregon question. . . ."[2]

On financial matters Gales and Seaton remembered Polk as the one who carried an important part of the fight against the Second United States Bank in 1834. But this constituted only part of their objection to Polk's financial policies, for the editors feared he favored "free trade."

On the last of Polk's major points the *Intelligencer* editors staked out the ground for their bitterest battles with the administration: manifest destiny. Gales and Seaton opposed expanding the country's boundaries under any circumstances until the nation developed its present holdings. Polk's address served notice that his eyes were on the West and strongly hinted that before his term was over the borders of the United States would be greatly altered.

Despite this opposition Gales and Seaton expressed a certain respect for the new president, and they hoped that Polk would be neither "cajoled nor terrified" into a course he did not desire. They especially wished he would not fall under the control of undesirable forces near the administration.[3] Memories of Jackson's Kitchen Cabinet remained fresh in the editors' minds.

If Gales and Seaton worried that the Polk administration would extend the Jacksonian era, they were mistaken. Even before the inauguration strong indications showed that no political leader—particularly Jackson—dominated Polk. The new president defeated the old Jacksonian, Van Buren, to

2. *National Intelligencer*, March 6, 1845.
3. Ibid., March 11, 1845.

gain the Democratic nomination, and Polk did his best to dissociate himself from the vestiges of the party remaining in Washington.

One of the strongest forces of Jacksonianism still on the Washington scene was Francis Preston Blair's *Globe*. This political warrior became one of the newspaper casualties of the 1844 election, which left the *Intelligencer* as the only newspaper survivor of the politically turbulent Jacksonian era.[4]

The conflict between the *Intelligencer* and the *Globe* diminished during Tyler's administration, since both newspapers opposed the president's politics.[5] With Polk's election, Blair once again stood ready to edit the official journal, but the president and his supporters suspected Blair's loyalties far too much to trust him with such a job. For one thing, Blair was friendly with such leaders as Thomas Hart Benton and Van Buren, who opposed Polk's nomination. Blair also personally opposed annexing Texas, an important issue to Polk.[6] Further, Blair was suspected of holding antislavery views.

By February 21 Blair was fairly certain Polk would not use the *Globe* as his official paper,[7] and by the end of February rumors circulated widely that the *Madisonian* would become the president's voice.[8] Before the March 4 inauguration, however, Blair was given the presidential address to publish; on this basis the *Globe* editor assumed his journal once again officially spoke for the federal administration.[9] But Polk intended no such commitment. A few days later Blair pointedly asked the president his intentions regarding the *Globe* and was informed that both Blair and his newspaper were unacceptable to the new administration.

The president cited several reasons, among them the close

4. For details of the circumstances which brought the change, see Jackson-Blair correspondence, Blair Family Papers, Library of Congress, Washington, D.C.

5. William Ernest Smith, *The Francis Preston Blair Family in Politics* (New York, 1933), 1:151-55.

6. Ibid., pp. 144-81.

7. Blair to Jackson, February 21, 1845, quoted in John Spencer Bassett, ed., *Correspondence of Andrew Jackson* (Washington, D.C., 1933), 6:370.

8. Jackson to Polk, February 28, 1845, Jackson-Blair Correspondence, Blair Family Papers.

9. Blair to Jackson, March 24, 1845, Jackson-Blair Correspondence, Blair Family Papers.

ties between Blair, Benton, and Van Buren, which made the editor unacceptable to Calhoun's proslavery wing of the party. Further, the president feared Blair might attempt to exert too much influence over the administration. Polk needed a unifying agent rather than a controversial one and therefore informed Blair that only if he removed himself as editor could the *Globe* become the official journal.[10]

Polk and his supporters discussed the possibilities of starting a new paper, but abandoned this plan. Instead, Blair and Rives were persuaded to sell the *Globe* and to retire from the Washington newspaper field. To replace Blair, Polk sought out an "experienced and talented" editor and Democrat strongly sympathetic to the southern wing of the Democratic party: Thomas Ritchie of the *Richmond Enquirer*. Ritchie, active in Virginia journalism since the first decade of the century, served with Seaton during their early days on Richmond newspapers.

The Virginia editor quickly made his decision to move to Washington after he heard of the possibility of such an opening the first week in February when Colonel R. W. Roberts, congressman from Mississippi, offered to advance $50,000 for a new paper. The proposition appealed to Ritchie.[11] Andrew Jackson Donelson, Jackson's former secretary, had been approached about the editor's job, but he preferred a diplomatic appointment.[12] Polk did persuade another Tennessean to join Ritchie, however—John P. Heiss, former editor of the *Nashville Union*, who became business manager.[13] Not even the name of the *Globe* remained, for the new paper flew the flag of the *Union*.

Gales and Seaton offered best wishes and expressed a kind feeling toward Ritchie. But the *Intelligencer* regretted that the new editor was "at his time of life, entering upon a new scene, with which he is not familiar, and in which we are apprehensive he will find himself ill at ease." They thought the move

10. Polk to Jackson, March 26, 1845, Jackson-Blair Correspondence, Blair Family Papers.

11. W. E. Wallach to Ritchie, February 1, 1845, Ritchie Papers, Library of Congress, Washington, D.C.

12. Polk to Jackson, March 17, 1845, quoted in Bassett, *Correspondence of Andrew Jackson*, pp. 382-83.

13. Eugene Irving McCormac, *James K. Polk: A Political Biography* (Berkeley, Calif., 1922), p. 333.

would increase rather than overcome Ritchie's financial troubles.[14] Politically Gales and Seaton opposed Ritchie as strongly as ever, particularly his views on states' rights and his interpretation of the Constitution, which they termed "more latitudinarian than Federalist of old ever dreamed of."[15]

Some spirit was lost from the *Intelligencer* editorial pages when Blair left the publishing field. No one could goad Gales into bitter comment as well as Blair, for the battles between the editors had been personal as well as political. And though the feuds diminished between the administration paper and the *Intelligencer* editors, evidently little friendship developed, at least between Gales and Ritchie. William L. Marcy, secretary of war, claimed he was instrumental in getting Gales and Ritchie to speak to each other. Marcy thought it might have been the first time the two men ever had spoken.[16]

The printing during the early years of Polk's administration went to the *Union*, but the contracts became even less attractive after the lower price schedule was approved in March, 1845. House printing during the twenty-seventh Congress amounted to about $200,000,[17] but the 1845 act lowered by 20 percent the prices a printer might charge. Despite the lower rates, Ritchie and Heiss were glad to receive the financial support for their new publishing venture.

Awarding the contracts to Ritchie and Heiss was unpopular with both the Whigs and the anti-Polk Democrats and resulted in the repeal of the 1819 method of letting contracts. Under the newly enacted bill, passed August 3, 1846,[18] the contracts went to the lowest bidder rather than to a political favorite. As a result, the printing passed completely from the hands of the Washington newspapers.

Wendell and Van Benthuysen of Albany, New York, a firm that owned no newspaper and only a small printing establish-

14. Considerable information on the *Union* policies and problems may be obtained through reading the Ritchie Papers covering this period. The correspondence shows that almost immediately disagreement between the editor and business manager hindered the effectiveness of the *Union*.

15. *National Intelligencer*, April 17, 1845.

16. Marcy to Gen. P. M. Wetmore, July 4, 1847, Marcy Papers, vol. 13, Library of Congress, Washington, D.C.

17. R. W. Kerr, *History of the Government Printing Office* (Lancaster, Pa., 1881), p. 21.

18. *United States Statutes at Large* (Boston, 1854), 9:113-14.

ment in the capital, received the new contract.[19] Their printing plant was rapidly enlarged but not without considerable
expense to the new government printer. Before the session
was over, Wendell and Van Benthuysen appealed and received from Congress financial relief on the basis that the
company lost money under the contract. The firm remained
in Washington and became the largest printer in the city by
handling most congressional printing on a subcontract basis.[20] The company lost the contracts to Ritchie and the *Union* for the 1849 session, but Ritchie, too, encountered financial difficulty in carrying out the contract, and only a $50,000
grant from Congress enabled him to escape without serious
loss.[21]

Although Gales and Seaton received no contracts under the
new system, they were concerned with the arrangements
made during the 1840s for handling congressional reporting.
By the end of Polk's administration, even the *Intelligencer* editors questioned the wisdom of running long columns of
House and Senate proceedings as they had done for nearly
fifty years. Gales and Seaton frankly explained that without
the printing contracts no newspaper could afford the great
expenditure necessary to publish detailed accounts of congressional proceedings.[22]

The Senate evidently agreed with Gales and Seaton and
accordingly provided for hiring a stenographer and printer
to report and publish its daily proceedings.[23] James A. Houston of New York received the job. Houston's reports were
issued in his *United States Reporter*, devoted entirely to congressional proceedings, but the job proved too much for one man,
and the publication was suspended after only one session.[24] Congress continued to hire the debates reported and
split the contract between the *Intelligencer* and the *Union*.[25]
Gales and Seaton at first welcomed the new source of income,

19. Kerr, *Government Printing Office*, p. 23.
20. Wilhelmus Bogart Bryan, *A History of the National Capital, 1790-1884* (New York, 1916), 2:410.
21. Kerr, *Government Printing Office*, p. 24.
22. *National Intelligencer*, December 25, 1848.
23. *The Congressional Globe*, Thirtieth Congress, First Session (Washington, D.C., 1848), 17:1011, 1049, 1050.
24. Bryan, *History of the National Capital*, p. 411.
25. *The Congressional Globe*, Thirty-First Congress, First Session (Washington, D.C., 1850), 19:1935.

for they felt they were being paid for a service they formerly had provided at their own expense. Indeed, they were "honored" to receive such a contract.[26] The *Intelligencer's* old adversary Blair opposed newspapers' receiving compensation for such reporting and termed the system another form of charity for the *Intelligencer* editors.[27]

The plan proved unsatisfactory, however. Complaints of partisanship flavoring the reporting were heard, and more than ever reporters were charged with incompetence. Solomon W. Downs of Louisiana complained bitterly of a report of his speech printed in the *Union.* He particularly regretted not being quoted accurately because " 'it was the paper which circulated most freely among his constituents, while the National Intelligencer, which contained more accurate reports, circulates little.' "[28] But undoubtedly more important than any criticism was the plan's failure to yield the expected financial return, and in March, 1851, Gales and Seaton relinquished their contract.[29]

John C. Rives, Blair's former *Globe* partner, stepped in and temporarily solved the reporting problem for Congress. Rives no longer published a newspaper but had continued with the annual publication of the *Congressional Globe.* In 1851 he issued the *Daily Globe,* a nonpolitical newspaper which contained little other than detailed accounts of congressional happenings. As such, the *Globe* became known as the official reporter for Congress.[30] Rives's paper reported the debates for the remainder of Gales's and Seaton's publishing career.

The passing of the congressional printing contracts from the hands of Washington printers marked the end of an era in the history of Washington journalism. For twenty-six years Congress had generously underwritten the political organs of the nation's capital, and no publication had received more generous treatment than the *National Intelligencer.* In those

26. Gales and Seaton to Willie P. Mangum, August 15, 1848, Mangum Papers, vol. 16, Library of Congress, Washington, D.C.

27. Blair to Rives, August 5, 1848, Blair and Rives Papers, vol. 5, Library of Congress, Washington, D.C.

28. Down's letter quoted from Elizabeth Gregory McPherson, "The History of Reporting the Debates and Proceedings of Congress" (Ph.D. thesis, University of North Carolina, 1940), pp. 148-49.

29. Ibid., p. 151.

30. Bryan, *History of the National Capital*, p. 412n.

twenty-six years during which the newspapers held these contracts, nearly $2,500,000 was received by Washington publishers. The newspaper receiving the most was the *National Intelligencer*, whose receipts showed about $1,010,000 from the regular congressional contracts. An additional $650,000 was paid for the *Annals* and the *American State Papers* before 1845, and major portions of these two jobs were still to be completed. Blair and Rives received a half million dollars in congressional contract money during their fifteen years in Washington. Duff Green was paid nearly $400,000 before he was forced from the scene in the 1830s, and he received an additional $54,000 for publishing documents relative to public lands. The other major recipient was Thomas Allen, editor of the *Madisonian*, whose income amounted to $258,000.[31]

Despite the loss of this government printing, Seaton attained his greatest popularity during the 1840s, for he edited one of the most important political papers in the country and served as mayor of the nation's capital between 1840 and 1850.[32] He also was committeeman for the Washington Monument Society and secretary of the Smithsonian Institute.[33]

Socially the Seatons presided at one of the most noted centers of hospitality in the city of Washington;[34] Seaton's days away from the office frequently were spent at Winston, his shooting box in the mountains of Virginia. There Seaton and Webster spent long hours in pursuit of wild game.[35] Seaton's pointer dogs were famous and much prized.[36]

Gales, on the other hand, devoted his energies to the *Intelligencer* and to his home at Eckington, located at 332 Seaton Place, N.E. Eckington covered 160 acres but not until Gales's

31. *United States House Document 83*, Twenty-Ninth Congress, First Session.

32. Allen C. Clark, "Colonel William Winston Seaton and His Mayoralty," *Columbia Historical Society Records* 29-30 (1928): 14; Josephine Seaton, *William Winston Seaton of the "National Intelligencer"* (Boston, 1871), pp. 286-87.

33. Seaton, *William Winston Seaton*, p. 287; Clark, "Colonel William Winston Seaton," pp. 88-90; Washington National Monument Society (mimeographed booklet).

34. Mrs. Hugh White's letter, quoted in Helen Nicolay, *Our Capital on the Potomac* (New York, 1924), p. 302; Harriet Weed, ed., *Autobiography of Thurlow Weed* (Boston, 1883), p. 180.

35. Seaton, *William Winston Seaton*, pp. 296-300. Seaton also contains a number of letters Webster wrote to Seaton which dealt mostly with hunting, cooking, or eating fish or wild game (see pp. 303-7).

36. Henry A. Wise to Josephine Seaton, July 10, 1867, quoted in Seaton, *William Winston Seaton*, pp. 319-21.

later years was the estate beautified and improved.[37]

The senior editor, who reached his sixtieth birthday in 1846, suffered from poor health, evidently a rheumatic condition. During the crucial year of 1846, when the *Intelligencer* so strongly opposed the Mexican War, Gales was dangerously ill, and the burden of publishing the paper fell on Seaton.[38] Gales, however, despite his affliction, usually dominated the editorial decisions of the *Intelligencer*.

Despite the disappointments and lack of great financial success Gales and Seaton found the period between 1845 and 1849 interesting. They fought hard against an administration they felt did its best to destroy the United States they had known. Free trade, the Oregon question, and the Mexican War provided the issues on which the *Intelligencer* battled President Polk.

Gales and Seaton abhorred what they considered the radical idea of free trade, which gained strength both in the United States and in Great Britain during the 1840s. The editors termed raising the tariff duties in 1842 as the work of true Whigs, but they sensed it was no lasting settlement. In 1844 the *Intelligencer* gave the tariff question a good deal of space, particularly after Polk's nomination. The Democratic platform said nothing about the tariff, but Polk's antitariff views were known.[39]

After his election Polk appointed to the Treasury post Robert J. Walker of Mississippi, who leaned toward the free-trade philosophy.[40] Gales and Seaton warned the public of the disaster that might prevail if lower tariffs were introduced and asked the president and his advisors to think in terms of the whole country and not just of one section. The editors argued that the consequences were too many and too great to even consider the possibility of lowering the tariff. There would be no money in the national treasury and no money to pay the army, navy, and volunteers. Then, too, lower tariffs would disturb business and drive hundreds of thousands out of employment, deprive wives of their "comforts," send chil-

37. Willis G. Briggs, "Two Pioneer Journalists," *National Republic* 18 (October, 1930): 18-19, 47.

38. Seaton to unidentified correspondent, November 12, 1846, quoted in Seaton, *William Winston Seaton*, p. 248.

39. McCormac, *James K. Polk*, pp. 664-66.

40. Ibid., p. 298.

dren to bed supperless, fill cities with beggars, and bring numerous other hardships to the country. Further, Gales and Seaton argued, every pledge the government had given to "industrial mechanics" would be broken.[41]

But the *Intelligencer* editors pleaded in vain, and on July 30, 1846, the paper's editorial column told of the triumph of the "free traders" over "a betrayed and terrified people." The editors claimed this fatal measure struck at the roots of the industry of the country, as well as at the laborers. It was a "misshapen and monsterous scheme, which its friends would not defend, and which some of them admitted could not be defended—[42] this measure, so pregnant of evil. . . ."[43]

The tariff was not changed again until 1857,[44] but the *Intelligencer* editors' prophecies failed to materialize. Gales and Seaton, however, never brought themselves to accept the Tariff of 1846, since to them it was as far away as possible from the ideals embodied in the American System. And to Gales and Seaton, the " 'American System' advocated by the Whig party is unquestionably the true policy of the country" and should have been the permanent law. "The Tariff of 1842," they said, "was not a perfect one; that of 1846 is believed to be the most imperfect one we ever had. . . ." The editors reasoned that somewhere between the two lay the ground for a judicious compromise.[45]

The *Intelligencer* publishers found Polk no more satisfactory on foreign relations. They thought that a sane policy toward the Oregon question would settle the problem without difficulty. They wrote: "Be our rights to the territory of Oregon what they may, it is quite possible to put ourselves in the wrong, by resorting to certain modes of asserting them." The editors warned that force would not settle the difficulty and also wrote that in their opinion the United States and not Great Britain was creating the crisis.[46] Gales and Seaton

41. *National Intelligencer*, July 21, 1846.
42. The *Intelligencer* referred here to the deflection of certain Pennsylvania and New York Democrats on the bill. They voted with the Whigs against it; see *Polk, The Diary of a President, 1845-1849*, ed. Allan Nevins (New York, 1929), pp. 132-34.
43. *National Intelligencer*, July 30, 1846.
44. Harry J. Carman, *Social and Economic History of the United States* (Boston, 1934), 2:46-48.
45. *National Intelligencer*, April 2, 1849.
46. Ibid., May 6, 1845.

thought the logical settlement of the boundary should be the forty-ninth parallel with a drop to the forty-eighth to accommodate the British claims to Vancouver Island.[47]

Polk, as anxious as the editors to end the Oregon difficulty, received this settlement warmly once it was negotiated.[48] Gales and Seaton offered the agreement as proof of what could be accomplished when nations had faith in each other's integrity. They gave the United States action no special praise, for the editors felt willingness on both sides made the agreement possible.[49] Gales and Seaton found praising the British role in the settlement as easy as praising the Democrats.

Such understanding again raised the charge that Gales was strongly pro-British. This view was strengthened by the *Intelligencer*'s arguments that the United States had little to fear from British interference in Texas and Mexican affairs. Ritchie of the *Union* claimed annoyance at the *Intelligencer*'s constant praise of Great Britain and consistent criticism of the United States.

Gales and Seaton replied: "The National Intelligencer is not, indeed, so far as known, *the organ* of the British Government; for such exclusiveness might conflict with its engagements to the Mexicans. It is, however, we believe, well informed as to the views of the British Ministry. . . ."[50]

With regard to the mention of Mexico, the editors continued: "The language of this passage is susceptible of no other construction than as an assertion that the National Intelligencer has 'engagements' of some sort 'with the Mexicans' if it be not 'the organ of the British Government.' To such an assertion there can be no reply other than that, by whomsoever made; it is detestably false, and without the shadow of foundation; nor less so is the *innuendo* which accompanies it."[51]

The references to Mexico came not by chance, for war with that nation seemed probable from the beginning of the Polk administration. Gales and Seaton felt certain that annexing

47. Ibid., February 24, 1846.
48. McCormac, *James K. Polk*, p. 609.
49. *National Intelligencer*, June 18, 1846.
50. Ibid., May 15, 1845.
51. Ibid.

Texas meant war, and they believed the Texas convention's final ratification on July 4, 1845, brought the conflict a step closer. During the summer of 1845 the president called for troops in order to protect the Texas border, a move described by the *Intelligencer* editors as "*offensive war*," and not necessary for the defense of Texas. They continued: "And should it prove . . . that the President has gone this additional length, then the President will be MAKING WAR, in the full sense of the word, on his own authority and beyond all plea of need, and even without any thought of asking legislative leave."[52] Gales's and Seaton's protests seemed futile as war formally was declared, and the *Intelligencer* vowed never to support the conflict.[53]

The *Intelligencer's* unrelenting opposition to the war with Mexico earned for it the ill feeling not only of the Democrats but also of the Whigs who backed the administration's stand. The *Intelligencer*, recognized spokesman for the old-time Whigs in Washington, embarrassed the party. Shortly after the declaration of war, several unidentified Whig senators who felt the sting of the *Intelligencer* barbs asked Gales and Seaton to cease the outspoken attacks. The letter writers cautioned Gales and Seaton that "persistence in a course so full in injustice toward them, will dissolve all the bonds that might otherwise embarrass them, in placing fairly and fully before the country the issue the Intelligencer has deemed it a duty to make with them."[54] The specifics of this threat are not clear, but the *Intelligencer* editors continued to oppose the war and its backers, whether Democratic or Whig.

The *Intelligencer's* criticism of the Mexican War also made its position difficult with regard to the slave states. Much opposition to the war came from northern states opposed to extending slavery further, and the *Union* quickly grasped at the idea that perhaps antislavery views also motivated the *Intelligencer*. The paper came to its own defense: "Slavery is too much interwoven with the whole social being of the South—with its habits, opinions, feelings, personal fortunes, and even personal safety, with its whole legal and public state,

52. Ibid., August 7, 1845.
53. Ibid., May 13, 1846.
54. Several senators to Gales and Seaton, May 16, 1846, Gales and Seaton Papers, Library of Congress, Washington, D.C.

present and possible—for it to be dealt with either justly or wisely by reproach, or by anything but time and patience." Gales and Seaton doubted that the South could abolish slavery if it wished.[55]

The editorial further stated that only "a simulated and most perfidious party flattery . . . and the political ambition of bad aspirants at home" made this play on sectional hate an issue. Gales and Seaton admitted that the South had acted badly in supporting the war and had taken "blind and fatal steps" subversive to the Constitution in attempting to expand at the expense of its neighbors. Though the editors agreed that the South was not wholly to blame for the Mexican War,[56] they thought it was "much to blame in aiding to pull down its only sure bulwark, the Constitution, in order to acquire a fallacious strength, by a momentary widening of slave territory, which must soon shrink back to its old proportion, and thus magnify . . . instead of diminishing, the existing inequality against it."[57]

Gales and Seaton spoke even more bitterly of the war as it progressed. They defended the Whig generals, Zachary Taylor and Winfield Scott, against Polk's attacks[58] and labeled the reasons for fighting the war "false issues." The editors went so far as to deny the accuracy of the United States charges made against the Mexican government. Gales and Seaton discarded such reasons as repelling invasion, seeking reparations for wrongs against United States citizens, and attempting to right diplomatic slights. "The lust of dominion, the greediness of acquisition . . . the passion which animates alike the spectator and the highwayman . . ." were in their eyes the "animating motive of this war, if not its true source and cause."[59]

President Polk naturally resented the *Intelligencer*'s role in opposing him and viewed the paper's criticism as a basic

---

55. *National Intelligencer*, October 16, 1846. For a discussion of the divergent southern views, see Charles M. Wiltse, *John C. Calhoun, Sectionalist, 1840-1850* (Indianapolis, 1951), pp. 287-302.

56. *National Intelligencer*, October 16, 1846.

57. Ibid., October 20, 1846.

58. Holman Hamilton, *Zachary Taylor: Soldier of the Republic* (Indianapolis, 1941), pp. 218-20; McCormac, *James K. Polk*, pp. 480, 495; Charles Winslow Elliott, *Winfield Scott: The Soldier and the Man* (New York, 1937), pp. 417-35.

59. *National Intelligencer*, March 20, 1847.

disloyalty to the United States. When Nicholas Trist was dispatched as a special envoy from Washington to begin peace negotiations, Polk confided to his diary the necessity for keeping the whole mission a secret. He wrote: "Had his mission and the object of it been proclaimed in advance at Washington I have no doubt there are persons in Washington, and among them the editors of the National Intelligencer, who would have been ready and willing to have despatched a courier to Mexico to discourage the government of that weak and distracted country from entering upon negotiations for peace."[60]

Polk felt the *Intelligencer* was so vindictive that its editors would rather continue the war than suffer his administration to negotiate a just and honorable peace. He thought the negative effect of the *Intelligencer*'s stand could not be underplayed: "The articles in the National Intelligencer . . . against their own government and in favour of the enemy, have done more to prevent a peace than all the armies of the enemy. The Mexican papers republish these treasonable papers and make the ignorant population of Mexico believe that the Democratic party will shortly be expelled from power in the United States, and that their friends (The Federal alias Whig party) will come into power." If the war continued, Polk wrote, it would be "attributed to the treasonable course of the Federal editors and leading men."[61]

Polk misunderstood Gales's and Seaton's devotion to their country. They fought to preserve a nation, not to expand it. The *Intelligencer* editors learned of Trist's mission, published reports on it, and newspapers throughout the country speculated on its success.[62] Eventually, through a complicated and highly unorthodox diplomatic procedure, Trist negotiated an acceptable treaty with Mexico even though he disobeyed Polk's recall orders to do it.[63]

Once the peace treaty was offered Gales and Seaton strongly supported its acceptance. Polk was as grateful to the *Intelligencer* editors for their help in gaining ratification of the

60. *Polk, The Diary of a President*, p. 218.
61. Ibid.
62. Norman Graebner, *Empire on the Pacific: A Study in American Continental Expansion* (New York, 1955), p. 195.
63. Ibid., pp. 195-216.

treaty as he was bitter in criticizing their opposition to the war. Most Whigs and a group of Democrats opposed to Polk set up a howl against the treaty, and Polk feared it might be rejected. On March 1, 1848, however, the president received word that Gales refused to follow some of his fellow Whigs in opposing the treaty and would not write against ratification. Polk was pleased and thought this an important factor in securing acceptance of the treaty.[64]

Gales and Seaton particularly were pleased that Mexico was to receive financial settlement for the property lost. One editorial read: "Had this unfortunate war not arisen, we might, in all probability, have purchased, if desired, for five millions of dollars, the territory now proposed to be added." The editors thought no one who valued national character could object to the large sum: "To close the bloody tragedy by a magnanimous act will be honorable in our country. It will raise us in our esteem and in that of the civilized world."[65]

The Mexican War soon was dropped from the editorial pages of the *Intelligencer* as a subject distasteful enough when comment had been necessary. The editors hailed the salve of money the United States so gingerly applied to the wounds of Mexico as great medicine, and the aggression that Gales and Seaton lamented throughout the war became somewhat more palatable.

64. McCormac, *James K. Polk*, p. 547.
65. *National Intelligencer*, February 27, 1848.

CHAPTER 16

Defeat in Compromise

Scarcely had the nation begun to relax from the tensions of the war with Mexico when the United States felt its muscles tighten once again to face a new crisis. The treaty that brought peace between the two nations fanned the flames of sectional discord and hate which eventually were to plunge the country into an internal holocaust. The roots of the new tensions were deep and old, but they received fresh fertilization from a disgruntled Pennsylvania Democrat who succeeded in injecting the slavery issue into the argument over the division of spoils resulting from the Mexican War.

The man was David Wilmot, whose Proviso sought to exclude slavery from any of the territory acquired from Mexico under the peace treaty. Both northern and southern Democrats rose to the bait offered by Wilmot, and slavery was thrust to the center of the political stage.

The climate was suitable for such a development for the country had seethed with social reform movements for years. In many ways these activities reached their climax in the 1840s, which saw female reformers marching through the streets of Seneca Falls, New York, to declare their independence from the male-dominated society. Such issues as temperance, education, and peace nearly obsessed the tireless reformers. But slavery was the topic that dominated the nation between 1848 and the outbreak of the Civil War.

Gales and Seaton had difficulty accepting this development, for somehow they sought to avoid this entire problem. They refused to recognize slavery as a political issue and avoided using their pages either to defend or attack the institution.

The election of 1848 helped set the stage for the bitter battle that lay ahead. The Democrats were badly divided on the slavery issue, with such prominent members as Van Buren on the brink of joining the free-soil movement. The northwestern Democrats were generally antislavery and free-soil, but much more moderately so, while the southerners developed a fanatic defense of slavery.[1]

The Whigs were no more united and once again turned to creating a leader rather than accepting one from their midst. Two Mexican War generals, Zachary Taylor and Winfield Scott, emerged as logical candidates, partially because of their feuds with President Polk over the conduct of the war.[2] The military victories of Taylor had attracted the most favorable attention, and he was the most likely prospect as the Whig candidate.

General Taylor was by no means the unanimous choice, for Clay still aroused enthusiasm from old-line Whigs. This support continued despite the fact that this was a period of general defeat for Whig policies. The Tariff of 1846 and the Mexican War were among the most serious setbacks.

The *Intelligencer* editors watched Taylor's political rise with misgivings. He never had been a politician, they contended, so how were they to be certain he was a Whig? They argued that the party had candidates who were tried and sound, but even Gales and Seaton knew that wide segments of the Whig party had wearied of following Clay to defeat. The editors

1. The division within the Democratic party is discussed in Clark E. Persinger, "The 'Bargain of 1844' as the Origin of the Wilmot Proviso," *Oregon Historical Society Quarterly* 15 (1914).

2. Polk, *The Diary of a President, 1845-1849*, ed. Allan Nevins (New York, 1929), pp. 185-86, 190-93; Eugene Irving McCormac, *James K. Polk: A Political Biography* (Berkeley, Calif., 1922), p. 467.

also realized they could not afford to oppose vigorously any Whig candidate and still hope to maintain their position as the Whig voice in the nation's capital.

Gales and Seaton found it extremely difficult to openly support Clay over Taylor, for in April, 1847, the *National Whig*, the party's other organ in the capital,[3] came out strongly in favor of the general. The *Intelligencer* editors scarcely could let such a weak newspaper challenge their position in Washington. The *Whig*, edited by Washington G. Snethen, spoke for the segment of the party dissatisfied with Clay and Webster, and General Taylor was the most attractive candidate to this party wing.

The *Intelligencer* was committed to no candidate before the Whig national convention, although the editors gave favorable notice to Clay and had defended Taylor both from the criticism of President Polk and from the attacks of Ritchie and his *Union*.[4] They gave just as cordial treatment to General Scott, a close friend of Seaton's, however, and warned that he should not be overlooked in the search for presidential candidates.[5] But, wrote the editors, they would not decide the issue, for only the national convention had the power or right to impose a candidate on the party.[6]

Gales and Seaton unemotionally accepted Taylor's nomination.[7] They admitted that not all elements of the party favored the general, but they pledged their newspaper's full support. They declared that Taylor would make a safe president and bring the United States closer to the platform of George Washington than at any time in twenty years, except for Harrison's brief administration.[8] Gales and Seaton were growing old and believed the past rather than the future marked America's golden age.

One can understand Gales's and Seaton's lack of en-

3. Wilhelmus Bogart Bryan, *A History of the National Capital, 1790-1884* (New York, 1916), 2:417.

4. See the *National Intelligencer*, February 2, 1847, and the *Union* for the month of April, 1847.

5. *National Intelligencer*, April 17, 1847.

6. Ibid., January 27, 1848.

7. For an interesting account of Taylor's selection as the Whig candidate, see Holman Hamilton, *Zachary Taylor: Soldier in the White House* (Indianapolis, 1951), pp. 67-97.

8. *National Intelligencer*, June 10, 1848.

thusiasm for Taylor by viewing his stand on the issues important to the editors. Taylor felt that there was no real sentiment for the United States Bank; that the tariff should be
increased somewhat from the 1846 schedule but not enough
to make it a money-raising tariff; that surplus funds from land
sales should not be distributed; and that internal improvements were not of major concern to the federal government.[9] This was not the Whig philosophy the *Intelligencer*
editors held.

The Democrats chose as their candidate Lewis Cass, former
territorial governor of Michigan and a party member of long
service in Washington. Gales and Seaton felt Cass had little
to recommend him, yet they warned their party followers not
to underestimate him. A slow starter, but an independent
thinker, Cass might be able to rise above the handicap of the
Democratic party, the editors said.

The *Intelligencer* played a rather diffident role in the 1848
campaign. During the early stages the newspaper contained
little support of Taylor, but once the editors pledged support
for his campaign, the *Intelligencer* carried several long and
carefully written political essays which argued for Gales's
and Seaton's Whig principles rather than directly for the
Whig candidate. In November they hailed the party victory
as a great triumph of Whig principles and gave thanks to
"the Almighty Ruler of Nations for having guided the minds
and hearts of the American People to a result which . . . is
the salvation of the nation." Gales and Seaton felt that a
revival of the heroic age meant a "bright day" ahead.[10]

Perhaps this burst of enthusiasm, sharply in contrast to the
Intelligencer's tone during the campaign, was inspired by the
editors' desire for close ties with the newly elected administration. No doubt they hoped to once again become the official journal and sought this goal socially as well as politically.
One of their first efforts included a letter to John Crittenden,
Kentucky senator who actively campaigned for Taylor, invit-
ing the newly elected president to stay at Mayor Seaton's
home before the inauguration. They reminded Crittenden
that General Harrison had done this. Seaton expressed the

9. Hamilton, *Zachary Taylor*, p. 45.
10. *National Intelligencer*, November 11, 1848.

hope that Crittenden would become Taylor's counselor, since it was important that "he should have some such safe guide & true friend near him in his new & difficult position."[11] Clay was a common friend to Crittenden and the *Intelligencer* editors, and undoubtedly Gales and Seaton counted on this friendship to work in their favor. Seaton was extending more than just a polite invitation involving his official position as mayor of Washington.

The president-elect and his close supporters had no intention of placing the new administration close to Gales and Seaton, largely because of Taylor's dissatisfaction with the *Intelligencer*'s part in the election. Further, Taylor and his supporters were uncertain of Gales's and Seaton's politics, although the editors considered themselves loyal Whigs well within the inner core of the party. In the view of the new administration the *Intelligencer* had to be replaced as Whig spokesman. A. T. Burnley, a liaison between Crittenden and Taylor, supported the idea of the new paper in Washington, and suggested, partly in jest, that he would make a worthy editor. Burnley said: ". . . judging by letters I have seen . . . I should judge there were a great many else where—who do not consider the Intelligencer a fit or desirable organ of Genl. Taylors administration—And I am quite sure another paper will be established." He wrote that a large majority in the New Orleans area was against the *Intelligencer*.[12]

Burnley pointed out more specific criticisms:

Some of the objections . . . against Gales & Seaton are—that they were opposed to Genl. Taylors nomination, & only came in at the 11th hour, & rendered no service, but to write some half a dozen very able, tho' very long winded articles, which few read. In fact when the contest was a hand to hand one, they were firing out a long *fuse* with a slow match, which did no good—That they are too slow & behind the times—That they are committed to ultra measures, & would give a luke warm support to an administration of moderate measures, & especially would they do so if Mr. Clay were to return to the Senate. That they would all the time have an eye to the succession of some *particular* individual. That they did

11. Seaton to Crittenden, November 14, 1848, Crittenden Papers, vol. 12, Library of Congress, Washington, D.C.

12. Burnley to Crittenden, January 12, 1849, Crittenden Papers, vol. 13.

Adams' admn. no good, & would be injurious to Taylor's. That they never did find out that Tyler was not a good Whig. That they have always taken the foreign side in every dispute the country has been in since the war with England, so much so, that many people suspect them of having been *bribed*—That it is all important the President should have some one as his organ, in whom he has the utmost confidence, a man of high character, great firmness, unquestionable ability & judgement, & whose real political opinions correspond with those of the President—That Gales & Seaton are not in that Catagory [*sic*], & that Bullett[13] is, etc. etc. etc.[14]

Burnley was trying to win support for bringing Alexander A. Bullett to Washington to edit an administration paper, and he may have exaggerated. He had another convincing argument: "In conversation with Genl. Taylor I *infer* he has no great confidence in Gales & Seaton, & I *know* he would like very much to have Bullett with him—in fact would prefer him to any one. . . ."[15]

Taylor's preference for Bullett gained wider circulation, and by April the *New York Evening Post* reported that Bullett of the *New Orleans Picayune* would start a new paper in Washington. The *Intelligencer* editors labeled the rumor false—as just another example of inaccurate reporting by Washington newspaper correspondents. Actually, Gales and Seaton explained, Bullett would join Nicholas Snethen in editing the *National Journal*.[16] Equally ridiculous, claimed the *Intelligencer*, were rumors that Gales had complained to the president because the editors had not been taken more into the executive's confidence. Gales and Seaton reported that Taylor read the *Intelligencer* and thought it a good paper. The editors were afraid the *Post* had fallen for a hoax in reporting the story.[17]

As Gales and Seaton well knew, the story was no hoax. On June 13, 1849, a new paper, the *Republic*, became the official journal of the Taylor administration with Bullett, one of Taylor's staunch supporters in the South, editing the paper. John O. Sargent was brought from the *New York Courier and En-*

13. This refers to Alexander A. Bullett of the *New Orleans Picayune*.
14. Burnley to Crittenden, January 12, 1849, Crittenden Papers, vol. 13.
15. Ibid.
16. *National Intelligencer*, April 17, 1849.
17. Ibid.

quirer to prevent the paper from being too prosouthern in tone.[18]

Gales and Seaton betrayed no disappointment at the loss of position and continued to support the Whig party. After all, there were still Clay and Webster, the leaders the editors had favored since 1832. But these two senators, as well as Gales and Seaton, were growing old and seemingly had lost control of the Whigs. Forces already were at work that would spell the final doom to that ill-fated political party, for Gales and Seaton stood ready to follow Clay and Webster in support of the compromise measures of 1850. The party, as well as the *Intelligencer*, found itself tied to a philosophy of compromise the people of the nation were no longer willing to accept.

Even if Gales and Seaton were disappointed at being passed over for the official newspaper position, they could not dwell long on the problem, for more serious matters needed consideration. The publishers had to decide first how to meet their financial needs now that the official printing and advertising were lost and second how to find a solution to the increasing sectional tensions threatening the nation.

The answer to the first problem once again came from a government printing contract. During the early years of Jackson's administration, before the plan for the *American State Papers* was fully developed, Gales and Seaton published the proceedings of the first session of Congress under the title of the *Annals of Congress*. After 1834 nothing was done with the project since congressional printing contracts and the *State Papers* kept the *Intelligencer* plant busy. In 1849 the *Annals* project once again was revived.

On March 2, 1849, Congress passed a bill calling for congressional subscription to the proposed volumes but not without a strong move by the Democrats to block what they considered another "gift" to the *Intelligencer* editors.[19] The opposition continued for years, with Senator August C. Dodge of Iowa contending that the project might cost as much as $150,000 and that no such worth could be gained

18. Bryan, *History of the National Capital*, p. 417; Hamilton, *Zachary Taylor*, pp. 170-71.
19. *Congressional Globe*, Thirtieth Congress, Second Session (Washington, D.C., 1849), 18:646.

from the volumes. Senator John P. Hale, of New Hampshire, was more politically practical in supporting the publishing. He argued the necessity of sustaining the press through government patronage, and he viewed the *Annals* project as a method of maintaining a strong Whig paper in the nation's capital.[20]

The exact cost of the *Annals* project is unknown, but $30,-000 was appropriated to cover the first four volumes.[21] The forty-two volumes published between 1849 and 1856 undoubtedly kept Gales and Seaton in the publishing business.

The other problem could not be solved so easily, for the future of the nation rested on its outcome. Gales and Seaton, while generally ignoring the slavery controversy in the *Intelligencer*, worked hard to bring about the gradual abolition of what they considered a "deciduous institution." Both editors actively participated in the American Colonization Society, and Seaton served as an officer from the society's beginning in 1817 until it gradually died out in the fiery attack on slavery climaxed by the Civil War.[22]

Both Gales and Seaton and their wives had southern backgrounds, and after 1807 none of them ever lived above the Mason-Dixon line. Seaton, particularly, was somewhat attached to that "Southern patriarchal institution," and admitted that he saw "the general benevolence of its operation and the happiness of the race subjected to its protecting administration."[23] Yet he also felt it wrong for one man to hold another in bondage, and all his humanitarian instincts cried out against the institution. Gales, probably even more strongly than Seaton, condemned slavery and hoped to see it abolished from the United States, but not through political means. He felt private individuals would have to do this in such a manner as not to upset "the whole framework and foundations of [southern] society."[24]

20. *Congressional Globe*, Thirty-First Congress, First Session (Washington, D.C., 1850), 19:1050.
21. *United States Statutes at Large* (Boston, 1854), 9:419. For other appropriations, see pp. 524 and 543.
22. Josephine Seaton, *William Winston Seaton of the "National Intelligencer"* (Boston, 1871), p. 264.
23. Ibid.
24. *National Intelligencer*, quoted in Seaton, *William Winston Seaton*, p. 266.

The editors attempted to set an example by freeing their slaves. Together the two were credited by one writer with having "emancipated more slaves at their own cost and out of their own pockets . . . than all the abolitionists put together between the Penobscot and the Potomac."[25]

Gales and Seaton thought antislave persons who spoke of immediate freedom for masses of slaves were unrealistic. The editors noted that the happiness of Negroes was "rarely increased by the change of their relation to society from dependence to freedom, while society certainly" suffered. They concluded: "If slaves were manumitted only when fitted for freedom, their manumissions in numbers would be less objectionable, but even then not harmless, unless the rule were universal."[26]

However much Gales and Seaton worked for gradually freeing slaves, the editors still were convinced the Negro was socially and racially inferior. They spelled out their feelings in broad terms following an army court hearing at which a Negro was allowed to testify. They were shocked by the ruling that took from the officers their "commanding superiority over a class of being which the regulations of society and the laws of the country have placed below them—which the instincts of nature render separate—a class whom ignorance, position and degradation place so easily within the reach of corrupt influences as ever to make them unsafe and dangerous witnesses against their superiors."[27] Gales and Seaton completely opposed any move that gave the Negro a voice "affecting the rights of persons OR property of the white man." The editors were sure that any admission of equality between the two races would shock the entire nation.[28]

With regard to sectional conflicts and as editors of a national paper in a border location, Gales and Seaton attempted to follow a neutral role; at the same time they sought to bring understanding to the extremists at both ends of the slavery controversy. The editors tried to keep the *Intelligencer* from becoming a journal for promoting slavery and for a period beginning in 1817 refused all advertisements offering slaves

25. Seaton, *William Winston Seaton*, p. 266.
26. *National Intelligencer*, August 12, 1829.
27. Ibid., June 25, 1840.
28. Ibid.

"for sale."[29] This policy gradually gave way to the pressures of the interests of slavery and during the last decades of the paper a sizable portion of the advertisements dealt either with "runaway slaves" or "slaves for sale."

Gales's and Seaton's attempt to bring understanding between the North and the South was no short-range project. The program was carried on for at least forty years as the editors argued for a policy of moderation. They warned the North that grave trouble was inevitable unless the antislavery workers were somehow brought under control, since the antislavery elements of the North did not understand the problems of the South. On one occasion the editors wrote: "The Intelligent free persons of color in the Southern States understand their own case much better than some of their overzealous white friends elsewhere."[30] Again the editors urged northern states to leave the solution of the problem to the South, because such interference could lead only to disaster.[31]

During the 1830s Gales and Seaton noted and condemned the increasing volume of abolitionist literature. Such emotional pleas would lead to bloodshed and revolt on the part of the Negro, *Intelligencer* editorials contended. Dissemination of such literature was "a crime which may be perpetrated by a single individual, who is reckless enough to imbue his hands in the blood of hecatombes by depositing incendiary publications in the mail, to inflame the whole country. . . ." The editors felt a Negro's attack on Mrs. William Thornton, prominent Washington social figure, resulted from such literature.[32] They also favored postal regulations to forbid mailing abolitionist material.[33]

But the editors realized that controlling dissemination of the literature would not solve the problem. They again stressed the point that the northern fanatics working for abolition, particularly in the District of Columbia, had to be silenced. Gales and Seaton appealed to what they termed the calm minds of the North and asked that the agitators be

29. Ibid., June 7, 1817.
30. Ibid., October 29, 1831.
31. Ibid., July 25, 1835.
32. Bryan, *History of the National Capital*, 2:144.
33. *National Intelligencer*, August 5, 1833.

quieted: "The peace of society will require that something be done effectually to put an end to the angry excitement, which every where attends their course."[34]

By the late 1840s even Gales and Seaton realized they had misjudged the climate of the nation and that the cry against slavery, rather than diminishing, seemed everywhere to be growing in intensity. The expansion of the country as a result of the Mexican War increased the tensions between the slavery and abolitionist elements, and the Wilmot Proviso forced slavery into the political arena. Still Gales and Seaton refused to admit the gravity of the problem facing the nation. They thought too much emotion was being given to the question of whether slavery should be extended into the newly acquired territories. They argued that the new areas were not geographically suitable for slaves and therefore Congress should let the people settling there make the decision.[35]

Especially annoying to the editors were the political segments such as the Barnburner element in the Democratic party which seemed bent on making slavery its sole reason for existence. Gales and Seaton felt that citizens in the two opposite sections of the country never would agree on the question and since discussion could do "no possible good, we have always . . . kept it out of our columns. In our mind, we have likened it to an inveterate ulcer in the body politic, which handling serves only to irritate, and we have let it alone."[36] Gales and Seaton hastened to explain four days later that their reference to an ulcer had been to the agitation about slavery rather than to the institution itself. Slavery, they argued, was not necessarily bad.[37]

Gales and Seaton wished in vain for the tumult to cease. Instead, it increased, building toward a climax in 1850 as the problem of slavery manifested itself in several different ways. California asked for statehood, and there was no slave state to balance this proposed free state of the West. Northern agitators demanded the end of slavery in the District of Columbia. The boundary in Texas, a slave state, still needed to be set, and the question was undetermined concerning

34. Ibid., July 29, 1835, and October 8, 1835.
35. Ibid., September 11, 1849.
36. Ibid., December 4, 1849.
37. Ibid., December 8, 1849.

whether slavery would be permitted in the new territories acquired from Mexico.

Calm, rational minds were needed to work out the solutions, but instead the northern abolitionists pushed their goals still harder, and the South once again raised the dread cry of nullification and secession. Although Gales and Seaton attempted to quiet the slavery agitation by maintaining an attitude of silence, their stand on nullification was clearly and carefully stated. From the Hartford Convention and throughout the remainder of their lives the editors relentlessly argued against nullification, secession, and any other theory for disrupting the union.

The *Intelligencer*'s early stand that the ties that bound the states into a federal union could not be broken incurred the wrath of southern political leaders. Since a great part of the paper's circulation was in the South, the editors tampered with the life of their paper when they opposed such southern views.

In general Gales's and Seaton's reasoning on nullification was this: ". . . since the establishment of the Constitution, there is no such thing as a Sovereign State, independent of the Union." Nullification, a real danger, could be put down only through the support of the rest of the country.[38] They viewed the doctrine as a seed capable of ripening into poisonous fruit.[39]

During the fall of 1831 the editors summarized their views in a long series of editorials entitled "The Crisis." "For ourselves," they said, "we here enter our solemn protest against a doctrine which we can compare only to the torch applied to our dwelling in open day, by a member, an esteemed member, of one's own family."[40]

That member was, of course, South Carolina. Gales and Seaton agreed that perhaps the tariff had faults, but that nullification would not remedy these: "We have no objection to yielding a modification of the Tariff to fair argument—but to threats of disunion, never!"[41]

Gales and Seaton explained their position on nullification

38. Ibid., January 4, 1831.
39. Ibid., December 6, 1832.
40. Ibid., August 27, 1831.
41. Ibid., October 12, 1831.

and its effects to Mathew Carey, Philadelphia publisher and economist, who criticized the editors for not publishing a series of essays he had written. They rebuked him: "You write as if Nullification were a new thing, or opposition to it. We have been opposing it these three years, and, losing the friendship of Southern Members of Congress, have been brought to the verge of ruin by it. So you will perceive that neither fear, favor, or affectation, has deterred us from our duty."[42]

Gales and Seaton assured their readers in 1850 that there was a way out of the difficulty. Compromise opened the way, for no problems were so serious they could not be resolved if both sides were willing to give. And with this thought, they turned to Clay and his old-line Whigs to lead the country back to safety. Both sides needed to stop testing the sharpness of their missiles, for such hate contests led only to disaster.[43]

The editors contended wrong existed on each side, but they assured their readers that slavery was not the core of the problem. The publishers had blamed the abolitionist agitators of the North for helping create this impression, and now Gales and Seaton condemned the defensive attitude of the South. They had wearied of the South's cry that its rights were being trampled. The editors felt the United States had trespassed on no rights of the South.[44]

Continuing their reasoning and attempting to draw some basic truths on which to build a compromise, Gales and Seaton pointed out that it was unsafe for either side to point a finger and say that the other side had started the trouble. Speaking of the work of the abolitionists, the editors reminded southerners "that agitation was met, if not preceded, by a counter-agitation from the opposite quarter, which was industriously prosecuted so long as political objects were hoped to be attained by means of it. . . ."[45]

The idea of maintaining a balance of power between the North and the South was scoffed at by the *Intelligencer* editors: "The idea of *an equilibrium* established by the Constitution is

42. Gales, Jr., to Carey, July 18, 1831, Edward Carey Gardiner Collection, Mathew Carey Section, Historical Society of Pennsylvania, Philadelphia.
43. *National Intelligencer*, February 2, 1850.
44. Ibid., February 9, 1850.
45. Ibid., March 11, 1850.

a theory, however ingenious, that has no foundation in the Constitution, nor any warrant in history." The *Intelligencer* argued that the Constitution recognized no division of race or territory—only union. The editors ridiculed Calhoun's idea of an amendment to maintain the "equilibrium."[46]

Gales and Seaton believed the only solution lay in Clay's compromise, supported by enough Democrats and Whigs to insure passage. If the editors were apprehensive about any of the compromise measures, they did not betray their feelings to their readers. Gales and Seaton, who supported the measure but devoted no great amount of space to its defense, were relieved once the final passage was achieved.[47] To them the compromise was a victory for the Whig party, but they failed to see that actually the measures fastened a stranglehold on the Whigs and hastened the death of the party that led the conservative forces during the 1840s. The compromise marked the end of an era. New faces replaced such venerable leaders as Clay and Webster. New ideas attracted the attention of the nation. Gone was the desire for compromise which Gales and Seaton felt was the only hope of saving the union.

46. Ibid.
47. For details of the compromise, see Allan Nevins, *Ordeal of the Union* (New York, 1947), 1:219-345. The actual compromise measures and the vote on each are found in the *Congressional Globe*, Thirty-First Congress, First Session, 19:1555, 1573, 1589, 1647, and 1817.

CHAPTER 17

Loss of
a Political Voice

The *National Intelligencer* and its editors, once young and liberal, were definitely old and conservative by the mid-nineteenth century. The paper itself, born in the revolution of 1800, celebrated its fiftieth birthday on October 31, 1850; it boasted the longest life of any Washington newspaper— more than five times as long as any other prominent political paper. During the 1850s each editor passed his seventieth birthday. By 1860 Gales had completed fifty-three years and Seaton forty-eight years on the paper. Such years of service extracted a toll from the editors, and Gales, particularly, become more infirm as the decade passed.

Even the building at Seventh and D streets, N.W., which housed the *Intelligencer*, was regarded as "ancient and dingy." Its architectural elegance, so much in vogue when built, seemed strangely out of place.[1] Inside the *Intelligencer* was even more archaic. One Washington observer described the offices: "On entering the door you find yourself in a lowbrowed, smoke-stained room, with discolored desks and counters. All the appendages seem old-fashioned, even to the aged clerk [Thomas Donohoe], who receives you with a politeness, alas! old-fashioned too." A narrow and rather gloomy flight of stairs led to Gales's office on the second floor. There the same atmosphere prevailed. A table covered with papers, pamphlets, and manuscripts was the room's principal piece of furniture, and behind it sat Gales.[2]

The senior editor's years showed plainly, for by the early 1850s the crippling disease that had plagued him for years had left his right hand paralyzed;[3] his legs were so badly crippled that he was forced to use crutches.[4] His entire appearance indicated advanced age, for his hair was completely white, although still plentiful and unruly. Glasses covered his bright and penetrating eyes, and his heavily wrinkled face seemed to make his large head somewhat smaller.[5]

Still, despite these infirmities Gales continued to exert a dominant influence on the *Intelligencer*. Probably at no time in his life did he write with greater conviction than when he attempted to calm the fiery tempers of those who threatened the union during the 1850s.

Gales's physical condition prevented him from playing too active a role in the social or political life of the community. He was building his country home, Eckington, into a place of great beauty, however. Indeed, as one writer contended, Gales made "a paradise out of originally very rough materials indeed. . . ."[6] From this beautiful estate he traveled daily to the *Intelligencer* building, a trip that became a legend in itself. Reportedly, Gales arrived, borne by the same carriage for

1. Mary Jane Windle, *Life in Washington, and Life Here and There* (Philadelphia, 1859), p. 218.
2. Ibid.
3. Ibid.
4. Henry A. Wise to Henry A. Wise, March 17, 1851, Wise Papers, Library of Congress, Washington, D.C.
5. O. H. Smith, *Early Indiana Trials: and Sketches* (Cincinnati, Ohio, 1858), p. 464.
6. *The Evening Star*, July 28, 1860.

thirty years, at the same hour every day for as long as anyone could remember. There to meet him was the *Intelligencer's* St. Bernard, rumored to have been "discerning enough to discriminate between a 'Whig' and a 'Democrat' "; the dog's eyes were said to glare in the presence of the latter.[7]

Old age was kinder to Seaton, who remained more physically active than his partner. Seaton refused to seek reelection as mayor in 1850[8] and retired to devote his time to the *Intelligencer*, although he still remained active in the Smithsonian and the Washington Monument societies. The Seaton home on E Street between Seventh and Eighth, N.E., continued as a social center, although most old-line Whig and National Republicans with whom the Seatons long had been intimate were either dead or retired.

Probably the highlight of the 1850s for Seaton was his trip to Europe, a journey he had planned for years. In August, 1855, he sailed for a busy three months of sightseeing in many western European centers. He particularly enjoyed England and Scotland.[9] In Sheffield, England, he visited his wife's birthplace and talked to an aunt of the family.[10] From England he moved on to Ireland, then to the cities of Paris, Manheim, Dusseldorf, Berlin, and Munich.[11]

Seaton's absence from the *Intelligencer* probably never would have been possible if it had not been for a highly capable young editor hired in 1850. James Clarke Welling started work as literary editor for the *Intelligencer*, but before he finished his editorial duties he was the guiding hand behind the newspaper. Born in New Jersey, Welling received a degree from the College of New Jersey, later Princeton University. He taught school in New York before moving to Virginia. In the same year in which he joined the *Intelligencer* staff he met and married Genevieve H. Garnett. Two years later Welling's wife died, leaving him an infant daughter.

7. Windle, *Life in Washington*, p. 220.

8. Josephine Seaton, *William Winston Seaton of the "National Intelligencer"* (Boston, 1871), p. 286.

9. See Seaton to Sarah Gales Seaton, September 7, 1855, quoted, ibid., pp. 324-26.

10. Seaton to Sarah Gales Seaton, September 15, 1855, quoted, ibid., p. 331.

11. For excerpts from his letters to his wife and friends, see Seaton, ibid., pp. 333-55.

After retiring from the *Intelligencer* staff in 1865, Welling went into college teaching and served as president of St. John's College at Annapolis, Maryland, in 1867. Later he became president of Columbia College in Washington, D.C., a forerunner of George Washington University.[12]

Welling was a highly literate person, and because of Gales's and Seaton's ages, he handled much news-gathering for the newspaper. The editorials, or leaders as they were called, continued in Gales's style for years after Welling joined the paper.[13]

Welling's youth little affected the general tone of the *Intelligencer*, for it continued to reflect the views of its elderly publishers. Even the circulation of the political journal lagged behind its competition in the nation's capital. The triweekly *Intelligencer*, which had 4,512 subscribers, continued to have the widest distribution of the three papers published by Gales and Seaton. The daily had 2,040 subscribers, and the weekly, started in 1841, was received by 2,784 readers.[14]

The top-circulation paper in Washington was the *Star*, which daily sold 4,975 copies, twice the number of *Intelligencers* distributed. Only 383 persons subscribed to the *Star*'s weekly edition.[15]

This was the first time in its history that the *Intelligencer*'s circulation figure was bested by another Washington paper, but even more significant was the general trend shown by the *Intelligencer* and *Star* figures. The *Intelligencer* circulation slowly declined, while the *Star* grew rather rapidly during the 1850s. The *Star*, begun in 1851 as the *American Daily Telegraph*, was edited by Thomas C. Conolly. The paper was devoted largely to District news and took a nonpartisan stand on political issues. It cost two cents an issue. Its name was changed to the *Star* after it was sold on July 14, 1852, to Joseph B. Tate. On July 5, 1853, W. D. Wallach and W. H. Hope

12. "James Clarke Welling," *Dictionary of American Biography* 19:633-34, 1956.

13. Allan Nevins speculated that Welling may have authored *The Diary of a Public Man*, which purportedly was written in Washington during the early part of the Civil War. I make no effort here either to prove or disprove this speculation. For the most thorough research on the *Diary*, see Frank Maloy Anderson, *The Mystery of "A Public Man": A Historical Detective Story* (Minneapolis, 1948).

14. Affidavit to the Post Office Department, January 11, 1855, signed by Horatio King, William H. Dundas, and J. Marron, Blair and Rives Papers, vol. 6, Library of Congress, Washington, D.C.

15. Ibid.

purchased the *Star* and built it into the leading circulation paper of the city.[16]

The *Star* and the *Intelligencer* were only two of eight dailies published in Washington during the 1850s. None of the others achieved a large circulation. At the beginning of the decade Ritchie, backed by the Democratic party, still published the *Union*, but age and finances forced him to retire in April, 1851, and his interest in the paper was sold to Andrew Jackson Donelson, who formerly served as secretary to his famous namesake.[17]

The *Republic*, begun under the Taylor administration, politically opposed the *Union*. Alexander Bullett and John Sargent edited the *Republic* until its sale to William M. Barwell on August 27, 1853. Barwell published the paper as a weekly for a short time, but it soon ceased publication.[18]

Two other dailies owed their existence to the battle raging over the slavery issue, and both served rather short and ineffective lives. The *Southern Press* was begun during the debate over the Compromise of 1850 and lasted from June 17, 1850, until August 9, 1852. Ellwood Fisher and Edwin de Leon edited the *Press*, which advocated the radical southern point of view but never gained wide circulation. Contributions from interested partisans kept the paper going during its lifetime.[19] The *Constitution*, begun on December 17, 1850, advocated the Compromise of 1850 as a means of ending the agitation over slavery.[20] Its life was exceedingly short.

In 1854 a new daily, the *Daily American Organ*, appeared. It was the spokesman for the American Know-Nothing party which won the city election in Washington in 1854. The political victory for the Know-Nothings marked a great defeat for the *Intelligencer*. For the first time in fifty years the official printing for the city of Washington was taken from Gales's and Seaton's newspaper.[21]

16. Wilhelmus Bogart Bryan, *A History of the National Capital, 1790-1884* (New York, 1916), pp. 420-21.

17. Ibid., pp. 407-8, 421-22; *National Intelligencer*, April 17, 1851; Winifred Gregory, ed., *American Newspapers, 1821-1936* (New York, 1937), p. 92; William E. Smith, *The Francis Preston Blair Family in Politics* (New York, 1933), 1:269-70.

18. Bryan, *History of the National Capital*, p. 417; Gregory, *American Newspapers*, p. 90.

19. Bryan, *History of the National Capital*, p. 418; Gregory, *American Newspapers*, p. 91.

20. Bryan, *History of the National Capital*, pp. 418-19.

21. Ibid., p. 426.

The remaining daily was the *Globe*, but it differed from the *Globe* of Jacksonian days. The paper was revived after Congress began paying for publishing the debates, but it never again served as a party organ. By that time Blair had sold his interest to his partner, Rives, who edited the *Congressional Globe* until it was replaced by the *Congressional Record*.[22] The daily circulation of the Globe in 1855 was 2,036, only slightly less than that of the *Intelligencer*, while the weekly *Globe* was distributed to 13,000 subscribers.[23]

Even though the *Intelligencer* remained in many ways the most respected and revered of the city papers, its influence declined with its circulation. New York newspapers, impatient with the *Intelligencer*'s deliberate method of reporting, succeeded in breaking the near monopoly on congressional news which the *Intelligencer* and leading city Democratic papers held for nearly fifty years. For the first time reporters from outside the city were admitted on an equal basis to the halls of Congress.[24]

Gales and Seaton surrendered no more graciously to the Washington correspondents from papers outside than they did to the telegraph.[25] The *Intelligencer* editors resented the hurried reporting they thought the telegraph encouraged, for they favored long deliberation on a subject before commenting for their readers. One Washington observer accused the *Intelligencer* of resembling a Sunday-school journal for grown-up sinners. Further, he contended, it refused to feel the slightest sense of urgency in dealing with the news. The president's message might go unreported for days while Gales and Seaton pondered the matter so that they could eventually present a thoughtful analysis. But, the writer conceded, the editors' comments were "meat" for all the conservative papers of the country.[26]

The editors believed delay was preferable to hurried and erroneous transmission. They informed their readers:

22. Smith, *Early Indiana Trials*, pp. 244-46.
23. Affidavit to the Post Office Department, January 11, 1855, signed by Horatio King, William H. Dundas, and J. Marron, Blair and Rives Papers, vol. 6.
24. Frederick B. Marbut, "The History of Washington Newspaper Correspondence to 1861" (Ph.D. thesis, Harvard University, 1950), pp. 155-265.
25. For a history of the extension of the telegraph, see Robert Luther Thompson, *Wiring a Continent* (Princeton, N.J., 1947), pp. 20-69.
26. Correspondent George Alfred Townsend, quoted in Allen C. Clark, "Joseph Gales, Junior, Editor and Mayor," *Columbia Historical Society Records* 23 (1920): 143.

"Hardly a day passes over our heads but it is setting the country in ferment with some strange news or some extravagant conceit" that would have been of little importance except for the telegraph's speedy transmission of information before the writers realized the full meaning of an event.[27]

More than just the method of transmitting news had changed by the 1850s. A whole new type of content dominated most newspapers. The human interest and gossip stories were enigmas to old political editors such as Gales and Seaton, who long had fed their subscribers a diet of hard news which originated from the nation's capital. They resented the fact that hired help wrote editorials and leaders and that personal journalism was losing its force. A newspaper became the voice of many reporters, most of whom were never known to the readers.

The Washington correspondents were Gales's and Seaton's main objects of criticism. The *Intelligencer* editors thought the reporters on the whole were rather thoughtless, careless, and irresponsible. Gales and Seaton appraised these new journalists: "Naturally eager to give interest to their letters, some yield a more ready credence to rumor than others, and are in constant danger of substituting fancy for fact. . . ."[28] Four years later the old editors again viewed these "outsiders" and thought their work generally was "falling into discredit," and justly so, for there were many "too careless about accuracy, or content with mere gossip." The editors admitted, however, that there were some careful reporters, but added that these were too few.[29]

Gales and Seaton realized that their resentment of the changes in the journalism field resulted largely from their inability to accept new ideas. They hesitated to express veneration for old customs for fear the younger journalists would think they were out-of-date.[30] The *Intelligencer* editors admitted, however, "that in some of the attributes of modern popular newspapers the journals of this city, and the Intelligencer amongst them, fall greatly behind not a few of their most energetic contemporaries at the North. . . ." But despite this, Gales and Seaton still opposed publishing such material as

27. *National Intelligencer*, August 31, 1848.
28. Ibid., April 7, 1849.
29. Ibid., March 24, 1853.
30. Ibid., December 26, 1853.

rumor and crime. In fact, they discontinued running all crime stories because they felt readers gained nothing from such accounts.[31]

Rather than expressing regret over their unwillingness to change their newspaper, the editors expressed pride in the fact that their paper was considered "Rococo" and "behind the age."[32] Indeed, Gales shrewdly observed that adherence to old-fashioned methods kept the *Intelligencer* alive. Noting the paper's fiftieth anniversary, the editors explained that they thought its success and longevity were due "not to any special amount of talent in the conducting of it, certainly not to its unscrupulous allegiance to any political party, but simply to a uniform adherence to decency and to truth, and a candid admission of excellence, whether found in friend or foe."[33]

In all probability those who continued to subscribe to the *Intelligencer* were like its editors: old and unwilling to change. Complimentary letters were still run occasionally in the paper, but the editors must have noted that the comments came from those who had read the paper for nearly as long as Gales and Seaton had published it. One reader, proud of the number of years he had subscribed to the *Intelligencer*, congratulated the editors for the pleasure they had given him for forty-seven years. The writer felt a kindredship through age: "I still feel a lively interest in the paper, and especially in the conservative news and principles which it puts forth and maintains with equal ability, good taste, and good feeling."[34]

Gales and Seaton optimistically faced the future during the waning months of 1850, but before the decade ended the world they had known for so many years seemed ready to explode and destroy itself while they looked on helplessly. Not all their problems seemed settled in 1850, but most of them seemed to be working toward solution. Zachary Taylor's death brought Millard Fillmore, a friend of the *Intelligencer*, to the presidency. Once again, and for the last time, the paper became the official organ of the president. But by 1850 the position gave little more than prestige, for gone were

31. Ibid., April 18, 1857.
32. Gales, Jr., to Charles Lanman, August 27, 1849, Lanman Papers, vol. 1, Library of Congress, Washington, D.C.
33. *National Intelligencer*, January 2, 1851.
34. Ibid., May 24, 1853.

the profitable printing contracts that so long had accompanied the role of official organ.

The nation's political situation caused the greatest anguish to Gales and Seaton during the decade. The editors watched with grave concern the breakup of the Whig party, the heated debate over the Kansas-Nebraska bill, the fight over "bleeding Kansas," the repeal of the Missouri Compromise, the Dred Scott decision, and the general snapping of ties that held the North and the South together as a nation.

The position Gales and Seaton took throughout the decade was based largely on legal arguments and betrayed a lack of reality on their part. They condemned sectionalism yet argued nearly completely from the point of view found most frequently in the border states. They were not unaware that many factors contributed to the unrest of the nation: quarrels over internal improvements, competing economic systems and philosophies, westward expansion, rapid population growth, and—always—slavery.

To Gales and Seaton two basic considerations dominated all problems that might face the country. First, the editors were convinced that the people of the country believed in union above all. The preservation of the Constitution was most important, and in order to achieve this aim Gales and Seaton played on their second theme: the preservation of law and order.

The editors argued that two major compromises—the Missouri Compromise and the Compromise of 1850—were largely responsible for preserving the peace of the country. The repeal of the Missouri Compromise and the unwillingness of large segments to adhere to the Fugitive Slave Law were interpreted by Gales and Seaton as examples of the lack of reason that plagued the country and that eventually would lead to armed conflict unless a more rational approach could be found. They termed William Lloyd Garrison a "lunatic"[35] and thought John Brown deserved no sympathy or understanding.[36] They were equally critical of such southern firebrands as W. L. Yancey.[37] The editors believed such extremists were polarizing each question and threatening the disruption of the union.

35. Ibid., February 2, 1850.
36. *Daily National Intelligencer*, October 19, 1859.
37. *National Intelligencer*, July 20, 1858.

The *Intelligencer* editors had definite ideas of what was reasonable and just in the entire fight that was developing within the nation. First, they argued that slavery could not be touched as far as the states already in the union were concerned. It was recognized by the Constitution, the law of the land. Second, they argued that the new territories were not suitable to slavery, and therefore it was futile to argue whether new states were to be admitted as free or slave. Given these two bases, the editors reasoned that there were really no problems that could not be handled. Reason rather than emotion was the key.

Still there was something unreal about the position of the *Intelligencer*. Gales and Seaton either failed or refused to recognize the changes that were taking place in the country and to admit the seriousness of the threat to the union. They misled their readers, either intentionally or through their own delusion, into thinking that through compromise and understanding the civil conflict could be avoided. They described for their readers an unreal picture of what was happening in the nation and probably erred seriously in leading subscribers into thinking that reasoning might prevail when the country had passed the point where calm, rational approaches were possible.

The decade had begun on a note of hope for the editors—the compromise measures of 1850. They applauded the action and hoped sectional strife was settled. But despite their belief that the measures were just, Gales and Seaton worried that the compromise never would receive a fair trial. As strongly as the publishers defended the southern position, they grew impatient with the radical elements of the South, which tended to keep agitation on the slavery issue alive.[38] Gales and Seaton held: "There is . . . nothing which the Southern States could reasonably desire—nothing within the Constitutional power of Congress which the South could reasonably ask to be done or omitted—that Congress did not do or omit at its last session."[39]

Gales and Seaton felt the North's reaction to the Fugitive Slave Law[40] was equally onerous. They argued that this was not a moral but a legal issue. No power existed above that of

38. Allan Nevins, *Ordeal of the Union* (New York, 1947), 1:346-79.
39. *National Intelligencer*, January 4, 1851.
40. Nevins, *Ordeal of the Union*, pp. 380-411.

the federal government to which those opposing the law could appeal: "Suppose that those ill-advised or malicious persons at the North, who have been disposed to interfere with the Execution of the Fugitive Slave Law, could be quite sure that they are beyond that reach or danger of actual punishment for so grave an infraction of the duties of a citizen, still they are bound, in our opinion, to obey the Law. . . ." Gales and Seaton argued that laws applied to everyone, for if one man resisted a statute then it meant nothing, even though it was designed to benefit society as a whole.[41]

The *Intelligencer* editors pressed for carrying out the compromise by showing the results that could be expected if it failed. They pleaded with South Carolina to recognize the position it would face even if it seceded and formed a southern confederacy with other states. The smallness of such a nation, the lack of raw materials, and the shortage of harbors would prohibit its becoming a great trade center. Gales and Seaton argued that the union had so much more to offer.[42]

The *Intelligencer* editors advised the North to think of slavery in terms of an economic rather than a moral issue. They reasoned that the northern communities did not find slavery profitable or it would not have been abolished. The strong antislavery segment, the editors continued, was really a small group which "unfortunately hold the balance of power between the two parties of the North, and both parties have courted their favor until we witness the sad effects of widespread agitation of the Northern mind upon the slavery question. . . ."[43]

Gales and Seaton thought the triumph of a unionist ticket in Alabama in the autumn of 1851 proved that the South was quieting down and accepting the 1850 compromise measures: "It is for the North to say whether . . . peace shall take the place of agitation, and harmony and fraternity the place of discord and hate. Let the North maintain the covenants of the Constitution firmly and in good faith, and we shall no more hear the harsh and hateful threat of disunion."[44]

Between 1850 and 1852 the Whig party as Gales and Seaton

41. *National Intelligencer*, January 4, 1851.
42. Ibid., December 1, 1851.
43. Ibid., January 7, 1851.
44. Ibid., November 1, 1851.

knew it died. The leaders whom they followed for so long were gone. The Compromise of 1850, which many Whigs hoped would bring success to their party, actually seemed to tear the political institution apart. Northern opposition to the Fugitive Slave Law daily grew stronger, and the Whigs were blamed for the odious legislation. Southern radicals never really accepted the compromise and continued to set forces in motion which would tear the nation apart.

The 1852 national election provided the strongest evidence possible that the Whig party had fallen apart at the seams. Gales and Seaton hoped their old friend Webster somehow would win the support needed to carry his party's banner in the election.[45] But the Whig party, copying its successful tactics of 1848, again nominated a general, Winfield Scott, a close personal friend of Seaton's but not a political ally.[46] Gales and Seaton were dismayed that all elements within the party failed to support Scott. The editors were impatient with Whigs such as Seward and his free-soilers who worried because Scott had not taken a stand on the Compromise of 1850. Gales and Seaton felt the general's views were well known enough that no party member need worry. The publishers feared that pressing the issue of slavery into the campaign would throw southern support to the Democratic candidate, Franklin Pierce.[47] Scott's defeat, more decisive than anyone expected, dealt a mortal blow to the Whigs. The party, made up of segments of slavery and antislavery men, each suspicious of the other, stumbled over the issue of slavery in 1852 while trying to pretend the problem did not even exist.[48]

Early in Pierce's term the divergent forces within the United States again began tugging at the foundations of the union. The issues of the Kansas and Nebraska bill[49] faced the country, and a new decision concerning which territories should be free or slave had to be made. This time Gales and

45. Nevins, *Ordeal of the Union*, p. 23.
46. Charles W. Elliott, *Winfield Scott: The Soldier and the Man* (New York, 1937), pp. 614-46.
47. For one of the most interesting descriptions of the campaign, see Roy F. Nichols, *Franklin Pierce: Young Hickory of the Granite Hills* (Philadelphia, 1958), pp. 205-15.
48. Nevins, *Ordeal of the Union*, 2:36-42; Henry H. Simms, *A Decade of Sectional Controversy* (Chapel Hill, N.C., 1942), pp. 56-57.
49. Nevins, *Ordeal of the Union*, pp. 78-121; Simms, *Sectional Controversy*, pp. 72-99.

Seaton felt the northern abolitionists had started the trouble. The editors reasoned that the Compromise of 1850 had worked fairly well and that times had been relatively tranquil. But now the abolitionists were working again: ". . . these mischievous forces are rallying on the issue of the Nebraska bill which would repeal the Missouri Compromise."[50]

Gales and Seaton looked for compromise, but no old champions of the legislative compromise were present. A new crop of congressmen and senators had taken their place, and these new men were unwilling to deviate from their positions. But Gales and Seaton felt a concession had to be made because neither side could afford a victory.

By late May, 1854, the *Intelligencer* editors mourned the end of the Missouri Compromise: "The final blow was inflicted on the venerable Missouri Compromise on Thursday night last, and the ancient Pacificator of the Country, this Healer of Discord, this Friend of the Union, was dispatched. . . ." The editors wrote that nothing had been gained but much lost. Gales and Seaton believed that the death of the compromise made disunion more probable.[51]

By the fall of 1854 Gales and Seaton realized that sectional political parties were gaining ground. The editors thought they could discern southern efforts to unite the South in the Democratic party to oppose the North: "What is this but a notice to all anti-slavery elements of the North to combine in the same way, but with the advantage of outnumbering the Southern organization?" Gales and Seaton wrote that only disunion could result.[52]

The editors saw what was happening to the nation. In their minds, passion was being substituted for reason, and no solution seemed evident. The two men, tired and considered old-fashioned, believed differences between the sections of the country could be settled without tearing it apart. So much of what the people in both the areas argued about could not be controlled anyway. The answer to the problem of "bleeding Kansas" already was determined, for "the inevitable and natural laws of natural growth and population would determine the character of the social and industrial system of Kan-

50. *National Intelligencer*, February 21, 1854.
51. Ibid., May 27, 1854.
52. Ibid., August 31, 1854.

sas with or without the excitement created in the country by the repeal of the Missouri Compromise."[53]

Gales and Seaton ridiculed Seward's idea that the nation would be in grave danger if slavery were not abolished. An answer could be worked out if only "calm deliberation" could prevail. Thus all disagreements could be settled; nothing could be accomplished by loss of temper and wild charges. The publishers pleaded for calm heads as the passions of the country rose higher with each new aspect of sectional strife.[54]

Although after 1852 the Whig party was dead for all practical purposes, Gales and Seaton refused to admit it editorially. In 1856 the Republican party emerged, absorbing many Whig elements.[55] Gales and Seaton acknowledged this event and thought "the Whig party should preserve its distinct organization, and . . . abide its proper time for making the weight of its influence felt in that decision which duty and patriotism shall call upon it to take in the present conjuncture of political events." The editors reasoned the party could not be dead until some other group had absorbed its principles.[56]

The antislavery elements of the Republican party especially worried Gales and Seaton. This tinge made the party one of section more than a party should be. Lack of southern support, Gales and Seaton warned, could spell disaster. The Republican party was no substitute for the national Whig party, the *Intelligencer* editors concluded, and continued their hopeless task of keeping the Whig party alive.

But no matter how much Gales and Seaton urged the Whigs to rise and take action, no movement resulted. The appeal from Kentucky's Whigs for a national conclave went unheeded. Even the *Intelligencer* editors realized the Whigs could never win the election against James Buchanan in 1856. The Kansas-Nebraska Act was the final death blow to the party.[57] But a minority could be influential if it supported the right cause, Gales and Seaton reminded their readers.[58]

53. Ibid., July 4, 1857.
54. Ibid., November 13, 1858.
55. Roy F. Nichols, *The Disruption of American Democracy* (New York, 1948), pp. 41-50.
56. *National Intelligencer*, April 22, 1856.
57. Simms, *Sectional Controversy*, p. 86.
58. *National Intelligencer*, May 26, 1856.

When the Whig convention met and supported Fillmore, even the *Intelligencer* editors could give only lukewarm approval. Despite the fact that Fillmore also represented the American party, Gales and Seaton thought he should be considered the head of the Whigs.[59] Actually Fillmore always was a bit too much of an antislavery man to suit the editors.

The pursuit of neutrality policies led Gales and Seaton away from the rising Republicans and more toward the Democratic party, because it was still national in composition. The editors did not feel comfortable in admitting it, but only a national party would allow them an effective vote of neutrality.[60]

But Gales and Seaton could not support the Democratic party. They could not bring themselves to follow the party that had presented such adversaries as Jackson, Van Buren, and Polk. Perhaps it was " 'a sense of duty' " or a " 'feeling of prejudice' " that prevented them from going the "length of the Democratic platform."[61]

Still Gales and Seaton toyed with the idea of supporting James Buchanan rather than the Republican, John Fremont, or Fillmore, the Whig. In September the editors announced that they could do nothing for the Whig party. They had little sympathy with the Democratic party, but they conceded that Buchanan had private virtue and high administrative ability. They never could support him politically, however. How could they possibly "rush with ardor to the support of a gentleman whose political opinions have for many years been antipodes of our own?"[62]

It must have been a difficult editorial for Gales and Seaton to write. They admitted that the *Intelligencer* lacked a political voice. The paper had principles, but they were not expressed in the framework of any party. In attempting to hold the union together at all costs, the *Intelligencer* had lost its voice and now found itself without political expression.

For all purposes the *Intelligencer*'s political life was dead. Never again did its pen support the leadership of a party. Other papers throughout the country had to look elsewhere

59. Ibid., September 23, 1856.
60. Ibid., August 12, 1858.
61. Ibid., July 7, 1856.
62. Ibid., September 4, 1856.

to find out what the leaders of the conservative party were thinking. Gales and Seaton contended their views were the same as always. The country itself had changed, and the editors had not changed with it. They felt people no longer were interested in internal improvements, protective tariffs, humanitarian reforms, and western lands. Readers no longer cared about congressional happenings as detailed by Gales and Seaton; they had turned to more frivolous reading. Slavery, an issue that had gnawed away steadily at the framework of the union, now threatened destruction.

The election returns gave Buchanan the presidency.[63] Gales and Seaton congratulated the Democrats and were pleased that the Republicans had not triumphed. The publishers also were glad Buchanan had triumphed over Fillmore. But, then, Fillmore's candidacy had been more "disinterested" than promising.[64]

But even the Whigs' disastrous showing in 1856 did not kill the editors' loyalty to their party. The next year Gales and Seaton again urged a movement to reorganize the old Whig group.[65] But the support given to this proposal was feeble, and the attempt to revive the party even weaker.

Gales's and Seaton's policy of neutrality at all costs on the slavery issue brought disagreeable aspects other than those which left them partyless. A northern Whig criticized the editors' contention that nature and not man would regulate the extension of slavery.[66] An "Old Reader" in Maryland agreed with the editors that such debates as that on the Nebraska bill did little but agitate the already-inflamed issues and settled nothing. The man had read the *Intelligencer* for over forty years and agreed with it on all points except the War of 1812.[67] On the other hand, southern readers criticized Gales and Seaton for being too tolerant of radical northern views and bitterly attacked them.[68]

Another long-time subscriber, a Democrat, explained he usually differed with the paper, particularly with the caution and reserve of its editorial policy. He admitted the paper was

63. Nevins, *Ordeal of the Union*, pp. 510-11.
64. *National Intelligencer*, November 15, 1856.
65. Ibid., June 23, 1857.
66. Ibid., November 13, 1855.
67. Ibid., February 25, 1854.
68. Ibid., August 1, 1857.

factually accurate and generally correct in deductions. He said that its influence on public opinion had been great. But he could not agree with Gales's and Seaton's refusal to take a stand on the growing sectional and political agitation: "Permit me to say that I, like some of your correspondents and contemporaries, am disposed to find fault with the present *cold neutrality* of your journal." He thought the apathy of the *Intelligencer* was criminal.[69]

An Indiana subscriber went even further and canceled his subscription because of his impatience with the *Intelligencer* editors and their refusal to take a stand. He was not an antislavery man, but he thought the paper should stand against the "lawless Extension" of slavery. He was tired of southern threats and the *Intelligencer's* failure to answer. Gales and Seaton admitted they were sorry to lose a subscriber, but said they had to maintain their views.[70]

The momentum of the nation toward a civil war continued, and Gales and Seaton continued to plead for a rational settlement of the crisis. They watched as the contending factions pounced on any event that might give the opposition an advantage, and they realized that sectional differences, particularly those dealing with slavery, became more exaggerated each day.

Gales and Seaton regretted the Dred Scott decision in 1857, because, they said, right or wrong, the ruling merely agitated the issues involved. They were sorry the Court felt called on to comment on points of political controversy, and they contended that the fact that the decision was not unanimous made the politics even more apparent. They thought citizens had to submit to the decision, however. If Chief Justice Roger B. Taney and his court had erred, time would point up these errors.[71] Gales and Seaton noted the Lincoln-Douglas debates with interest, for they regarded Douglas's views as an important indication of the thinking of the Democratic party. Also, Lincoln's ideas indicated a rising political element in the West.

No matter how Gales and Seaton tried to point the way to peace through compromise, the elements within the country

69. Ibid., September 4, 1856.
70. Ibid., August 11, 1855.
71. Ibid., May 30, 1857.

became more polarized. The extremes rather than the broad bases of middle ground made gains. Gales and Seaton approached 1860 with apprehension and misgiving. Their dream of a United States built on the basis of Clay's American System seemed far away.

CHAPTER 18

The Passing of
the *Intelligencer*

The world in which the *Intelligencer* had operated for more than sixty years fell apart between 1860 and 1865. The very foundations of the venerable old newspaper crumbled, and efforts to erect new buttresses failed. The America that had supported the *Intelligencer* had changed, and the paper, like its editors, had been in a state of decline for years. The paper's demise was inevitable; only the time of death remained a mystery. The political newspaper of the *Intelligencer* type no longer was profitable, particularly when there was no political party to support.

The greatest personal loss for the *Intelligencer* came during the summer of 1860 when, soon after seven o'clock on the evening of July 21, Joseph Gales died in his home. His life, which began in Eckington, England, ended at the Eckington he had built in America. The illness that had disabled Gales for much of his last fifteen years finally took its full toll in the editor's seventy-fifth year. He had been critically ill for months.[1]

Gales's death was felt throughout the nation but especially by the city of Washington, D.C., where he had lived and worked for fifty-three years. This was Gales's city, for he had watched it grow from a small collection of roughhewn huts and unfinished buildings to one of the great metropolitan centers of the nation. The city recognized the personal contribution Gales had made to this growth and responded accordingly. The *Intelligencer*, edged in a black border, added solemnity to the sorrow expressed throughout the city. President Buchanan and his cabinet attended the funeral, as great a tribute as the city and nation could pay. All of the members of the Board of Aldermen and the Common Council from the city of Washington also were present at the final rites. The entire City Council of Alexandria, Virginia, arrived too late for the funeral but paid its respects. The Columbia Typographical Society and the Book Binder Association represented Gales's fellow printers and publishers.

After services at Eckington the funeral procession moved through crepe-draped streets on its way to the Congressional Cemetery. Employees of the *Intelligencer* and members of the Typographical Union participated. For hours large throngs gathered to pay their last tribute, and schools and stores were closed by order of the City Council. The crowd was especially heavy near the *Intelligencer* building. Other buildings similarly hung in black included the campaign headquarters of Bell and Everett and the *Congressional Globe* office, still operated by one of the *Intelligencer*'s most bitter antagonists, John C. Rives.[2] The showy aspects of the occasion would have embarrassed such a modest man as Gales, but he could not have escaped observing that the tribute rested on genuine affection.

One of the last notices of Gales as a person to appear in the *Intelligencer* came a few days later when Philip and Solomon's Metropolitan Bookstore capitalized on the emotion of the occasion and offered likenesses of the late editor for only one

1. *National Intelligencer*, July 23, 1860.
2. Ibid., July 26, 1860.

dollar. Gales's only remaining contribution to his old publishing firm was the title, for the business name continued as Gales and Seaton.

Undoubtedly because of his illness, Gales's influence was absent from the *Intelligencer* for months and perhaps years before his death. Still Gales symbolized a fair and responsible type of journalism which in many ways marked the high point of nineteenth-century publishing. The most vital issue for which he contended, preservation of the union, still remained an obtainable goal. Within a few months, however, his partner saw the world the Gales and Seaton firm had known crumble completely.

Numerous editorials from all sections of the country commented on Gales's death. The editor of the *New York World* reflected on the editor's contributions and concluded that the *Intelligencer* under Gales had performed well in providing documents and articles of information but had left readers to make up their own minds. The *World* editor felt only a moderate amount of editorial material was published, and, in his eyes, this "meagreness" of discussion of public issues was the greatest failure of the old Washington newspaper. He thought Gales and Seaton had presumed that their readers' minds were far more active than they really were.[3]

The *World* editor had in some ways failed to understand the *Intelligencer*. Not many long articles in the old paper bore the title of editorial, but scarcely a story in the whole paper, other than the congressional reports, did not bear recognizable expressions of the editors' opinions. Happenings were not described as cold, objective facts. Events had meaning, and Gales and Seaton interpreted these events for their readers. Their opinions could not be avoided by even the most casual reader of the paper.

Seaton, annoyed by the comments, betrayed his complete lack of sympathy with the newspapers of large circulation that had grown up throughout the country. To him, a newspaper still functioned "to furnish facts and arguments to the studious and thoughtful rather than the superficial 'skimmings' and impressions designed for those who 'have no use for them except for the casual conversation of the day.' "[4]

3. *New York World*, quoted in the *National Intelligencer*, July 30, 1860.
4. *National Intelligencer*, July 30, 1860.

Gales's death did not bring immediate or obvious changes in the *Intelligencer*. Not even the staff changed, although James Welling was named associate editor. Welling, whose ten years on the paper well qualified him for the position, was a strong support for Seaton. Many felt Welling was the key force in the *Intelligencer*'s policies during its last years under Gales and Seaton. At the time the Welling promotion was made the paper again pledged to support its long-standing principles of constitutionality and conservatism: peace and friendship with all nations; noninterference in foreign affairs; arbitration of difficulties; preservation of the union; respect for the rights and authority of states; freedom of religion and conscience; individual rights; freedom of the press; adequate military protection; promotion of agriculture and manufacturing; improvement of science; and the diffusion of information.[5]

There seems little doubt that Welling was the chief force behind the *Intelligencer*'s editorial policy during its remaining years under Seaton. In newspaper circles at least, Welling was recognized as the "principal editor of the Intelligencer."[6] Welling himself admitted that his duties on the *Intelligencer* were so great that he could not accept other work offered him.[7] But whatever responsibilities Welling assumed, no doubt he did little to take Gales's place as far as Seaton was concerned. All Seaton's old party and business friends were gone—Webster, Clay, Calhoun, Adams, and now even Gales.

Since 1860 was an election year, the *Intelligencer* naturally devoted a good deal of its space to the crucial issue facing the nation. The campaign was well underway even before Gales's death, and the *Intelligencer* had taken its stand. The choice was not difficult for the old editors, although in many ways it was impractical.

The *Intelligencer* never could support the Republican party, that maturing new political force rising in the North and West. Such old-line Whigs as Gales and Seaton believed men like William Seward branded the Republicans with a strong

5. Ibid., August 30, 1860.
6. George Adams to Manton Marble, November 10, 1860, Marble Papers, vol. 3, Library of Congress, Washington, D.C.
7. Welling to Marble, February 20, 1864, Marble Papers, vol. 6.

antislavery tinge and that a victory for this party was the surest way of tearing the nation apart.

Gales's and Seaton's attitude toward Lincoln is difficult to determine. They certainly had heard of him before the campaign of 1860 and may have known him personally or at least met him when he served a term as congressman from Illinois in the 1840s. If in no other way, Gales's and Seaton's capacity for incurring debts brought them in contact with the Illinois attorney. In January, 1849, Lincoln was engaged by a Thomas French to collect from Gales and Seaton on overdue notes totaling $1,476.70. Records do not indicate whether or not Lincoln succeeded.[8]

Lincoln was well aware of the *Intelligencer* long before he gained prominence as a politician, for he had read Gales's and Seaton's paper throughout most of his years.[9] The *Intelligencer* was credited with being Lincoln's main source of information during his famous debates with Stephen A. Douglas.[10] The newspaper, in turn, paid scant attention to Lincoln until the Lincoln-Douglas debates, when the editors wrote that Lincoln, "who so arduously stumped his State last autum[n] as the Republican Antagonist of Senator Douglas . . . handled the honorable Senator's doctrines without gloves."[11]

Gales and Seaton might have favored Lincoln as a man, but they never could support his party. However, neither could they back either wing of the Democratic party that emerged following the Charleston convention in 1860.[12] Douglas the Democrat had little in common with Gales and Seaton. At the same time John Breckinridge, the southern Democrats' candidate, represented antiunion views which were as odious to Gales and Seaton as those of the antislavery segments of the North.

This left only one choice, and despite the weakness of the party, it was the logical place for Gales and Seaton in the campaign of 1860. John Bell and Edward Everett as candidates of the National Constitutional Union party represented

8. Lincoln to Gales and Seaton, January 22, 1849, quoted in Roy P. Basler, ed., *The Collected Works of Abraham Lincoln* (New Brunswick, N.J., 1953), 2:24.

9. Edgar Lee Masters, *Lincoln the Man* (New York, 1931), pp. 33, 111.

10. Ibid., p. 282.

11. *National Intelligencer*, September 22, 1859.

12. Allan Nevins, *The Emergence of Lincoln* (New York, 1950), 2:261-86.

everything Gales and Seaton had stood for. As Lincoln described it, the party consisted of " 'the nice exclusive sort' " of Whigs who were inclined to ignore everything that had happened in the United States after 1848. The fires that raged throughout the country and threatened the very structures of the nation would die out, according to the Bell followers, if only the country would adhere to the Constitution, the union of states, and the enforcement of laws.[13]

The vice-presidential candidate knew both Gales and Seaton personally, and this certainly influenced the paper to support Bell and Everett.[14] The choice was made before Gales's death, and undoubtedly the overwhelming reason for the decision was the belief that this party could best preserve the union. It is doubtful that Seaton ever held any real hope for the Constitutional Union party, but any positive stand against disunion was desirable.

The *Intelligencer* for the most part refused to discuss any real possibility of secession and looked to the West and to the border states along the Ohio River as the elements that would hold the nation together. But the Ohio Valley would have to ignore the southern wooing that was taking place. One editorial concluded: "From all such horrors and excesses, and from all other lamentable consequences which would undoubtedly attend the secession of any State from the Union, may Heaven protect and defend the People of every State."[15]

Seaton admitted that he hoped the 1860 election would go to the House of Representatives for solution. Then his candidate might have a chance. He hoped that Breckinridge and Douglas would cooperate to help defeat Lincoln. Bell might be the compromise candidate needed to save the nation from a Republican victory.[16] Seaton kept hoping his candidates would win and shared this hope with his readers.[17]

Such wishes were in vain as the Republican party elected a president, and Seaton calmly accepted the fact. His paper urged that Lincoln and his party be given a chance to solve

13. Samuel Eliot Morison and Henry Steele Commager, *The Growth of the American Republic* (New York, 1962), 1:663.
14. *National Intelligencer*, July 21, 1860.
15. Ibid., July 24, 1860.
16. Ibid., July 27, 1860.
17. Ibid., August 1, 1860.

this great clash of sectional interests. Seaton knew he would have to wait to see what developed before deciding on any definite course for the *Intelligencer.*

At the beginning of the march of states from the union in 1861, Seaton pleaded for compromise of differences between the sections. He thought there still was ground for a just settlement of differences that would save the union, and he made his proposals accordingly. First, Congress should have no power to regulate or control established and recognized slavery. Second, the United States could not abolish slavery in military establishments of any state. Further, slavery should remain within the District of Columbia until Maryland and Virginia, as well as the residents of the District, should consent to its abolition. Congress would not regulate or interfere with moving slaves between states. Importing slaves was to be prohibited, and no territory was to be annexed to the United States without a two-thirds vote of both houses of Congress or by a treaty ratified by a two-thirds vote of the Senate.[18]

Seaton suggested nothing new, and all but two of his points favored the South. But, then, he felt the South needed wooing because it was taking dramatic action in leaving the union. Behind each of Seaton's points lurked the question of slavery, an institution the venerable Whig editor hoped would become less embroiled in the minds of residents of the two sections of the country. Instead, a plea for calm and rational action seemed out of place.

Seaton's willingness to compromise did not stem from his inability to choose between the union or secession, for his stand was firm and unequivocal. He chose the union. He was horrified with the suggestion of some southern papers that Washington, D.C., be seized to prevent Lincoln from taking office. He labeled this idle talk and assured any who held these ideas that the people of the District stood prepared to fight any such move.[19]

The possibility of averting war seemed more remote each day as the inauguration neared, and Seaton viewed with grave misgiving the spectacle of the Republican party taking over the nation. The secession of southern states meant the surren-

18. Ibid., January 12, 1861.
19. Ibid., January 3, 1861.

der of the legislative branch to this new and as yet untried political party. To Seaton, this did not look promising for the nation.

Lincoln's inaugural address expressing his willingness to take a conciliatory view of the separation of the states gave Seaton hope.[20] "The Incoming President," said Seaton, "reaching the Presidential chair under circumstances of peculiar embarrassment, asks at the hand of his countrymen, in all sections, a candid hearing and a fair trial. Is he not entitled to these?"[21]

While urging caution, Seaton surveyed the holocaust that threatened and again cited the border states as the last hope of keeping the union intact. To them he made one of his final conciliatory appeals, and at the same time he confessed that extreme forces were at work which he failed to understand. The middle ground offered the solution, both politically and geographically. Let the Southern Gulf states go, he urged, for they had no adequate economic basis upon which to support themselves. If the border states stayed in the union, they would have an economic advantage over the seceding states in selling cotton outside the confederacy.[22]

By the latter part of March the *Intelligencer* directed its policies at preventing war at all costs. Since no guns had yet been fired, Seaton felt that perhaps a peaceful settlement might be reached even if it meant letting the secessionists depart in peace. Perhaps it took an old and less-alert mind to still urge patience, but Seaton felt the departing states should be given a year to determine their final attitude toward the United States. If the developments of the ensuing year left no doubt that the people in the seceded states were determined in their attitude toward the United States, "we shall advocate the policy of their recognition by our Government, and this, among other questions might be referred to the arbitrament of a National Convention. . . ."[23]

Seaton's attempt to maintain the union and at the same time not offend the secessionist states brought attacks on the frail old political journal from both sides. Seaton hesitated to

20. Ibid., March 5, 1861.
21. Ibid., March 7, 1861.
22. Ibid., March 9, 1861.
23. Ibid., March 21, 1861.

take such a personal problem to his readers, but he asked why it was considered traitorous to see more than one side. Not all papers thought it was. The Milledgeville, Georgia, *Southern Recorder* felt the *Intelligencer* was " 'by far the most able and courtly journal ever published in this country. . . .' "[24]

Seaton was surprised that so many southern journals imputed to the *Intelligencer* a lack of sympathy "calculated . . . to estrange from it that large support which Southern Readers have so cheerfully accorded to it during the sixty years of its existence." Seaton was hurt by the accusations: "It is impossible for it [*Intelligencer*] ever to become destructive in its principles or teachings without ignoring all its former labors, and without betraying a mental and moral infirmity which had never been suspected to exist" at any period in its editorial management.[25]

Probably the bitterest blow against the old *Intelligencer* editor came when the *Richmond Whig* charged Seaton with "apostasy," contending he had surrendered to the Republican party. The Richmond editor thought " 'the late Joseph Gales, died none too soon. . . .' " The Virginian added that he could " 'almost wish the surviving partner [Seaton] had been spared the excruciating humiliation of the present day. . . .' " Seaton countered with expressions of regret that such men as the Whig editor had abandoned "not only the principles for which they once contended, but even the Government . . . every good citizen is pledged to uphold against all enemies, domestic or foreign." Seaton assured the Richmond editor that Gales always had been against secession and that the two editors would have stood together on the issue.[26]

Even before Seaton had hurled this defense at an old southern compatriot the guns of Fort Sumter had sounded, and the active shooting phase of the Civil War started. Three days later President Lincoln issued a call for seventy-five thousand volunteers to put down this threat which was "too powerful to be suppressed by the ordinary course of judicial proceedings." Seaton's hope of avoiding war was nearly gone as he warned, in a brief note accompanying Lincoln's message, that "this important document gives a new phase to the probable

24. Ibid., March 30, 1861.
25. Ibid.
26. Ibid.

issues of the momentous crisis which has been precipitated upon the country by the rash act of South Carolina. . . ."[27]

Seaton stared at the reality of the situation and yet still slightly shied from it. He thought his readers could no longer hide from the "melancholy truth that the American people stand hesitatingly at the brink of a civil war." Still, if the border and northern states remained calm, Seaton thought something might be worked out. He rationalized that the forces Lincoln called for might be for defense purposes only.[28]

The steps leading to the actual military engagements of the war had been difficult for Seaton to understand, but somehow he hoped his paper had maintained a quiet dignity throughout. There was no surrender to the mad emotions that seemed to characterize all sections of the nation. Even the opening battle failed to jar the *Intelligencer* from its staid, emotionless recounting of a civil war. The Battle of Bull Run, fought in July of 1861, received little more than passing notice, except for an editorial praising the Union troops in the battle. Seaton also observed that the fight offered a warning of the strength of the Southern Confederacy. He was certain the Union would need more troops to meet this menace.[29]

The *Intelligencer*'s treatment of the battle caused the editor of the *Albany Argus* to charge Seaton and other Washington editors with apathy. The Albany writer contended the battle might as well have been fought in Moscow as far as the Washington papers' coverage was concerned. Seaton admitted his coverage differed from that of the New York City papers, but he explained that this resulted from the three-story technique used by the more sensational papers. The first two accounts speculated, and only the final report was correct. Seaton was convinced that his method of carefully researching the stories was preferred.[30]

In contrast to northern criticism, Seaton was flattered by notes from southern subscribers asking him to find a way for their papers to be received. After the states seceded regular deliveries no longer were possible. One Alabama subscriber

27. Ibid., April 15, 1861.
28. Ibid.
29. Ibid., July 27, 1861.
30. Ibid., August 1, 1861.

suggested that his paper be sent to Louisville, Kentucky, and forwarded from there to his home in Sumner, Alabama. A reader from Tuscaloosa, Alabama, said he had subscribed for forty years and wanted to continue. Seaton explained it was impossible to get the papers to him and that the reader would have to acquiesce to civil necessity.[31]

Seaton's views on Lincoln changed as the administration progressed, and by the fall of 1861 the *Intelligencer* editor defended the president and his policies against criticism. But there always was the feeling that President Lincoln represented the element that really had caused the war. For no matter what Seaton said on the war and its conduct, his heart was not in it. The world he had known for so long was gone. His native state, his relatives, and his friends were now the enemy. His wife's nephews helped lead the southern fight. Seaton must have felt isolated in the Union. He no doubt found it difficult to applaud anything Lincoln did, since he stood for a party made up of so many things Seaton opposed.

Seaton probably agreed with his daughter, who wrote Buchanan that in her eyes he was the last constitutional president the country would have. To her the Civil War was a "conflict which has uprooted friends & families, severed the dearest ties" and spelled disaster to the country. She was sorry Buchanan's term of office was not just beginning.[32]

Seaton disagreed with those who felt Lincoln had assumed unnecessary powers, but the editor did resent the president's failure to disclaim any connection with the antislavery people.[33] The *Intelligencer* held tight to the view that this was a war with only one purpose—preservation of the union.

The days just before the issuance of the Emancipation Proclamation marked the closest harmony between the *Intelligencer* and Lincoln. There even was speculation that the president might use the *Intelligencer* as his spokesman, but this was short-lived. After Horace Greeley published his famous "Prayer of Twenty Millions," a plea for freeing the slaves, Lincoln chose the *Intelligencer* in which to publish his reply.

31. Ibid., July 20, 1861.
32. Josephine Seaton to James Buchanan, June 23, 1862, Buchanan Papers, Historical Society of Pennsylvania, Philadelphia.
33. *National Intelligencer*, August 23, 1862.

The president again emphasized his stand that the war was fought to preserve a nation; he was not yet ready to admit that it might be necessary to free the slaves in order to gain the support needed to achieve the primary aim of the conflict.[34]

One sentence, which in many ways summarized Lincoln's feelings on the subject, was deleted at Seaton's and Welling's request. This passage, referring to the states that had seceded, read: "Broken eggs can never be mended, and the longer the breaking proceeds the more will be broken." Here Lincoln wished to express his fear that even those border states that remained in the Union might leave. Welling recalled: "The omitted passage . . . was erased, with some reluctance, by the President, on the representation, made to him by the editors, that it seemed somewhat exceptional, on rhetorical grounds, in a paper of such dignity." Years later Welling retold the story to reveal the "homely similitude" that Lincoln originally had proposed to reenforce his political warnings.[35]

Those who interpreted Lincoln's reply as a break with the Greeley forces and a comfort to the border states soon were disappointed. The "border states theory" of the war was losing ground with the strong wing of the Republican party, and Lincoln was pressured to remove "proslavery" generals from command of the army and to push an avowedly antislavery policy throughout the entire war. As Welling saw the struggle, Lincoln was caught between the two wings of the Republican party and had to go to the side that could give the greatest support.[36]

On September 22, 1862, Lincoln issued his preliminary Emancipation Proclamation, a surrender to the radical Republicans as far as Seaton and Welling were concerned. The editors were aware of the events surrounding the issuing of the preliminary draft of the plan for freeing slaves through Edward Stanly, military governor of North Carolina. Stanly was called to Washington for conferences with Lincoln and was told that the proclamation was being forced in order to "prevent the Radicals from openly embarrassing the Government in the conduct of the war. The President expressed the

34. Ibid.
35. James C. Welling, "The Emancipation Proclamation," *The North American Review* 130 (January, 1880): 167-68.
36. Ibid., p. 171.

belief that, without the Proclamation for which they had been clamoring, the Radicals would take the extreme step in Congress of withholding supplies for carrying on the war—leaving the whole land in anarchy."[37]

Lincoln was sorely troubled by the dilemma and told Stanly he "had prayed to the Almighty to save him from this necessity, adopting the language of our Saviour, 'If it be possible, let this cup pass from me,' but the prayer had not been answered."[38]

Issuance of the preliminary proclamation marked the end of cordial relations between Lincoln and the *Intelligencer*. The paper sympathized with the president as long as he sought to keep the border states in the Union by avoiding the slavery issue entirely. The war took on a different complexion as Seaton informed his readers: "With our well-known and oft-repeated views respecting the futility of such proclamations, it can hardly be necessary for us to say that, where we expect no good, we shall be only too happy to find that no harm has been done by the present declaration of the Executive." The editors thought that perhaps the president had taken "this method to convince the only class of persons likely to be pleased with this proclamation of the utter fallacy of the hopes they have founded upon it." The overt injection of the slavery issue into the war, in the eyes of Seaton and Welling, robbed the struggle of its greatest meaning.[39]

Three days later the editors again attacked the proclamation. Only two things possibly could be gained from the order. First, it would test the sagacity of the men who had predicted the declaration would end the rebellion. Also it would test the sincerity of those northerners who contended the enlistments never would be filled until the war attacked the real villain: slavery. The editors admitted they were watching with interest to see if these hopes would be fulfilled.[40] Seaton and Welling hoped, even after Lincoln's message to Congress on December 2, that the Emancipation Proclamation might be withheld. An *Intelligencer* editorial read: "The merely incidental manner in which he refers to the

37. Ibid., pp. 171-72.
38. Ibid.
39. *National Intelligencer*, September 23, 1862.
40. Ibid., September 26, 1862.

Proclamation of last September 22, especially when taken in connexion [*sic*] with the expansion he has given to his favorite project for 'compensated emancipation,' sufficiently indicates the direction in which he looks for a beneficent melioration in the condition of the African race now held in bondage."[41]

But Seaton's and Welling's hopes never were realized. On January 1, 1863, the proclamation went into effect. This was more than just a political defeat for Seaton. It was to him in some ways the negation of his basic philosophy of the United States. Seaton devoutly believed in the states' rights concept of the government, and the federal government had merit only as long as it helped preserve those rights. The proclamation established law that before only the states had the power to create. Now the editor seemed in doubt about the aims and wisdom of the whole conflict and perhaps the whole United States experiment.

The remainder of the war years was difficult indeed for Seaton. Not only was there the calamity of the war but within his own family there were deep personal tragedies. Probably the saddest event Seaton endured during his entire life was the death of his wife, Sarah, on December 23, 1863. A close friend of Seaton's sensed the deep feeling of the old editor: "Having lived in great love and harmony with that excellent woman, for more . . . than Fifty years, I know not how he can bear the loss of such a companion." He saw the editor as alone and "very desolate" because he had only grandchildren to comfort him, and they could give little but respect and reverence. "He is a philosopher," he said, "and will shew no signs of impatient and clamorous grief; but this calamity will silently sap the foundation of his existence—And I am prepared to see him sink rapidly and die soon."[42]

Two of the three mainstays in Seaton's life were gone, his partner and his wife. Within the next year he also severed the last support to his career: the *National Intelligencer*.

Seaton's newspaper had declined since the death of the Whig party. In 1864 the *Intelligencer* as a political voice died,

41. Ibid., December 2, 1862.
42. Bates's diary, December 25, 1863, in "The Diary of Edward Bates, 1859-1866," ed. Howard K. Beale, *American Historical Association Annual Report*, 1930 (Washington, D.C., 1933), 4:324.

or rather committed suicide. The paper's stand during the political campaign of 1864 marked its last desperate attempt to wield some political power. This try failed, and the dignified old *Intelligencer* lost much of the "high reputation" it once enjoyed.

The Emancipation Proclamation still rankled the *Intelligencer* editors, and the break in their relationship with Lincoln never was healed. The editors were not committed to Greeley and his followers, who attempted to defeat Lincoln and bring about a quick settlement to the war. Still Seaton never again could support strongly a president who made slavery a key issue of the war.

Following this thinking, the *Intelligencer* announced in late August[43] that it would back the Democratic candidate, General John McClellan, for the presidency. This may have been mainly Welling's decision, but Seaton must have at least assented to it. The *Intelligencer*'s support of a Democratic candidate was nearly beyond belief. Edward Bates, Lincoln's attorney general, was close to both Seaton and Welling and was extremely upset by the action. Bates wrote: "I do not doubt that Mr. W[elling] has acted conscienciously [*sic*] in this thing. But I think he has committed an unfortunate error, both for himself and his paper." Bates was certain that the paper would suffer more by the choice of McClellan than would Welling: "And for the glorious old Intelligencer, I grieve when I fear that it will lose, in its old age much of that high reputation which it has long maintained for wisdom, principle, moderation and prudence."[44]

Bates was right, for Seaton and Welling followed McClellan to a disastrous defeat, and the *Intelligencer* stood more alone and isolated than at any time during its existence. The paper had suffered losses before, seven presidential defeats after 1824 compared to two victories, but this setback came at a time when no resilient strength remained in the journal. Two important sources of strength, Seaton's wife and partner, were gone. The Seaton who remained was tired, old, and sick. Even the nation that had provided the strength for the *Intelligencer* had changed much. On December 31, 1864, Sea-

43. *National Intelligencer*, August 26, 1864.
44. Bates's diary, September 16, 1864, quoted in Beale, *AHA Annual Report*, pp. 408-9.

ton sold his paper to Snow, Coyle and Co., a Washington, D.C., publishing firm. On this date the publishing company of Gales and Seaton ceased to exist.

The main reasons for the sale were financial. The declining support, through the war and through the loss of prestige, was more than the *Intelligencer* could bear. Seaton and Welling clung to the format of a political newspaper long after all other major political newspapers in the country were dead. The times had changed. People no longer wanted a steady diet of congressional proceedings, government documents, and unemotional explanations of the political situation in the nation. Even Seaton finally admitted that the demand for such a journal was gone. With a great deal of feeling, Seaton wrote to an old friend, George S. Hilliard, Boston publisher, about the sale of the *Intelligencer*. Seaton looked back over the years stretching to 1807 when he wrote: "The parting with my old paper was painful in the extreme; But the reverses experienced from secession and the intolerance of party had reduced it to the point of extinction and no alternative was left but to see it expire or to accept the offer of some business men, who thought that by withdrawing the paper from the sphere of politics and converting it into a mere news and advertising sheet they could make it pay."[45]

Seaton admitted he would have preferred to see the paper die, but he had to consider others, particularly the friends who had given financial aid in keeping it alive. The price paid by the purchaser was an "insignificant sum." It was a defeated and bewildered Seaton who wrote of the loss of two-thirds of his paper's circulation caused by the secession of the states, of the lack of business support, and of the failure of the paper to attract northern readers. He concluded: "The country does not seem to regard it of importance to support a paper at the seat of Government which presumed to have a conscience and an independent Judgement. . . ." Perhaps, he surmised, the paper was not worthy of support. Perhaps in the United States of the future there was no place for the *Intelligencer*. It was the friends of the past who gave it meaning: "In the high character of the friends who . . . have stood by the old paper through all the mutations of party and cheered

45. Seaton to Hilliard, January 11, 1865, Charles Lanman Papers, vol. 2, Library of Congress, Washington, D.C.

its editors with approval in periods of trial, I find a consolation which I would not exchange for better fortune, although I end fifty two years of labor with nothing."[46]

Seaton did not live to see the final disposition of the *Intelligencer*, for he died June 15, 1866. The editor, who had remained active and healthy through more than eighty years of his life, suffered a slow and painful death as cancer, affecting largely his face, destroyed the once-active body. So extreme was the suffering that his mind gave way during the final stages of the disease, and at death he little resembled the once handsome and commanding figure so prominent in Washington.

Funeral services were held June 18, 1866, in the Church of the Epiphany with two Episcopal clergymen officiating. Although Seaton was a member of the Unitarian church throughout most of his adult life, he was returned to the Episcopal church for burial. Among the pallbearers were Seward, former secretary of state; Judge James M. Wayne; Thomas S. Donohoe, business manager of the *Intelligencer*, and Peter Force, former editor of the *National Journal* and mayor of Washington. Although the roster of those attending the funeral was not as impressive as at Gales's, still considerable honors were paid the former editor. Schools and some businesses were closed, and flags were flown at half-mast from the City Hall, school buildings, and other public offices.[47] A man who had helped write and preserve the history of the city and nation for over half a century was gone.

The attempts to make the *Intelligencer* into a "mere news and advertising sheet" never really succeeded. The format was changed, but somehow the modern makeup, the bolder headlines, and the flashier style of writing did not suit a paper of its vintage. The "aristocrat" of Washington, D.C., journalism was a bit too old and set in its ways to change without tragic effects. The *Intelligencer* lingered on until 1869 and then died.[48] But it really died in 1864 when Seaton signed his last editorial and laid down his pen.

46. Ibid.
47. Allen C. Clark, "Colonel William Winston Seaton and His Mayoralty," *Columbia Historical Society Records* 29-30 (1928): 100.
48. Winifred Gregory, ed., *American Newspapers, 1821-1936* (New York, 1937), p. 89.

Few newspapers in the United States played as vital a role in the politics of the nation as the *National Intelligencer* during its lifetime. The *Intelligencer* served important educational and policy-making functions in relation to the federal government from the time it was born to fight for the cause of Thomas Jefferson's liberalism until it died espousing a conservatism that had no party to support it.

Throughout its life the *National Intelligencer* was dependent on the federal government for financial support, yet it achieved an independence that few papers ever reach. It was founded on money borrowed from his family by Samuel Harrison Smith and rested on the hope that within a short time the Jefferson administration would provide financial aid. That hope was not an idle one, for not only did the executive printing go to the *Intelligencer* in 1801, but Smith also executed the printing for the House of Representatives from 1801 to 1804. During this period the printing was not the rich patronage plum it later became, but still it was a most welcome financial aid to a struggling young publisher.

But it was not the congressional printing that enabled the *Intelligencer* to remain in business during the period before 1820. During this time the *Intelligencer* functioned mainly to support the presidential office and received the executive printing in return. It was Smith's duty, and later Gales's and Seaton's, to convey to the nation the president's position and to win support for his measures. This supportive role was important immediately preceding the War of 1812, when the youthful Joseph Gales counseled with the inner circles of the executive branch and then through his newspaper sought to win congressional as well as public favor for the war measures. Gales did not find such a propaganda position satisfying, and moved to expand the role of the *Intelligencer* in the years following the War of 1812.

Throughout its life the *Intelligencer* played one role of great importance—as a vehicle of public record. The amount of news or editorial opinion carried by the paper at any time during its existence was relatively small compared to the space devoted to the documents of public record. The most important single item was the congressional debates, faithfully, and generally accurately, detailed in each issue of the newspaper. There is little doubt that newspapers of all political persuasions found the *Intelligencer*'s reports the most complete and accurate of any published.

By 1819 the duties of the *Intelligencer* were enlarged considerably. In addition to serving as the presidential organ, the *Intelligencer* took on the duties of spokesman for the dominant party in the two houses of Congress. It was in this role as congressional spokesman that the *Intelligencer* served during most of its life. It was especially effective in leading the opposition to the profound changes brought about by Jacksonian democracy and to such unpopular conflicts as the war with Mexico.

The period during which Gales and Seaton served as both congressional and presidential spokesman was brief, 1819-24, for the quarrel with John Quincy Adams during the campaign removed the *Intelligencer* as presidential spokesman. Gales and Seaton were then free to develop their role of congressional spokesman. Had its position been limited to that of presidential spokesman, the *National Intelligencer* in all probability would have ceased publication shortly after the 1824 election. This was the rule of publishing in Washington, D.C.: a newspaper stayed alive only as long as it had an administration to support it.

Between 1824 and 1828 the test of whether a newspaper could survive in Washington was not presidential patronage but congressional patronage—and this support the *Intelligencer* held. It was also during this period that Gales and Seaton formed the strong personal ties that were so important in their political role until after 1850. Henry Clay's American System became the basic political philosophy of the editors, and Daniel Webster's strong defense of the union fitted in well with their distaste for the threats of nullification and secession.

During this period, also, the policies and philosophies to which the *Intelligencer* editors adhered for nearly forty years were defined. Clay's American System became the basis for much of the domestic program Gales and Seaton advocated. The adoption of this program marked the movement of Gales and Seaton from the liberal political party within the country to the role of leading spokesman for the conservative party. For nearly all of their remaining publishing days, until the issues involved in the Civil War drove all others to the background, Gales and Seaton espoused a national bank, a protective tariff, and federal aid for internal improvements as the issues vital to the country. Yet both editors would have been disillusioned had they lived into the period following the Civil War and seen the bitter fruits produced by the implementation of Clay's system.

The most important contribution the 1819 law made was to help the *National Intelligencer* to remain in business as the leading opposition paper during the years when the United States was dominated by the vigorous Jacksonian democracy. Jackson, after his break with the Calhoun wing of the party, was never able to dominate Congress as he had during his first years, and Blair and Rives were forced to share the congressional printing with such rivals as Gales and Seaton or Duff Green.

This opposition in the anti-Jackson newspapers demonstrated how clearly the 1819 legislation had created congressional spokesmen to counter the strong voice of the presidency. The anti-Jackson papers represented separate wings of the Whig party after 1834 and never spoke with anything approaching unity. Yet the important function served by the papers was that of opposition—opposition built on the divergence of views within Congress and opposition which stressed the difference of opinion growing within the country.

The Jacksonian period marked great changes in the political functioning and institutions of the country. The electorate was expanded, the congressional caucus was killed, and the political convention was begun in response to the people's demands for greater participation in the selection of candidates. Probably at no other time in the history of the United States was the dialogue as continuous or on as high an intellectual level as during this period. Each Washington paper supported a political party or a faction of a political party. Blair and Rives represented Jackson and his party. Duff Green backed the dissident wing of the Democratic party representing the nullification views of the South. Gales and Seaton spoke for the nationalist wing of the Whig party.

Each of the papers existed to serve the interests of its party or faction of a party. Each sought to educate, to inform, and to persuade the reader of the justice of its political cause. The dialogue was made more lively by the penetrating attacks on the opposition's point of view.

In addition, each of the editors sat among the highest councils of his party or faction. Blair counseled regularly with President Jackson and his Kitchen Cabinet. Green was among the closest friends and political advisers of Calhoun and his southern followers, and the *Intelligencer* editors were friendly, both socially and politically, with nearly all members of the Clay-Webster wing of the Whig party. The *Intelligencer* offices frequently served as the caucus room for Whigs wrestling with matters of policy and party direction. All these editors not only were fully informed of what the party's policies were but often contributed to formulating these policies. With such editorial knowledge of the philosophies and policies of the major political factions in the country, it was not surprising that the Washington City newspapers of the period were rich and valuable sources of information, comment, and policy statement.

The factionalism during the Jackson period, coupled with Gales's and Seaton's realization that a paper in Washington City after 1819 could not thrive without some form of government patronage added many years' life to the *Intelligencer*. Politicians thought that once the *Intelligencer* lost its position as spokesman for the presidency during John Quincy Adams's administration and then lost the congressional printing as the Jackson party took office that the *Intelligencer* was doomed. Had Jackson been able to prevent the split within his own party, such a result would have been likely. But the division within the party and the eventual formation of the opposition elements into the Whig party in 1834 enabled Gales and Seaton to piece together a tenuous coalition which carried on the opposition to Jackson and looked to the *Intelligencer* as its main organ.

This backing of the *Intelligencer* was given partially through the congressional printing contracts, but considering the heavy debts of the *Intelligencer*, these contracts would have been insufficient to continue publication of the paper. Partial support also was received from the backers of the Second Bank of the United States in the form of large printing orders of speeches and other documents favorable to the bank. Such contributions also helped, but again would have been insufficient to have sustained the paper.

The printing plan that enabled the Jacksonian opposition to maintain the *Intelligencer*, of course, included the backing of the *American State Papers* and the *Annals of Congress*, the two most costly printing projects handled by private printers for the United States government. Although few today would argue the value of these two collections of documents as historical sources in United States history, they were no more important than some other publishing proposals during the period preceding the Civil War. The *Intelligencer's* projects, however, continued to receive support and enabled the paper to remain in existence for years. This was partly because of the prestige of the dean of Washington newspapers and because of the role it served during most of the life of the Whig party. But much credit also must be given to the insight and shrewdness of the editors in devising the publishing plan and to the quality of their firm's work, which enabled their friends to maintain support for the *Intelligencer* and its valuable publication series.

Members of Congress were not unaware that they performed an important function to the nation when they provided the patronage that enabled the Washington, D.C., press to function. Congressmen were not worried about the role of government in supporting the vital informational function of the nation. There were positive advantages to the system, and probably no one put them in better perspective than that arch rival of Gales's and Seaton's, John C. Rives, when he argued for the continuation of the system during the early 1840s:

I recommend it because it keeps up two daily papers here, advocating the principles and interests . . . of the two great parties into which the Union is happily . . . divided; each of them giving full and fair reports of the debates in Congress, which . . . is worth more to the government, or the people, for each and every year, than the printing of both houses of Congress costs in ten years. If the printing were let out to the lowest bidder, or executed at a government office, the debates would not be published as they are now. A daily paper, publishing the debates . . . would sink from $7,500 to $12,000 a year; and I do not think that two editors could be found in the United States patriotic enough to sink that much money a year. If *one* could be found who would do it, he would probably so report the proceedings as to subserve his party, or some great manufacturing interest, which would pay him well for his support. If the government were to attempt to report the debates, a large minority if not a majority of the people would repose but little confidence in the debates so published, as the reporters would be selected by the dominant party of Congress.[49]

Rives was certain that the patronage system brought the press independence rather than subservience to government.

In many ways the patronage system on which the *Intelligencer* was dependent for its existence gave the newspaper an independence few papers in the nation have ever achieved. It was dependent on no industrial or commercial advertising, and the political party it supported for much of this period was sufficiently diverse to enable the *Intelligencer* to exercise great independence of action as long as it opposed Jacksonian democracy and supported a national bank. Not even Clay and Webster were able to demand backing from the *Intelligencer* if the support conflicted with the deep convictions of Gales and Seaton.

During the 1850s, after the demise of the Whig party, Gales and Seaton received allegiance from no major political faction and supported none. The beliefs expressed in the *Intelligencer* represented the editors' own conclusions. They were the strong nationalist views of two elderly editors who, as publishers, had observed the nation for nearly half a century and who feared that all the achievements of this period were to be swept to ashes in the flames of civil conflict. The editors' strong humanitarian principles were apparent. They favored the eventual abolition of slavery, but only within the law. Since the Constitution allowed slavery, it was a subject that was not debatable—not to be tampered with. The editors felt they did not have to offer their own views on the slavery question. They had opposed it, had freed their own slaves, and had purchased the freedom of others; but they had done this as private individuals and did not expect the government to interfere. They were liberal men for their day, but in many ways they also represented their period. For all their liberal feeling, the editors considered the Negro an inferior being. He should be helped and patronized, but he certainly was not the equal of a white man. Freedom for the Negro was not, in their eyes, sufficient cause to rend the nation apart.

49. *United States House Report 754*, Twenty-Ninth Congress, First Session.

Gales and Seaton worshipped the Constitution with awe and reverence. They believed that this document created one nation, a nation that could not be set aside by nullification. A war to prevent secession was just, but a war to free slaves was unconstitutional; and it was on this line that the *Intelligencer* withdrew its support from the Lincoln administration.

Throughout its lifetime the basic philosophy of the *Intelligencer* rested on an appeal to reason. The editors used economic reasoning to try to dissuade Jackson against the actions he took with regard to the banking system of the United States. It was moral reasoning Gales and Seaton used to try to persuade Polk that his motives in waging war against Mexico were immoral. It was an appeal to the basic reasonableness of man that Gales and Seaton used to attempt to persuade the nation that it was folly to settle its differences through war. The reasonableness of Gales and Seaton had much to offer in the days of the Civil War, but few had time to listen to two elderly men who published a quaint little newspaper—a newspaper that seemed strangely out of place in the new world that was to be fashioned out of a civil war and the industrial revolution.

Gales and Seaton never could have edited a paper in which the tone of the content was set by the commercial advertisers; in which a corporate board, rather than leading political figures in consultation with the editors, was the policy-determining body; and in which the function of the newspaper was to observe rather than participate in the political life of a nation.

The death of the *Intelligencer* as a political newspaper marked the end of an era in journalism in the United States —an era that in many ways has not since been equalled on an intellectual level.

Bibliography

Manuscript Material

William Allen Papers. vol. 3. Library of Congress. Washington, D.C.

American Statesmen Papers, Dreere Collection. Historical Society of Pennsylvania. Philadelphia.

Bank of the United States Papers, Dreere Collection. Historical Society of Pennsylvania. Philadelphia.

James Barbour Collection. New York Public Library. New York.

Nicholas Biddle Letterbooks. nos. 3, 4, and 5. Library of Congress. Washington, D.C.

Nicholas Biddle Papers. vols. 25, 26, 27, 28, 30, 34, 36, 45, 48, 57, and 64. Library of Congress. Washington, D.C.

Blair and Rives Papers. vols. 2, 3, 5, and 6. Library of Congress. Washington, D.C.

John Leeds Bozman and John Leeds Kerr Papers. Library of Congress. Washington, D.C.

David Campbell Papers, Flowers Collection. Duke University Library. Durham, N.C.

Mathew Carey Section, Edward Carey Gardiner Collection. Historical Society of Pennsylvania. Philadelphia.

Henry Clay Papers. vols. 3, 17, and 21. Library of Congress. Washington, D.C.

William Crawford Papers. Library of Congress. Washington, D.C.

J. J. Crittenden Papers. vols. 12 and 13. Library of Congress. Washington, D.C.

Dialectic Society Minutes, University of North Carolina, 1798-1804. University of North Carolina Library. Chapel Hill, N.C.

347

Dialectic Society Papers, University of North Carolina, 1782-1808. University of North Carolina Library. Chapel Hill, N.C.

Andrew Jackson Donelson Papers. vol. 3. Library of Congress. Washington, D.C.

Etting Collection. vol. 3. Historical Society of Pennsylvania. Philadelphia.

Phillip Fendall Diary, Flowers Collection. Duke University Library. Durham, N.C.

Peter Force Papers. vols. 1, 2, and 3. Library of Congress. Washington, D.C.

Peter and William G. Force Papers, Southern Historical Collection. University of North Carolina Library. Chapel Hill, N.C.

Joseph Gales, Sr., Diary. North Carolina Department of Archives and History. Raleigh, N.C.

Gales Papers. North Carolina Department of Archives and History. Raleigh, N.C.

Gales and Seaton Papers. Historical Society of Pennsylvania. Philadelphia.

————. Library of Congress. Washington, D.C.

Winifred and Joseph Gales' Recollections, Gales Family Papers, Southern Historical Collection. University of North Carolina Library. Chapel Hill, N.C.

Simon Gratz Collection. Historical Society of Pennsylvania. Philadelphia.

Duff Green Papers and Letters. Library of Congress. Washington, D.C.

Wood Jones Hamlin Papers. North Carolina Department of Archives and History. Raleigh, N.C.

Andrew Jackson Papers. New York Public Library. New York.

Thomas Jefferson Papers. vols. 116, 142, 151, 164, 179, 180, 181, 188, 190, 191, 199, 202, 203, 220, 224, and 225. Library of Congress. Washington, D.C.

J. S. Johnston Papers. Historical Society of Pennsylvania. Philadelphia.

Charles Lanman Papers. vols. 1 and 2. Library of Congress. Washington, D.C.

John McLean Papers. vol. 7. Library of Congress. Washington, D.C.

Nathaniel Macon Papers. North Carolina Department of Archives and History. Raleigh, N.C.

James Madison Papers. vols. 21, 59, 65, 69, 75, and 87. Library of Congress. Washington, D.C.

Willie P. Mangum Papers. vols. 1, 2, 4, 12, and 16. Library of Congress. Washington, D.C.

Manton Marble Papers. vols. 3 and 6. Library of Congress. Washington, D.C.

William L. Marcy Papers. vols. 6 and 13. Library of Congress. Washington, D.C.

Miscellaneous Collection. New York Public Library. New York.

James Monroe Papers. vol. 20. Library of Congress. Washington, D.C.

————. New York Public Library. New York.

Joseph Nicholson Papers. vol. 3. Library of Congress. Washington, D.C.

William Plumer Diary. Library of Congress. Washington, D.C.

George Poindexter Letters. Duke University Library. Durham, N.C.

J. R. Poinsett Collection. vol. 9. Historical Society of Pennsylvania. Philadelphia.

James K. Polk Papers. vol. 4. Library of Congress. Washington, D.C.

John Randolph Papers. Library of Congress. Washington, D.C.

Thomas Ritchie Papers. Library of Congress. Washington, D.C.

Margaret Bayard Smith Diary. Library of Congress. Washington, D.C.

Margaret Bayard Smith Papers. vols. 6, 7, 8, and 9. Library of Congress. Washington, D.C.

Samuel Harrison Smith File. Alumni Records Office, University of Pennsylvania. Philadelphia.

Samuel Harrison Smith Papers. Library of Congress, Washington, D.C.

Mrs. William (Anna Maria Brodeau) Thornton Diary, William Thornton Papers. Library of Congress. Washington, D.C.

United States Bank, collection of papers relating mainly to the First Bank of the United States. Box 4. Library of Congress. Washington, D.C.

University of North Carolina Student Records, 1795-1809, May Term, 1801. University of North Carolina Library. Chapel Hill, N.C.

Martin Van Buren Papers. vols. 6 and 7. Library of Congress. Washington, D.C.

Daniel Webster Papers. vols. 5 and 7. Library of Congress. Washington, D.C.

Thurlow Weed Papers. Library of Congress. Washington, D.C.

Henry A. Wise Papers. Library of Congress. Washington, D.C.

Contemporaneous Newspapers and Magazines

Boston Courier, 1824-64.
Columbia Centinel (Boston), 1807-15.
Daily National Intelligencer (Washington, D.C.), 1813-69.
The Evening Star (Washington, D.C.), 1852-65.
Gales's Independent Gazetteer (Philadelphia), 1796-97.
Gazette of the United States (Philadelphia), 1792-94.
The Globe (Washington, D.C.), 1830-45.
The Independent Gazetteer or Chronicle of Freedom (Philadelphia), 1792-96.
The Madisonian (Washington, D.C.), 1837-45.
The Minerva (Raleigh, N.C.), 1799-1805.
National Intelligencer, 1810-65.
National Intelligencer and Washington Advertiser, 1800-1813.
National Journal (Washington, D.C.), 1823-32.
New York Evening Post, 1802-65.
New World (Philadelphia), 1796-97.
Niles' Register (Baltimore), 1811-49.
Philadelphia Aurora and General Advertiser, 1795-1800.
Raleigh Register (N.C.), 1799-1848.
Richmond Enquirer (Va.), 1804-45.
United States Telegraph (Washington, D.C.), 1826-37.
Union (Washington, D.C.), 1845-59.
Universal Gazette (Philadelphia), 1797-1800.
Washington Federalist, 1800-1809.
Washington Gazette, 1815-26.
Washington Republican and Congressional Examiner, 1822-24.

Public Documents

American State Papers. 21 vols. Washington, D.C.: Gales and Seaton, 1832-34.
Annals of Congress. 42 vols. Washington, D.C.: Gales and Seaton, 1834-56.
The Congressional Globe. 29 vols. Washington, D.C.: Blair and Rives and John C. Rives, 1834-60.
A Deed of Trust and Power of Attorney By and Between Joseph Gales, Jr., et al., Grantors, and Richard Smith, Grantee, Dated the 24th Day of May, 1833, and Recorded on the 29th Day of May, 1833, in Liber. No. W B 46, Folio 157, Office of the Recorder, District of Columbia.
Journal of the House of Representatives of the United States, Sixth Congress, First Session, to Thirty-First Congress, Second Session. 52

vols. Washington, D.C.: Gales and Seaton, Duff Green, Blair and Rives, and Thomas Allen, 1815-52.

Journal of the Senate of the United States, Sixth Congress, First Session, to Thirty-First Congress, Second Session. 52 vols. Washington, D.C.: Gales and Seaton, Duff Green, Blair and Rives, and Thomas Allen, 1815-52.

Pennsylvania Archives. ser. 1, vols. 5, 6, and 11, and ser. 2, vol. 3. Philadelphia: Joseph Severns & Co., 1852-55.

Register of Debates in Congress. 14 vols. Washington, D.C.: Gales and Seaton, 1825-37.

A Trust By and Between Joseph Gales, Grantor, and Richard Smith, Grantee, Dated the 24th Day of June, 1818, and Recorded on the 11th Day of September, 1818, in Liber. No. A S 43, Folio 134, Office of the Recorder, District of Columbia.

A Trust By and Between Joseph Gales, et al., Grantors, and Richard Smith, Grantee, Dated the 6th Day of January, 1826, and Recorded on the 7th Day of January, 1826, in Liber. No. W B 15, Folio 222, Office of the Recorder, District of Columbia.

United States House Document 111, Twenty-Sixth Congress, First Session.

United States House Document 92, Twenty-Seventh Congress, Third Session.

United States House Document 83, Twenty-Ninth Congress, First Session.

United States House Report 90, Twentieth Congress, First Session.

United States House Report 298, Twenty-Sixth Congress, First Session.

United States House Report 754, Twenty-Ninth Congress, First Session.

United States Senate Document 99, Fifteenth Congress, Second Session.

United States Senate Document 114, Twenty-Seventh Congress, First Session.

United States Senate Records 1D-A3 and 2A-F2, Original Reports of the Treasury Department, Third Congress, First Session to Fourth Congress, Second Session, Treasury Department Contingency Expenses for 1795. National Archives, Washington, D.C.

United States Senate Record 8D-B1, Senate Section. National Archives, Washington, D.C.

United States Senate Records 19D-21, Sen 30D-B2, Records of United States Senate, Record Group, 46. National Archives, Washington, D.C.

United States Senate Report 18, Fifty-Second Congress, First Session.

United States Statutes at Large. vols. 1-13. Boston: Charles C. Little and James Brown, and Little, Brown, and Company, 1845-66.

Printed Correspondence, Memoirs, Diaries, and Contemporaneous Publications

Abigail Adams, New Letters of, 1788-1801, ed. Stewart Mitchell. Boston: Houghton Mifflin Company, 1947.

John Quincy Adams, 1794-1845, The Diary of, ed. Allan Nevins. New York: Longmans, Green & Co., 1928.

John Quincy Adams, Memoirs of, comprising portions of his diary from 1795-1848, ed. Charles Francis Adams. vols. 1-12. Philadelphia: J. B. Lippincott Co., 1874-77.

John Quincy Adams, The Writings of, ed. Worthington Chauncey Ford. 7 vols. New York: Macmillan Co., 1913-17.

"James Allen, Esq., Diary of, of Philadelphia, Counsellor-at-Law, 1770-1778." *The Pennsylvania Magazine of History and Biography* 9 (1885): 176-96, 278-96, 424-41.

"Edward Bates, The Diary of, 1859-1866," ed. Howard K. Beale. *American Historical Association Annual Report, 1930.* Washington, D.C.: The Association, 1933. 4:1-57.

"James A. Bayard, Papers of, 1796-1815," ed. Elizabeth Donnan. *American Historical Association Annual Report, 1913.* Washington, D.C.: The Association, 1915. 2:11-516.

Thomas Hart Benton. *Thirty Years' View; or, A History of the Working of the American Government for Thirty Years, from 1820-1850.* 2 vols. New York: D. Appleton and Company, 1854-56.

Nicholas Biddle, The Correspondence of, Dealing with National Affairs, 1807-1844, ed. Reginald Charles McGrane. Boston: Houghton Mifflin Company, 1919.

John C. Calhoun, The Papers of, ed. W. Edwin Hemphill. 3 vols. Columbia, S.C.: University of South Carolina Press, 1959-67.

Henry Clay, Works of, ed. Calvin Colton. 7 vols. New York: Henry Clay Publishing Company, 1897.

William Cobbett, The Life and Letters of, in England and America, ed. Lewis T. Melville. 2 vols. London: J. Lane Co., 1913.

"William H. Crawford, The Journal of," ed. Daniel Chauncey Knowlton. *Smith College Studies in History* 11 (October, 1925): 5-64.

George M. Dallas. "The Mystery of the Dallas Papers, Diary and Letters of, December 4, 1848–March 6, 1849." *The Pennsylvania Magazine of History and Biography* 73 (July, 1949): 349-92.

The Diary of a Public Man. New Brunswick, N.J.: Rutgers University Press, 1946.

"William Duane, Letters of," ed. Worthington C. Ford. *Massachusetts Historical Society Proceedings,* 2nd series, 20 (May, 1906): 257-394.

Ninian Edwards. *The Edwards Papers,* ed. E. B. Washburne. vol. 3. Chicago: Fergus Printing Company, 1884.

"William Findley to William Plumer, Esqr.," January 17, 1812, in "In Original Letters and Documents." *The Pennsylvania Magazine of History and Biography* 8 (1884): 343-47.

Herbert Friedenwald. "The Journals and Papers of the Continental Congress." *American Historical Association Annual Report.* Washington, D.C.: The Association, 1897. 1:83-135.

————. "The Journals and Papers of the Continental Congress." *The Pennsylvania Magazine of History and Biography* 21 (1897): 171-84, 361-75, 445-65.

"Joseph Gales on the War Manifesto of 1812," ed. Gaillard Hunt. *American Historical Review* 13 (January, 1908): 303-10.

"Joseph Gales, Sr., The Diary of, 1794-1795." *The North Carolina Historical Review* 26 (July, 1949): 335-47.

Mrs. Winifred (Marshall) Gales. *Matilda Berkeley, or, Family Anecdotes; by the author of Lady Emma Malcombe and her family, etc.* Raleigh, N.C.: J. Gales, 1804.

Peter Harvey. *Reminiscences and Anecdotes of Daniel Webster,* ed. G. M. Towle. Boston: Little, Brown, & Company, 1921.

"Jacob Hiltzheimer, Extracts from the Diary of, 1768-1798." *The Pennsylvania Magazine of History and Biography* 16 (1892): 160-77.

Andrew Jackson, Correspondence of, ed. John Spencer Bassett. 7 vols. Washington, D.C.: Carnegie Institution of Washington, 1926-35.

Thomas Jefferson, The Writings of, ed. Paul Leicester Ford. vols. 7-10. New York: G. P. Putnam's Sons, 1896-99.

Thomas Jefferson, Writings of, ed. A. A. Lipscomb. 20 vols. Washington, D.C.: Thomas Jefferson Memorial Association, 1903-4.

Mrs. Jane Kirkpatrick. *The Light of Other Days: Sketches of the Past.* New Brunswick, N.J.: J. Terhune, 1856.

Charles Lanman. "The National Intelligencer and Its Editors." *The Atlantic Monthly* 6 (October, 1860): 470-81.

————. *The Private Life of Daniel Webster.* New York: Harper & Brothers, 1852.

Abraham Lincoln, The Collected Works of, ed. Roy P. Basler. vols. 1-8. New Brunswick, N.J.: Rutgers University Press, 1953.

James Madison, Writings of, ed. Gaillard Hunt. vols. 7-9. New York: G. P. Putnam's Sons, 1908-10.

Willie P. Mangum, Papers of, ed. Henry Thomas Shanks. vols. 1-4. Raleigh, N.C.: State Department of Archives and History, 1950-56.

James Montgomery, Memoirs of the Life and Writings of, ed. James Holland and James Everett. 5 vols. London: Brown, Green, and Longmans, 1854.

"The 'National Intelligencer' and Its Editors." *Harper's Weekly* 2 (January, 1858): 45.

Clark E. Persinger. "The 'Bargain of 1844' as the Origin of the Wilmot Proviso." *Oregon Historical Society Quarterly* 15 (1914): 137-46.

William Plumer's Memorandum of Proceedings in the United States Senate, 1803-1807, ed. Everett Sommerville Brown. New York: Macmillan Co., 1923.

James K. Polk, The Diary of, during his presidency, 1845 to 1849, ed. Milo Milton Quaife. 4 vols. Chicago: A. C. McClurg and Company, 1910.

Polk, The Diary of a President, 1845-1849, ed. Allan Nevins. New York: Longmans, Green, & Co., 1929.

Benjamin Perley Poore. *Perley's Reminiscences.* 2 vols. Philadelphia: Hubbard Brothers, 1886.

David Robertson. *Reports of the Trials of Colonel Aaron Burr.* 2 vols. Philadelphia, 1808.

Margaret Bayard (Mrs. Samuel Harrison) Smith. *The First Forty Years of Washington Society,* ed. Gaillard Hunt. New York: Charles Scribner's Sons, 1906.

————. "Washington in Jackson's Time with Glimpses of Henry Clay, from the diaries and family letters of Mrs. Samuel Harrison Smith (Margaret Bayard)," ed. Gaillard Hunt. *Scribner's Magazine* 40 (July–December, 1906): 608-26.

————. "Washington in Jefferson's Time, from the diaries and family letters of Mrs. Samuel Harrison Smith (Margaret Bayard)," ed. Gaillard Hunt. *Scribner's Magazine* 40 (July–December, 1906): 292-310.

————. "Washington in the Hands of the British, from the diaries and family letters of Mrs. Samuel Harrison Smith (Margaret Bayard)," ed. Gaillard Hunt. *Scribner's Magazine* 40 (July–December, 1906): 425-40.

————. *What Is Gentility? A moral tale . . .* Washington, D.C.: Pishey Thompson, 1828.

————. *A Winter in Washington; or, Memoirs of the Seymour Family.* 2 vols. New York: E. Bliss and E. White, 1824.

Oliver Hampton Smith. *Early Indiana Trials: and Sketches.* Cincinnati, Ohio: Moore, Wilstach, Keys & Company, 1858.

Samuel Harrison Smith. *History of the last session of Congress, which commenced on the seventh of December, 1801. Taken from the National Intelligencer.* Washington, D.C.: Rapine, Conrad & Company, 1802.

———. *Memoir of the life, character and writings of Thomas Jefferson.* Washington, D.C.: S. A. Elliott, 1827.

———. *Oration, pronounced in the City of Washington on Monday, the Fifth of July, 1813.* Washington, D.C.: Roger C. Weightman, 1813.

——— and Thomas Lloyd. *Trial of Samuel Chase.* 2 vols. Washington, D.C.: Samuel Harrison Smith, 1805.

"John Steele, The Papers of." *Publications of the North Carolina Historical Commission,* ed. H. M. Wagstaff. vol. 1. Raleigh, N.C.: Edwards & Broughton Printing Company, 1924.

"Mrs. William Thornton, Diary of, Capture of Washington by the British." *Columbia Historical Society Records* 18 (1916): 172-82.

Lyon G. Tyler. *The Letters and Times of the Tylers.* 3 vols. Richmond, Va.: Whittet & Shepperson, 1884-85, 1896.

"Martin Van Buren, The Autobiography of." *American Historical Association Reports,* vol. 2, ed. John C. Fitzpatrick. Washington, D.C.: The Association, 1920.

George Washington, Writings of, ed. Jared Sparks. vols. 10-11. New York: Russell, Shattuck and Williams, 1836.

Daniel Webster. *Private Correspondence,* ed. Fletcher Webster. 2 vols. Boston: Little, Brown, & Company, 1875.

Daniel Webster, The Letters of, ed. C. H. Van Tyne. New York: McClure, Phillips & Company, 1902.

Daniel Webster, The Writings and Speeches of, ed. Fletcher Webster. vols. 4, 15, and 16. Boston: Little, Brown, & Company, 1903.

Thurlow Weed, Autobiography of, ed. Harriet A. Weed. vol. 1. Boston: Houghton Mifflin Company, 1883.

James C. Welling. "The Emancipation Proclamation." *The North American Review* 130 (January, 1880): 163-85.

John C. Williams. *History of the Invasion and Capture of Washington.* New York: Harper & Brothers, 1857.

Henry A. Wise. *Seven Decades of the Union.* Richmond, Va.: J. W. Randolph & English, 1881.

General Sources

Thomas Perkins Abernethy. *The Burr Conspiracy.* New York: Oxford University Press, 1954.

"Accessions." *The Pennsylvania Magazine of History and Biography* 63 (October, 1939): 487-88.

Henry Adams. *History of the United States of America.* vols. 1-9. New York: Charles Scribner's Sons, 1931.

Herbert Baxter Adams. *The Life and Writings of Jared Sparks.* vol. 1. Boston: Houghton Mifflin Company, 1893.

"Thomas Allen." *Dictionary of American Biography* 1: 206-7, 1958.

Charles Henry Ambler. *Thomas Ritchie.* Richmond, Va.: Bell Book and Stationery Company, 1913.

Frank Maloy Anderson. *The Mystery of "A Public Man": A Historical Detective Story.* Minneapolis: University of Minnesota Press, 1948.

Katharine Susan Anthony. *Dolly Madison, Her Life and Times.* Garden City, N.Y.: Doubleday & Company, 1949.

W. H. G. Armytage. "The Editorial Experience of Joseph Gales, 1786-1794." *The North Carolina Historical Review* 28 (July, 1951): 332-61.

Thomas A. Bailey. *A Diplomatic History of the American People.* New York: Appleton-Century-Crofts, 1958.

John Spencer Bassett. *The Life of Andrew Jackson.* 2 vols. Garden City, N.Y.: Doubleday, Page & Company, 1911.

"James Asheton Bayard." *Dictionary of American Biography* 2:66-67, 1958.

"Jonathan Bubenheim Bayard." *Dictionary of American Biography* 2:67-68, 1958.

"Samuel Bayard." *Dictionary of American Biography* 2:69-70, 1958.

Francis F. Beirne. *The War of 1812.* New York: E. P. Dutton & Co., 1949.

Samuel Flagg Bemis, ed. *The American Secretaries of State and Their Diplomacy.* vols. 3 and 4. New York: Pageant Book Company, 1958.

————. *John Quincy Adams and the Foundations of American Foreign Policy.* New York: Alfred A. Knopf, 1949, 1957.

————. *John Quincy Adams and the Union.* New York: Alfred A. Knopf, 1956.

————. *A Diplomatic History of the United States.* New York: Henry Holt & Co., 1936.

————. *The Latin American Policy of the United States.* New York: Harcourt, Brace & Co., 1943.

Albert J. Beveridge. *The Life of John Marshall, Conflict and Construction, 1800-1815.* vol. 3. Boston: Houghton Mifflin Company, 1919.

Alfred Hoyt Bill. *Rehearsal for Conflict: The War with Mexico, 1846-1848.* New York: Alfred A. Knopf, 1947.

Ray Allen Billington. *Westward Expansion: A History of the American Frontier.* New York: Macmillan Co., 1950.

Gist Blair. "Lafayette Square." *Columbia Historical Society Records* 28 (1926): 133-73.

Morton Borden. *The Federalism of James A. Bayard.* New York: Columbia University Press, 1955.

Claude G. Bowers. *Jefferson in Power: The Death Struggle of the Federalists.* Boston: Houghton Mifflin Company, 1936.

————. *The Party Battles of the Jackson Period.* Boston: Houghton Mifflin Company, 1928.

Irving Brant. *Madison the President 1809-1812.* vol. 5. Indianapolis: Bobbs-Merrill Company, 1961.

Willis G. Briggs. "Two Pioneer Journalists." *National Republic* 18 (October, 1930): 18-19, 47.

Clarence S. Brigham. *History and Bibliography of American Newspapers, 1690-1820.* 2 vols. Worcester, Mass.: American Antiquarian Society, 1947.

Wilhelmus Bogart Bryan. *A History of the National Capital, 1790-1884.* 2 vols. New York: Macmillan Co., 1914, 1916.

Francis Von A. Cabeen. "The Society of the Sons of Saint Tammany of Philadelphia." *The Pennsylvania Magazine of History and Biography* 25 (1901): 433-51, 26 (1902): 7-24, 207-23, 335-47, 443-63.

Harry James Carman. *Social and Economic History of the United States.* 2 vols. Boston: D. C. Heath & Company, 1934.

W. S. Carpenter. "Repeal of the Judiciary Act of 1801." *American Political Science Review* 9 (August, 1915): 519-28.

E. Malcolm Carroll. *Origins of the Whig Party.* Durham, N.C.: Duke University Press, 1925.

Clarence C. Carter. "The United States and Documentary Historical Publication." *The Mississippi Valley Historical Review* 25 (June, 1938): 3-24.

Ralph Charles Henry Catterall. *The Second Bank of the United States.* Chicago: University of Chicago Press, 1903.

Mrs. J. R. Chamberlain. "Two Wake County Editors Whose Work Has Influenced the World." *Proceedings of the Twenty-Second Annual Session of the State Literary and Historical Association of North Carolina, Raleigh, December 7-8, 1922.* Raleigh, N.C.: Bynum Printing Company, State Printers, 1923. Pp. 45-52.

William Nisbet Chambers. *Old Bullion Benton, Senator from the New West: Thomas Hart Benton, 1782-1858.* Boston: Little, Brown, & Company, 1956.

Edward Channing. *A History of the United States.* vol. 5. New York: Macmillan Co., 1936.

James B. Childs. "Disappeared in the Wings of Oblivion." *Papers of the Bibliographical Society of America* 58 (Second Quarter, 1964): 91-132.

———. "The Story of the United States Senate Documents, First Congress, First Session, New York, 1789." *Papers of the Bibliographical Society of America* 56 (Second Quarter, 1962): 175-94.

Oliver Perry Chitwood. *John Tyler, Champion of the Old South.* New York: Appleton-Century Company, 1939.

Allen C. Clark. "Colonel William Winston Seaton and His Mayoralty," *Columbia Historical Society Records* 29-30 (1928): 1-102.

———. "General John Peter Van Ness, A Mayor of the City of Washington, His Wife, Marcia, and her Father David Burnes." *Columbia Historical Society Records* 22 (1919): 125-204.

———. "General Roger Chew Weightman, A Mayor of the City of Washington." *Columbia Historical Society Records* 22 (1919): 62-104.

———. "Joseph Gales, Junior, Editor and Mayor." *Columbia Historical Society Records* 23 (1920): 86-146.

———. "Richard Wallach and the Times of His Mayoralty." *Columbia Historical Society Records* 21 (1918): 195-245.

Bennett Champ Clark. *John Quincy Adams: "Old Man Eloquent."* Boston: Little, Brown, & Company, 1932.

Freeman Cleaves. *Old Tippecanoe: William Henry Harrison and His Time.* New York: Charles Scribner's Sons, 1939.

Margaret L. Coit. *John C. Calhoun.* Boston: Houghton Mifflin Company, 1950.

E. S. Corwin. *John Marshall and the Constitution.* The Chronicles of America Series, vol. 16. New Haven, Conn.: Yale University Press, 1921.

Major General George C. Cullum. "The Attack on Washington City in 1814." *American Historical Association Papers* 2 (1887): 54-68.

Noble E. Cunningham, Jr. *The Jeffersonian Republicans in Power: Party Operations, 1801-1809.* Chapel Hill, N.C.: University of North Carolina Press, 1963.

———. *Jeffersonian Republicans: The Formation of Party Organization, 1789-1801.* Chapel Hill, N.C.: University of North Carolina Press, 1963.

Richard N. Current. "Webster's Propaganda and the Ashburton Treaty." *Mississippi Valley Historical Review* 34 (September, 1947): 187-200.

George Dangerfield. *The Era of Good Feelings.* New York: Harcourt, Brace & Co., 1952.

Henry E. Davis. "A Celebrated Case of an Early District Day:

United States vs. Henry Pittman." *Columbia Historical Society Records* 21 (1918): 246-62.

―――. "The Seaton Mansion." *Columbia Historical Society Records* 29, 30 (1928): 291-94.

Davis Rich Dewey. *Financial History of the United States.* New York: Longmans, Green & Co., 1931.

William E. Dodd. *The Life of Nathaniel Macon.* Raleigh, N.C.: Edwards & Broughton Printing Company, 1903.

W. A. Newman Dorland. "The Second Troop Philadelphia City Cavalry." *The Pennsylvania Magazine of History and Biography* 49 (1925): 75-94, 163-91, 367-79.

Margaret Brent Downing. "Literary Landmarks: Being a Brief Account of Celebrated Authors Who Have Lived in Washington, the Location of Their Homes, and What They Have Written." *Columbia Historical Society Records* 19 (1916): 22-60.

Theodore Dwight. *History of the Hartford Convention.* 2 vols. New York: N. & J. White, 1833.

Ninian W. Edwards. *History of Illinois, from 1778 to 1833; and Life and Times of Ninian Edwards.* Springfield, Ill.: Illinois State Journal Company, 1870.

Charles Winslow Elliott. *Winfield Scott: The Soldier and the Man.* New York: Macmillan Co., 1937.

"Jonathan Elliott." *Dictionary of American Biography* 6:92-93, 1931.

Robert Neal Elliott, Jr. "The Raleigh Register, 1799-1863." Ph.D. thesis, University of North Carolina, 1955.

―――. *The Raleigh Register, 1799-1863.* James Sprunt Studies in History and Political Science, vol. 36. Chapel Hill, N.C.: University of North Carolina Press, 1955.

Edwin Emery and Henry Ladd Smith. *The Press and America.* New York: Prentice-Hall, 1954.

Fred A. Emery. "Banks and Bankers in the District of Columbia." *Columbia Historical Society Records* 46, 47 (1947): 267-99.

Max Farrand. "The Judiciary Act of 1801." *American Historical Review* 5 (July, 1900): 682-86.

The Federal Writers' Project of the Federal Works Agency, Work Projects Administration. *North Carolina: A Guide to the Old North State.* American Guide Series. Chapel Hill, N.C.: University of North Carolina Press, 1939.

"Phillip Fendall." *Appleton's Cyclopaedia of American Biography* 2:429-30, 1888.

Edgar Estes Folk. "W. W. Holden and the North Carolina Standard, 1843-1848." *The North Carolina Historical Review* 19 (January, 1942): 22-47.

"Peter Force." *Dictionary of American Biography* 6:512-13, 1931.

Early Lee Fox. *The American Colonization Society, 1817-1840.* Baltimore: John Hopkins Press, 1919.

Claude Moore Fuess. *Daniel Webster.* 2 vols. Boston: Little, Brown, & Company, 1930.

"Joseph Gales, Jr." *Dictionary of American Biography* 7:100-101, 1956.

"Joseph Gales, Sr." *Dictionary of American biography* 7:99-100, 1956.

"Winifred (Marshall) Gales, 1761-1839, Author," in *North Carolina Authors.* vol. 18, no. 1. Chapel Hill, N.C.: Joint Committee of the North Carolina English Teachers Association and the North Carolina Library Association, 1952. Pp. 42-43.

John Graham Gillam. *The Crucible: The Story of Joseph Priestley, LL.D., F.R.S.* London: Robert Hale, 1954.

Dorothy Burne Goebel. *William Henry Harrison.* Indianapolis: Historical Bureau of the Indiana Library and Historical Department, 1926.

J. P. Gordy. *Political History of the United States,* vol. 2. New York: Henry Holt & Co., 1902.

Thomas Payne Govan. *Nicholas Biddle, Nationalist and Public Banker, 1786-1844.* Chicago: University of Chicago Press, 1959.

Norman Graebner. *Empire on the Pacific: A Study in American Continental Expansion.* New York: Ronald Press Company, 1955.

"Duff Green." *Dictionary of American Biography* 7:540-42, 1931.

Fletcher M. Green. "Duff Green, Militant Journalist of the Old School." *American Historical Review* 52 (January, 1947): 247-64.

Winifred Gregory, ed. *American Newspapers, 1821-1936.* New York: The H. W. Wilson Company, 1937.

Robert Gray Gunderson. *The Log-Cabin Campaign.* Lexington, Ky.: University of Kentucky Press, 1957.

Holman Hamilton. *Zachary Taylor.* 2 vols. Indianapolis: Bobbs-Merrill Company, 1941, 1951.

George D. Harmon. *Sixty Years of Indian Affairs.* Chapel Hill, N.C.: University of North Carolina Press, 1941.

Benjamin H. Hibbard. *A History of the Public Land Policies.* New York: Macmillan Co., 1924.

Homer C. Hockett. *The Constitutional History of the United States, 1776-1826.* New York: Macmillan Co., 1939.

Anne Holt. *A Life of Joseph Priestley.* London: Oxford University Press, 1931.

Gaillard Hunt. *The Life of James Madison.* New York: Doubleday, Page & Company, 1902.

Charles Hurd. *Washington Cavalcade.* New York: E. P. Dutton & Co., 1948.

Marquis James. *Andrew Jackson: The Border Captain.* New York: Literary Guild, 1933.

———. *Andrew Jackson: Portrait of a President.* Indianapolis: Bobbs-Merrill Company, 1937.

Guion Griffis Johnson. *Ante-Bellum North Carolina: A Social History.* Chapel Hill, N.C.: University of North Carolina Press, 1937.

Hugh Llewellyn Keenleyside. *Canada and the United States.* New York: Alfred A. Knopf, 1929.

Robert W. Kerr. *History of the Government Printing Office.* Lancaster, Pa.: Inquirer Printing and Publishing Company, 1881.

Oscar Doane Lambert. *Presidential Politics in the United States, 1841-44.* Durham, N.C.: Duke University Press, 1936.

Lewis Gaston Leary. *That Rascal Freneau: A Study in Literary Failure.* New Brunswick, N.J.: Rutgers University Press, 1941.

Hugh Talmage Lefler and Albert Ray Newsome. *North Carolina.* Chapel Hill, N.C.: University of North Carolina Press, 1954.

Norval Neil Luxon. "H. Niles, The Man and The Editor." *Mississippi Valley Historical Review* 28 (June, 1941): 27-40.

———. *Niles Weekly Register.* Baton Rouge, La.: Louisiana State University Press, 1947.

Walter Flavius McCaleb. *The Aaron Burr Conspiracy.* New York: Dodd, Mead & Co., 1903.

Eugene Irving McCormac. *James K. Polk: A Political Biography.* Berkeley, Calif.: University of California Press, 1922.

Andrew C. McLaughlin. *A Constitutional History of the United States.* New York: D. Appleton-Century Company, 1935.

John MacLean. *History of the College of New Jersey.* 2 vols. Philadelphia: J. B. Lippincott Co., 1877.

Elizabeth Gregory McPherson. "The History of Reporting the Debates and Proceedings of Congress." Ph.D. thesis, University of North Carolina, 1940.

A. T. Mahan. *Sea Power in Its Relations to the War of 1812.* 2 vols. Boston: Little, Brown & Company, 1905.

Howard Mahan. "Joseph Gales and the War of 1812." Ph.D. thesis, Columbia University, 1957.

Frederic B. Marbut. "The History of Washington Newspaper Correspondence to 1861." Ph.D. thesis, Harvard University, 1950.

Lynn L. Marshall. "The Strange Stillbirth of the Whig Party," *American Historical Review* 72 (January, 1967): 462.

Robert Powell Marshall. "A Mythical Mayflower Competition: North Carolina Literature in the Half-Century Following the Revolution." *The North Carolina Historical Review* 27 (April, 1950): 178-92.

John Hill Martin. *Martin's Bench and Bar of Philadelphia.* Philadelphia: R. Welsh & Company, 1883.

Edgar Lee Masters. *Lincoln the Man.* New York: Dodd Mead & Company, 1931.

Bernard Mayo. *Henry Clay.* Boston: Houghton Mifflin Company, 1937.

William Montgomery Meigs. *The Life of John Caldwell Calhoun.* 2 vols. New York: The Neal Publishing Company, 1917.

John C. Miller. *Crisis in Freedom: The Alien and Sedition Acts.* Boston: Little, Brown, & Company, 1951.

"James Montgomery." *Dictionary of National Biography* 38:317-20, 1894.

Robert J. Morgan. *A Whig Embattled: The Presidency under John Tyler.* Lincoln, Neb.: University of Nebraska Press, 1954.

Samuel Eliot Morison. *The Life and Letters of Harrison Gray Otis, Federalist, 1765-1848.* 2 vols. Boston: Houghton Mifflin Company, 1913.

———— and Henry Steele Commager. *The Growth of the American Republic.* 2 vols. New York: Oxford University Press, 1962.

Frank Luther Mott. *American Journalism: A History of Newspapers in the United States through 250 Years, 1690-1940.* New York: Macmillan Co., 1950.

Winthrop and Frances Neilson. *Verdict for the Doctor: The Case of Benjamin Rush.* New York: Hastings House, 1958.

Allan Nevins. *Ordeal of the Union.* 2 vols. New York: Charles Scribner's Sons, 1947, 1950.

————. *The Emergence of Lincoln.* vol. 2. New York: Charles Scribner's Sons, 1950.

————. *The Evening Post: A Century of Journalism.* New York: Boni and Liveright, 1922.

Roy Franklin Nichols. *The Disruption of American Democracy.* New York: Macmillan Co., 1948.

————. *Franklin Pierce: Young Hickory of the Granite Hills.* Philadelphia: University of Pennsylvania Press, 1958.

Helen Nicolay. *Our Capital on the Potomac.* New York: Century Company, 1924.

Samuel Dean Olson. "The Washington, D.C., Press in the Election of 1824." Master's thesis, University of Washington, 1962.

J. H. P. "The Gorsuch and Lovelace Families." *The Virginia Magazine of History and Biography* 25 (January, 1917): 85-98.

James Parton. *Life of Andrew Jackson.* 3 vols. Boston: James R. Osgood, 1876.

Samuel W. Pennypacker. "The University of Pennsylvania in Its Relations to the State of Pennsylvania." *The Pennsylvania Magazine of History and Biography* 15 (1891): 88-100.

George Rawlings Poage. *Henry Clay and the Whig Party*. Chapel Hill, N.C.: University of North Carolina Press, 1936.

James E. Pollard. *The Presidents and the Press*. New York: Macmillan Co., 1947.

John Harvey Powell. *The Books of a New Nation: U.S. Government Publications, 1774-1814*. Philadelphia: University of Pennsylvania Press, 1957.

————. *Bring Out Your Dead*. Philadelphia: University of Pennsylvania Press, 1949.

Julius W. Pratt. *Expansionists of 1812*. New York: Peter Smith, 1949.

Harvey Putnam Prentiss, "Pickering and the Embargo," *Essex Institute Historical Collections* 69 (April, 1933): 97-136.

Proceedings of the American Philosophical Society. vols. 3, 22, and 27. Philadelphia: The Society, 1885-93.

John Clagett Proctor. "Christian Hines, Author of 'Early Recollections of Washington City,' with Notes on the Hines Family." *Columbia Historical Society Records* 22 (1919): 36-61.

William Reitzel. "William Cobbett and Philadelphia Journalism: 1794-1800." *The Pennsylvania Magazine of History and Biography* 59 (July, 1935): 223-44.

————. "William Cobbett." *Litell Living Age* 61 (Spring, 1854): 61-78.

Robert Vincent Remini. *Andrew Jackson*. New York: Twayne Publishers, 1966.

————. *Andrew Jackson and the Bank War: A Study in the Growth of Presidential Power*. New York: W. W. Norton & Company, 1967.

————. *Martin Van Buren and the Making of the Democratic Party*. New York: Columbia University Press, 1959.

————. *The Election of Andrew Jackson*. Philadelphia: Lippincott, 1963.

Fremont Rider. *Rider's Washington*. New York: Macmillan Co., 1924.

James A. Robertson, ed. *Louisiana Under the Rule of Spain, France and the United States, 1785-1807*. 2 vols. Cleveland, Ohio: The Arthur H. Clark Company, 1911.

Joseph Sabin and Wilberforce Eames. *Bibliotheca Americana*. vols. 1-20. New York: Bibliographical Society of America, 1868-1928.

Nathan Schachner. *Aaron Burr*. New York: Frederick A. Stokes Company, 1937.

————. *Thomas Jefferson*. 2 vols. New York: Appleton-Century-Crofts, 1951.

J. Thomas Scharf and Thompson Westcott. *History of Philadelphia,*

1609-1884. 3 vols. Philadelphia: L. H. Everts & Company, 1884.

Arthur M. Schlesinger, Jr. *The Age of Jackson.* Boston: Little, Brown, & Company, 1945.

Carl Schurz. *Life of Henry Clay.* American Statesmen Series, vols. 1 and 2. Boston: Houghton, Mifflin Company, 1887.

Jennie W. Scudder. *A Century of Unitarianism in the National Capital, 1821-1921.* Boston: Beacon Press, 1922.

Louis Martin Sears. *Jefferson and the Embargo.* Durham, N.C.: Duke University Press, 1927.

———. "The Middle States and the Embargo of 1808." *South Atlantic Quarterly* 21 (April, 1922): 152-69.

———. "Philadelphia and the Embargo of 1808." *Quarterly Journal of Economics* 35 (February, 1921): 354-59.

———. "The South and the Embargo of 1808." *South Atlantic Quarterly* 20 (July, 1921): 254-75.

Josephine Seaton. *William Winston Seaton of the "National Intelligencer."* Boston: James R. Osgood and Company, 1871.

"William Winston Seaton." *Dictionary of American Biography* 16:541-42, 1956.

"William Winston Seaton." *Smithsonian Miscellaneous Collections* 18 (1880): 308-15.

Morrison Shaforth. "The Aaron Burr Conspiracy." *American Bar Association Journal* 18 (1895): 669-72.

John Edgar Dawson Shipp. *Giant Days; or, The Life and Times of William H. Crawford.* Americus, Ga.: Southern Printers, 1909.

Henry H. Simms. *A Decade of Sectional Controversy, 1851-1861.* Chapel Hill, N.C.: University of North Carolina Press, 1942.

Culver Haygood Smith. "The Washington Press During the Jackson Period." Ph.D. thesis, Duke University, 1931.

Edgar F. Smith. *Priestley in America, 1794-1804.* Philadelphia: P. Blakiston's Son & Company, 1920.

James Morton Smith. *Freedom's Fetters: The Alien and Sedition Laws and American Civil Liberties.* vol. 24. Ithaca, N.Y.: Cornell University Press, 1956.

"Jonathan Bayard Smith." *Appleton's Cyclopaedia of American Biography* 5:574-75, 1888.

"Jonathan Bayard Smith." *Dictionary of American Biography* 17:308-9, 1956.

Justin Harvey Smith. *The War with Mexico.* vol. 2. New York: Macmillan Co., 1919.

"Margaret Bayard Smith." *Appleton's Cyclopaedia of American Biography* 5:574-75, 1888.

———. *Dictionary of American Biography* 17:318-19, 1956.

"Samuel Harrison Smith." *Appleton's Cyclopaedia of American Biography* 5:574, 1888.

———. *Dictionary of American Biography* 17:343-44, 1956.

———. *The National Cyclopaedia of American Biography* 20: 295-96, 1929.

William Ernest Smith. *The Francis Preston Blair Family in Politics.* vol. 1. New York: Macmillan Co., 1933.

A. R. Spofford. *Columbia Historical Society Records* 2 (1899): 218-33.

"Arthur J. Stansbury." *Appleton's Cyclopaedia of American Biography* 5:647, 1888.

Anthony Steel. "Impressment in the Monroe-Pinkney Negotiation, 1806-1807." *American Historical Review* 57 (January, 1952): 352-70.

Nathaniel W. Stephenson. *Texas and the Mexican War: A Chronicle of the Winning of the Southwest.* The Chronicles of America Series, vol. 24. New Haven, Conn.: Yale University Press, 1921.

Madeleine B. Stern. *Imprints on History: Book Publishers and American Frontiers.* Bloomington, Ind.: Indiana University Press, 1956.

Kenneth Stewart and John Tebbel. *Makers of Modern Journalism.* New York: Prentice-Hall, 1952.

Robert Luther Thompson. *Wiring a Continent.* Princeton, N.J.: Princeton University Press, 1947.

Mary Lindsay Thornton. "Public Printing in North Carolina, 1749-1815." *The North Carolina Historical Review* 21 (July, 1944): 181-202.

Charles Burr Todd. *The Story of Washington.* New York: G. P. Putnam's Sons, 1889.

Washington Topham. "The Benning McGuire House, E. Street and Neighborhood." *Columbia Historical Society Records* 33-34 (1932): 87-130.

George A. Tracy. *History of the Typographical Union.* Indianapolis: International Typographical Union, 1913.

George Macaulay Trevelyan. *England Under the Stuarts.* New York: G. P. Putnam's Sons, 1946.

Frederick Jackson Turner. *The United States, 1830-1850: The Nation and Its Sections.* New York: Henry Holt & Co., 1935.

University of Pennsylvania General Alumni Catalogue, comp. W. J. Maxwell. Philadelphia: Alumni Association, 1922.

Frank van der Linden. *The Turning Point: Jefferson's Battle for the Presidency.* Washington, D.C.: Robert B. Luce, 1962.

Glyndon Garlock Van Deusen. *The Life of Henry Clay.* Boston: Little, Brown & Company, 1937.

P. J. Wallis. "A Further Note on Joseph Gales of Newark, Sheffield, and Raleigh." *The North Carolina Historical Review* 30 (October, 1953): 561-63.

Richard Walser. "The Mysterious Case of George Higby Throop (1818-1896)." *The North Carolina Historical Review* 33 (January, 1956): 12-44.

"Robert Walsh." *Dictionary of American Biography* 19:391-92, 1956.

Raymond Walters, Jr. *Albert Gallatin: Jeffersonian Financier and Diplomat.* New York: Macmillan Co., 1957.

————. "The Origins of the Jeffersonian Party in Pennsylvania." *The Pennsylvania Magazine of History and Biography* 66 (October, 1942): 440-58.

Samuel H. Wandell and Meade Minnigerode. *Aaron Burr.* 2 vols. New York: G. P. Putnam's Sons, 1925.

"Washington National Monument Society, A Brief History of, 1833-1953." Mimeographed. Washington, D.C.: The Society, 1953.

"James Clarke Welling." *Dictionary of American Biography* 19: 633-34, 1956.

Anne Hollingsworth Wharton. *Social Life in the Early Republic.* Philadelphia: J. B. Lippincott Co., 1902.

Gen. Jas. Grant Wilson. "Colonel John Bayard (1738-1807) and the Bayard Family of America." *The New York Genealogical and Biographical Record* 16 (April, 1885): 49-72.

Louis R. Wilson, comp., and R. D. W. Connor, ed. *A Documentary History of the University of North Carolina.* vol. 1. Chapel Hill, N.C.: University of North Carolina Press, 1953.

Charles M. Wiltse. *John C. Calhoun, Nationalist, 1782-1828.* Indianapolis: Bobbs-Merrill Company, 1944.

————. *John C. Calhoun, Nullifier, 1829-1839.* Indianapolis: Bobbs-Merrill Company, 1949.

————. *John C. Calhoun, Sectionalist, 1840-1850.* Indianapolis: Bobbs-Merrill Company, 1951.

Mary Jane Windle. *Life in Washington and Life Here and There.* Philadelphia: J. B. Lippincott Co., 1859.

J. A. Woodburn. "The Historical Significance of the Missouri Compromise." *American Historical Association Annual Report.* Washington, D.C.: The Association, 1894. 1:251-97.

Margaret Woodbury. "Public Opinion in Philadelphia, 1789-1801." *Smith College Studies in History* 5 (October, 1919): 7-138.

James Sterling Young. *The Washington Community 1800-1828.* New York: Columbia University Press, 1966.

Index

[367]